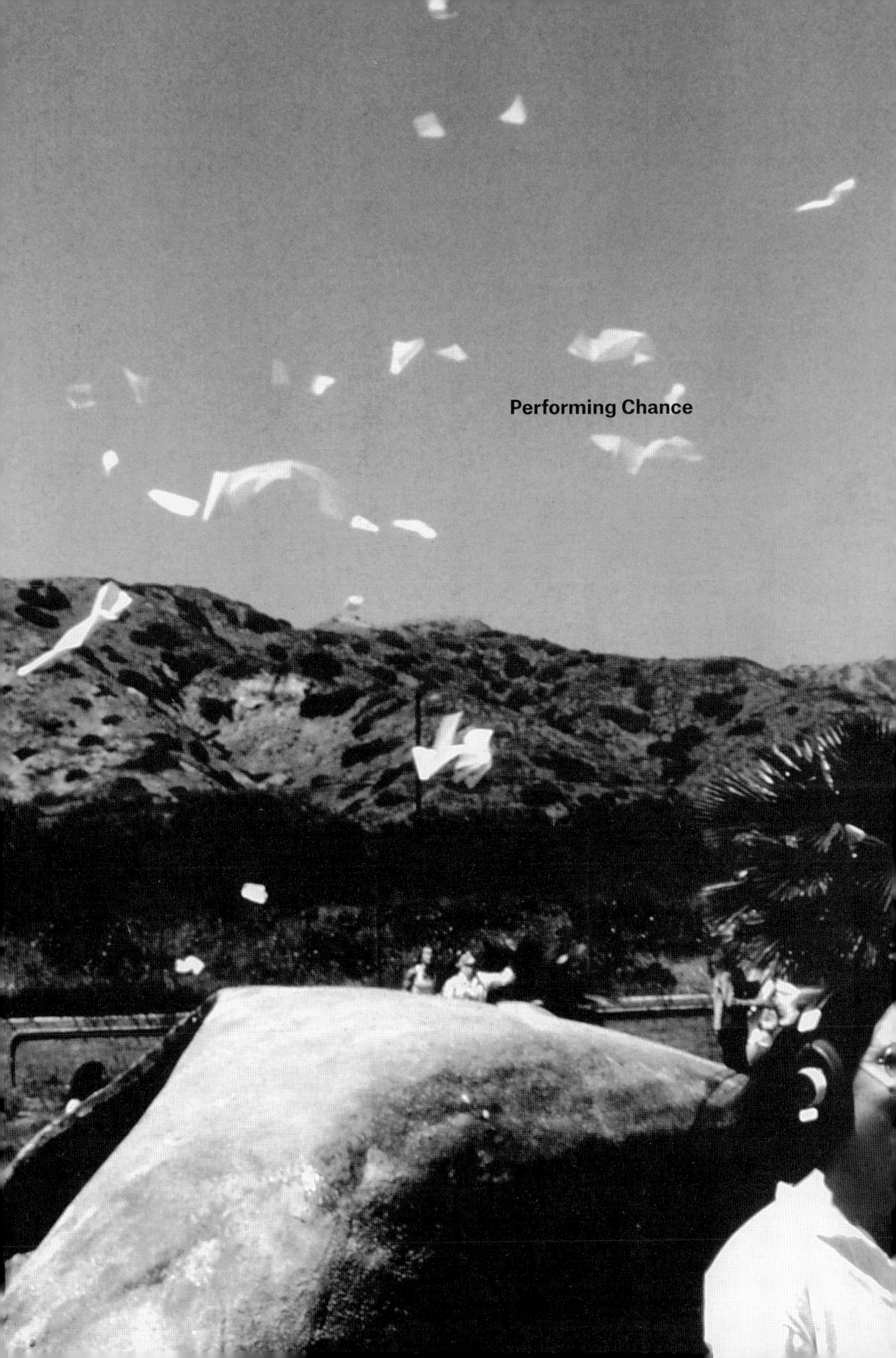

# Performing Chance

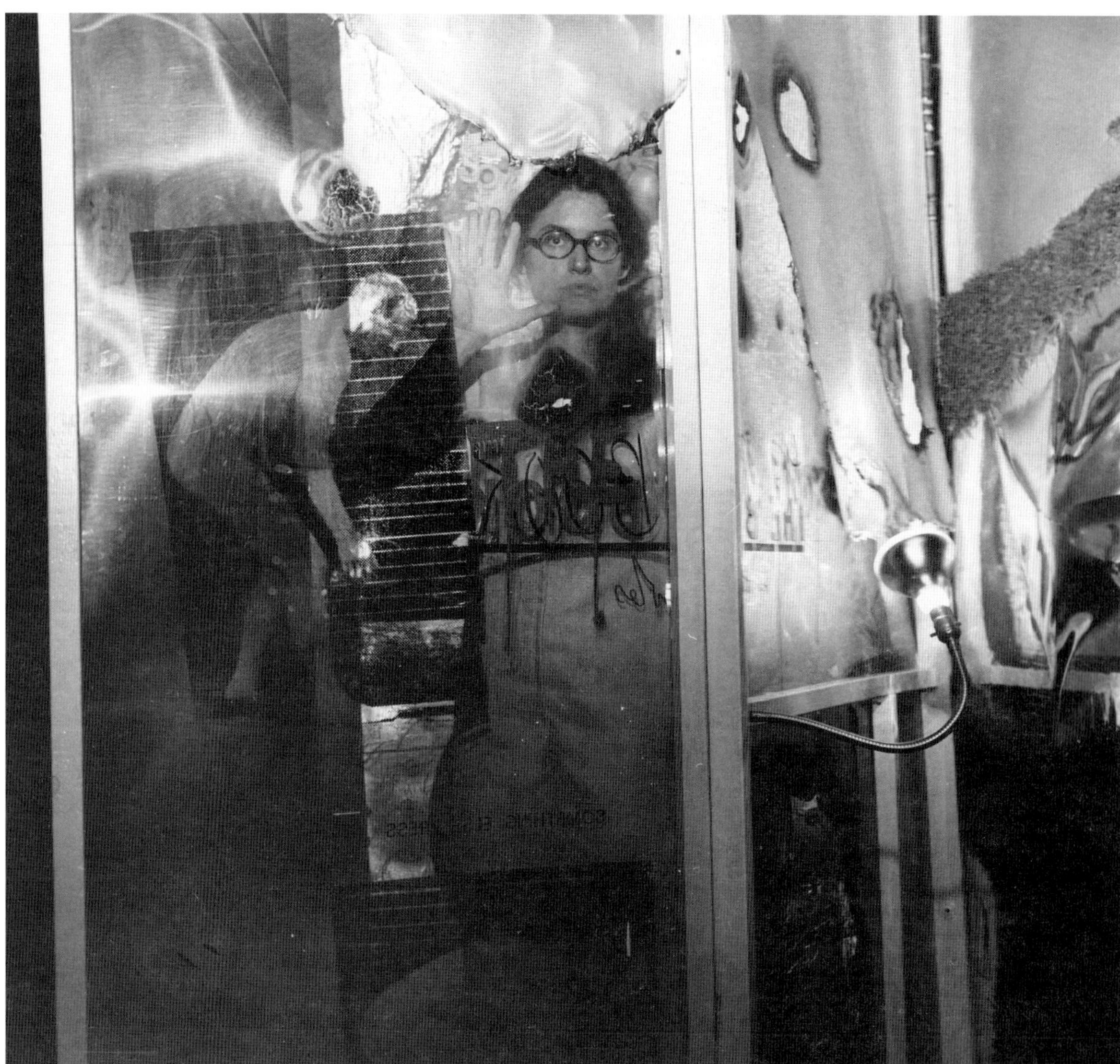

# PERFORMING CHANCE

## The Art of Alison Knowles In/Out of Fluxus

Nicole L. Woods

The University of Chicago Press
Chicago and London

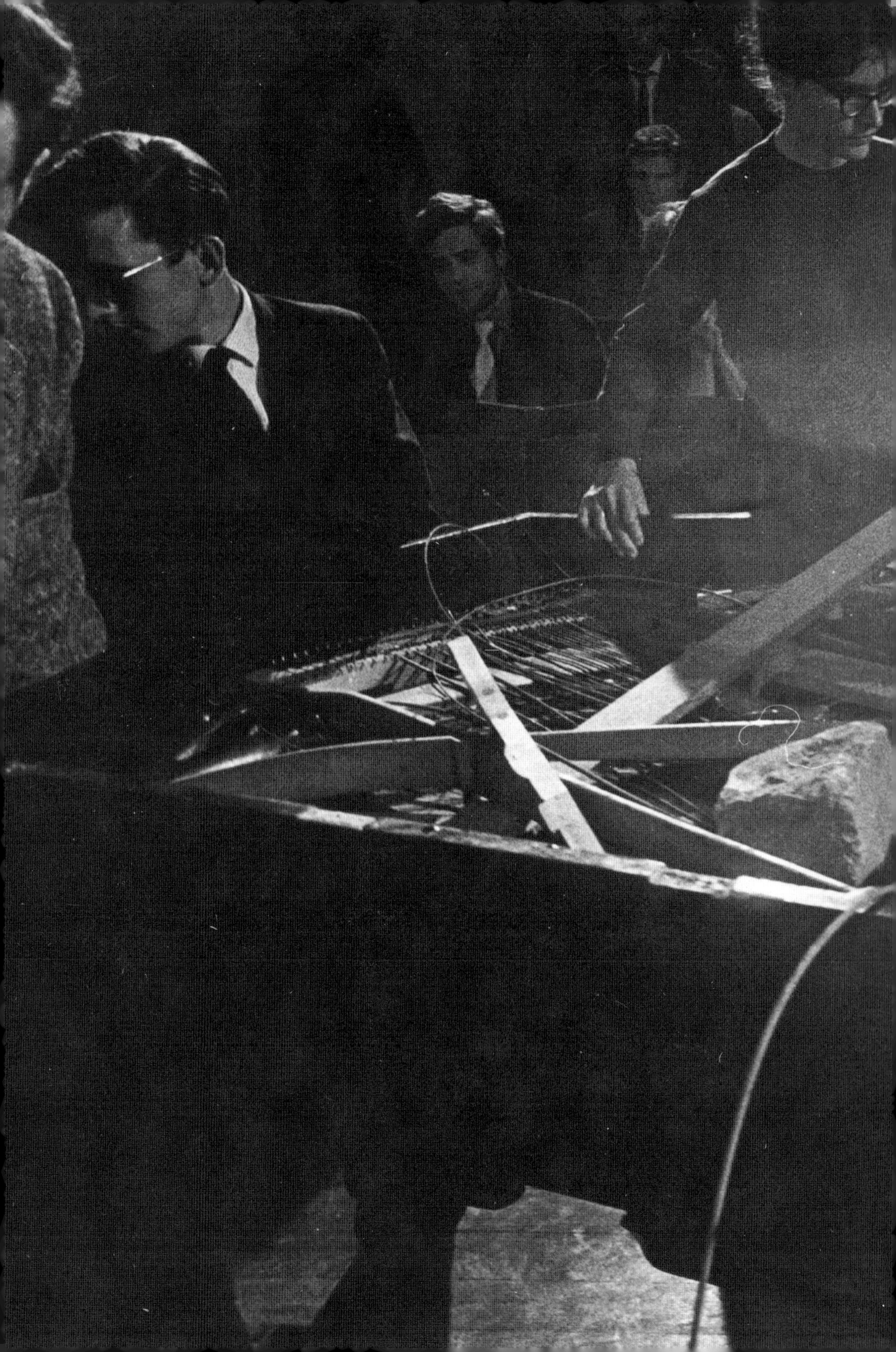

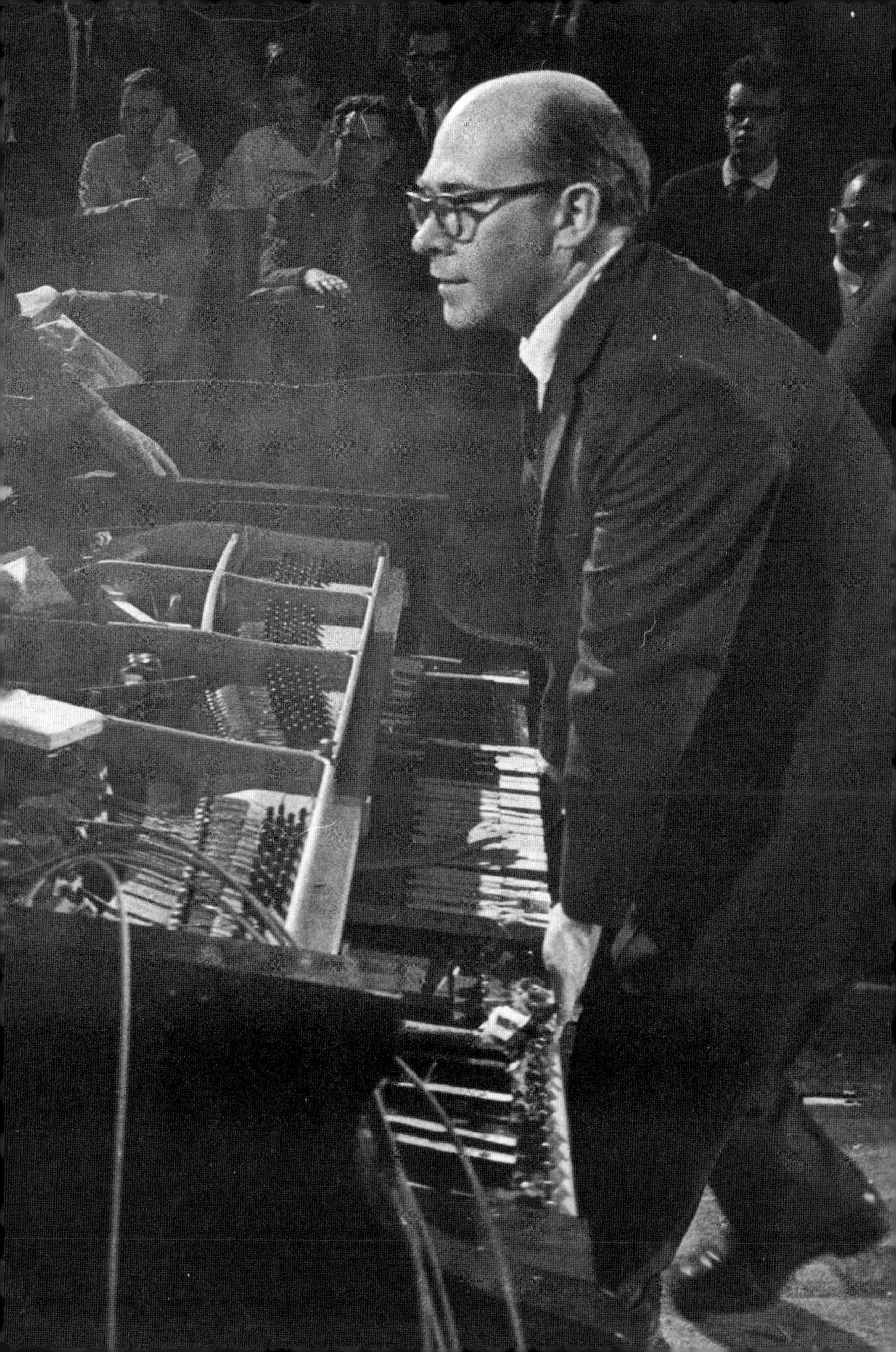

The University of Chicago Press, Chicago 60637
The University of Chicago Press, Ltd., London

Published 2026
Printed in the United States of America

35 34 33 32 31 30 29 28 27 26    1 2 3 4 5

ISBN-13: 978-0-226-65494-2 (cloth)
ISBN-13: 978-0-226-65513-0 (ebook)
DOI: https://doi.org/10.7208/chicago/9780226655130.001.0001

Front-matter image credits: Page i, Alison Knowles with Norman Kaplan, *Poem Drop Event at The House of Dust*, CalArts, 1971 (detail of fig. 5.12); courtesy California Institute of the Arts Library & Institute Archives. Page ii, Alison Knowles with *The Big Book*, 1967; © Alison Knowles, courtesy Staatsgalerie Stuttgart, Archiv Sohm, AS 2022/1032. Pages iv–v, Philip Corner, *Piano Activities*, at Fluxus Internationale Festpiele Neuester Musik, Wiesbaden, Germany, 1962 (detail of fig. I.3); image © The Museum of Modern Art, licensed by SCALA/Art Resource, NY.

Library of Congress Cataloging-in-Publication Data

Names: Woods, Nicole L., author.
Title: Performing chance : the art of Alison Knowles in/out of Fluxus / Nicole L. Woods.
Description: Chicago : The University of Chicago Press, 2026. | Includes bibliographical references and index.
Identifiers: LCCN 2025035957 | ISBN 9780226654942 (cloth) | ISBN 9780226655130 (ebook)
Subjects: LCSH: Knowles, Alison, 1933- —Criticism and interpretation. | Knowles, Alison, 1933- | Performance art—United States—History—20th century. | Installations (Art)—United States—History—20th century. | Fluxus (Group of artists) | Women artists—United States.
Classification: LCC N6537.K623 W66 2026
LC record available at https://lccn.loc.gov/2025035957

♾ This paper meets the requirements of ANSI/NISO Z39.48-1992 (Permanence of Paper).

# CONTENTS

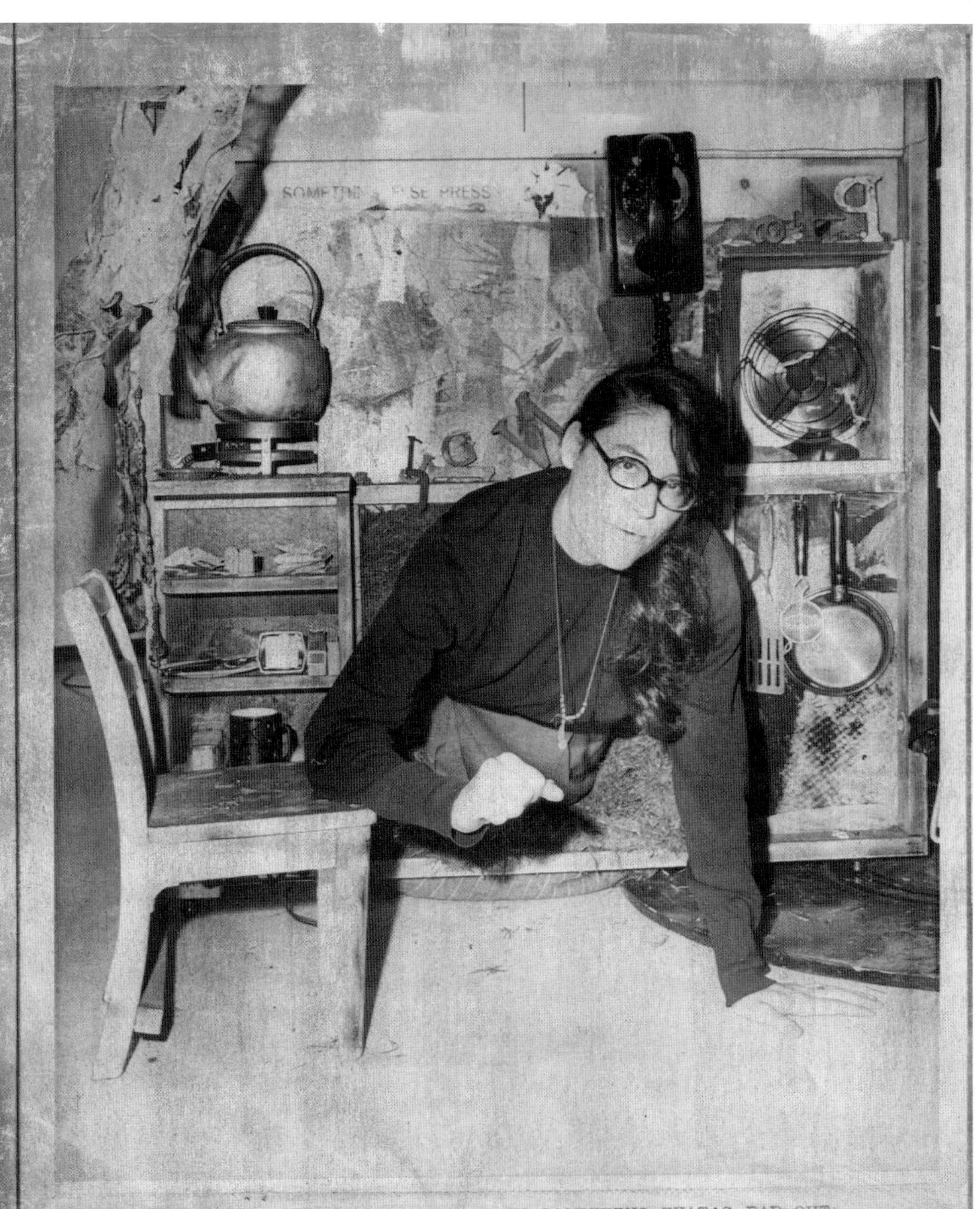

(CX5) CHICAGO, Oct. 20--SHE'S CLOSE IN SOMETHING THAT'S FAR OUT--
Contemporary art such as "The Big Book" here has creator, Alison
Knowles, very much a part of it today at museum given over to display
of controversial exhibits. This, among other things, went on display
at the Museum of Contemporary Art in Chicago. (AP Wirephoto) 1967
(fww61500esk-stf)(See story by Charles-Gene McDaniel)

# INTRODUCTION

In October 1967, New York–based artist Alison Knowles was photographed in a curiously staged domestic tableau (fig. I.1). With her left hand on the floor and right elbow on the seat of a small chair, she appears wresting her lower body through a tight portal. A hot plate and kettle sit atop a shelf on one side; on the other, cooking utensils hang below an electric fan. A rotary telephone is mounted just above her head. Close inspection reveals more eclectic items, including letterpress blocks—oversize letters and numbers—which, given Knowles's training as a painter and printmaker, suggest a habitat of both work and sustenance. Looking up at the camera, mouth slightly agape, she appears to be caught off guard.

**Figure I.1.** Associated Press wirephoto showing Alison Knowles with *The Big Book*, installed at the Museum of Contemporary Art, Chicago, October 1967. © Alison Knowles.

The Associated Press wirephoto, taken at a preview for *Pictures to Be Read/ Poetry to Be Seen*—the inaugural exhibition at Chicago's newly founded Museum of Contemporary Art (MCA)—records the first museum presentation of Knowles's large-scale installation *The Big Book*, which she'd constructed piecemeal in her New York home.[1] Measuring over eight feet high and comprising individual "pages" that pivoted on a steel spine, *The Big Book* provided an entryway with a grass tunnel, the makeshift kitchen, a small library with a typewriter, and an art gallery showing commissioned prints by artist friends and intimates, including George Brecht, Dick Higgins, and Carolee Schneemann (plate 1). Its immersive scale and evocation of functional spaces of everyday life exemplify Knowles's determination that art be composed to be lived in, not just looked at. Her physical demonstration at the press event not only illustrated how museumgoers might move between the monumental work's sections but underscored the expectation that they should (fig. I.2).

The AP distributed the photograph with a caption that pithily positioned Knowles's contribution within *Pictures to Be Read/Poetry to Be Seen*: "She's close in something that's far out." The MCA itself, it said, was given to "controversial exhibits."[2] That *The Big Book* was seen as "far out," even within a

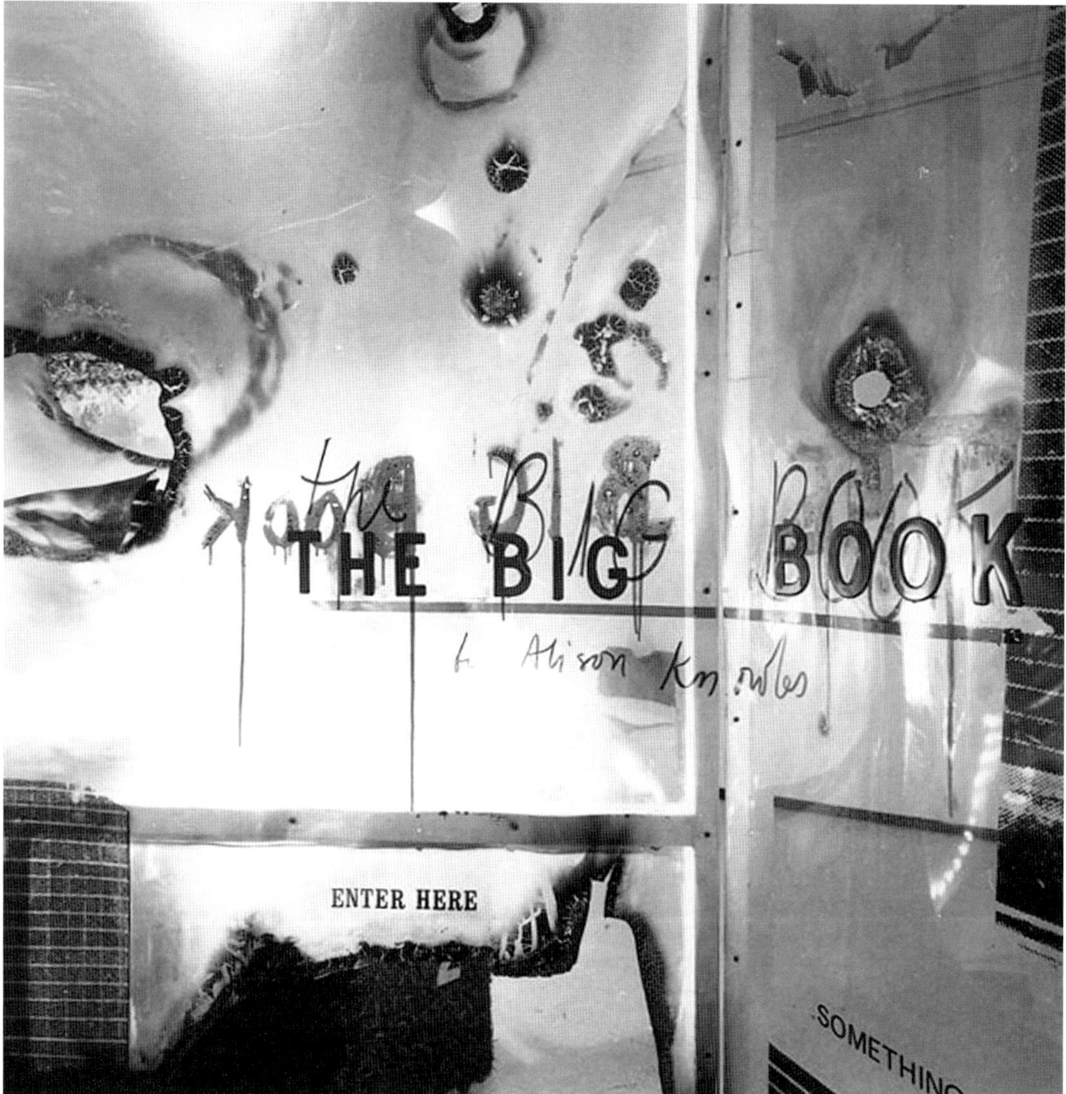


**Figure I.2.** Alison Knowles, *The Big Book*, 1967. Installation view showing entrance page, *Pictures to Be Read/Poetry to Be Seen*, Museum of Contemporary Art, Chicago. Photo: Dan Van Riper, © MCA Chicago. Artwork © Alison Knowles.

show whose title promised a radical inversion of image and text, speaks to both the thrill and the anxiety of cultural deracination; the work defied the conventional parameters of sculpture and, thus, confounded familiar, passive viewing. As one reviewer of the exhibition noted, "You can crawl into it, listen to it talk, read snippets of literature on its wall, scrutinize the pictures, and even settle down and have a cup of tea in its kitchen."[3]

By the time of the Chicago exhibition, Knowles had established herself as a full-fledged member of the post–World War II neo-avant-garde. A rather inchoate category, the term *neo-avant-garde* has been applied to artists, in the United States and abroad, whose disparate practices after 1950 transformed the aesthetic criteria set forth by the historical avant-garde—developing, as Hal Foster has argued, a "critique of the conventions of the traditional mediums" instigated by Dadaists and their kin, circa 1916, into "an investigation of the institution of art, its perceptual and cognitive, structural and discursive parameters."[4] Knowles's standing within this ontological recalibration centered primarily on her role in the founding of Fluxus in 1962 in Wiesbaden, Germany (figs. I.3–I.4), where she performed in now-canonical pieces of experimental art and music.

Fluxus was a loose, itinerant coalition of visual artists, poets, composers, and musicians working in Western Europe and North America whose core practitioners shared poetic "correspondences" (as Baudelaire might have put it), a general dissatisfaction with established art mediums and their prescribed hierarchies, and a particular antipathy, tinged with boredom, toward the restrictive economy of abstract expressionism, which had served as lingua franca for many in the previous generation of artists. Original Fluxus members Knowles, Brecht, Higgins, George Maciunas, Nam June Paik, Benjamin Patterson, and Emmett Williams turned away from their formal disciplinary training to work instead in the generative spaces *between* visual, textual, and musical forms. Writing three years after the group's first "Newest Music" festival in Wiesbaden, Higgins theorized the concept of "intermedia"—a neologism intended to expand and delimit the multifarious hybrid genres initiated within Fluxus, Happenings, minimalist music and dance, experimental film, concrete poetry, and other creative expressions of the period's dissident energy.[5]

The works and teachings of experimental composer John Cage were central to Higgins's intermedia schema and to the Fluxus artists' assault on the conventions of painting, sculpture, theater, and music. Artists who knew or worked closely with Cage applied his assiduous experimentalism across a broad swath of the arts.[6] Nonmusicians and visual artists—Higgins, Brecht, Al Hansen, and Happenings pioneer Allan Kaprow, among others—populated his courses at the New School for Social Research, hungry for transgression and dispirited by what they perceived as an exclusionary art world. In his "Experimental Composition" class, Cage instructed his pupils to embrace "everyday sounds," placing them on par with musical ones, and to eschew the "false" security of mastery, releasing themselves from the bonds of professional obligation.[7] When the MCA invited Knowles to exhibit *The Big Book* in its maiden show, she and her Fluxus compatriots had already toured Western Europe spreading the gospel of Cagean experimentalism. She and Cage had also begun to assemble and edit *Notations*, a publication of experimental scores that would be the first of many collaborations.[8]

As a founding member of Fluxus, Knowles stands out among its mostly male cadre. Yet she has remained a mystery, a minor character in the history of art whose accomplishments are generally noted but woefully understudied. Across six decades of pioneering conceptual and performance art, she has been the subject of analytical essays, journal articles and book chapters, and exhibition catalogs but, until now, no monographic study.[9] As with her contemporaries Simone Forti, Shigeko Kubota, Charlotte Moorman, and

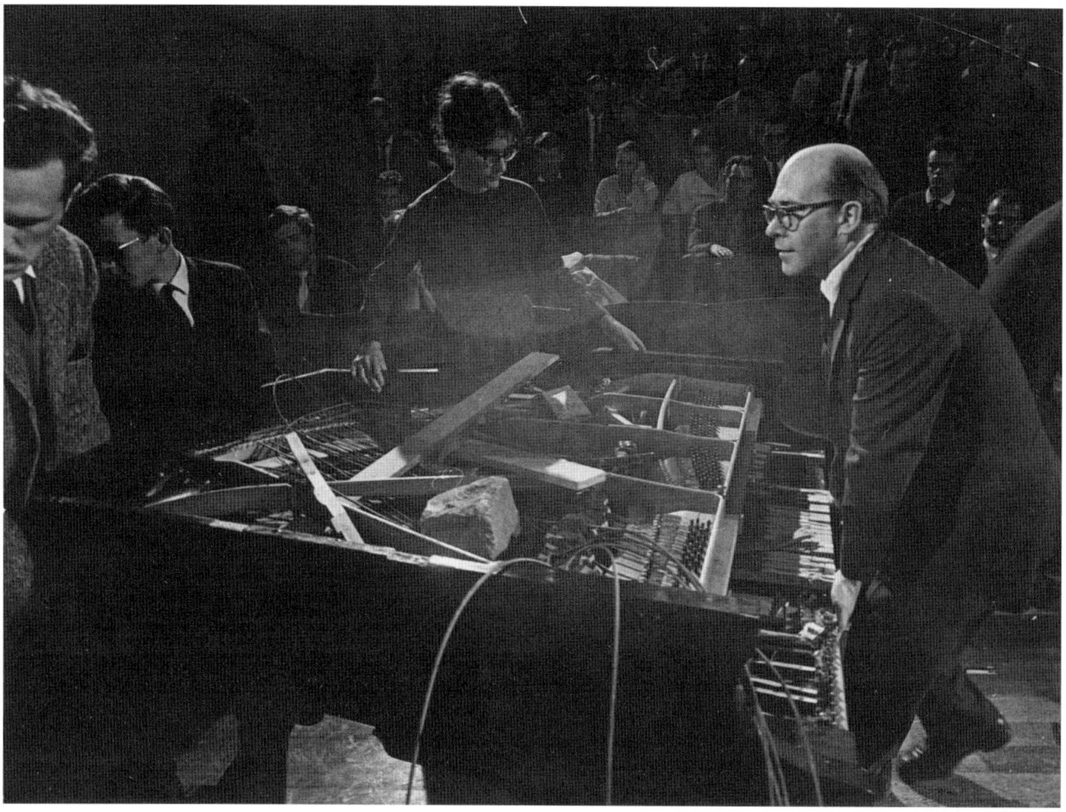

**Figure I.3.** Philip Corner, *Piano Activities*, performed during Fluxus Internationale Festpiele Neuester Musik, Hörsaal des Städtischen Museums, Wiesbaden, Germany, September 1, 1962. Performers: Dick Higgins, Alison Knowles, George Maciunas, Benjamin Patterson, Emmett Williams. Image © The Museum of Modern Art. Licensed by SCALA/Art Resource, NY.

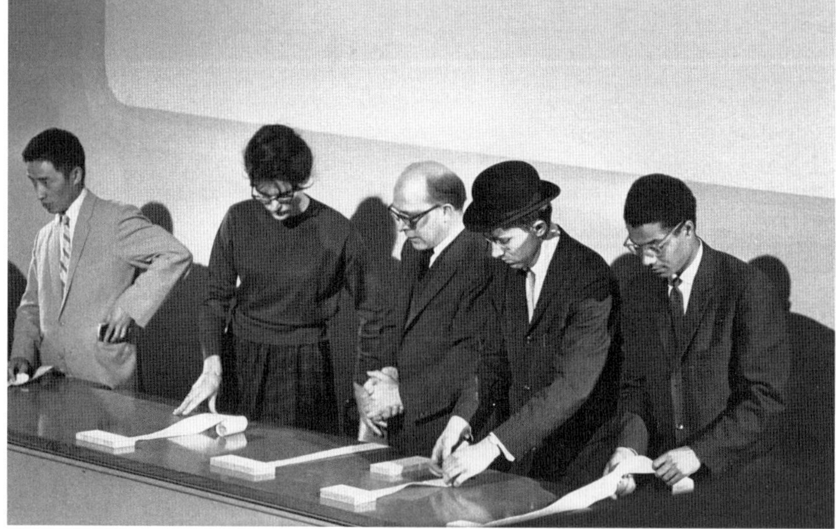

**Figure I.4.** Nam June Paik, Alison Knowles, Emmett Williams, George Maciunas, and Benjamin Patterson performing Maciunas's *In Memoriam to Adriano Olivetti* during *Concert No. 5*, Fluxus Internationale Festspiele Neuester Musik, Hörsaal des Städtischen Museum, Wiesbaden, September 8, 1962. Image © The Museum of Modern Art. Licensed by SCALA/Art Resource, NY.

Mieko Shiomi, Knowles's clever and groundbreaking production has suffered a double exclusion: first, because of the work's often ephemeral character and, second, because of her marginalized position relative to Fluxus men.[10] Curiously, her early collaborations with Paik and French Fluxus artist Ben Vautier are widely known and have been amply reproduced, albeit with little salient context or commentary, in the exhibition catalogs and other publications that served for decades as the foundational literature on Fluxus (see figs. 2.13, 3.3, 3.4, and 3.6). Even when the topic is specifically Fluxus's problematic gender politics, Knowles has been passed over, often in favor of women who were not involved in the originary European Fluxus concerts or listed in any major texts or broadsides stateside.[11]

Complicating the historical record are the symbolic and material purges conducted by George Maciunas, the self-appointed "chairman" and organizer of all manner of Fluxus activities. Maciunas maintained meticulous diagrams, newsletters, and object inventories, from which he periodically eliminated artists he no longer deemed suitable for the Fluxus brand.[12] For one reason or another, mainly to do with perceived disloyalty, petty jealousies, and heated exchanges between Maciunas and Higgins around the latter's establishment of Something Else Press as an alternative to Fluxus publishing ventures (including clashes over contributors and copyrights), Knowles and her artworks were for a time erased from the group's official chronicles, only to be reinstated once tempers had cooled.[13] Higgins, whom Knowles had married in 1960, admonished Maciunas in August 1966 for dragging her into their personal conflict, writing, "Really George, if you are mad at me, don't bring poor Alison into it."[14] In another letter a week later, he criticized Maciunas's actions more broadly, as "personal cultism and aggrandizement":

> While you invented the term "Fluxus" (and nobody will deny you that) you have consistently destroyed its utility, antagonized your real friends, and misused the whole situation . . . But Fluxus means too much (and I insist on that) to allow any individual person to reduce it to a means of confinement of people's work based on your own personal taste . . . I made a grievous error in 1963 not to perform the Stockholm Fluxus without you, and in so doing, for the first time, established a precedent on the basis of which you have been able systematically to reduce the most important artistic tendency of the last half century (with Dada, of the last century) to a personal fief.[15]

Knowles, though frustrated by the conflict, has often rationalized it as part and parcel of the combustible mixture of strong personalities among the Fluxus set, and she recalls being taken seriously by her closest male peers, especially Brecht and Williams.[16] In contemporaneous correspondence with Higgins, however, she confessed to feeling estrangement and disconnection, despite enjoying "exceptional access" to mentors like Cage.[17]

Art historical neglect and Fluxus infighting notwithstanding, some writers and literary critics have attended to and lauded Knowles's work. Poets Charlie Morrow, Jerome Rothenberg, and George Quasha were among the first to hail her heterogeneous approach to social performance and the thicket of language in the domestic everyday, including or referencing her work in several groundbreaking anthologies in the late 1960s and early 1970s.[18] Their rich interpretations, affording critical space to Knowles's notational scores, performances, and book installations, situate her verbal-visual constructions firmly within the literary avant-garde. She has, indeed, in various contexts, referred to herself as a "visual poet" or "performance poet"—hybrid designations that again reject any rigidly medium-specific working method.[19] And for years she collaborated closely with another early affiliate of Fluxus, composer and experimental poet Jackson Mac Low.

Yet Knowles's practice in and beyond Fluxus—as a prolific author (in various media), bookmaker (at all scales), and printmaker (of every technical process)—evinces, as this book aims to demonstrate, a thoroughgoing aesthetic commitment to questions of *translation in form*: propositional recipes for physical action; word collages to be read out of sequence in fragmented, staccato cadences; book-objects and installations to be activated by reader-viewers; and computational poetry and paper sculptures that presage new genres.[20]

*Performing Chance* is the first in-depth look at Knowles's influential but insufficiently examined career.[21] Acknowledging earlier raconteurs' and curators' groundbreaking chronicles of Fluxus artists' collective achievements, it argues the necessity of a monographic focus that can hold Knowles's art and life in productive tension.[22] It considers, for example, that for the first two decades of her practice, Knowles labored to create an artistic life as a woman—or, as she prefers, an artist who *happened to be a woman*—and as a woman artist who happened to be a mother. Confronting both structural and softer forms of sexism in the art world necessitated a nimble approach—a position of professional precarity felt acutely by Knowles and artist friends like Schneemann, as well as Kubota and Shiomi, both of whom she collaborated with in the 1960s.[23]

Recent scholarship on Fluxus has jettisoned wide-ranging genealogies of the movement in favor of examinations of specific artworks and artists.[24] This book contributes to this development by establishing the groundwork for Knowles's emergence within the group. Through a series of interconnected close readings of her Fluxus scores of the early 1960s, I argue, for example, that a study of the material conditions of their making (both historical and conceptual) reveals an aesthetic preference for a subtle account of institutions imbricated with the banality of daily habits. One form this takes is Knowles's persistent plea that we examine how we know and sustain the material world; how our bodies are inscribed in a process of object-subject formation; and how these interventions are negotiated between public and private spheres. A related aim is to show how Knowles made her durational, ephemeral working method a viable medium for artistic representation—and one that is profoundly, if not obviously, political. As her work emerges from painting into live-art practices, her adoption of open-ended procedures and readymade (even edible) materials participates in and expands an exploratory discursive space, shared with other artistic projects, that facilitates social interaction.

The following chapters establish a chronological scaffolding for Knowles's diverse output across two decades, roughly 1958 to 1975, contending with the concerns and artistic strategies that underscore her entire oeuvre, namely, the changing status of the art object (and art maker) in postwar American society as filtered through various techniques of the body. Putting key works into conversation with Cage and her Fluxus cohorts, as well as contemporaries like Schneemann, Philip Corner, Annea Lockwood, and James Tenney, the book aims to give a fuller account of Knowles's radical shift from painting to performance, installation, and computational art.

Chapter 1 sets the stage, charting Knowles's career from the mid-1950s to the early 1960s. I examine key details of her family life, her training with Adolph Gottlieb at Pratt Institute as an abstract expressionist painter, and her deepening involvement with Lower Manhattan's various avant-garde circles (Happenings, Beat poetics, experimental theater, etc.). This chapter examines her early work in greater depth than any previous presentation in the Fluxus literature and lays the foundation for her embrace of nontraditional forms of making. Chapter 2 fleshes out her performance life in Fluxus, delineating her preoccupation with the language of notational scoring and the conceptual framework of indeterminacy by thematically analyzing major propositional pieces like *Make a Salad* (1962; fig. 2.1) and *Nivea Cream Piece* (1962–1963; fig. 2.9). Her inventive interpretation of the propositional event score set her apart from her peers, resulting in presciently incisive meditations on quotidian routines and the politics of the everyday.

Chapter 3 focuses on two works concerned with food and sound: the early book project *Bean Rolls* (1963; fig. 3.9), a handheld canned work distributed within Maciunas's *Fluxkits*, and *The Identical Lunch* (1967–1973)—a durational score, edible performance, and eventual series of canvases (figs. 3.14–3.22). Delving into Knowles's interest in public space, portability, and emergent technologies (including computers), chapters 4 and 5 reconstruct the histories of, respectively, *The Big Book* (1966–1969; fig. 4.2) and *The House of Dust* (1967–1975; fig. 5.8) and consider formative collaborations from the period in which those monumental works were realized, including her time as a professor at California Institute of the Arts and her founding of a feminist workshop and publication.

Formally, Knowles's use of time-based events and durational media to probe notions of artistic authority and control released her into an exploratory mode of practice that could both specify and generalize corporeal experiences—hence, the move toward demonstrations of shared biosocial rituals like eating. By freeing the *work*—both the labor and the object of art—from traditional procedures of making, she not only disengages from conventional questions about color, shape, and form but, I argue, enacts an aesthetic wherein chance and the temporal-durational multiply compositional choices. Importantly, Knowles's artistic comportment in the 1960s and 1970s did not align directly with the strategies of US feminist activism still being formulated at the start of her career—her interest in intersubjectivity and perceptual systems of the body was at times only elliptically political. Yet in small-scale objects, for example, a poetics of touch, sensation, and texture—sentient knowledge in Knowles's hands—translated to a form of sociopolitical engagement wherein chance was not only a technique but a life practice.

## Toward a Protofeminist Dialectic of Chance

Knowles's inclusion in *Pictures to Be Read/Poetry to Be Seen* came at a remarkable moment in her personal and professional life. Her twin daughters Hannah and Jessica, born in August 1964, were by 1967 active toddlers. At the same time, the artist was comanaging Something Else Gallery and Something Else Press, both based in her Chelsea home, as well as other projects—all while mourning the unexpected death of her father Ned.[25] And her late-1950s shift toward chance and intermedia was crystallizing into a sustained artistic sensibility, as she effected her shift from Fluxus performances to monumental public environments (in *The Big Book*), aleatory computational poetics (*The House of Dust*), and everyday routines (*The Identical Lunch*).

Another notable occurrence in 1967, under the auspices of Something Else Press (SEP), afforded Knowles the chance to collaborate with Marcel Duchamp to reissue a 1936 print. A photograph by art critic and historian William S. (Bill) Wilson documenting one of their meetings in Duchamp's Tenth Street apartment shows the artists in a state of mutual concentration, Knowles leaning over Duchamp's shoulder to flip through colored paper swatches (fig. I.5). The revivified *Coeurs Volants*—the "fluttering hearts" image originally published in the French artistic and literary journal *Cahiers d'Art*—was to grace the dust jacket of *Sweethearts*, a book of concrete poetry by fellow Fluxist Emmett Williams (fig. I.6).[26] According to an SEP announcement card, there would also be a limited edition of twenty-four copies, screen-printed by Knowles on black proof paper and signed and numbered by Duchamp.[27] Higgins, who was also present at a second meeting, remembers Knowles's process:

> Using an available screen of a simple disk of color she had printed, on a brilliant matte-surface silk screen paper, a disk of red and a disk of blue, overlapping, the one directly above the other, matching the colors of the original printing of *les coeurs volants* as exactly as possible.[28]

Decades later, Knowles vividly recounted her symbiotic exchange with the famed provocateur, pointedly noting the arbitrary, even comical, nature of the final selection process:

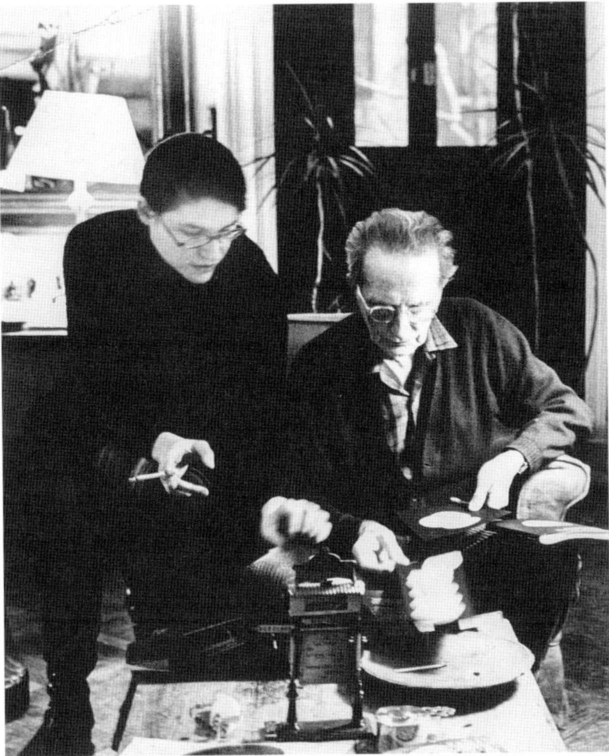

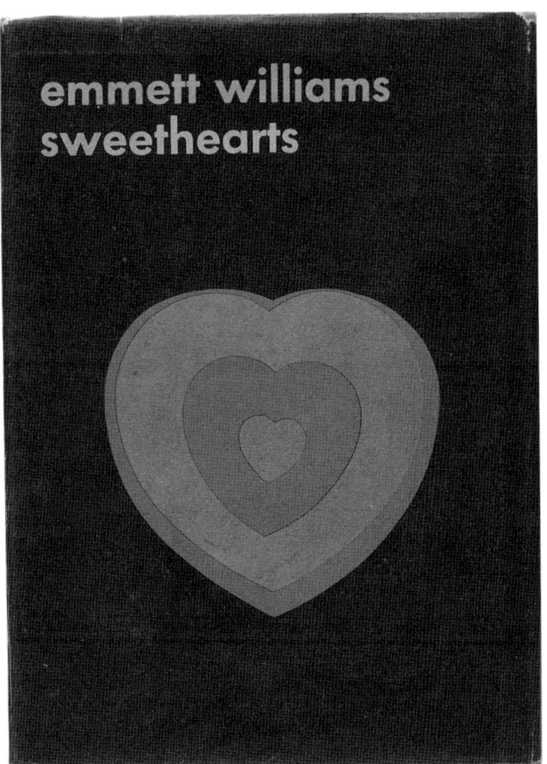


**Figure I.5.** William S. Wilson, "Alison Knowles and Marcel Duchamp working on *Coeurs Volants*, New York, 1967." Courtesy Estate of William S. Wilson.

**Figure I.6.** Emmett Williams, *Sweethearts* (Something Else Press, 1967). Cover design and image are by Alison Knowles.

> Some visits later I arrived at his door with eleven color swatches on black paper, each with two overlapping circles in red and blue in slightly different tints and hues . . . He chose one and set it aside on the buffet. After lunch, his wife Teeny picked up the swatch and said, "Oh Marcel, when did you do this?" He smiled, took a pencil and signed the swatch. The following year, Marcel died. Arturo Schwarz wrote me suggesting I had the last readymade. Teeny and Richard Hamilton assured me that I did not, but that I had a piece of interesting memorabilia.[29]

Higgins contested that assessment, insisting that the signed swatch should count as a veritable readymade. He attempted to have it insured as a Duchamp work and argued to Schwarz—documenter, cataloger, and reproducer of readymades—that Knowles's artistic remaking was more than a mere facsimile or an arresting souvenir.[30] In a letter to Schwarz, who had requested one or two copies of the signed and numbered edition to be included in Duchamp's 1969 catalogue raisonné, Higgins explained that the collaborative limited-edition poster "was an outgrowth of the project of putting LES COEURS VOLANTS on the cover of Emmett Williams's sweethearts."[31] Significantly, such entanglements of originality, reproduction, and the question of what constitutes a work of art were key to Knowles's investigations of experimental activities and cooperative invention.

This convergence with one of the most prolific and influential artists of the historical avant-garde was but one of many encounters that would shape Knowles's artistic practice. Collaborating with Duchamp provided the formative, almost didactic experience of seeing his process up close and reaffirmed her sense of the exquisite, sometimes humorous possibilities of unintentional choices, aesthetic and otherwise. Moreover, it demonstrated that one could revitalize old works under new conditions, new contexts, even new "thoughts," as Duchamp once claimed for the readymade. As coauthor of the new fluttering hearts, Knowles made her own use of the image, silk-screening it, for example, onto T-shirts and baby onesies, some of which, years later, she sold at various art auctions or gave away as gifts.

The aleatory procedures Knowles developed throughout the 1960s and 1970s frame an ongoing exploration of everyday sensorial data that appears in various manifestations—from language-based notational scores and Fluxus performances to *objet trouvé* experiments within her lived spaces to one of the first computer-generated poems to large-scale installations like *The Big Book*. Many of the arguments put forth in this book are grounded in the assertion that, whatever the materials, Knowles conceives of and practices chance-derived processes through two primary means: first, the isolation of everyday routines and, second, an openness to perception that refashions our understanding of the relay between an artist and her public. She has amplified, for instance, the traditional format of musical notation into an elegantly understated and deeply pensive mode of working, often involving physical interaction with and mental penetration of readymade found and manufactured objects—beans, shoes, paper, and other stuffs of the domestic sphere. In key works under study here, we observe material activations of the canvas, of the street, of the word, of body and gesture, and of the abundant sources of everyday experiences. Within the *iterative* space of these experiences, I view Knowles's most richly inflected works as an exploration of the significance of concrete action that slyly unveils, among other insights, a politics of form amidst the tremendous complexity of social life. Her disruption of art's hermetic nature—its adherence to conventional means, exhibitionary tactics, and distribution processes—informs the core readings throughout.

To consider Knowles's embrace of chance aesthetics as it flowered in the early 1960s is to point to how the artist inflected both Duchampian and Cagean terms with what I call a *protofeminist dialectic of chance*. This dialectic is best expressed not in any direct involvement in the activist politics of the era—Knowles never participated in women's marches for equality, for example—but in the formal economy of her work: the task-based structure of her propositional scores and their live iterations, which observed an acute awareness of the domestic sphere in both its public and private operations. Antispectacular, language-centered, and coded to the terrain and objects of daily existence, Knowles's aesthetic of minimally produced events and scores, I argue, is premised on the notion that openness, where performers/viewers carry out simple actions, *expands* the method of chance operations (and autonomous subjectivity) set into motion by Cage by adding a recognition of gender and its relation to the body in social space. Knowles's integration of chance and domesticity (in the form, for example, of food and food preparation, shoes, hand cream, children's art, caretaking, homemaking, etc.) is characterized, via protofeminist dialectical procedures, by a set of shifting terms: immediate and measured, public and private, literal and metaphorical, practical and imaginative, modest and confident, intelligent and humorous, simple and complex.

While Knowles undoubtedly owes much to Cage and repeatedly cites him as an early model and champion of her work—"he brought in joy and revolution"—this book asserts a nuanced counternarrative alongside that of yoking visual art with aleatory aesthetics.[32] In fact, works created by Knowles in and outside of Fluxus constitute a remarkable response to a diverse array of source material and theoretical influences. It is worth noting Knowles's prolonged commitment to multicultural literary and spiritual praxis. Asked in 1991 for "a list of books that have retained significance," she included texts by Cage but also Henry David Thoreau's *Journals*, translations of the *I Ching* and *The Book of the Hopi*, and D. T. Suzuki's *Essays on Zen Buddhism*.[33] Other conceptual emissaries invoked over the course of her career include French symbolist poet Stéphane Mallarmé, James Joyce's epics *Ulysses* and *Finnegans Wake*, and the concrete poetry of Emmett Williams, one of her most intimate confidantes. Different authors served variously as models for amplifications of semantic visuality and thus were foundational to her own artistic maturation.[34]

*Performing Chance* thus aspires to address a curious blind spot in more traditional accounts of Fluxus, and by extension, to reposition Knowles's remarkable oeuvre as paradigmatic of the kind of rigorous experimentalism developed among the neo-avant-garde. To those ends, I closely inspect primary source materials extracted from numerous archives, as well as unpublished photographs, ephemera, and rarely seen artworks.[35] Drawing too on interviews with the artist conducted over the course of several years, this study discloses the ways in which Knowles's work instituted a range of chance-based formal tactics whose ends were little concerned with the legacy of painting, for example, and more conscious of an ever-changing political age rife with conflict and social change.

In what follows, I contextualize and narrativize episodes in her artistic evolution from the late 1950s to the mid-1970s in relation to aesthetic, institutional, and political developments surrounding the formation of a viable postwar American avant-garde. By concentrating on Knowles as a crucial yet overlooked player within this matrix, my objective is to offer a more complex account of the histories of performance, conceptual, and women's art. In mobilizing the figure of Knowles and her multifaceted work bridging experimental visual and acoustic arts, we gain as well an expansive rereading of both Fluxus and late modernist art history.

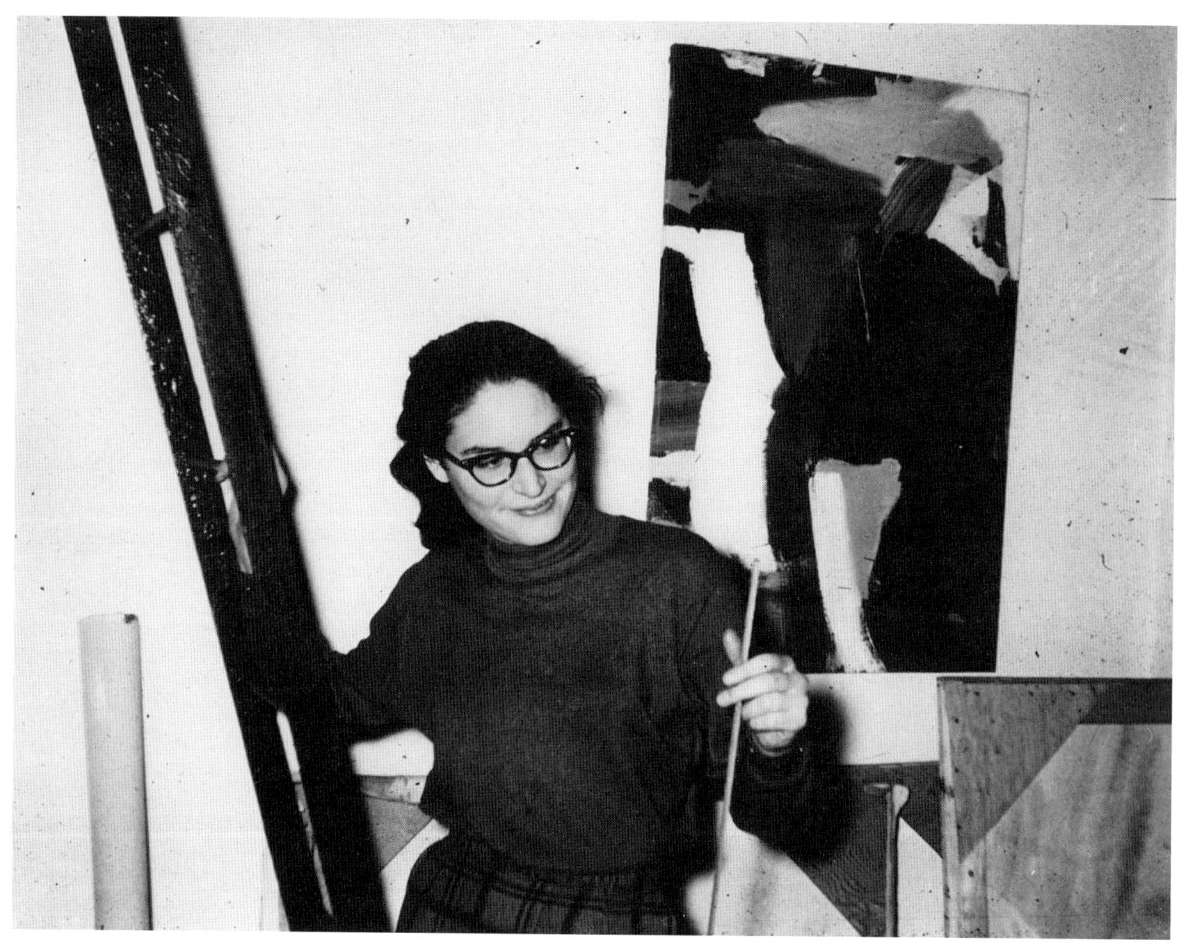

**Figure 1.1.** Dick Higgins, *Alison Knowles in Context*, 1959. Getty Research Institute, Los-Angeles (940003). © Estate of Dick Higgins.

# 1 FROM PAINTING TO PERFORMANCE

> She had a loft, which she adored. No two boards were parallel, no corners were square. There were angles everywhere. She was just emerging from *tachisme*, and her paintings were like her loft.
> **Dick Higgins**[1]

Alison Knowles is pictured in her New York studio. The photograph, from 1959, shows her from the waist up, dressed in a turtleneck sweater and tartan pants. She sports thick-rimmed glasses, and her long hair is pulled back into a soft ponytail (fig. 1.1). A paint-spattered ladder angles through the frame to her right; seen edge-on, it warps the sense of depth in the picture field. One arm rests on a rung of the ladder; the other lightly grasps a thin maulstick used to steady a painter's hand. Other than the stick, no working tools are in sight, but a finished painting hangs over her left shoulder, below which several canvases lean against the stark white wall. Knowles does not look directly at the camera; her bemused smile seems directed toward the end of the stick. The black-and-white snapshot, taken by fellow artist Dick Higgins—her partner, at that point, in a budding but complicated romance—implies an intimate and tender playfulness.[2]

Knowles's artistic formation originated in the dialogic space of post–World War II modernist abstraction, and the large rectangular canvases visible in the loft portrait and another photograph taken during the same period (fig. 1.2) display gestural affinities with the late-career paintings of Hans Hofmann, a German immigrant and respected art teacher working in Greenwich Village. We see, in Knowles's canvases, patchworks of taut, multihued shapes, assertive swaths of pigment layered across the fabric ground, even spilling onto its tacked sides. In both photos we see other paintings turned toward the wall, their bare wooden stretchers revealing no sense of any obverse renderings. The withholding piques one's curiosity: Do these canvases too bear sweeping forms, striking layers of viscid materiality, or are they simply taut supports awaiting the artist's hand? Are the paintings unfinished or unsatisfying? Is their being turned away from the camera concealment? The presence of numerous frames is evidence of prolific output, while the absence of pictorial

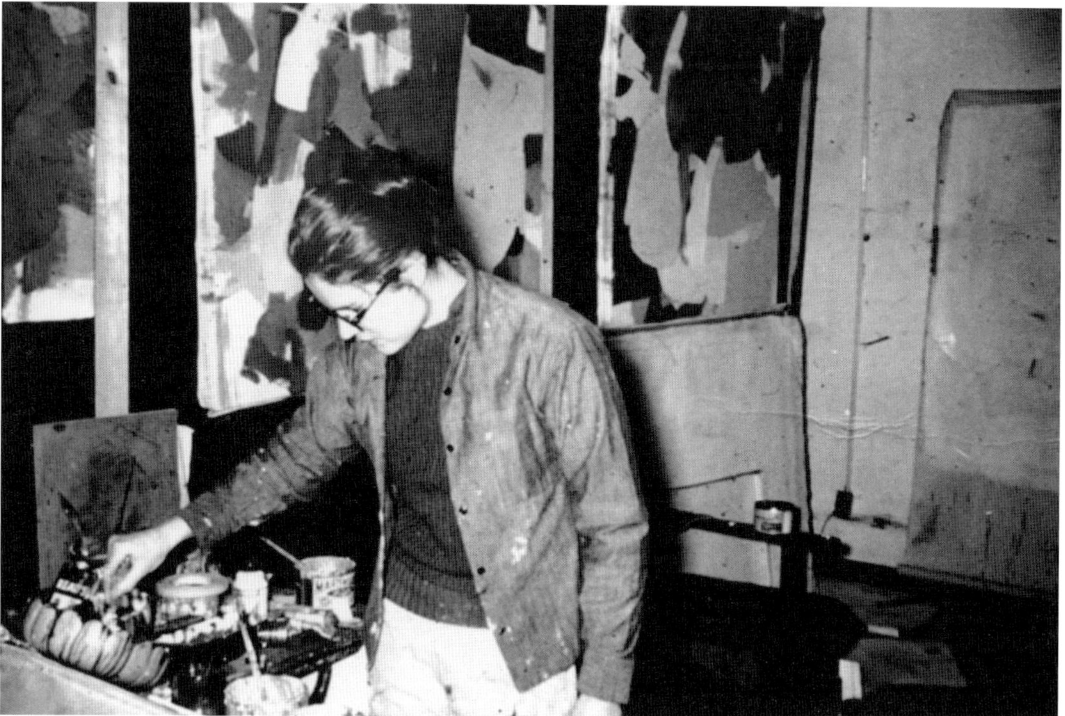

**Figure 1.2.** Alison Knowles in her studio, New York City, ca. 1956–1958. Black-and-white photograph, 12 × 18 in. (approx.). Photographer unknown. Collection of the author.

content speaks *to* arrested action, for both the canvases under cover and the artist as producer. Visual documentation of Knowles's life as a painter, the studio images also beckon a moment when her professional work was beginning to shift toward the burgeoning realm of experimental art via individual and collaborative activities in the early Happenings, aleatory music, and nontraditional theater of the later 1950s.

This chapter traces the contours of Knowles's early artistic life through vignettes of an emerging critical practice in the late 1950s and early 1960s. The period saw her disavowals, first, of abstract expressionism and its exclusionary politics and, second, of the dogmatic modernist framework that then still insulated the domain of visual art from the direct incorporation of source material from the external world. Knowles's appropriation of poetic language, cast-off objects, images from popular print media, and diurnal rituals, and her exploration of the intersection of food and performance, would thereafter form the crucible of her oeuvre. Moreover, in adopting a heterogeneous approach to making art outside of extant categories or histories, she contributed to both the extension of post–World War II neo-avant-garde experimentalism and the diversification of work made by women artists. Indeed, Knowles's pursuit throughout these years of an open-ended, iterative, inherently generative practice fostered an aesthetic evolution that provides a new model for the painterly subject and its performative differentiation. Her instrumental role in the formation of Fluxus, and within late modernism more generally, lies precisely in her engagement with everyday speech and quotidian actions and materials, foregrounding, as it were, a subtly gendered critique and rigorous expansion of the Cagean program.

## The Artist as Painter

Alison Knowles was born April 29, 1933, in New York City. She was raised in a modest colonial house in Scarsdale, a suburban enclave thirty miles northeast of Manhattan, where her family struggled financially amid the area's rising affluence. Her father, Edwin (Ned) Knowles, shuttled between academic posts at Queens College and New York University before becoming a professor of English and dean of general studies at Pratt Institute in Brooklyn in the late 1940s. A scholar of Thomas Shelton, who published the first English translation of *Don Quixote*, Ned specialized in Spanish-English literary relations but published little else on account of a heavy teaching load.[3] Her mother, Lois (née Beckwith) Knowles descended from a middle-class family in Lancaster, Pennsylvania, and studied at Goucher College in Baltimore, Maryland. While Alison and her older brother Lawrence (Larry) were children, Lois contributed to the family's tight budget by working part-time in nursery schools and as a hospital technician. Occasional tensions between Alison, who had no interest in being a housewife, and her mother were often smoothed over by her good-natured father and brother.

Her parents' bourgeois aspirations were apparent in the family's move to Scarsdale, in pursuit of "good schools." But Knowles has especially praised Ned for his "very ambitious" focus on her education and for encouraging her interest in literature, visual art, and music.[4] It was for Ned that she crafted, almost daily, small, hand-drawn books casting Walt Disney characters in invented stories.[5] Ned's research on *Don Quixote* further inspired an interest in the enchantment of episodic novels, narrative invention, and stylizations of language, including French, which she studied seriously in high school.[6]

After graduating from Scarsdale High School in 1951, Knowles majored in fine art and French literature at Middlebury College in Vermont. Per the terms of her scholarship—and to subsidize her living expenses—she worked at Le Chateau, the dining room in the francophone residence hall, where students communicated exclusively in French.[7] Knowles's aesthetic interest in wedding art and poetry is apparent already in her undergraduate coursework. In a fine arts seminar, for example, Knowles examined William Blake's *House of Death* illustration for book XI of John Milton's *Paradise Lost*—a paper that was graded down for being "perhaps too literary."[8] The course was taught by Arthur K. D. Healy, then chair of the Art Department and an artist celebrated in Vermont and New York for his exquisite watercolor landscapes. Throughout the mid-1940s and 1950s, Healy taught fine art, was an active critic, and exhibited his paintings and drawings at the Macbeth Gallery on East Fifty-Seventh Street.[9] Healy was a popular professor, sympathetic and encouraging, and Knowles enjoyed his classes. Overall, however, her experience at Middlebury left her feeling alienated, restless, homesick, and bored. When her scholarship ended, in 1954, she moved back to New York, to the basement of her parents' new residence at 278 West Fourth Street in Greenwich Village, and switched to painting full-time at Pratt, where she could pursue her education for free thanks to her father's teaching position.[10]

Having studied with several artist-teachers at Pratt, including painters Adolph Gottlieb and Richard Lindner, watercolorist Roger Crossgrove, and lithographer Leander Fornas, Knowles graduated with honors in 1956 with a BFA in painting and illustration.[11] She continued taking classes there for the next two and a half years, closely working and occasionally socializing with abstract expressionists Gottlieb and Franz Kline, who often substituted for Gottlieb in the evenings.[12] With uninterrupted training and recognition from supportive mentors, there was a palpable sense that she could become, in her words, "the next Helen Frankenthaler," a New York–based artist whose ethereal abstractions Knowles greatly admired. Born in 1928, Frankenthaler was just five years older than Knowles but by the mid-1950s had several solo shows at Tibor de Nagy Gallery and had been written up in *Life* magazine as one of four "notable artists who happen to be women."[13]

At Middlebury, Knowles typically painted with thin washes. At Pratt, Gottlieb encouraged her to paint with a palette knife, sweeping broad, viscous strokes across an all-over ground on larger canvases. Gottlieb "said very little to anyone," Knowles recalls, "but spoke directly in front of the work to each person so it [became] a personal critical dialogue about art with each one of us. He made me feel I could be a great painter."[14] Describing his personality and teaching approach further, she notes:

> Certainly, Gottlieb had a kind of mystery about himself. [During] most of the class at Pratt, in the night school, he would read the *New York Post* and then stand up for the last half hour and go to each student. And it was effective because I had been through the struggle of trying to draw the figure, the human figure, for years at Pratt, and I distinctly remember the night he told me that I could be a painter without drawing the perfect charcoal nude. It was one of those memorable things someone says to you. That was very exciting.[15]

Gottlieb also purportedly advised her to find an abandoned loft and convert it into a studio space fit for painting and storing enormous canvases. Knowles agreed and took the loft at 423 Broadway—thus becoming among the first in a generation of artists to reside in Lower Manhattan's SoHo neighborhood.[16]

While at Pratt, Knowles also collaborated on several graphic arts projects. Flexing newly acquired technical skills in layout and type design, she was for a time part of the production staff for *ADLIB*, a student-run publication supported by the Art School's Department of Graphic Arts and Illustration. The 1956 issue, one of very few surviving works from her student days, offers key insights into her aesthetic temperament (fig. 1.3).[17] Knowles helped design the issue and created an original woodcut to accompany an abridgment of American bard Carl Sandburg's prosodic free-verse poem "Upstream" (1922).[18] Sandburg might seem a peculiar choice, but in the 1950s he was an immensely popular cultural figure widely known through recordings of his poems on vinyl LPs.[19] Knowles cited his popularity, his poetry albums, and her reading of his books as a child in a contributor's note—a highly selective choice that signaled a sophisticated cultural-literary acumen.[20] In her *ADLIB* spread, Knowles sets five of Sandburg's original seven lines in sans serif type and enfolds the text with bold, black expressionist strokes (fig. 1.4). Her imagery, while certainly abstract, responds to the poem's content and can easily be read as suggesting an advancing central figure. When queried about the decision to elide lines 4 and 5, "The strong mothers pulling them on . . . / The strong mothers pulling them from a dark sea, a great prairie, a long mountain," Knowles later cited limited space and time constraints in the production deadline.[21] While she now considers this a "poor" student project, the imagery documents her early training in visual communication and evidences an investment in fusing the graphic arts with painting and poetry.

After Pratt it took more than two years of soliciting exposure before Knowles was offered her first solo painting exhibition, at the Nonagon Gallery at 99 Second Avenue near Sixth Street, in spring 1958.[22] An eccentric and versatile space in the East Village founded by artists Dorothy Podber and Eunice (Skid) Shality, the gallery would, the following winter, host the performance recorded as Charles Mingus's live album *Mingus in Wonderland*.[23] Knowles's show immediately followed Black Mountain poet and ceramist M. C. Richards's pottery Happening and exhibit *Clay Things to Touch . . .*, and both shows were featured in a gallery review in the *New York Herald Tribune* (fig. 1.5).[24] From an accompanying photograph, it is clear that Knowles presented the type of large abstract canvases evident in loft photographs from this era and that the opening was attended by her parents and her first husband, James ("Jim") Ericson.[25] Ericson, a New York–born son of a New England Episcopal minister whom Knowles met at Middlebury, graduated from Haverford College and was studying social work at NYU when they were married just days after Knowles graduated from Pratt.[26] During their union, which lasted just two years, they lived in Knowles's downtown loft.

Responses to Knowles's show were mostly positive, save for one acerbic review by Robert Warren Dash, the in-house critic at *Arts* magazine, who decried the "angry" artist's "leaden and weary" brushwork, its eclectic strokes "unrelated to the whole," and mocked her alleged failure to deliver sufficiently nonobjective paintings: "pathetic realities of the figurative chunkily crouch" in compositions evoking the "furiously tangled emptiness of crowds." However laudable Knowles's color palette and formal choices, Dash could not sanction the supposed intrusion of not just gravity but discourse—"a desire for speech border[ing] on the lip-edge of calligraphy"—into the sacred space of purified

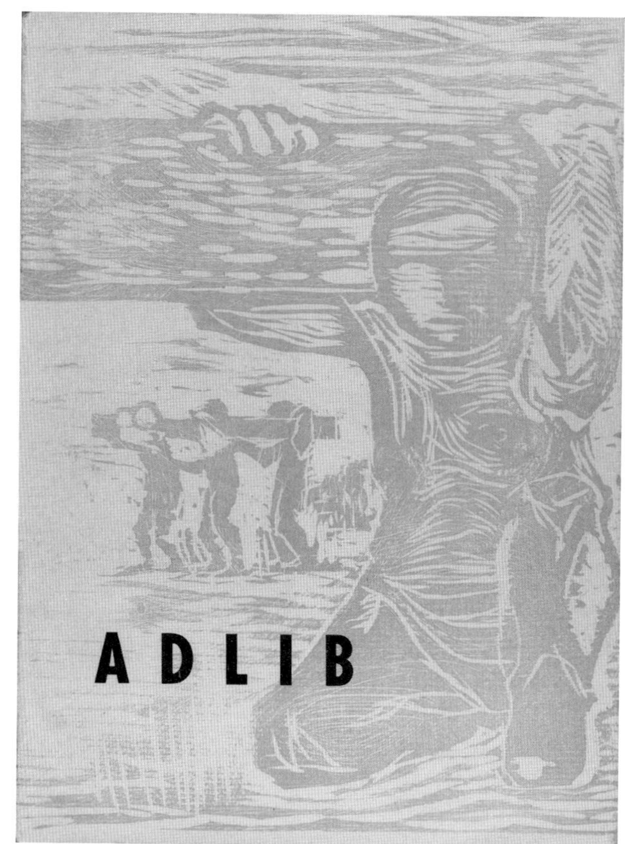


**Figure 1.3.** *ADLIB*, no. 4 (1956), cover. Layout and woodcut prints by Alison Knowles. Photo: Evan Graham. Courtesy Pratt Institute Archives, Brooklyn, NY.

**Figure 1.4.** *ADLIB*, no. 4 (1956), pages 32–33. Layout and woodcut print by Alison Knowles. Photo: Evan Graham. Courtesy Pratt Institute Archives, Brooklyn, NY.

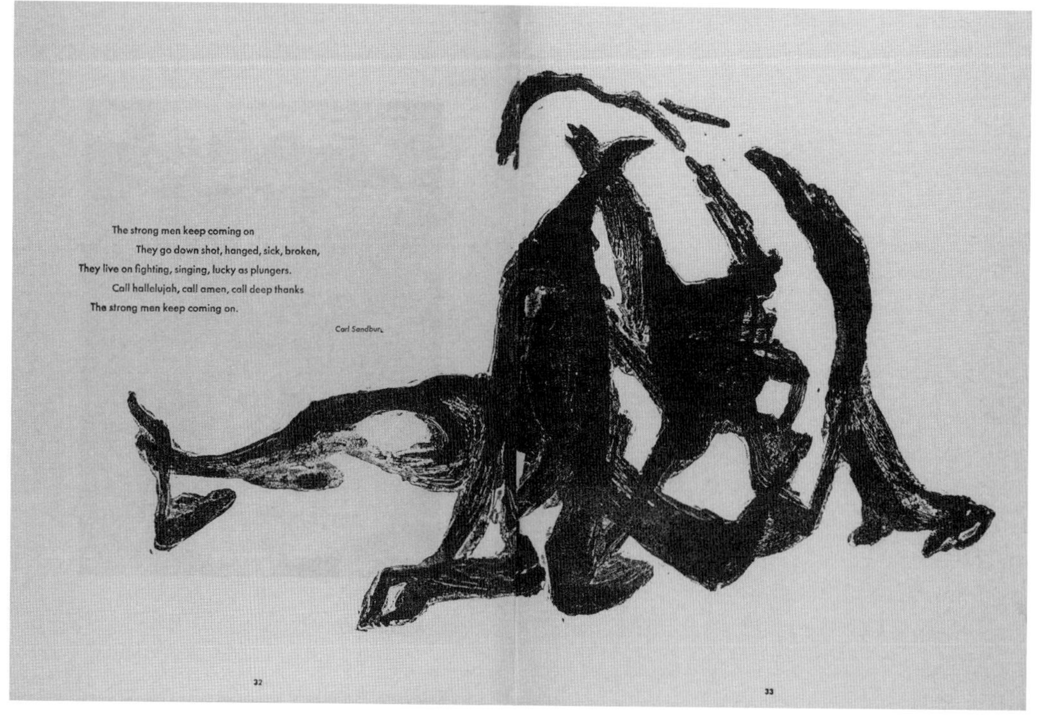

All the Arts
In One House

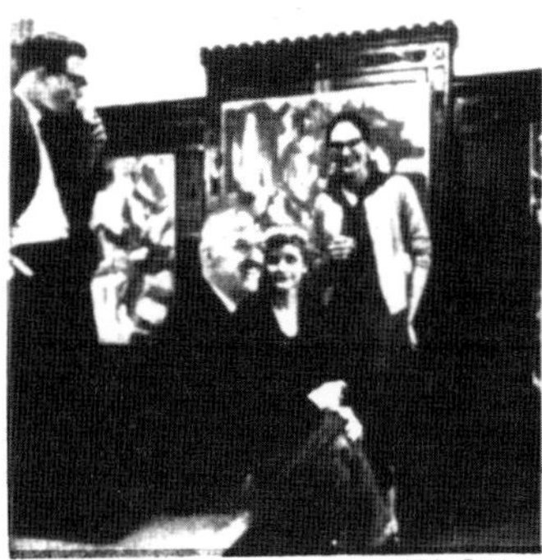

Photos by Mitchell Chatalian and Walter Rosasco

Informal punch parties mark openings of new art shows at The Nonagan, an off-beat gallery on lower Second Ave., which exhibits new music and handcrafts as well as painting. Plans are under way, too, to add poetry readings. At right: The two girls who started it all, Dorothy Podbar, on the left, and "Skid" Shality, pose among ceramics by M. C. Richards. Above: Painter Alison Knowles with husband and parents at opening of her show.

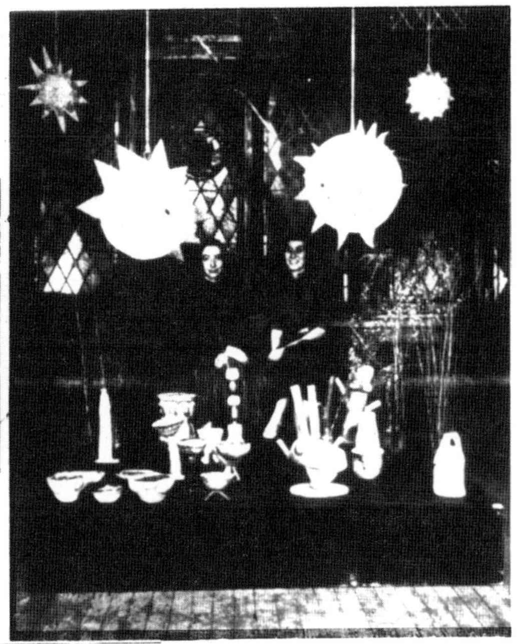

**Figure 1.5.** "All the Arts in One House: Gallery Shows Music." *New York Herald Tribune*, November 19, 1958. Photo on left shows Alison Knowles, Jim Ericson, and Knowles's parents; on right, Dorothy Podber and Eunice Shality with ceramics by M. C. Richards.

form.[27] The ontological gestures of abstraction instantiated in the brushwork are here reduced by Dash to decorative writing.

Much as Michael Fried would later critique minimalist sculpture as inherently theatrical, Dash identifies aesthetic menace in the rude insertion of external objects, like "screaming, distraught insects, swirling around," into the transcendent field of vision. It is worth noting that in a separate review in the same issue, Dash accused another woman artist of similar transgressions in similarly overwrought, misogynistic terms: Nanae Momiyama, he wrote, was also "angry," an "emotional Tokyo painter" who lazily "permits gravity" onto her canvases. He was not alone, however, in this sort of response to artists who—like Knowles and, apparently, Momiyama—blurred the boundaries of traditional representation and abstraction. Many critics directed their ire or suspicion at other artists, like Robert Rauschenberg, who consciously expanded the syntax of modernist painting, including allusions to the vernacular and even to the desires of the body and their political realities.[28] In other words, emerging artists who rejected determinist theories of art, deviating from the strict formalist modernism associated with the New York School, were received as adversaries.

The month after her solo exhibition, Knowles was included in a group show, *8 Painters*, also at Nonagon.[29] By then her growing dissatisfaction with the strict terms of abstract painting was beginning to find form. That summer, she audited a graduate-level painting course at Syracuse University titled "Pictorial Design," under the tutelage of the famous disciplinarian of art instruction, Bauhaus émigré Josef Albers.[30] Knowles recounts being forced by

Albers to paint in the art school's basement for refusing to engage in his lessons on abstract unity and the dynamic tension between monochromatic color and the square. Though deflated by the separation from her classmates, Knowles came to cherish the quiet of her makeshift studio. She began to experiment with a new system of chance-derived techniques in which dice thrown onto a canvas determined the order and arrangement of brushstrokes—a kind of aleatory paint-by-numbers paradigm she would soon extend, using a translation of the *I Ching*, the ancient Chinese book of changes, at the suggestion of her future mentor John Cage (detailed later in this chapter). When Albers occasionally visited to offer feedback, he was alternately severe and polite, wishing to help but ultimately unable to reconcile the scale of her pieces with their bold gesturalism and unusual compositional process.[31] While Knowles remembers these exchanges fondly, as testimony of Albers's serious approach to teaching, one particularly dispiriting interaction sparked a new sense of urgency. She finished the course for credit and returned to her Lower Manhattan loft at the close of August. In retrospect, she recalls, "I just didn't want to pursue the traditional methods of art making anymore."[32] Partly, it was the abstractionists' suspicious, imperious demand for fealty to formalist procedures that excluded the material messiness of daily life—and by extension its social and political isolationism—that pressed Knowles to realign her engagement with nonrepresentational art.[33]

More practically, Knowles was frustrated by the limited professional opportunities for women artists in the tightly controlled, male-dominated art world. She recalls the hypermasculinity often on display at the Cedar Tavern and other Greenwich Village artists' haunts, where Willem De Kooning, Mark Rothko, and other painters she met through Gottlieb and Kline were polite if sometimes dismissive toward her.[34] Her experiences in these spaces speaks to the paradox confronting the first postwar generation of US women artists: an increase in postsecondary education brought social mobility and the potential for autonomous, middle-class employment; at the same time, the commercial reach of their work remained limited within a virulently patriarchal value system. In *Abstract Expressionism: Other Politics*, Anne E. Gibson examines the politically and culturally conservative climate that pervaded the 1940s and 1950s, persuasively arguing for a reckoning of creative activity in relation to gender, race, sexuality, familial bonds, and artistic reception. The collective pathos of existential suffering, she observes, yielded enormously productive results, creatively and professionally, for many artists of the New York School, but it also served to reaffirm values that supported an "aesthetic elite of white heterosexual males" by effacing the broader potential power to be derived from anxieties shared by "other identities, other experiences, and other relations to power."[35] Knowles's lived experience of precisely this marginalization (social and commercial) belies the premise that nonobjective form and "appropriate" expressionist brushwork could authenticate anything except the stabilization of certain modes and privileges of power. By late 1959, Knowles's determination to become "the next Frankenthaler"—by assimilating an abstract formula bound to the careers of (mostly) male artists and their institutional benefactors—had lost its allure.[36]

"I felt the influence of new winds from all sides and stopped painting," Knowles recalls.[37] In place of her previous material propositions, expressed with oil on canvas, came pulsating textual surfaces, disjointed visual narratives comprising nonart, graphic art, and pop-culture ephemera. Grace Hartigan and Joan Mitchell, among other contemporaries of the second-generation abstractionists, also referenced urban environments in richly pigmented, energetic canvases that retained some representational elements.[38] Knowles became acquainted with Hartigan's work through the Museum of Modern Art's exhibition *12 Americans*, in 1956, and Mitchell's through her solo show at Stable Gallery in 1958. Though she shared with them a program of complex abstract figuration and poetic sensibilities (not to mention close professional ties and friendships with poets), Knowles was ultimately desensitized to the emotive compositions and rhythmic atmospheres that appeared to propel contemporary painting, at least in terms of its discursive operations (especially the more narrowly rigid interpretations of Jackson Pollock).[39] In her stretched canvases and, from the late 1950s onward, silk-screen image transfers, there is a deliberate reinscription of everyday signifiers that at first sweep connect to the scale of her abstract works but achieve a more dynamic circuitry of reference and signification.

## Recalibrations

Amid profound disappointment surrounding the dissolution of her first marriage, Knowles chanced to meet a promising playwright and composer, Richard (Dick) Higgins, in 1959.[40] The two were introduced at a party "of mostly gay men" at Higgins's apartment at 84 Christopher Street in the West Village by mutual friends Dorothy Podber (of the Nonagon Gallery) and artist Ray Johnson.[41] "I went to this party that was just men, and the women were from the underworld, so to speak, and I simply got really turned on to the whole group," Knowles later reminisced. "The level of conversation was very interesting and so I just decided to stay."[42] They were an unlikely couple. Knowles and Higgins's daughter Hannah Higgins, herself a Fluxus scholar, also describes the occasion of their meeting, citing her father's unpublished autobiography, as a party "that was running too loud and late, so Dick called the police on himself and hid under his bed until his apartment cleared out. Alison found him there, crawled under the bed with him, and stayed for three days." Higgins, who identified as gay, and Knowles, who was informed of his sexual orientation by Podber, decided to "let the plumbing take care of itself in its own way."[43] He quickly moved into her SoHo loft—which had already been condemned by the city—and set up an improvised studio in the basement coal bin. The two married on May 31, 1960.[44] Their bond was a source of deep affection and plenitude but also a vexed entanglement. Never wishing to perpetuate traditional marriage, the couple tacitly agreed to a committed but flexible relationship.[45]

For Knowles, their partnership was driven by love and a realist's understanding of the limited options for women in the era. In Higgins she intuited an equal and steadfast artistic companion, whose complicated sexuality and progressive politics ensured she would never carry the expectations of a typical housewife.[46] Marriage to Higgins, the son of a wealthy New England industrialist, also brought economic advantages. Higgins's family money and eventual inheritance meant both could exist as relatively carefree agents. Dedicated to a Bohemian lifestyle of art, music, poetry, film, and theater, they enjoyed extensive travels to Turkey and Western Europe (detailed in chapter 2), supported by their commercial design work but also, vitally, by Higgins's personal fortune. In effect, Knowles found with Higgins an alternative to the systematic oppression and patriarchal mores (strictly enforced in conservative 1950s America) that ensured, as Carole Pateman has noted, that "single women lack[ed] a defined and accepted social space; becoming a man's wife [was] still the major means through which most women [found] a recognized social identity."[47] That Knowles considered Higgins's sexuality as a fact to be negotiated and (for a time) a perfectly acceptable complication, ultimately fostered their dedication to each other's emotional well-being, artistic temperament, and financial security—and, more broadly, to an experimentalist ethos in art and life.[48]

Knowles, flush with their exciting new intimacy and girded by its social and economic stability, earnestly began to seek out nontraditional models of creative work. Having spent years in the hotspots of abstract expressionism, she took an autodidact's approach to her cultural reeducation, exploring other sites in the downtown scene. She frequented jazz clubs like the Village Vanguard and the Five Spot, attended poetry readings at the E-pit-o-me Coffee House (where Higgins performed) and the Poetry Project at St. Mark's Church on the Lower East Side. These community spaces served as "self-consciously inscribed meeting grounds, think tanks," nurturing a "fascinating microcosm of a counterculture that helped define the 1960s as a time when experiments in community building were crucial to forming an alternative and at times dissident sensibility."[49] Within this context, Knowles cultivated close friendships with local eccentrics like Podber, Johnson, and early Happenings artist Al Hansen, with whom she felt common cause. She also began experimenting with silk-screen painting and printmaking in her studio.

By 1960, Knowles had begun taking courses at the Manhattan School of Printing, extending her graphic studies from Pratt. Founded in 1949 for returning soldiers in need of work and civilians looking for a new trade, the school was situated in the heart of Greenwich Village and for a time was the only privately owned educational institution in the country offering courses in all branches of the printing industry, including courses open to women interested in the commercial trades. It boasted a "diverse student body" of local and international students taught by experienced journeymen who developed an intensive curriculum that required a minimum of six months of coursework and training for each class.[50] Knowles studied linotype, commercial layout, paper cutting, and older techniques like palladium printing, mezzotint, and cyanotype, which she began incorporating into her canvases. The school also operated an in-house placement bureau, which guaranteed positions in local firms. Between 1960 and 1962, Knowles held layout jobs at several advertising agencies and design studios, including Salzman Company, Edward Banks Association, and Meshekoff Mural Studio.[51] This training would serve her well, not only in her own practice (her first silk-screened paintings predate Andy Warhol's) but a decade later during her stint as the first director of the Graphic Prints Lab at the newly founded California Institute of the Arts.[52] Access to a supportive creative environment, the use of equipment after hours, and plentiful source material in studio castoffs and lightly used remnants and silk screens allowed Knowles to experiment with various techniques, including transferring Photostat prints directly onto canvas. Freed from the formality of an art school education designed to propagate the "proper" use of tools and the vocabulary of painterly formalism, Knowles shed any residue of the "purely optical experience" of transcendent brushwork and henceforth deployed decidedly technological and modest means to make her art.[53]

Knowles's embrace of the supposedly tainted world of mass commodities idealized in commercial advertising and graphic print culture was both a crucial and a risky move within her immediate artistic community. In the late 1950s, as post–World War II North America developed an increasingly refined aesthetic, printmaking was anathema to abstract expressionism's sublime romance of the studio. Caroline Jones demonstrates the degree to which a categorical opposition between public and private spheres was felt and strictly maintained, citing an instance in which Kline, Knowles's intermittent teacher at Pratt (who was also included in MoMA's *12 Americans* show), scoffed at an invitation to make prints: "Printmaking concerns social attitudes, you know—politics and a public . . . I can't think about it; I'm involved in the private image."[54] It was this self-containment, which Kline desired, that Knowles rejected.

Far from accommodating her artistic practice to "the private image," Knowles invoked chance methods and commercial sources precisely to expunge any trace of the subjective hand. We see this directly in a small two-sided triptych on archival paper she created around this time, wherein she combined the tense dynamism of sweeping gestural lines with stock typographic signage—the language of abstraction meeting its degraded other in a single material source (fig. 1.6). On one side of each sheet, entangled black calligraphic marks are rendered in ink. The reverse of the middle sheet exhibits a different sort of readymade, the advertising phrase "BUY NOW ON LAYAWAY" screen-printed in Futura type within a pale aqua circle and partially

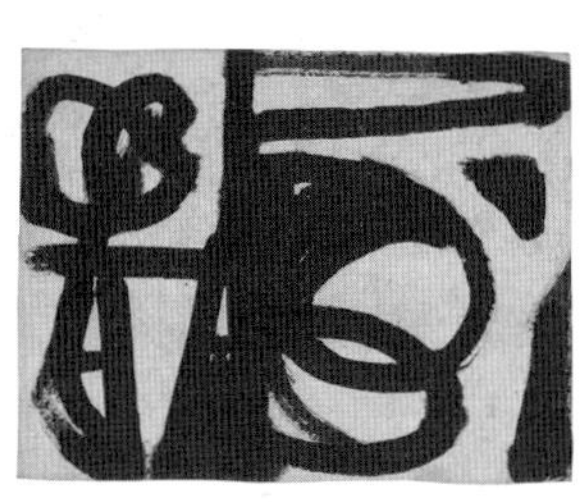

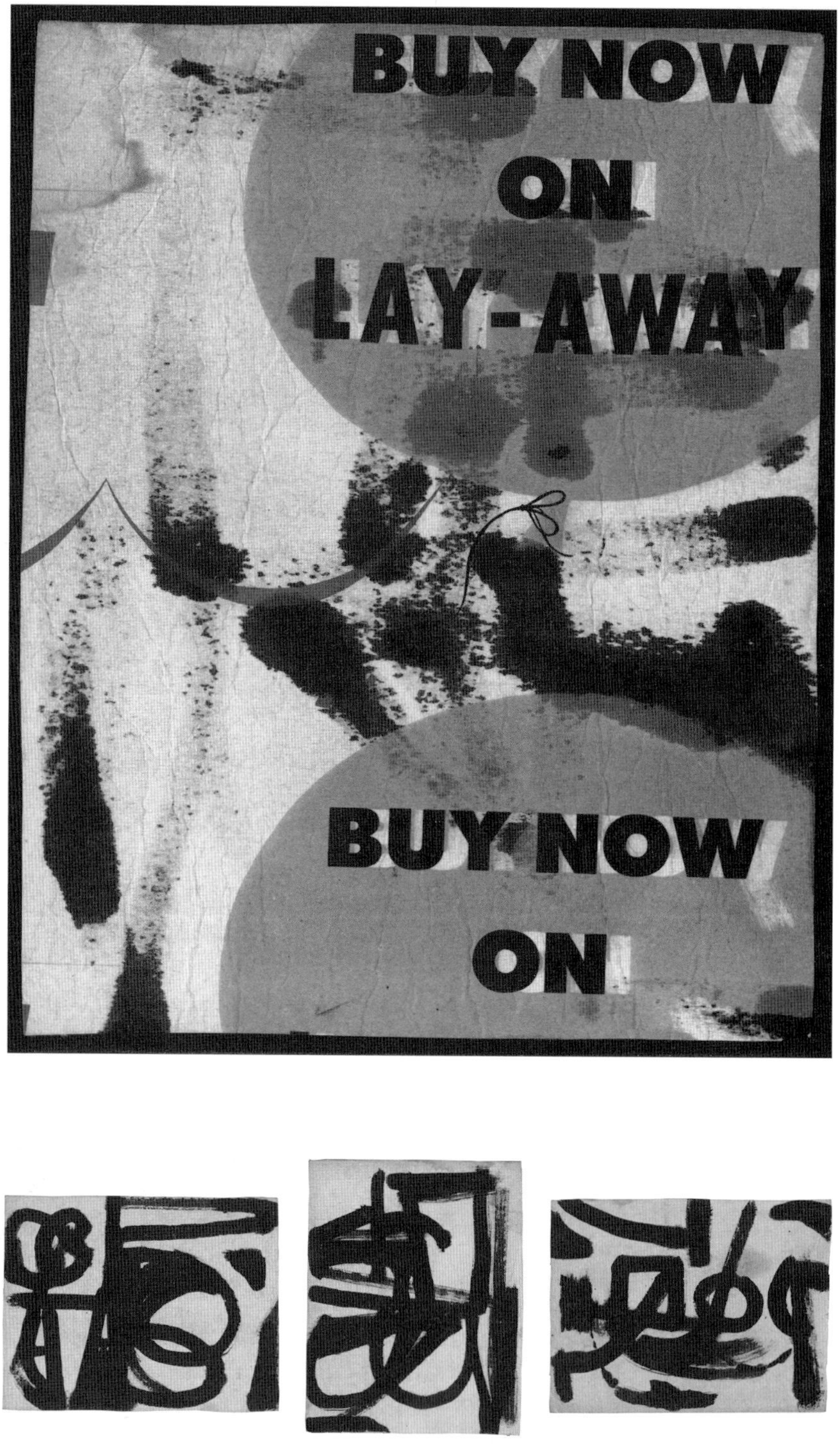

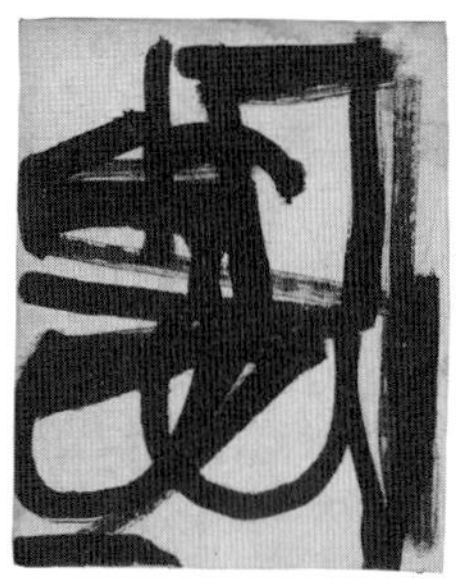

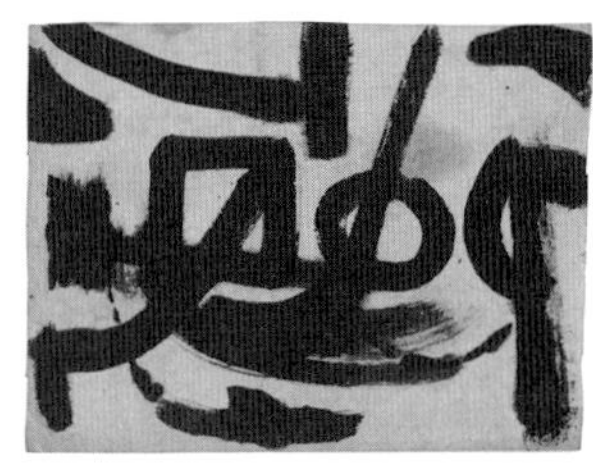

**Figure 1.6.** Alison Knowles, *Untitled (Triptych)*, ink and print on paper, n.d. (*Bottom*) side one of the three panels; (*top*) side two of central panel. Courtesy Fluxus West Collection, Special Collections & Archives, University of Iowa Libraries.

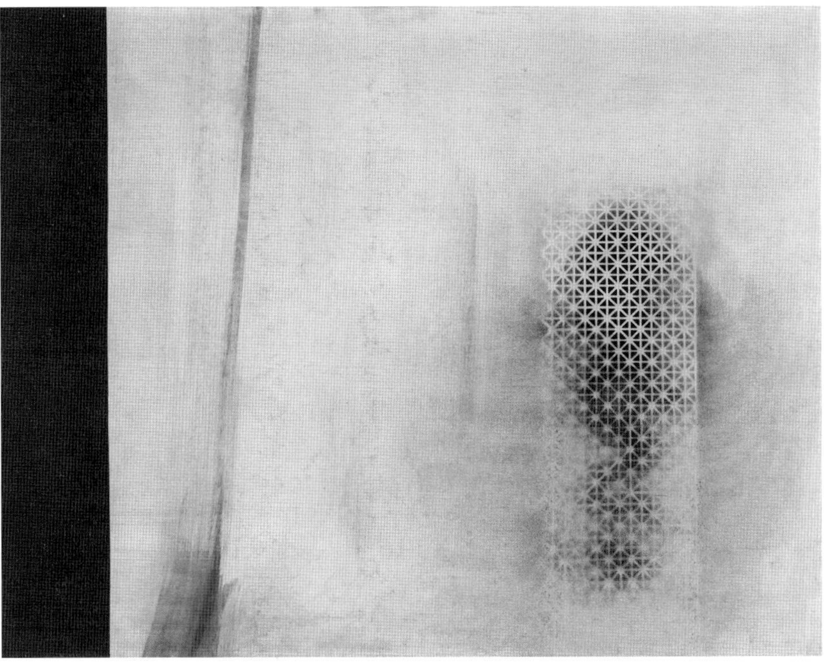

**Figure 1.7.** Alison Knowles, *Untitled*, 1961. Screen print on canvas. Courtesy Hermann Braun Fluxus Collection, Museum Ostwall at the Dortmunder U, Dortmund. Photo: Jürgen Spiler, Dortmund.

repeated, complemented with curved red swashes resembling supermarket bunting and a thin navy-blue bow whimsically caught between the shapes and the black strokes pervading the page. With the simplicity and immediacy of this stark juxtaposition, Knowles offers a novel investigation of fine art and mass media forms akin to Cubist *papier collé* experiments at the turn of the twentieth century.

The recalibration toward visual-techno fusion in Knowles's transitional work from this era can also be seen in two proto-Pop silk screens, *Taxis and Busses* (1959–1960; plate 2) and *Untitled* (1961; fig. 1.7). The bold gestural sweeps of previous works are now gone, replaced by word-image composites appropriated from leftover prints and commercial cutouts found on the floor at her design-firm day jobs. The surface of *Taxis and Busses*, larger in scale even than her earlier nonrepresentational paintings (roughly ninety-six by fifty-four inches), is built up of overlapping graphic fragments from disparate past and present commercial sources. The imagery includes interlocking chains, formal-looking male portraits, clowns, cats, a coffee pot, and text in a variety of colors and stenciled fonts: "JELL-O," "Circus," "Charleston," "Mercury," "UNION Dissolved!" Knowles used leftover tear sheets and randomized newspaper headlines to produce chance-derived juxtapositions. The inclusion of what appear to be portraits of Civil War generals, including James Longstreet and Winfield Scott, alongside "Charleston" and "UNION Dissolved!" may allude to the persistence of racial injustice in the US and the struggle for civil rights—manifested in the 1950s in forms including student-led demonstration marches and sit-ins.[55] Invoking historical urgency through experimental collage, *Taxis and Busses* is a montagelike patchwork of disconnected signage not unlike that experienced in clogged urban landscapes. Reminiscent of Walter Benjamin's notion of a picture's moving "not *out of* the instant, but *into* it," the creeping in of language, a transgression decried by Dash in the pages of *Arts*, begins to take full form in Knowles's expanded aesthetic field.[56]

For *Untitled*, Knowles placed a radiator screen on the canvas and spray-painted through it to register "the 'straight' design of the repetitious pattern," then created an "atmospheric effect" by smudging and crumpling the canvas before applying a gesso substrate.[57] A thick, even band of cobalt blue runs vertically along the painting's left edge, and lighter, less precise strokes of the same hue punctuate the mostly-white field. The composition, balancing an element reminiscent of a color-field abstraction with the material imprint of an industrial product, might be regarded as a merging of her fine-art and commercial training within the space of representation—a type of visual caesura bridging mutually beneficial sensibilities. Ever the recycler of forms, Knowles again used the radiator screen as a stencil in works in the later 1960s, including *Blue Ram* (1966), a large notational score for four performers consisting of six silk-screened prints on cardboard that was reproduced for her and John Cage's collaborative *Notations* project (1969) and exhibited at the Drawing Center in New York in 1979.[58]

On the strength of these new canvases, Knowles was offered a solo show in January 1962 at the Judson Gallery at 239 Thompson Street, just south of Washington Square, to showcase her "huge paintings of street signs [with] objects projected large," including *Taxis and Busses*, *Untitled*, and *Mother, or the Great Train Robbery* (1959–1961; fig. 1.8).[59] In an *ARTnews* review, critic Jill Johnston applauded Knowles's multilayered method of projecting a single image, placing objects directly on the canvas and spray-painting over them, and silk-screening clustered images and stenciled letters.[60] Knowles's embrace of light-image projection spoils the customary operations of figure/ground and obviates the artist's obligation to sketch any underdrawings directly onto the canvas. This new, nimble method of stripping any evidence of painterly labor from the layered ephemera was most evident in *Mother, or the Great Train Robbery*, where Knowles employed the Bell-Opticon light projector to magnify found ads, letters, more radiator screens, and drawings directly onto the material surface—a fresh technological take on image making that she modified from Kline.[61] In a related painting, Johnston discerned reproductions of letters from a cigar box, a newspaper clipping about a film, a photograph of a favorite aunt, postmarks, and a small grid of found advertisements disarticulated from their primary sources.[62]

Knowles extended this collagist practice by installing a Bell-Opticon projector within the gallery during the run of the Judson show, affording visitors a chance to *participate* in the process of making rather than simply admiring completed artworks from a respectable distance. This move anticipates a

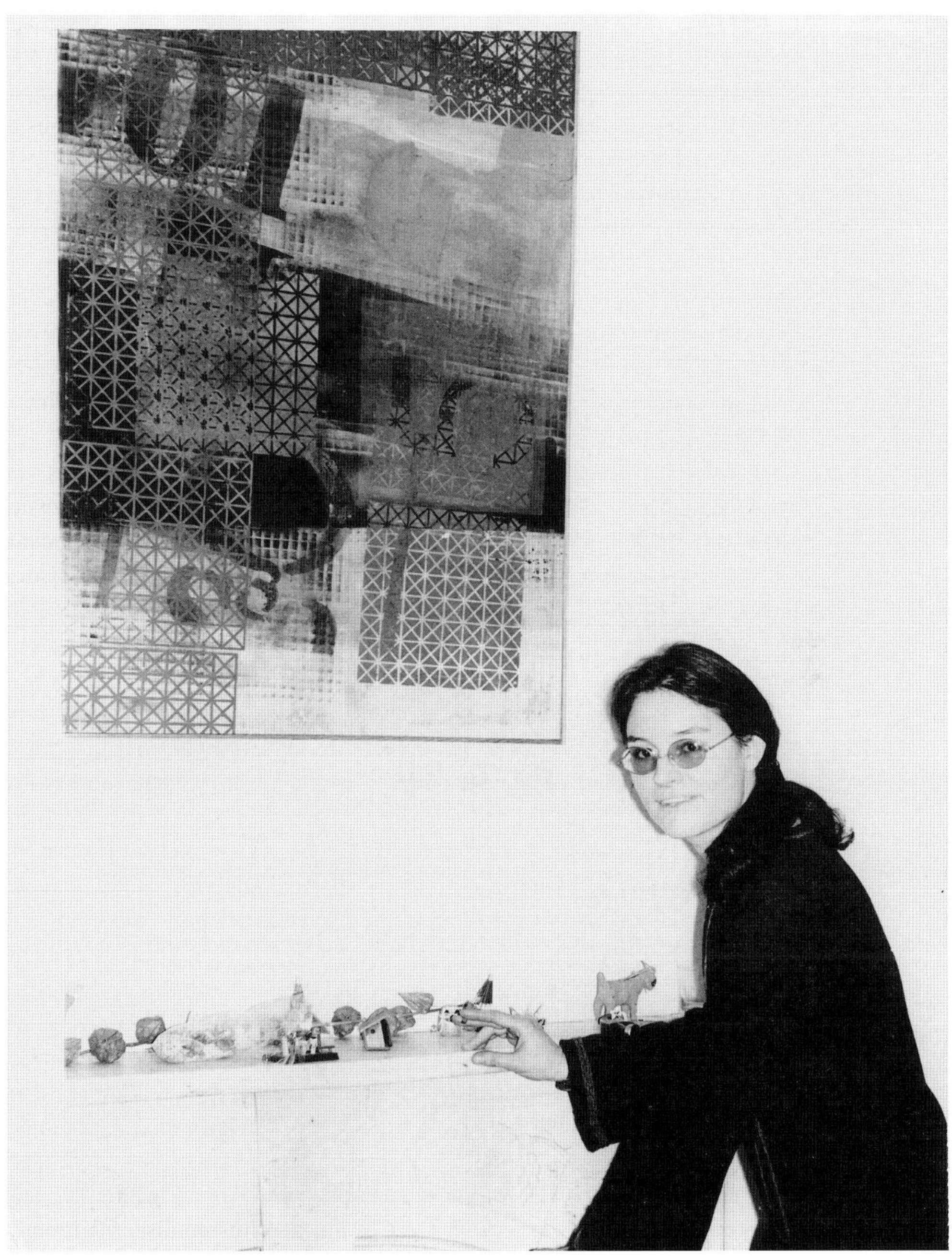

**Figure 1.8.** Alison Knowles with her painting *Mother, or the Great Train Robbery* (lost and presumed destroyed), December 24, 1969. Photo: Hans Sohm. Courtesy bpk Bildagentur/Archiv Sohm, Staatsgalerie Stuttgart/Hans Sohm/Art Resource, NY.

throughline in Knowles's work in the 1960s, which integrated various visual technologies; *Do You Remember* (1968; plate 3), for example, dedicated to Fluxus confidant and concrete poet Emmett Williams in response to a lyrical poem he wrote for her bearing the same title, incorporates a film projector.[63] And certainly it is remarkably unlike the way Kline deployed the same Bell-Opticon projector. Knowles's direct projection of randomly sourced images from her repertoire was more akin to the Combine paintings and transfer drawings Robert Rauschenberg was making between 1952 and 1964. Intervening in the "ceaseless flow of urban message," Rauschenberg altered images and reconfigured ephemera to present "the picture conceived as the image of an image."[64]

Knowles's visual palimpsests also enact a remove from her more traditionally abstract works. Here complexly animated zones of layered pictures, letters, objects, and scraps of paper effectively replace the earlier canvases' exaggerated, tangled bands of paint as a series of ghostly images. Indeed, several paintings appear re-formed as a kind of screen-memory, bridging two perceptual experiences simultaneously: the literal process of making and the sensorial act of viewing—a kind of body/mind transmission challenged by the scale and overlay of competing pictures, each a relic from the artist's personal storehouse blown up to monumental size.

By intentionally playing with new forms and compositional patterns, Knowles rejected the ethos of nonobjective abstraction in favor of a more complicated picture plane, one that "got a strong injection of print culture."[65] Of course, she had already experimented with graphics from commercial studios, as in *Taxis and Busses*, and briefly worked designing window displays for Bloomingdale's.[66] In numerous works from these early years, including those she exhibited in 1966 in *Object Poems*, the first show Higgins curated for the Something Else Gallery in their New York home (fig. 1.9), Knowles consolidated her expertise in graphic techniques and engaged advertising and other aspects of mass culture in ways that had a lasting effect on her art.[67]

In attending to postwar consumption and its detritus, Knowles and other neo-avant-garde artists posited that the accidental, external, and quotidian could articulate the changing social, cultural, and political milieu more profoundly than the anguished interiority demanded by North American abstract painting. Within Knowles's newly open, indeterminate process, the visceral was not opposed to the conceptual. *Taxis and Busses*, for example, uses a large-scale, all-over orientation that, like a Pollock, disperses meaning and signification, but its projected and painted ensemble of words, colors, and textures skillfully evokes the senses of sight, touch, and sound. Throughout the formative decade 1960–1969, Knowles's silk-screen canvases, performances, and other object-based works consciously and confidently incorporated the rawness of commercialism and the codes of capitalist consumption as a means of emphasizing the contingent nature of speech and its potential politics. Pollock remained a point of reference, but Cage was ascendant.

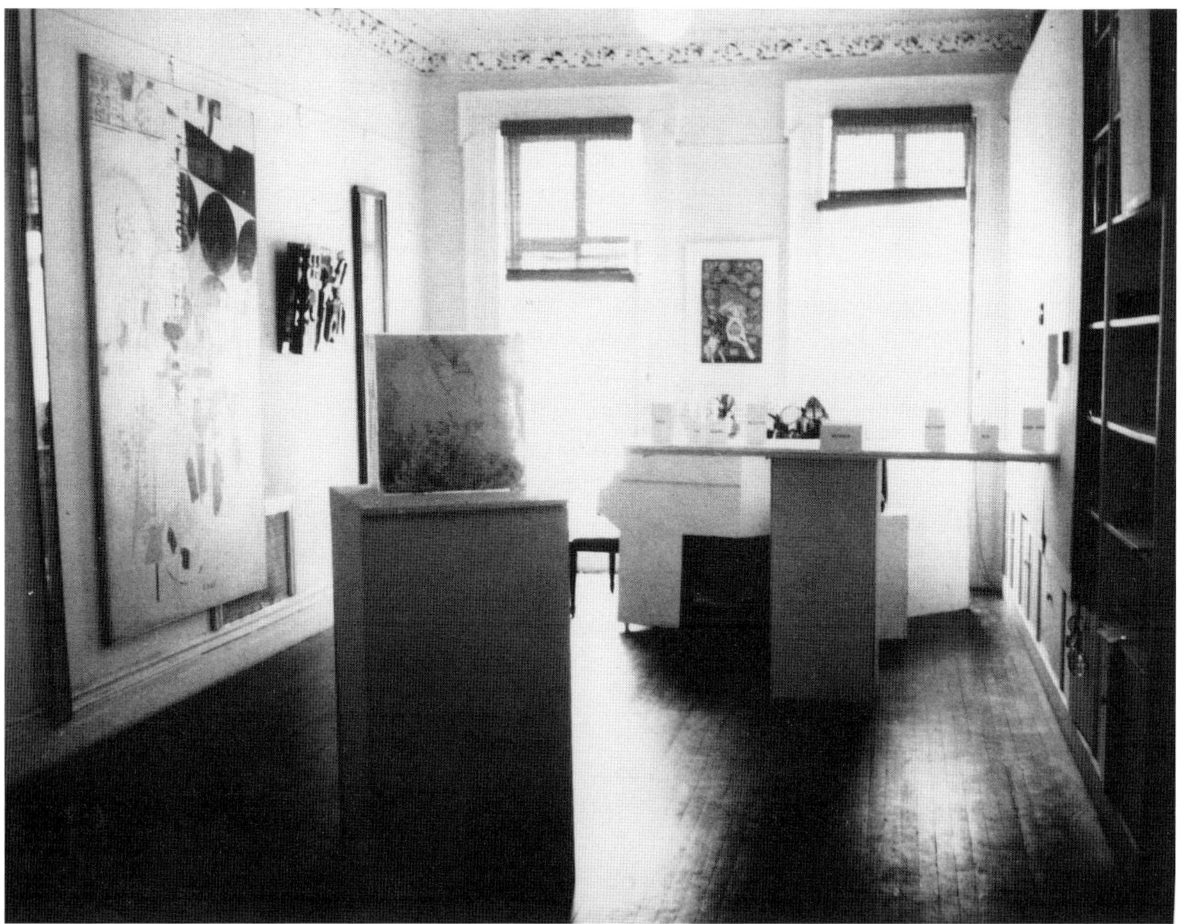

Figure 1.9. Installation view of *Object Poems*, Something Else Gallery, New York, 1966. Archiv Sohm, Staatsgalerie Stuttgart, AS 2024/1009. Photo © Staatsgalerie Stuttgart.

## By Way of Chance

Knowles's turn from abstract painting to silkscreens and action-based, live performance was in part a reaction to the spatial sequestration entailed by painting—being huddled in the studio for days at a time brought on bouts of profound loneliness and a painful sense of detachment from the world. This physical and psychic isolation was exacerbated by the dearth of gallery representation and professional mentorship available to women artists in the 1950s; as frustration with gender politics mounted, so too did her indifference toward abstract expressionism. Then, amid these occupational hindrances, came a fortuitous introduction to pioneering composer John Cage, whom she met through Higgins.[68]

In their courtship, Higgins conveyed to Knowles the concrete lessons he derived from Cage's famously influential class at the New School for Social Research, which he had taken in the summer of 1958.[69] The composer's pedagogical approach moved beyond the simple transmission of skills or facts from master to apprentice; his students were encouraged, rather, to conduct independent "experiments" using a diverse array of chance procedures, to be followed by a group discussion of the "philosophical and practical implications of each piece."[70] As Cage later told art critic Barbara Rose, he emphasized the role of practice and the potential for "inventiveness" among students with no previous musical training: "The only thing I warned them about was that I was interested in experimentation and that if they weren't experimental enough then I would tend to criticize them."[71] Having thus dismantled the standard instrumental premises of composition, he sought to sharpen the nonmusicians' perception of "other components of sound," such as duration, timber, amplitude, and morphology. Ultimately, the course, with its emphasis on experimentation; the use of words rather than numbers, musical notes, or graphs to construct performance scores; and speech to explain the notation to the class *before* a work's presentation produced far-reaching renegotiations of music's traditional procedures, which would become important precursors for Knowles's later Fluxus practice.

While Knowles never enrolled in the New School class, she absorbed Cage's theories on chance procedures and indeterminate outcomes by proxy and through direct exchanges with the composer. Knowles and Cage developed a deep bond of friendship during their mushroom-hunting trips with the New York Mycological Society between the early 1960s and the late 1970s. "I began to talk with John a little . . . to walk with him privately in the woods and [to] have conversations about what was going on in art, what I was doing."[72] These privileged conversations, she recalls, revealed striking similarities between her and Cage's artistic concerns and dissatisfactions with modernist idioms. "Cage was this fresh guy with these great ideas, loving to talk to people, delighted to give dinner parties all the time, always going off to other people's performances too."[73] Knowles received informal instruction on, for example, Cage's principles of imagist graphic notation, the development of chance patterning through the hexagram logic of the *I Ching,* and the devotional literature of Zen Buddhism and other Eastern religious traditions and philosophies. To Cage, in turn, Knowles explained the graphic pleasure of "happy accidents" in screen-printing, the granularity of French poetry, and, later, macrobiotic cooking.[74]

Decades on, Knowles credited Higgins with animating connections between her and Cage, and between subjective openness and conceptual rigor. But by 1959, even before the fruitful encounter with Cage, Knowles had begun to intuit that abstract painting, as a professional pursuit, could not sustain her intellectually or psychologically.

There were, of course, precedents, long predating Cage, for expansive experimentation, the collaging of sound and language, found objects, and other quotidian materials. Knowles, an intuitive student of art history, had by the late 1950s pored over the synthetic fragments of Cubist constructions, the readymades of Marcel Duchamp, and, most importantly, the collisions of image and text in the *Merz* pictures of early twentieth-century German Dada artist Kurt Schwitters. Schwitters's 1920 essay on the subject was reprinted in Robert Motherwell's influential anthology *The Dada Painters and Poets* (1951), of which Knowles owned a copy—the volume was widely read by artists of her day. Describing the formal breakthrough of fusing graphic and textual media, Schwitters imagined his practice as a necessary realignment of the structural elements of painting: "I take any material whatsoever if the picture demands it. When I adjust materials of different kinds to one another, I have taken a step in advance of mere oil painting, for in addition to playing off color against color, line against line, form against form, etc., I play off material against material."[75] For Schwitters, the process of collage painting readjusted his inclination away from naturalistic or mimetic image making.

It is this Schwitters—the proto-intermedia artist whose work consciously obscured the boundaries among traditional mediums—who made a lasting impression on Knowles's practice. "His painting and collages are particularly close to my way of thinking . . . especially the street and photo fragments."[76] Knowles had occasion to view the Dadaist's *Merz* in 1961, in the exhibition *Art of Assemblage* at the Museum of Modern Art. The idea of his "making collages out of train tickets" appealed to her sense of visual texture and the aesthetic potential of unruly and unconventional materials. The careful study of *Merz*-textured planes—of Schwitters's deployment of chance and "adjustment" of linguistic fragments and concrete materials—coupled with painterly frustration and fatigue, reinforced the formal experimentation of Knowles's evolving pictorial and spatial vocabulary.[77]

Formal and informal lessons and professional and personal relationships thus contributed to the material and theoretical transformation of Knowles's work. In the early 1960s, Knowles collaborated on set design and construction for experimental productions across Lower Manhattan. She had an active presence in several of Higgins's works, including the premiere of *Edifices, Cabarets & Contributions* as part of Claes Oldenburg's "Ray Gun Spex" series, held at Judson Memorial Church in winter 1960 (fig. 1.10); *Stacked Deck* (1958) at Cooper Union in 1961; and *Graphis 82* (1960; fig. 1.11) and *Two Generous Women* at The Living Theater in 1962.[78] She arranged the lighting and built props and sets for Higgins's *Inroads Rebuff'd; or, The Disdainful Evacuation* for the Poets Theater at Judson (1962) and fabricated gigantic dice screen-printed with appropriated images (a blue ram, a goat's head) for his *The Tart* (1965) at Sunnyside Garden Boxing Arena in Queens.[79] Knowles had first met and become friendly with Oldenburg at a May Day party at artist George Segal's farm in New Brunswick, New Jersey. The various events at Segal's farm, Judson, and other downtown spaces were localized instantiations of performance art's emerging aesthetic, establishing, as Johanna Drucker has argued, "the elements which would become characteristic of Happenings from that point onward," such as "simultaneity of actions" and "collective activity."[80]

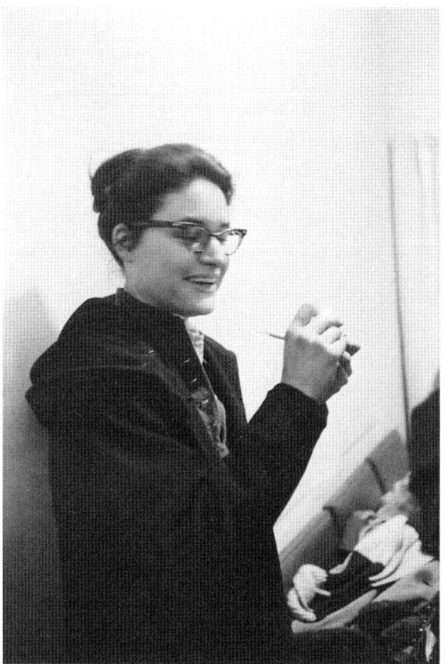

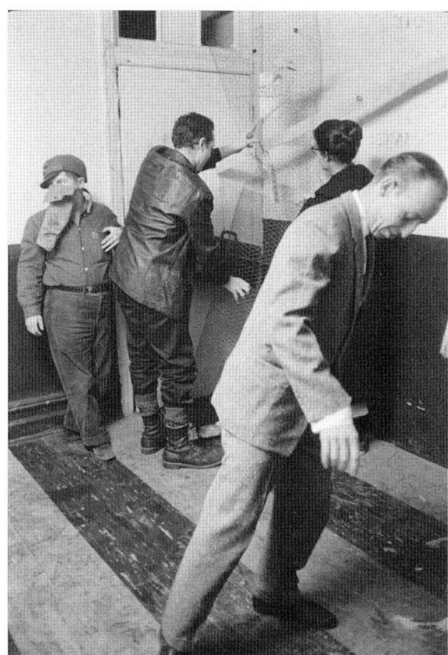

**Figure 1.10.** Alison Knowles performing in Dick Higgins's *Edifices, Cabarets & Contributions* (1960). The event was part of Claes Oldenburg's "Ray Gun Spex" series of Happenings at Judson Memorial Church, February 29–March 2, 1960. Photo: Robert R. McElroy, © J. Paul Getty Trust. Getty Research Institute, Los Angeles (2014.M/7).

The growing influence of Cage, too, and his methods "of orchestration and coordination were drawn on very loosely," with results that were more "purely performative" than later events staged in the city and elsewhere.[81]

Knowles's developing aesthetic crystallized, then, within a context of sharing and collaborative merrymaking, disruptive to the autonomous modernist tradition, where it was possible to meet and mingle with like-minded artists who were also refusing "product-oriented" art practices—like painting—and works that could be exchanged on the art market. She was still earning a meager living as an itinerant silk-screen camera technician in downtown studios and design firms, where she worked on logos and signage for Air France and other commercial clients.[82]

In these pre-Fluxus days, the former painter actualized her own Happening-type events too, often as the only female artist in the group. Knowles's earliest performance-based work came in August 1962, when she presented *Light House* in Bridgehampton, New York, for the Ergo Suits Festival—a landmark show of site-specific works by Kaprow, Hansen, Walter De Maria, and La Monte Young. The performance may have involved incinerating her expressionist canvases.[83] Emmett Williams recalled that after her "second one-man show in Manhattan, at the Judson Gallery in 1962," some paintings were ceremonially burned and "almost all the unsold large canvases were given away . . . to anyone who came to carry them away." As he explained it, "she was through with them . . . and didn't want to clutter up her studio with unfinished business."[84] Whatever the circumstances, purging evidence of a former artistic self was not an unusual impulse among artists in the 1960s who turned from traditional painting to a conceptually based practice.[85] The aesthetic lessons

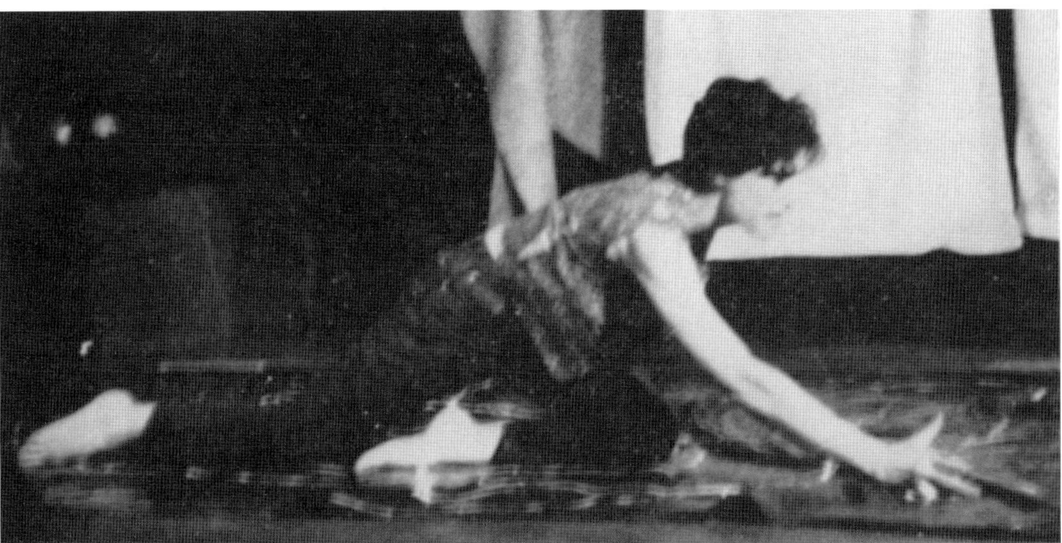

**Figure 1.11.** Alison Knowles, "throwing dice at losing money," in Dick Higgins's *Graphis 82* (1960) at The Living Theater, New York, May 1–2, 1962. Photographer unknown. Courtesy Charles Deering McCormick Library of Special Collections, Northwestern University.

Knowles absorbed in this richly productive community of artists, poets, and musicians as she moved beyond New York School painting would provide, as she later explained, the theoretical baseline and temporal-durational structure for her ongoing experimentation with chance methods of composition:

> Abstract expressionism was dependent on a person, was dependent, say, on Pollock . . . or a critic like Clement Greenberg . . . so it needed a lift off to be looked at the way one could look at a readymade—the way Duchamp looked at things. What was wonderful about Cage and Duchamp was that they didn't hang onto the theory as if it was theirs only . . . [Our small] group just kept growing because there was this need, this kind of theory, [that] was desperately needed as a response to abstract expressionism. The concept of "chance operations" was needed. We *needed* it.[86]

The aspiration toward *something else*—a clear desire for the transformation of aesthetic, social, and political orders—was widespread in the early 1960s. What is notable about Knowles's articulation of this unmet need is that it hinges on chance operations as a *form*, tied to notions of progress. Cage's personal affect—his reputation for being a generous and approachable mentor, ever open to conversation about students' ideas—was not only an antidote to Albers's disciplinary dogmatism but a counter to assertions that alternative conceptions of art and performance could not be mapped. For Knowles, this encouragement was paramount. After all, this was still a time when an attentive and supportive male colleague could be an important ally.

The reconfiguration of durational processes was particularly effective for artists working within Cage's orbit who were, like Knowles (at least at that time), decidedly nonmusical but still attentive to their environment and its temporalities. The premise of *process* as a compositional method and material developed in the context of a broadly felt ennui with traditional musical structures. Cage pitched this "indeterminacy" as a renunciation of mastery and aesthetic control. In stark contrast to conventional modes of production, which he dismissed as "the presentation of a whole as an object in time having a beginning, a middle, and an ending [and] possessed of a climax," his aleatory procedures left the performance of a score open to randomness and unpredictability but not without precision. "An experimental action," he wrote, "is one the outcome of which is not foreseen. Being unforeseen, this action is not concerned with its excuse."[87] In effect, the point was to free musical notation from any obligation to provide a coherent narrative structure. "It is thus possible to make musical composition free of individual taste and memory (psychology) and of the literature and 'traditions' of the art. The sounds enter the time-space centered within themselves, unimpeded by service to any abstraction."[88]

The archetypal, much-analyzed example of how chance methods operate within the larger structure of Cage's oeuvre is undoubtedly *4′33″* (1952), which he composed after a summer residency at Black Mountain College. The score was first performed by pianist David Tudor at the Maverick Concert Hall, an auditorium in the middle of a forest near Woodstock, New York, as part of a series of performances to benefit the Artists Welfare Fund. On the evening of August 29, 1952, Tudor entered the hall, walked directly to a piano placed at center stage, quietly sat down, and lifted the lid of the keyboard. He then proceeded to mark off time, in three movements, without playing a single note for the duration of the piece—exactly four minutes and thirty-three seconds. What the audience heard, Cage later recalled, was not silence but "accidental sounds" that heightened the physical experience of the setting: "You could hear the wind stirring outside during the first movement. During the second, raindrops began pattering on the roof, and during the third the people themselves made all kinds of interesting sounds as they talked or walked out."[89] If offering unintended sounds rather than carefully ordered notes as a musical stimulus presumed attentive listening, doing so in an isolated, natural location turned the performance into an unexpectedly vivid "visual event" that in itself "constituted the work of art," through a process analogous to what surrealist André Breton termed "objective-chance"—chance with a purpose not readily available to the conscious mind.[90] By amplifying ambient and "found" sounds into the substance of composition and performance, Cage leveled any traces of artistic control with a far more profound gesture than other experimentally inclined composers of his era, such as Pierre Boulez and Edgard Varèse.[91]

By the late 1950s, Knowles was aware of the buzz and art-world gossip surrounding *4′33″*—publication notices and reviews supplemented by firsthand accounts and scandalous chatter. What piqued the young painter's interest were questions regarding authorship, including who and what constructed the meaning and artistic value of a piece like *4′33″*. Knowles's appropriation of indeterminate, open procedures in much of her career from the 1960s onward would permit an aesthetic liberation. She would "escape the ravening jaws of abstract expressionism" by orchestrating the possibility of infinitely open structures diffused across a body of objects and ritual practices.[92] She later mused, in a journal entry, "I think sound has always been a very strong ingredient once the painting stopped."[93]

As Julia Robinson has noted, the concept of indeterminacy—"the source of the earliest affinity" between Knowles and Cage—effectively demarcated artists who "felt liberated" by Cage's techniques from those who felt restrained by them.[94] My research shows that Knowles had ample contact with Cage's contemporaneous work, beyond *4′33″*, including the premiere of *Theatre Piece* (1960)—one of his earliest works using time brackets—at a downtown composer's showcase at the Circle in the Square theater, 159 Bleecker Street.[95] She experienced Cagean dynamics, then, via primary and secondary interactions.

One noteworthy conceptual link between Knowles and Cage, sometimes overlooked in the critical literature but detailed throughout this book, is their shared use of the *I Ching*. The core conceit of this ancient "book of changes" is the balancing of opposites through a process of events that accepts the inevitability of accidents and random occurrences. Impressed by the idea that a single notation could generate so much variability, Cage drew from the *I Ching* the abiding structure and supplementary material for his chance-derived *Music of Changes* (1951) and for *Variations II* (1961)—scores that, Branden W. Joseph has argued, highlight the period of the composer's work "recognized as central, indeed, fundamental, to the breakdown of the modernist project and the advent of postmodernism."[96] Cage's teachings based on the *I Ching* and the ninth-century Zen master Huangbo, found expression in Knowles's screen paintings, when she began using a rudimentary system of indeterminate occurrences to score their composition.[97] One technique, she recalls, involved creasing a piece of fabric to delineate numbered squares: "Dick was on the phone telling me the probabilities available, giving me my local visual vocabulary at the time. I made hard divisions on this canvas that I could not overstep. If I threw a two, the area must be blue."[98] Knowles thus extended the process Cage described as throwing "sound into silence" by constructing whole fields of painterly form predicated on visualizing chance operations.

## Collaborative Authorship

Returning to *Taxis and Busses* and *Untitled*, we see how the ways in which Knowles adopted prosaic and depersonalized graphic materials could be identified with Cage's incorporating found sounds into chance compositions. Her transition from gestural painting to a more performative activation of the canvas thus demonstrates that the "breakdown of the modernist project" Cage initiated could be transmitted to artists who were not directly part of his class. A decade later, as previously noted, Knowles and Cage would collaborate on *Notations* (1969), a Something Else Press book of commissioned visual-musical scores that was formatted using, among other experimental tools, the *I Ching* and chance procedures.[99]

More pertinently, the scores she later wrote for Fluxus performances, or as she termed them, *propositions*, closely followed Cage's model yet effectively deviated from it. Knowles often composed these scores—conceptually flexible, linguistically sparse, formally chance-derived, free of preprogrammed outcomes—during weekend train excursions to and from Fluxus concerts. Jotted down hastily and later typed up by Higgins, Knowles's propositions were textually unpretentious, at times necessarily site-specific, and predicated on an aspirational engagement with the viewer/listener (who was not necessarily a direct participant). Generative and generous, Knowles's propositional scores, detailed in the next chapter, integrated heightened audiovisual phenomenon and quotidian objects in situ or, in her framing, an art experience simply "as experience."[100] In *The Identical Lunch* (fig. 3.14) and *Proposition 2: Make a Salad* (fig. 2.1), for example, "in the first case one eats a tunafish sandwich and in the second one makes a salad, but as an art experience, as a performance . . . As I eat the sandwich, does it taste any better? Does that fact that I'm nourished physically negate it as art? My opinion is that perceiving it as art puts our feet 'just a little off the ground.'"[101] In Knowles's nimble adaptation of Cage's environmentally sensitive aesthetics, chance structures bodily experience through temporal, durational, diurnal means. In early canvas experiments like *Taxis and Busses*, throwing dice to determine aesthetic outcomes served to negate the sanctified terms and universalist assumptions of traditional easel painting, wherein imagery is predetermined via a sketch or outline, or at least conceived as a formal thought ahead of its material realization. It is useful here to quote Knowles in an interview decades later:

> I was still trying to do some painting by throwing dice to divide the canvas and make this part blue and that part red . . . I had a canvas and I wanted to know how to start out with it, so I just needed a place to begin . . . I was throwing dice, perhaps in one-third of the canvas I could have six things—six blue areas there, throw again, get a yellow, etc. . . . so I was still struggling with painting . . . the mechanisms of structure discussed in that [Cage] class helped me [by proxy] escape the ravening jaws of abstract expressionism . . . The *immediacy* of these new ideas convinced me to stop painting in the New York style of abstraction. I burned thirty paintings out at my father's house in East Hampton.[102]

The symbolic act of erasure and effacement of patriarchal structures in burning her paintings, whether at her father's or brother's home or among other experimentally minded artists at the Ergo Suits Festival, signals Knowles's reimagining of the framework of her own art production.

At the same time, the changing nature of postwar New York City, especially downtown, fostered both a budding political consciousness and the language with which to articulate it. Key to this were several other friendships Knowles developed with artists, including George Brecht. Brecht was a research chemist, painter, and close confidant of Knowles, and his understanding of chance operations was a decisive pivot between the procedures advanced in Cage's New School courses (of which he was a student) and the instigation of language as a specifically postwar material approach to art.[103] Brecht's 1959 Reuben Gallery solo exhibition *Toward Events: An Arrangement*, which Knowles and Higgins attended, was an important occasion for their shared concerns, wherein he formally introduced his concept of the "event score."[104] Brecht had written a related essay in 1957 that traced the use of randomness in twentieth-century art and proffered the term "chance-imagery" to characterize a deliberate erasure or "lack" of conscious design displacing traditional painting with indiscriminate procedures. Seeking to "eliminate bias" and other limiting strictures of aesthetic labor, Brecht posited that the "degree of randomness of the finished image can be made as great as the artist's desires and capabilities allow" and that its "open-endedness . . . embraces all of nature."[105] The potentials of chance-imagery were not the sole domain of figures like Pollock, he argued; rather, the concept could be extended to diffuse disciplinary apparatuses: to "the selection and arrangement of sounds by the composer, to movement and pace by the dancer, to three-dimensional form by the sculptor, to surface form and color by the painter, to linguistic elements by the poet."[106] Similarly, Knowles has noted a "field of possibilities" inhabited by many artists at this time, something "important in the air" as it pertained to Cage's widely read writings on chance procedures and notational scoring. Indeed, while Brecht's chance-imagery essay was not published until 1966 by Knowles and Higgins's Something Else Press, she was in constant conversation with Brecht and others beginning in the fall of 1959 about its implications.

One example of Knowles's remixing of found, chance imagery with text and print culture is *ROOM*, a collaborative silk-screen print on canvas that she made with Brecht in 1960 (fig. 1.12). A taut, square composition, *ROOM* depicts three numbered side views of male swimmers, line drawings possibly culled from an illustrated swimming manual. *ROOM* echoes *Taxis and Busses* in pasting found imagery from popular, sometimes didactic sources directly into the visual field, where it is paired, however enigmatically, with stenciled language. It departs from the earlier work in that it is much smaller and includes just one word of text: ROOM, in bold, sans serif letters, superimposed between the upper two figures. For Knowles and Brecht, the choice of a noun ("room") inserted between two bodies may act as a slyly displaced linguistic signifier for wholly different physical experiences—alluding not to the public act of swimming but to private spaces where any manner of bodily encounters can be had. Viewed in the context of a proto-Pop annexation of mass media imagery, Knowles and Brecht anticipated a broader cultural drive toward appropriation as a means of scrambling certainties of originality, authenticity, and authorship in the postmodern era.

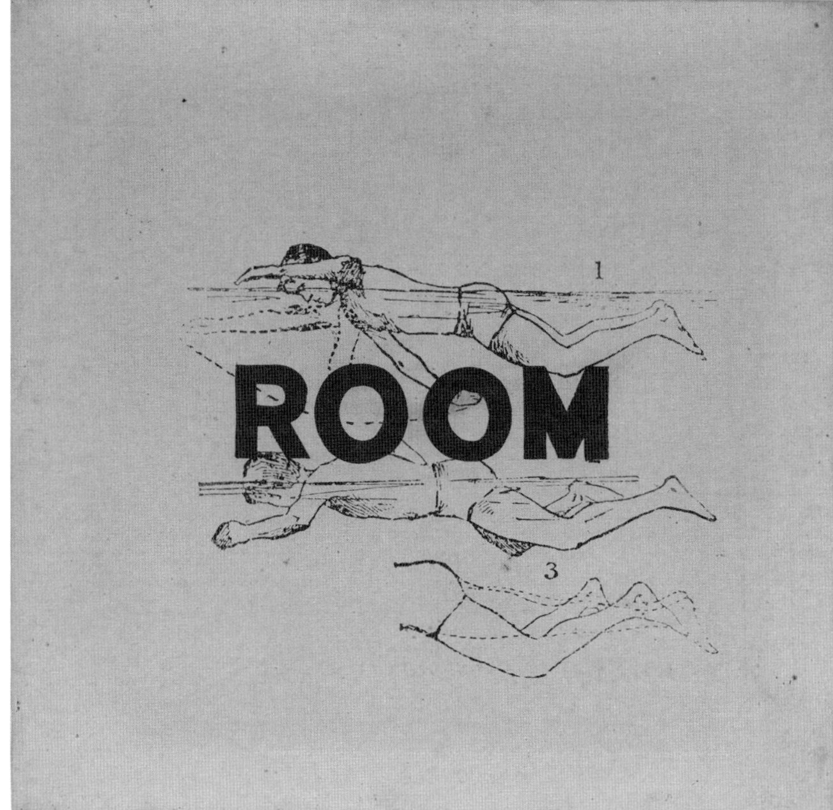


**Figure 1.12.** Alison Knowles and George Brecht, *ROOM*, 1960. Screen print on canvas, 18⅟₁₆ × 18⅟₁₆ in. (45.8 × 45.8 cm). Museum of Modern Art, New York. © 2024 Artists Rights Society (ARS), New York/VG Bild-Kunst, Bonn. Image © The Museum of Modern Art. Licensed by SCALA/Art Resource, NY.

Another collaborative painting, *BLINK*, was created by Knowles, Brecht, and Robert (Bob) Watts in 1963, following the initial Fluxus concerts (plate 4). Each artist contributed a third of the visual material, which was printed onto square canvases over a yellow ground: at the top, a halftone image of a New Guinean ritual wedding dance, supplied by Watts; in the middle, the word BLINK in red block letters, from Brecht; and, across the bottom, three pairs of open silver scissors, from Knowles.[107] Individual authorship of the three sections was, at the time, never publicly revealed, though it is clear from Knowles's later use of scissor imagery that she was responsible for the bottom portion.[108] The image was printed by Knowles in her studio onto a series of fifty canvases, which subsequently hung on the walls of Watts's New York loft apartment, all unsigned. Knowles also reproduced the tripartite image on various cheap commodities, including clothes, gloves, bedding, hosiery, lunch boxes, record labels, bottles, floor mats, stationery, and stamps.[109] The goods were modeled by Lette Lou Eisenhauer and photographed by Peter Moore at Watts's loft (fig. 1.13) before being shipped to Los Angeles for exhibit at the Rolf Nelson Gallery under the anonymous collective name Sissor Bros. Warehouse (sometimes spelled "Scissor").[110] Knowles, Brecht, and Watts had met

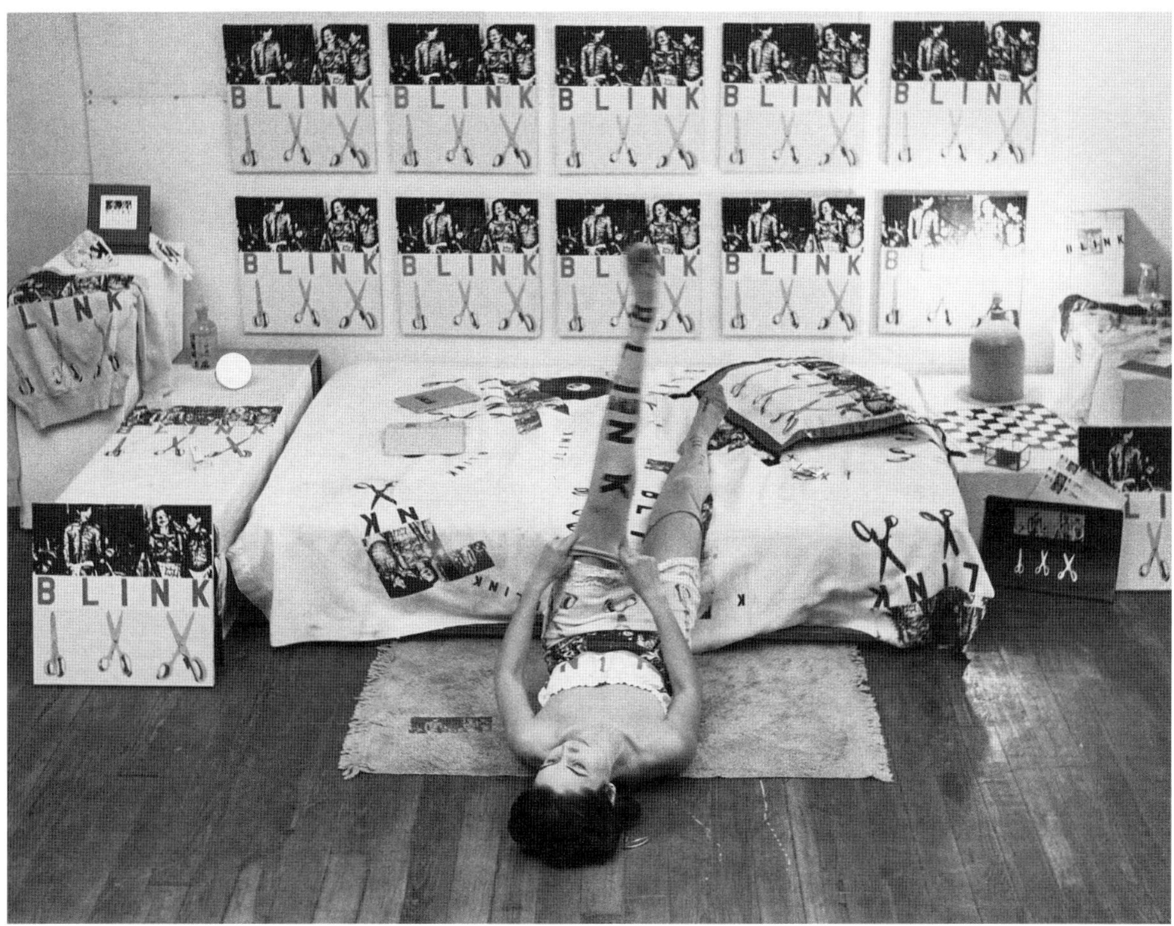


**Figure 1.13.** Lette Lou Eisenhauer modeling *BLINK* merchandise in Robert Watts's loft, New York, August 29, 1963. Photo: Peter Moore, © Northwestern University. Getty Research Institute, Los Angeles (2010.M.38).

Nelson earlier in the decade through the Martha Jackson Gallery in New York, where he began his career. Nelson moved west in 1962 and opened his own space on La Cienega Boulevard a year later. The trio's Pop-esque show was in line with his gallery's promotion of other emerging Pop artists such as George Herms and Jess, and it happened to coincide with Marcel Duchamp's 1963 retrospective at the Pasadena Museum of Art.[111] A review in the *Los Angeles Times* characterized the *BLINK* exhibition as "full of duplicated silkscreens [that are] one giant step beyond pop art," while a reviewer in *Artforum* referred to the works on view as a "stunt."[112] Brecht randomly priced the identical canvases ("one would be forty cents and one would be five hundred dollars," Knowles later recalled), with buyers unsure of their unit's cost until purchase.[113] Watts, in a letter to Emmett Williams, said the artists intended that the installation's appearance be "that of a supermarket discount store" and thus, intentionally or not, aligned their show with Claes Oldenburg's presentation of art goods in The Store on the Lower East Side of New York (under the name of Ray Gun).[114] Knowles, likewise writing to Williams in 1963, went further:

> We feel the spirit of Sissor Bros. and the merchandise is international. . . . The idea of this is something like an anti-gallery thing, anti-painting too. These paintings could be easily duplicated for anyone at 10 or 15 bucks a piece. Since they are scrupulously identical, all the gallery has, Ferus or 3rd Rail, or Kornblee what have you, is one or a few examples. It sort of undermines the whole gallery prestige thing entirely.[115]

Knowles viewed the trio's attentiveness to postwar consumption and its material sameness as a fundamental shift, for it presumed that the accidental, external, and quotidian, rather than the predetermined, interior, and anguished self, articulated the changing nature of the cultural-political milieu in ways that officially sanctioned Pop art only began to hint at.

The late 1950s and early 1960s were heady times in Los Angeles and Lower Manhattan, and Knowles was active in the emergence of SoHo and the West/East Village as preferred locations for artists and musicians, including the avant-garde jazz scene populated by Charles Mingus, Ornette Coleman, and Cecil Taylor, among others.[116] Through friends and acquaintances around her Broadway loft, Knowles encountered a social awareness unfamiliar from her relatively sheltered middle-class upbringing. Dorothy Podber ran an illegal abortion service from her apartment and, in the late 1950s, often asked artist friends for help in securing safe spaces for the procedure.[117] Knowles, sympathetic to the plight of young, desperate, and impoverished women faced with limited choices regarding their own health and bodies, briefly allowed an acquaintance who was a nurse to provide early-term abortions services in the bathroom of her loft. "My studio was separate from the bathroom where there was a cold stove," she remembered decades later. "I think it only happened a few times, but it put me in touch with a whole group of underworld figures that now, seems to me, that I was very extraordinarily lucky to know."[118]

While she questioned whether her involvement was truly subversive—she was not, of course, the one carrying out the procedure—the transgressive nature of providing a space in which a life untied to maternal obligations might be imagined, before the 1973 watershed Supreme Court ruling in *Roe v. Wade*, speaks to the fundamental imperative of liberation within postwar critical praxis. In relation to Knowles's chance-based work, we might retroactively view this action as emblematic of her Fluxus and conceptual art practice of the 1960s, wherein the performer's freedom to choose a path, select an object, perform a score—in public or in private—was at least an aesthetic sign of emancipation from the limits of gendered subjectivity at a time when it was common for women artists to deemphasize their authorship, minimizing their roles in the art-making process or in politicized acts to achieve status and recognition equal to that of their male peers.

Within the context of her early career, Knowles's serious study of chance and experimentation held political potential in the sense that it absolved her from replicating abstraction's idiom of existential (male) suffering. By detaching herself from the space of the traditional painter's studio in works like *Taxis and Busses*, *Untitled*, *Mother, or the Great Train Robbery*, *ROOM*, and *BLINK*, she pursued a trajectory that was less alienated, less reified, less controlling. Knowles's complicated relationship to subjectivity can also be tied to the influence of Cage, who's anti-egoic tendencies and allegiance to Zen and anarchism point toward the nonmilitant, more nuanced and humble approach of her later feminist (anti)politics.[119] It seems a logical choice, then, that Knowles would move away from "American-type" painting and into the fortuitous zones of indeterminate outcomes, where the accidental encounter provided by chance aesthetics and capacious authorship renders the artist's intentionality less momentous, less stupefying. Moreover, the trace of a "woman's hand"—an autonomous gesture coded in the dynamics of gender politics in the art world and beyond—is displaced in the technical process of silk-screening and generative use of the *I Ching*

While most second-wave feminists might have vied for greater external visibility, Knowles's desubjectivized approach rejected the angstful rhetoric of abstract expressionism in favor of the displacement and negation of her own ego within the space of representation. In less conventional ways, as this book argues, the neo-avant-garde has a politics, and for Knowles this can be seen in her prefeminist awareness of the materials and opportunities available in her orbit, and in her attendance to private and public operations.

Initiation into Cage's model of chance as a means of liberation from the bounds of compositional intentionality and control remained a transformational experience for Knowles. His all-encompassing openness to the external, sociable world, for example, stirred Knowles's aesthetic interest in the ordinary goods and detritus in her immediate neighborhood.[120] Canal Street's bustling commercial district became a fertile source of materials—rocks, scraps of metal, used tea bags, shoe heels, cheap containers—that connoted, in the patchwork planes of Knowles's early paintings and her later, small-scale objects, sculptures, and Fluxus performances, the teeming energy of the urban landscape.

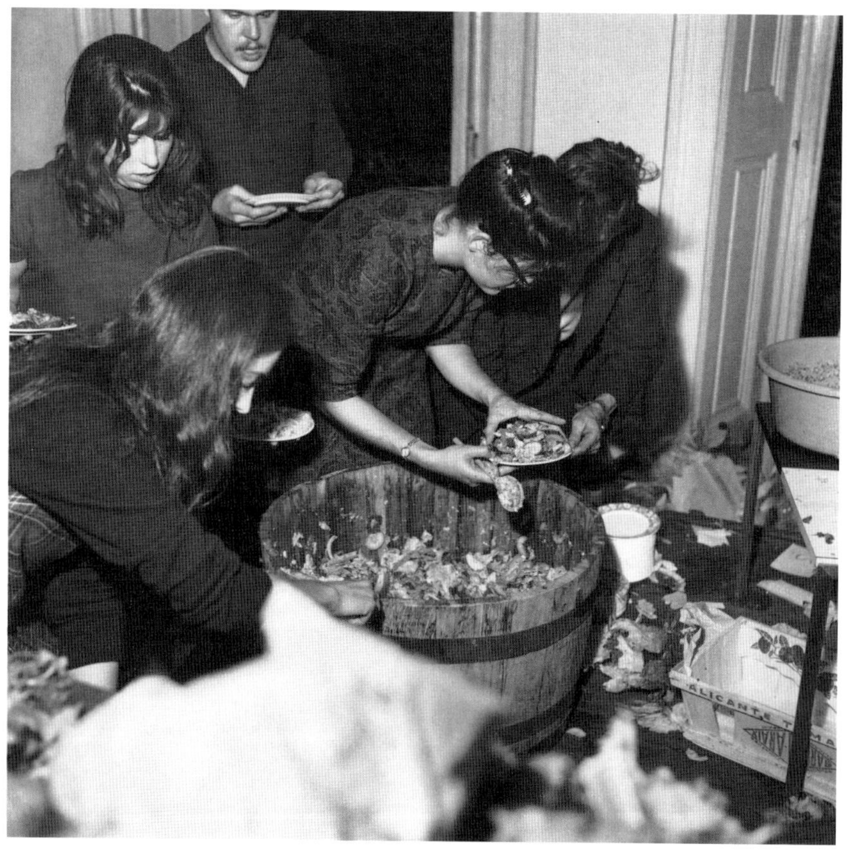

**Figure 2.1.** Alison Knowles serving *Proposition #2: Make a Salad* at the Festival of Misfits, Institute of Contemporary Arts, London, October 24, 1962. Photo: Bruce Fleming. Image © The Museum of Modern Art. Licensed by SCALA/Art Resource, NY.

# 2 TOWARD A FEMINIST FLUXUS SCORE

The environment is ever ready, but we have to make a bridge to it.
The simpler the score the better.
**Alison Knowles**[1]

On October 24, 1962, at the Institute of Contemporary Arts (ICA), just off Trafalgar Square in London, Alison Knowles premiered her now-celebrated piece *Proposition #2: Make a Salad*.[2] Standing onstage in a small concert hall before an audience accustomed to both traditional musical performances and progressive programming, Knowles enacted a literal demonstration of the work's directive (fig. 2.1). Simply put, she composed a salad for the attendees using fresh produce collected that day from a local market. No recipe for the salad was provided, nor did she specify how many servings should be prepared or whether it should be offered to the audience; she simply directed that an action be completed.

Knowles shared the bill with other Fluxus artists who had traveled to London from across Western Europe. The raucous evening, which extended into the morning hours, was part of the Festival of Misfits, an evening of events accompanying an exhibition curated by poet and art dealer Victor Musgrave at Gallery One in nearby Hyde Park. The exhibition, introducing the Fluxus group to Great Britain, came one month after the end of the first series of Fluxus concerts, in Wiesbaden, Germany, and featured artists from continental Europe and the US, including Robert Filliou, Dick Higgins, Arthur Køpcke, Gustav Metzger, Robin Page, Benjamin Patterson, Ben Vautier, and Emmett Williams. The London festival was somewhat different from previous Fluxus events, most organized in advance by George Maciunas, but was nonetheless officially sanctioned under the Fluxus moniker. Musgrave tasked Nouveau Réaliste Swiss artist and Fluxus affiliate Daniel Spoerri with bringing "the first important manifestation in this country of the avant-garde 'Happenings Movements' that has swept America" and coordinated the international coterie of artists and their mix of objects, performances, and installation-based work into a cohesive theme.[3] Musgrave later recalled that the show was quickly arranged in the gallery "over a period of about a week" and "included

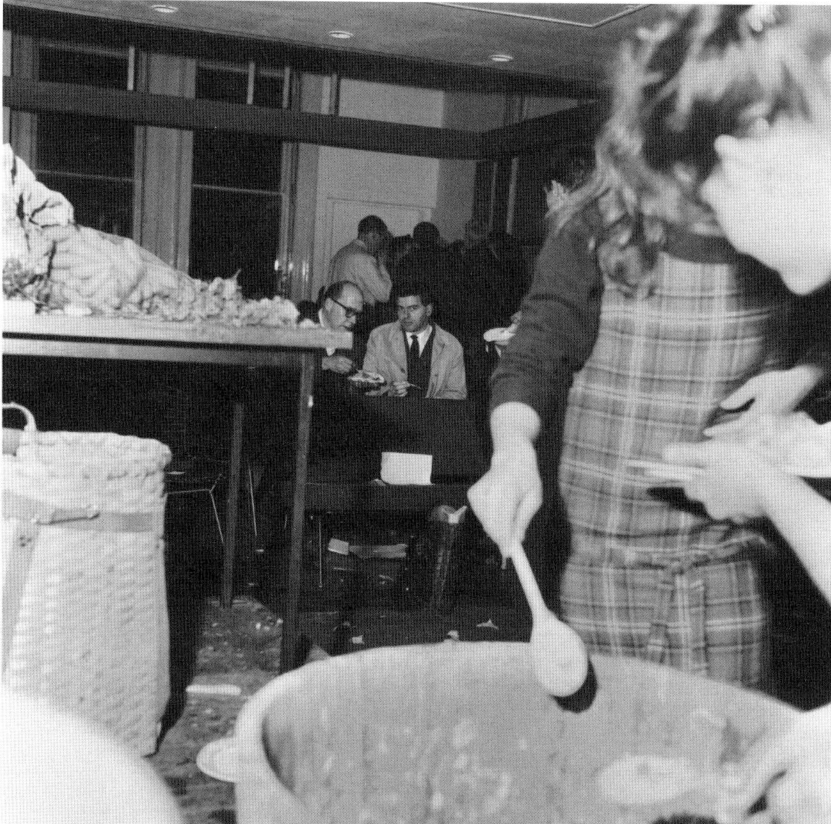

**Figure 2.2.** Alison Knowles serving *Proposition #2: Make a Salad* at the Festival of Misfits, Institute of Contemporary Arts, London, October 1962. Photo: Bruce Fleming. Gilbert and Lila Silverman Fluxus Collection Gift, Museum of Modern Art, New York.

a labyrinthine black-out room, a fun-making machine shop and the artist Ben Vautier living and sleeping in the window. Nothing was for sale, although small objects were given away for free."[4]

For Spoerri and the other artists, audience participation was a key ingredient.[5] This was especially true for Knowles, who transformed *Proposition #2: Make a Salad* from a concept piece into a consciously multisensory occasion (figs. 2.2–2.3). Participants experienced not just sights, smells, and tastes but a cacophony that announced something more radical than mere hospitality: the rhythmic hum of slicing—a noise so distinctive that, according to the artist, you could "hear every crack of the knife"—together with the aural merriment of those watching and eating, effected a subtle mimicry of orchestral labor.[6] Undermining habits and expectations of conventional spectatorship, Knowles refused to produce what an audience in 1962 might reasonably require: a discrete modernist art object obliging singular contemplation and transcendent quietude. Instead, the former abstract painter offered a common experience extracted from everyday life and subjected her public to chaotic viewing and fleshy consumption.

This chapter revisits Knowles's *Make a Salad* and other key propositional scores created during her most active performance days in Fluxus. These note-

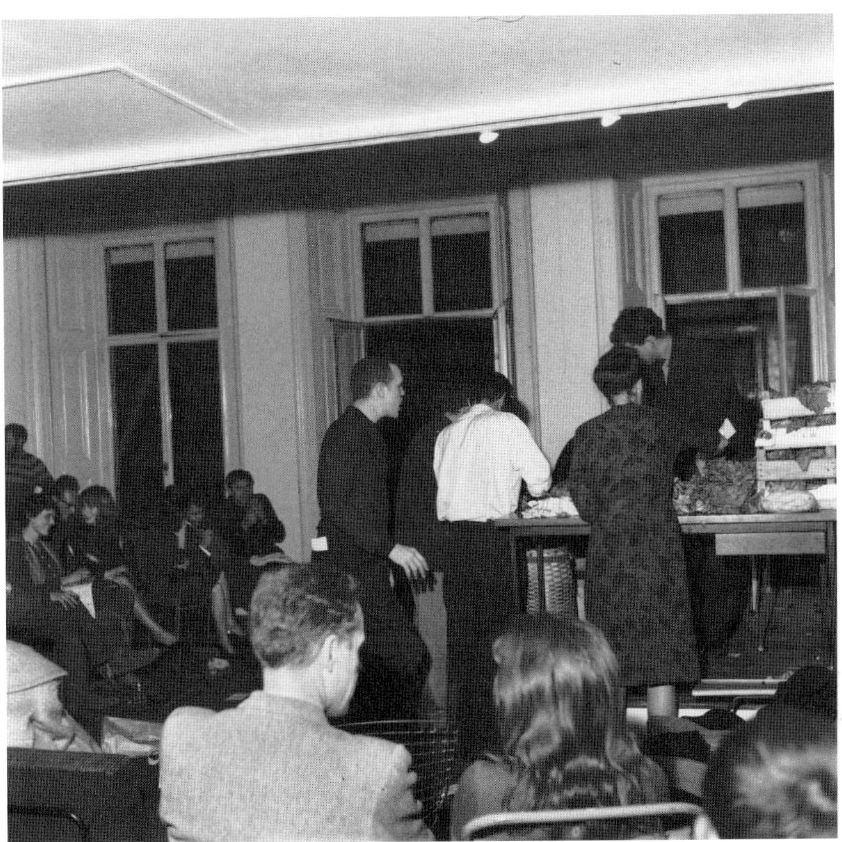

**Figure 2.3.** Alison Knowles serving *Proposition #2: Make a Salad* at the Festival of Misfits, Institute of Contemporary Arts, London, October 1962. Photo: Bruce Fleming. Gilbert and Lila Silverman Fluxus Collection Gift, Museum of Modern Art, New York.

worthy works from the early 1960s expand John Cage's program of chance-derived aesthetics into an artistic praxis whose increasingly evident political aspect includes an elliptic feminist attitude toward investigations of the everyday. We will see this more clearly in the next chapter when, in the mid- to late 1960s, her modest scores investigate the intimate choices and habits of the daily world, reflecting larger cultural anxieties around the status of gender. Shifting away from studio painting and printmaking toward temporality as a medium circumscribed in public performances, Knowles's Fluxus propositional model resituates the self in relation to the social world.

In a very few years, Knowles's artistic production evolved from abstract expressionist paintings to silk-screen collages, still created largely in private, to collaborative happenings, conceptually rigorous scores for performance that could be enacted (or not) in concert with the spectator. Fluxus, Happenings, and other temporal and body-based artistic actions of the 1960s strategically incorporated (and in some cases aggressively solicited) audience participation to complete the work, and the propositional format Knowles originated in Fluxus implicitly acknowledge that it is the public—freely defined—who weaves together the work's formal procedures.

While this merging of artistic intention with public address would be the crux of Knowles's post-painting career, her major Fluxus scores, thematically detailed in this chapter, magnified the notion of engagement through protofeminist dialectics of chance that did *not* dogmatically insist on the audience's direct participation. Rather, I argue that the propositions are often open-sourced instigations—urgings, spaces, desires, pitches. Existing as minimalist solo undertakings, collective performances, or temporal/durational compositions that may remain purely textual, these pieces were a remarkable response to the increasingly interdisciplinary demands of the era. Heterogeneous in nature and perpetually iterative, Knowles's propositional scores manifest more complex remedies to the supposed divide between artist and spectator than have heretofore been credited to her in critical narratives of Fluxus and late modernist art history.

## Knowles's Fluxus Origins

In September 1962, Alison Knowles and Dick Higgins made the long journey from New York City to Wiesbaden, Germany, arriving just as the Fluxus Internationale Festspiele Neuester Musik (Fluxus International Festival of Very New Music) was getting under way at the Städtisches Museum.[7] The trip promised a rare opportunity to finally meet in person artists with whom both had been exchanging letters. Higgins had kept abreast of contemporary music in Europe, especially in Germany, thanks to dispatches from composer Earle Brown's detailing of the unusual performances by US expatriates like Benjamin Patterson, a virtuoso double bassist from Pennsylvania who toured with the Seventh Army's symphony orchestra and had recently resettled in Europe (commuting between Paris and West Germany), and Southern-born Oscar (Emmett) Williams, a poet then living in Darmstadt, who worked as the features editor of *Stars and Stripes*, the US Army newspaper. Korean-born composer Nam June Paik, in Germany since the late 1950s, was also active in the experimental music scene, as was North American composer and musician La Monte Young, with whom Knowles and Higgins were in regular contact before the trip.

Prior to Wiesbaden, an alliance to alternative art, dance, and theater happenings in New York's Lower Manhattan (at Cooper Union, The Living Theater, Judson Memorial Church, and auxiliary venues) provided Knowles with a supportive base for her own conceptual interests, as well as her budding collaborations with Higgins and others. Interactions within this creative milieu arguably cemented her connection to the community of avant-gardists who would eventually form the "American contingent" of the Fluxus group in Europe.[8] As noted in chapter 1, she contributed to various productions staged by Higgins, who was a founding member of a few artist-directed experimental clusters, including (with Al Hansen) the New York Audio-Visual Group.[9] And she regularly attended the six-month series of events co-organized, starting in December 1960, by Young and Yoko Ono at 112 Chambers Street, a downtown loft where Ono (Tokyo-born and New York–based) lived with her first husband, composer Toshi Ichiyanagi, both of whom were friends of Cage.[10] Featuring a disparate cast of visual artists, poets, dancers, playwrights, and musicians, the Chambers Street Loft series, as it came to be known, was a tremendously generative forum and testing ground for artistic exploration and exchange, not to mention an increasingly intricate constellation of contacts. Knowles witnessed, for example, choreographer Simone Forti's evocative task-based *Five Dance Constructions and Some Other Things* (1961), including *Slant Board*, an experience that both reinforced Knowles's emerging aesthetic sensibilities regarding space and somatic motility and sparked a lifelong friendship with Forti.[11]

The Chambers Street loft was also where Knowles first got to know Maciunas, a Lithuanian-born graphic designer and antique musical instruments dealer who was then managing AG Gallery. Named after its two business partners, George Maciunas and fellow Lithuanian Almus Salcius, AG Gallery was a modest space at 925 Madison Avenue, between Seventy-Third and Seventy-Fourth Streets on the Upper East Side. The storefront gallery presented art exhibitions (including early work by Ono), concerts of classical and avant-garde music, and poetry evenings run by Frank Kuenstler, a filmmaker, poet, and editor of the literary journal *Bread&*, which Knowles attended. She also witnessed there Higgins's electronic music and films, included in a Maciunas-curated series entitled *Concerts of New Sounds and Noises*.[12]

Around this time, Maciunas was invited by Young (whom he met at electronic music composer Richard Maxfield's course at the New School for Social Research) to design the compilation of avant-garde musical scores, manifestos, concrete poetry, and artworks Young had been assembling for a small zine to be called *Beatitude East*. Poet Jackson Mac Low (a student of Cage's influential 1958 course on experimental music) joined the production team, and the volume was ultimately published as *An Anthology of Chance Operations, Concept Art, Anti Art, Indeterminacy, Plans of Action, Diagrams, Music, Dance Constructions, Improvisation, Meaningless Work, Natural Disasters, Compositions, Mathematics, Essays, Poetry* in 1963.[13] The visually striking pages Maciunas designed featured sans-serif type in mixed sizes and orientations set on various sorts of paper—a look that would become a signal feature of his Fluxus "brand" and style.[14] Funds for its publication came through a crowd-sourced effort that included benefit concerts co-organized by Young and Higgins at The Living Theater in January and February 1962.[15] Higgins was included in the original *Anthology*, and Knowles was invited by Maciunas, alongside others like Ono and George Brecht, to contribute material for a future second compilation to be called *Fluxus*, after which he envisioned a succession of publications.[16] Maciunas, thwarted by significant private and public debts incurred promoting AG Gallery, was forced to close its doors in August 1961, having by then produced the mechanicals for the layout of *An Anthology*. He fled the US, landing first in Austria and then in Wiesbaden, where he procured a graphic design position as a civilian contractor at the US Air Force Exchange.

By spring 1962, Knowles, Higgins, and Williams were receiving frequent communiqués from Maciunas, typed or printed on index cards and long paper scrolls, and mailed from his APO address in Wiesbaden.[17] Maciunas provided his interlocutors with updates and announcements of the many artistic activities happening on the Continent and solicited ideas for public programs. He declared himself manager of a global enterprise, spanning three continents (Europe, North America, Asia), and laid out plans for Fluxus yearbooks to promote its performances, experimental music concerts, and visual-poetry events.[18] Thus, even before Fluxus coalesced as an experimental performance group, it originated as a name, a fluid sign, and a polysemic brand for a collective of like-minded individuals lacking institutional support for their avant-garde tastes and forms. Chosen for its breadth of meaning and linguistic flexibility, "Fluxus" indeed proved an ideal moniker, a deliberately elusive designation for the earlier publishing venture that quickly gathered momentum in unintended ways.[19] Notwithstanding the extensive articulation of administrative and conceptual procedures, Fluxus—as a working practice—remained largely undefined when the group began performing under its name in Wiesbaden. Like Knowles's propositional scores, it remained a concrete yet indeterminate suggestion for action passing through the hands of potential actors.

In Germany, Knowles and Higgins shared a house with Maciunas in Ehlhalten, a village outside Wiesbaden. At the time they were more interested in pursuing screenings for Higgins's feature-length cinematic portrait of metropolitan New York, *The Flaming City*—an "anti-semantic love story" in which Knowles appears—than in founding an international group.[20] Nonetheless, having corresponded with Maciunas, Paik, Young, and Patterson, they arrived bearing the compositions and event scores of US-based artists and composers (like George Brecht, Philip Corner, and Robert Watts) who could not attend the Fluxus festivals and fairs that would take place in major European cities over the course of the next year. According to Watts and Corner, Knowles and Higgins each suggested that they send Maciunas some of the events they were then producing.[21] Neither Young nor Corner ever formally joined Fluxus, but their notational compositions were performed at the first festival in Wiesbaden and would do much to define a recognizable Fluxus aesthetic. This striking confluence of exploratory artistic trends in New York, Japan, and Western Europe (e.g., Happenings, experimental music, Cagean aesthetics, concrete poetry, Lettrisme, COBRA, the Gutai Group), coupled with Maciunas's organizational skills, graphics acumen (as demonstrated in *An Anthology*), and indefatigable work ethic, all aided in the establishment of the discursive ground for Fluxus.

## The Propositional Score

In early fall 1962, posters, announcements, and mailers promoted the inaugural concert of the Wiesbaden Fluxus festival, listing the performers and their pieces. An article previewing the series even appeared in the US Army's *Stars and Stripes*.[22] In practice, the concerts rarely followed the programs circulated beforehand. More importantly, while the public concerts, scheduled on weekends, presented the promised ensemble pieces (e.g., Maciunas's *In Memoriam to Adriano Olivetti* (fig.I.4) and Williams's *Four-Directional Song of Doubt for Five Voices*), much of significance occurred during the week: Individual artists developed their scores, and brainstorming sessions at Maciunas's house delved into discussions of what exactly participants were trying to accomplish—what kind of transgressive wave they hoped to unleash across postwar Germany.[23]

Years later, Knowles related public reactions to the Fluxus performances with her own sense of artistic transformation:

> In 1962 performing in Wiesbaden, Germany, I became shocked out of painting as my medium of expression. Out of necessity and almost overnight, we began composing and performing "event scores" for a starved German public, under the banner of Fluxus. Our audience was astonished to find daily events in kitchens and markets, in offices and street wanderings suddenly looked at by artists. On our second night, the audience was divided into those picketing and shouting us down and those fervently defending what we did on the stage. My *Make a Salad* or *Shoes of Your Choice*, Dick Higgins's *Scream*, and Ben Patterson's *Cello Variations* were of tremendous value to our audience: to wrest the German stage from the jaws of Grand Opera! The newspaper headlines the next day read "the Crazies have come to town." After that the theatre was packed each night.[24]

While Knowles appears here to conflate her first Fluxus concert, in September, with the October performance of *Make a Salad* at the ICA in London, her statement of the performer's collective ambitions is striking. The relation of the conceptual and the political was cemented early on. Knowles was keen to stage events (at the time, all performances) based on a perceived need, grounded in the moment but already extrapolated as a resistance to conservative retrenchment and backlash. Before she and Higgins arrived in Germany, he and Maciunas had exchanged letters outlining which performances the couple planned on doing. In one, from 1962, Higgins wrote, "Alison says she's game to perform almost anything."[25]

In retrospect, Knowles's initial Fluxus work clearly reflects both fatigue with abstract expressionism, widespread among artists in the late 1950s; her Bohemian milieu; and the influence of experimental composer John Cage. Her propositional scores like *Make a Salad* were Cagean in their minimalism, indeterminacy, and openness to the new realizations temporally uncertain actions may generate. "The events I perform, the prints I have made and the environments I build," she wrote later, "are designed to put the spectator/

performer in touch with him/herself and the real world. Since all feelings reside in the individual sensibility, I am interested in touching, awakening and activating certain of my own and your own personal responses."[26] Knowles's elucidation here of her compositional method is tied to a convergence of materiality and sonic substance in her propositional scores. Improvisational in nature and often written down hastily, her contemporaneous notes nevertheless set out an orderly intellectual framework that simultaneously allows for engagement with each new public and for continual recalibration based on circumstances on the ground.

This flexibility is illustrated in previously unpublished notes related to *Make a Salad*, long lost in the archives.[27] Handwritten on what appears to be a fragment of a press release related to the ICA's second major exhibition, *40,000 Years of Modern Art: A Comparison of Primitive and Modern* (1948–1949), Knowles's notes provide detailed instructions, beyond the title imperative, for *performing* the salad (fig. 2.4). From seating arrangements for her Fluxus coperformers to the preparation of ingredients to decisions rethought and scratched out, Knowles instructed each participant to abide by certain duties:

> Then the other performers get up from seats and take a plastic bag from the kitchen area. One bag per person. With exception of Ben [Vautier] and Robert [Filliou] who will only help out later, or if needed—in front row. Empty your vegetable into the tub of water, clean thoroughly and replace cleaned fruit in plastic bag. Find a cutting board and knife on the table and proceed to ~~clean~~ prepare your vegetable. If you finish help Oscar [Emmett Williams] with the onions etc. When vegetables are cleaned and cut, replace in plastic bag. ~~The 1st vegetable for cleaning is the lettuce.~~ Lettuce—Daniel [Spoerri]'s basket out on cloth on table . . . I'm [Alison] making dressing on small table. As you clean, put parings into waste bags. When all vegetables are cleaned, Ady [Arthur Køpcke] and Oscar [Emmett] and helpers empty the tub in the studio sink, dry out, replace tub on table. Then Spoerri adds his lettuce, Oscar his onions etc. until all vegetables are added. Perhaps two halves if tub is too small, in which case add only half your vegetables. Dressing last. All will serve onto the small plates. ~~Filliou and Ben will get up then~~ and hand each member of audience a salad with fork, when there is no salad left the piece is over. Ady and Oscar take the tub to kitchen.[28]

The event was shared with a specific art public and with her fellow performers—all of whom participated in, as directed, making a salad. As a female artist leading a nearly all-male cast in food preparation, she effectively inscribed into her instructions the subject position of authority and protofeminist intentionality.

In a letter to Allan Kaprow, written soon after the performance, Higgins recounted the evening's program. After opining on contributions by Williams, Metzger, Page, Køpcke, and Filliou, he ends on Knowles's piece:

Salad 1

chief: - Alison Knowles

assistants;

Dick Higgins
Addi Køpcke
Oscar Williams
Daniel Spoerri
Robin Page
. Robert Filliou
. Ben Vautier

procedure:

following intermission the tables to be used will be beside the stage to begin Oscar and Addi will set these up end to end the long way on the stage, and the small tables beside the stage on either side. Then these two will go to the kitchen area and carry the large tub to the tables. Dick and I will carry two or three buckets with water to the tub and fill it. They also set out the available knives and cutting boards.

then the other performers get up from seats and take a plastic bag from the kitchen area. One bag per person. [illegible]

2

with exception of Ben and Robert who will only help out later, or if needed — in front row.

empty your vegetable into the tub of water, clean thoroughly and replace cleaned fruit in plastic bag. Find a cutting board and knife on the table and proceed to prepare your vegetable. If you finish help Oscar with the onions etc. when vegetables are cleaned and cut, replace in plastic bag.

lettuce — Daniel, basket out on cloth on table. Alison making dressing on small table.

as you clean, put parings into waste bag. When all vegetables are cleaned, Addi and Oscar and helpers empty the tub in the studio sink, dry out, replace tub on table. Then Spoerri adds his lettuce, Oscar his onions etc. until all vegetables are added. Perhaps two halves if tub is too small, in which case add only half your vegetables. Dressing

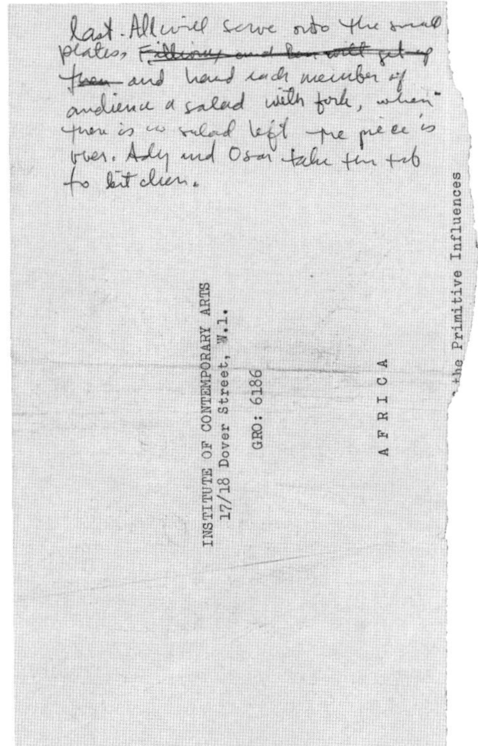
last. All will serve onto the small plates, and hand each member of audience a salad with fork, when there is no salad left the piece is over. Addi and Oscar take the tub to kitchen.

INSTITUTE OF CONTEMPORARY ARTS
17/18 Dover Street, W.1.
GRO: 6186

A F R I C A

the Primitive Influences

**Figure 2.4.** Alison Knowles, notes for propositions, ca. 1962. John Cage Notations Project. Courtesy Charles Deering McCormick Library of Special Collections, Northwestern University.

> At the end, we did Alison's very nice "Proposition," which goes simply, "Make a Salad." Crosse & Blackwell donated a lovely pickle barrel—what a marvelous aroma! And at 4:30 AM before [the] performance we went to Covent Garden & bought the loveliest, freshest vegetables you ever saw. We got enough for 200 people but there were only 100 there, since that was the day of the Cuban [Missile] Crisis. But what a salad! Everybody got some. All the artists even [Gustav] Metzger & Ben [Vautier] helped. All told it was one of the finest evenings I've ever been involved with, much better than our other European one-shot, at Amsterdam.[29]

Higgins's letter contextualizes Knowles's salad performance as being presented amid a terrifying nuclear showdown. He attributes the smaller than expected audience (and hence, our relative lack of available witnesses) to geopolitical tensions and, in doing so, situates Fluxus within the Cold War, its anticommunist hysteria, and its intersection with public art making (and even frivolity). At the height of a global crisis, Knowles decided to conclude the "Misfits" performance series with a public meal. Her maneuver (intentionally or not) demonstrates that artistic labor and communal, even political, experience are not mutually exclusive. Her proposition, in other words, shifted the presumed authority of the artwork as object to the artist as live performer and conductor of a pleasurable, convivial atmosphere.[30]

Knowles's notion of propositional scores at first aligned with Maciunas's understanding of the purpose of early Fluxus concerts. In a letter written to the German artist Tomas Schmit in 1963, after the festivals had concluded, Maciunas emphasized that "Fluxus people must obtain their 'art' experience from everyday occurrences, eating, working, etc.," with concerts serving "only as educational means to convert the audiences to such non-art experience in their daily lives."[31] A year later, however, Maciunas posited a revised imperative: "*Fluxus objectives* are *social* (not aesthetic)" and directed toward the "*gradual elimination of fine arts* (music, theater, poetry, fiction, painting, sculpt—etc., etc.). This is motivated by the desire to stop the waste of material and human resources (like yourself) and divert it to *socially constructive ends*."[32] Despite such axiomatic assertions, it is not so easy to specify Fluxus practitioners' individual or collective objectives. In the case of Knowles, she forged a unique practice that troubled Maciunas's presumptions by investing in new aesthetic terrains, building upon the insights and innovations of the historical avant-garde and contemporary developments in her immediate orbit. She pursued, in other words, *both* aesthetic and social ends, motivated less by the "gradual elimination of the arts" than by the potential richness of their interdisciplinarity.

In this model of aesthetic exchange, the viewer bears some responsibility; accordingly, their engagement or refusal to engage more or less determines the artwork's value, if not exactly its interpretation. The propositional structure, as a *form* of offering, is clearly laid out in the enaction of *Make a Salad* (chopping and serving) but also in the historical reception of other notational scores and performances from Knowles's early days in Fluxus. As part of an evolution that includes, most dramatically, the turn from painting to performance, Knowles's modest, seemingly mundane scores fixed the terms for a multimedia practice that disrupts the very categories of postwar taste (aesthetic, philosophic, gastronomic). With *Make a Salad*, Knowles materially and conceptually augments the performance model of Fluxus concerts as it was forming into her own orchestration; closer to collaged elements, the effects produced a space where sound, smell, and taste were simultaneously perceived.

At the most basic level, the very presentation of a *proposition* as a directive in the imperative voice (Make a salad) is a singular "creative act" that can instigate a sequence of further actions.[33] The template of Fluxus concerts in Wiesbaden, for example, had relied, to a certain extent, on instruments and props for sound. The coincidence of the chance cab ride conversation with Higgins rendered the line between art and life indistinct and instigated the epigrammatic structure Knowles came to favor in her Fluxus scores. As she noted later, "Because these event pieces are so simple the audience projects their own political or artistic frame. Each person must flesh it out."[34]

It is significant that Knowles, unlike many of her cohort, rarely composed what became her published Fluxus propositions as comprehensive scripts or typed notecards prepared in advance of a performance. She arrived in Europe with ideas for work, "game" to perform almost anything, but no preplanned scores. Rather, assessing the demands of a given situation and available local materials, she devised outlines for an evening's events more or less on the spot. As in *Make a Salad*—jotting down notes before the performance and directing the makers as ingredients were being prepared—Knowles produced a formalized score only after the fact.[35] Knowles recalls Higgins saving the slips of paper she used throughout the run of the original Fluxus tour, and publishing them in spring 1965, two years after their return to New York, as the Great Bear Pamphlet *by Alison Knowles* (fig. 2.8).[36] The propositional scores listed in *by Alison Knowles* can thus generally be said to have been composed in 1962–1964 (with variations added later), though their association with specific locations may align them with a more exact timeline.

The extent to which Knowles aesthetically developed the poetic possibilities of the scored form often goes unremarked in the Fluxus literature. The propositional relationship is, in fact, a grammar of choice. At the ICA event in London (and elsewhere later), audience members had several options. They could watch the salad being made, focusing their perceptual attention on the overlapping rhythms of food being sliced and the smell of fresh ingredients, and then partake in its consumption. Yet the proposition itself does not address the spectator's response or specify any reciprocal action.

In 1964, back in New York, Knowles reperformed *Make a Salad* score and modified it with *Variation #1: Make a Soup* for friends and audience members of George Brecht and Robert Watts's performance series "Monday Night

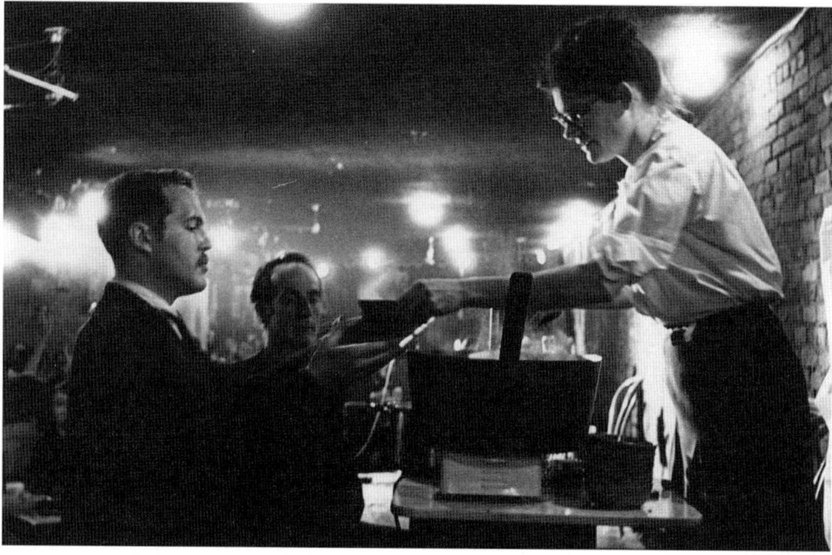

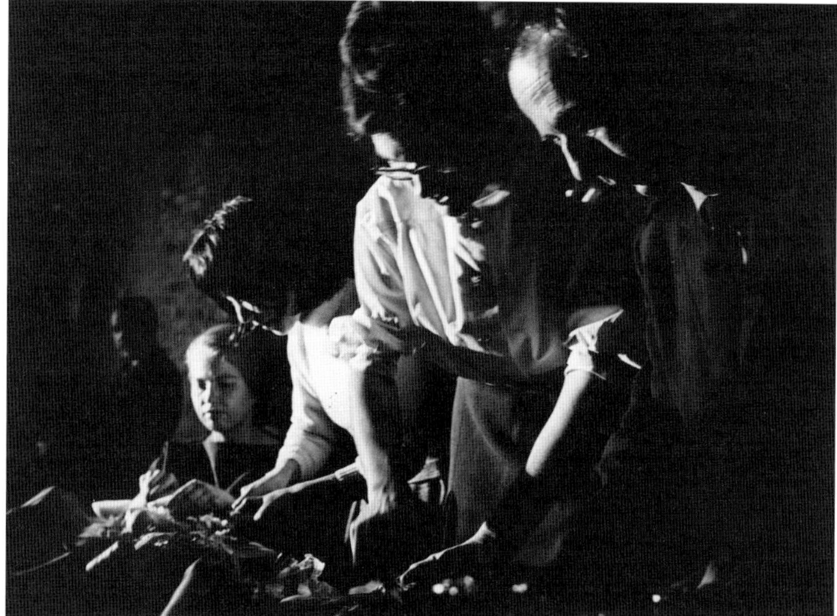

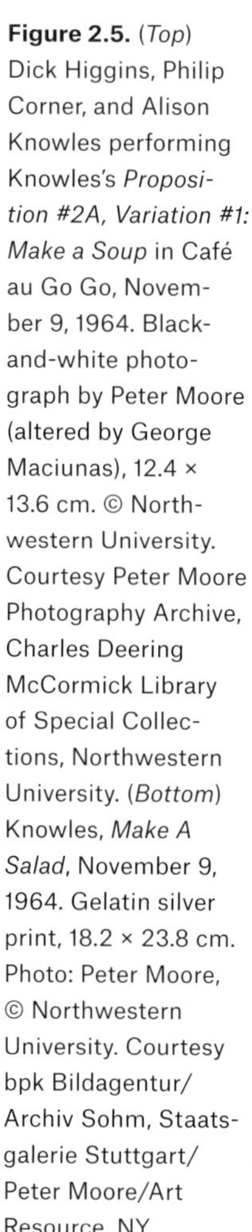

**Figure 2.5.** (*Top*) Dick Higgins, Philip Corner, and Alison Knowles performing Knowles's *Proposition #2A, Variation #1: Make a Soup* in Café au Go Go, November 9, 1964. Black-and-white photograph by Peter Moore (altered by George Maciunas), 12.4 × 13.6 cm. © Northwestern University. Courtesy Peter Moore Photography Archive, Charles Deering McCormick Library of Special Collections, Northwestern University. (*Bottom*) Knowles, *Make A Salad*, November 9, 1964. Gelatin silver print, 18.2 × 23.8 cm. Photo: Peter Moore, © Northwestern University. Courtesy bpk Bildagentur/Archiv Sohm, Staatsgalerie Stuttgart/Peter Moore/Art Resource, NY.

Letters" at the Café au Go Go at 152 Bleecker Street in Greenwich Village (fig. 2.5). The café was infamous for featuring irreverent comedians like Lenny Bruce and George Carlin and jazz acts like Bill Evans and the New Stan Getz Quartet, as well as stateside Fluxus events and film and video screenings by the likes of Warhol and Paik.[37] Knowles, too, executed her own works and participated in cooperative events with other close artist friends, including Corner, Patterson, Spoerri, and composer and choreographer Meredith Monk.[38]

Wherever their presentation, Knowles's propositional scores within Fluxus ultimately reveal the nature of the relation between artist and public to be lively, unpredictable, and subject to context (location, time of day) but not inevitably codependent. This point is especially crucial to Knowles's understanding of the fugitive or revolutionary potential of Fluxus. In yoking chance to live-art practices, she craved a "slackening [of] the hold of the [artist's] ego" and imagined that Fluxus could invest in the "real world spectator [as] the moving ingredient."[39] However, despite the industriousness implicit in Maciunas's program and the rhetorical virtuosity of his 1963 manifesto, the general tone of his post-European missives and newsletters struck Knowles as inconsistent with her own sensibilities, and she refused to fully endorse his aims.[40] As Maciunas's idea of the collective hardened (for a time) into a more overtly activist politicized agenda, Knowles and others demurred. Knowles agreed with Higgins when he argued that "no creed" was necessary and the possibility of a "Fluxus Group . . . would probably have driven every one of us away—[we wanted] nothing but the rostrum and the material."[41] This is not to suggest that Fluxus work was devoid of political or social content. Indeed, it is the intention of this study to demonstrate otherwise through a close study of many works developed by Knowles within and beyond the Fluxus paradigm.

In one memorable collaboration, in Wiesbaden (fig. 2.6), Knowles acted as principal, on the rostrum, for Higgins's score *Danger Music No. 2* (1961), which reads, "Hat. Rags. Paper. Heave. Shave."[42] Richard O'Regan, an Associated Press correspondent, reviewed the evening for *Stars and Stripes*:

> The opening work that night was "Danger Music No. 2" by a New Yorker, Dick Higgins. Higgins entered and took a bow. He sat himself beside a bucket. His wife, Alison Knowles, appeared with a pair of scissors. She began to cut his hair. Higgins looked content. After 15 minutes, the audience grew restless. Paper airplanes circled from the back row. Conversation took over. "I'm sure I don't know what it is all about or what it is supposed to mean," commented one of Germany's well-known abstract painters. "I tell you Higgins is performing a rare work," said Emmett Williams, a part-time performer and composer of this Very New Music living in Germany. "He could play a Chopin etude every night. But Higgins can't give another performance like this for six months, until his hair grows back." "But there is no music," we protested naïvely. "Is this parody or protest?" "You have to understand," said George Maciunas, the American promoter of the festival, "that in new music the audible and the visible overlap. That is what is called action music."[43]

What are we to make of this collaborative performance, one that proposes a new definitional term, "action music," and provokes spectators, whether professional critics or chance attendees, to make their own music by turning their boredom and confusion into *new actions* or debating the merits of what they are seeing? Further, what are we to make of Knowles's action here—

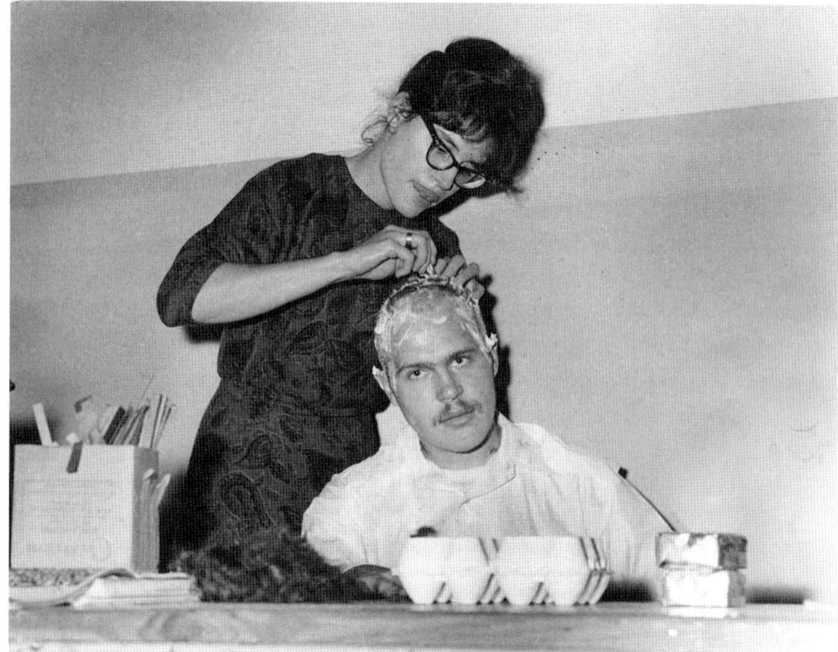

**Figure 2.6.** Dick Higgins and Alison Knowles performing Higgins's *Danger Music Number Two* at Fluxus Internationale Festspiele, 1962. Black-and-white photograph, 9½ × 11 in. (23.9 × 30.2 cm). Photo: Hartmut Rekort, © Staatsgalerie Stuttgart.

methodically shaving Higgins in front of a post–World War II German audience? Or of Higgins throwing "Strike for Peace!" political pamphlets at the audience afterwards?[44]

On a practical level, it makes sense that Higgins would choose Knowles as a performance partner; their marital status seems to guarantee her caution in wielding a razor. The couple was at once performing an act of domestic care (one spouse taking care of the other) and wittingly speaking to more broadly shared experiences. The audience's purported irritation and boredom might mean they had not fully understood the piece, or perhaps boredom was the point.[45] Within the tedious enactment of mundane chores in Fluxus performances, actions that are refreshingly "unpretentious and nonconformist," Kristine Stiles detects an air of ironic humor, the "appearance of chaos."[46] This slightly anarchic, deliberately droll theatricality characterizes much of the early Fluxus oeuvre. Interpreted more critically, *Danger Music No. 2* symbolically speaks to the murderous trauma wrought upon Jewish citizens across Germany and much of Europe during the Nazi regime just two decades earlier, where the shaving of heads was a potent visual means of marking and humiliating ethnic others.[47] Perhaps, then, we might view Higgins and Knowles's performance as a condemnation of bourgeois passivity (alluding, at least obliquely, to Hannah Arendt's "banality of evil") and a warning to never forget. Unlike most Fluxus pieces, which were repeated in other Western German cities, to my knowledge, Knowles and Higgins never repeated *Danger Music No. 2* during their Fluxus tour (even after his hair grew back), marking the performance in Wiesbaden as especially psychologically and politically charged.[48]

Despite abundant discourse on audience activation and participation, few sources record Fluxus events from the perspective of the viewers. A score or composition played out like an event to be consumed—an invitation, not to participate directly onstage but, rather, to watch and listen, to take in the action sensorially, live and unmediated. O'Regan's review is, in this regard, a standout exception.[49] The noisy frustration he reports recalls the similar reaction ten years earlier to Cage's *4′33″*—the sonorous movements of boredom composed by the audience as they watched David Tudor open and close a piano lid. During Fluxus events, Higgins once noted that the spectators' responses "varied from enormous to tiny, from explosive (we had two riots) to docile and indifferent to sympathetic."[50]

The earliest Fluxus festivals, however unevenly attended, still enabled the artists to work on their craft, to perform their pieces, if only for each other. At its phenomenological base, art viewing is always experiential. We see this in several performances. In their rendition of Maciunas's *In Memoriam to Adriano Olivetti* (fig. I.4), Knowles squatted down behind a long table on the stage each time the number four was read on her tickertape, and in Corner's *Piano Activities*, she rubbed the piano strings with a sandal while Patterson and Maciunas hammered on the keys and soundboard to amplify their collective sounds and vibrarions (fig. I.3). What Knowles and other pioneers of Fluxus performance activated was a more textured experience, one that deliberately engaged the multisensorial capacities of the body, merging visual, aural, olfactive, and tactile. While some scores, such as Higgins's *Danger Music No. 2*, do not overtly carry these stimuli to an audience, others, like *Make a Salad*, incorporate as well the gustatory.

Owen F. Smith argued that event works like *Make a Salad* evince an "operation of egalitarianism" within Fluxus, shifting focus from the performative nature of making art to the lived rituals of daily nourishment.[51] Similarly, David Doris contends that early Fluxus work more generally was premised on the "exposition of the path [of doing] itself, the restructuring and presentation of a process of meaning-production."[52] Yet, while the performance may not rely on the presence of an audience or need the "structures of artistic presentation to be extraordinary," Knowles's propositional format and its corporeal realization still require that the structure be understood as art. *Make a Salad* is site-specific, Doris perceptively notes, in that it depends on its surrounding to enable its performance *as* art.[53]

After London, Knowles went on to perform *Proposition #2: Make a Salad* during European concerts under the Fluxus aegis.[54] In November 1962, as part of what came to be referred to as the Nordic Festum Fluxorum in Copenhagen, she performed the score for an audience of reportedly five hundred people and found herself "confronted with all of these angry Danes." She noted, in particular, the ire of the head of the music school, who had personally subsidized the purchase of vegetables, presumably believing she was "going to [just] make something in a little bowl."[55] Instead, Knowles prepared a salad big enough for all the attendees and even accepted their help in washing, chopping, and tossing the ingredients in a "dynamic feminist twist."[56]

Curiously, the *political* implications of her Fluxus instruction pieces, grounded in the language of daily experience and gendered domesticity, are often lost or overlooked. *Make a Salad*, informed by the emerging discourse around second-wave feminism, covertly critiqued the monotonous, repetitive nature of household labor and the relation between women and the maintenance of the self and the familial (and political) body. Yet her work is not generally included in feminist, or even protofeminist, art histories. I view Knowles's exploration of everyday labors as a specific effort to instigate a dialogue about gender, the distinctions between private and public, and not just class but the attendant refinement of taste and cultivation.

On this level, the intimacy of the performance and its invocation of domestic service—shopping for the salad, preparing the salad, sharing the salad—allowed Knowles to operate beyond the limits of traditional art making and exchange. Even when its realization was collaborative, her proposition invited a singular meditation on (early feminist) authorship by effectively foregrounding the conditions of *how* an artist shares her work with her audience, with her publics.[57] We see this in a suite of previously unpublished photographs documenting the original 1962 performance in London. These photographs show Knowles preparing the salad, but also Knowles orchestrating the work of others, including Spoerri, Williams, and Higgins, and the salad's messy aftermath (fig. 2.7).

Any work of art (live or otherwise) premised on edible consumption is necessarily intended to disappear. Knowles's propositional performance must have struck her audiences as outside any extant artistic category. There was little chance its aesthetic remainders—the empty pickle barrel, bags of parings, unconsumed leftovers—would persist as profitable commodities.[58] Even as the impetus for the salad was generated by chance, as she later recounted to an interviewer, the fact that Knowles's name was not included on the distributed flyer announcing the "Misfit" events at the ICA speaks to, at best, an inattentive anticipation of her contribution to the evening's planned events. We are left wondering what Musgrave or Spoerri expected from her involvement, in her singular role as the sole Fluxus woman artist among a roster of men offering their own works and ideas.

Of course, Knowles's audiences in London, Copenhagen, and New York might have performed the action they witnessed—preparing and eating a simple salad—every day. But her choice to execute it in a museum or other edifying space, under the conditions and pretext of art making and reception, satisfied her desire to connect private durational activities (like cooking and eating) to the demands of cultural institutions looking for innovative content. *Make a Salad* and other propositions predate by decades the "artistic service" model, outlined by contemporary artists like Andrea Fraser and structured around ephemeral "project work"—installations, collaborations,

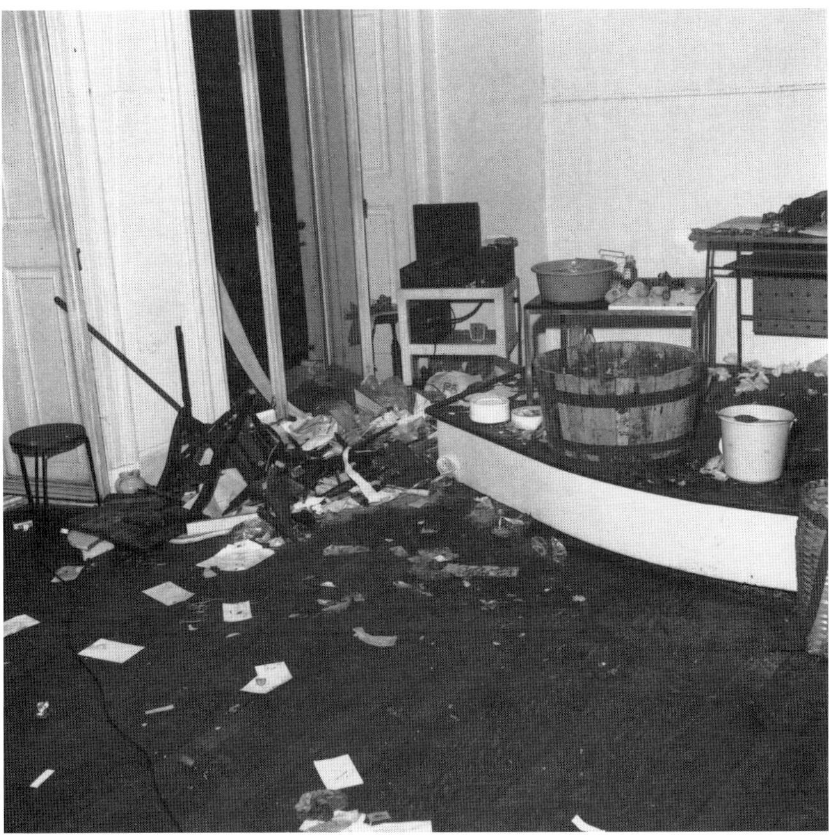

**Figure 2.7.** Alison Knowles, *Proposition #2: Make a Salad*, after performance. Institute of Contemporary Arts, London, October 1962. Photo: Bruce Fleming. Gilbert and Lila Silverman Fluxus Collection Gift, Museum of Modern Art, New York.

residencies, and so on—carried out in coordination with curated spaces.[59] By contrast, the "service" Knowles provided was primarily a tangible, edible exchange between the artist and her assembled audience, whose reaction was wholly unpredictable. Meditating on making a salad while doing so for oneself, in the privacy of one's own domestic sphere, elicits a range of responses based on any number of contingent factors (hunger, pleasure at the freshness of a tomato, say, or disgust at oil gone rancid). Performing the action in a museum or other public context (thus multiplying its indeterminate reactions) foregrounds the paradoxically unintentional yet purposeful spirit of Knowles's propositional score format.

Consistently, Knowles's collaboration with her Fluxus peers in public is predicated on an implied task to be performed, by her or the present viewer or a future reader, and while the performers are given instructions, there is no explicit statement as to *how* the task should be accomplished. I view this as an openness that aligns with emerging feminist sensibilities of the era, in which expanded notions of art, and one's own liberation from moral and aesthetic formulae, are tantamount to expressions of and searchings for a more profoundly personal liberation. In a certain way, then, in Knowles's embrace of daily acts of care, iterated as art, the artist is *displaced* but never fully obliter-

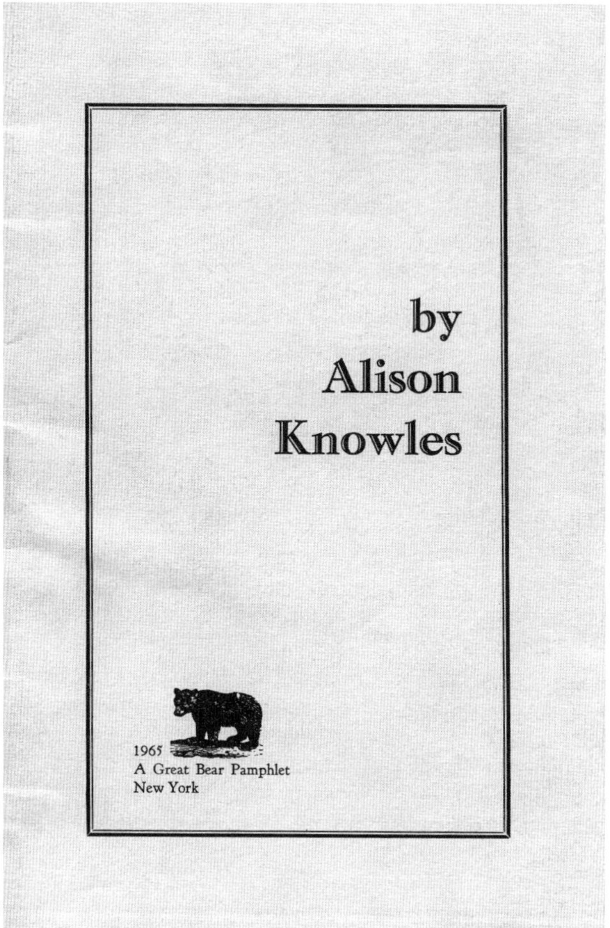


**Figure 2.8.** Alison Knowles, *by Alison Knowles*, A Great Bear Pamphlet (Something Else Press, 1965).

ated. Each proposition in *by Alison Knowles* differently accomplishes this self-generating practice for others to consider, interpret, and complete.

## Bodily Elicitations

The movement of *bodies* oriented by space, task, or touch is central to the propositional scores Knowles conceptualized under the Fluxus rubric. *Proposition #1: Shuffle Piece*, for example, calls for an indeterminate number of performers to quietly "shuffle into the performance area and away from it, above, behind, around or through the audience." The collective shuffling through a venue not only evoked the flavor of Fluxus performances but paralleled the matter-of-fact dance moves performed by Judson Dance Theater in New York.[60] *Proposition #3: Nivea Cream Piece (for Oscar Williams)* (1962; fig. 2.9) further explores corporeal sensation and group dynamics, hinting at an erotics of the score. Knowles debuted the score at the Alle Scenen Theater in Copenhagen

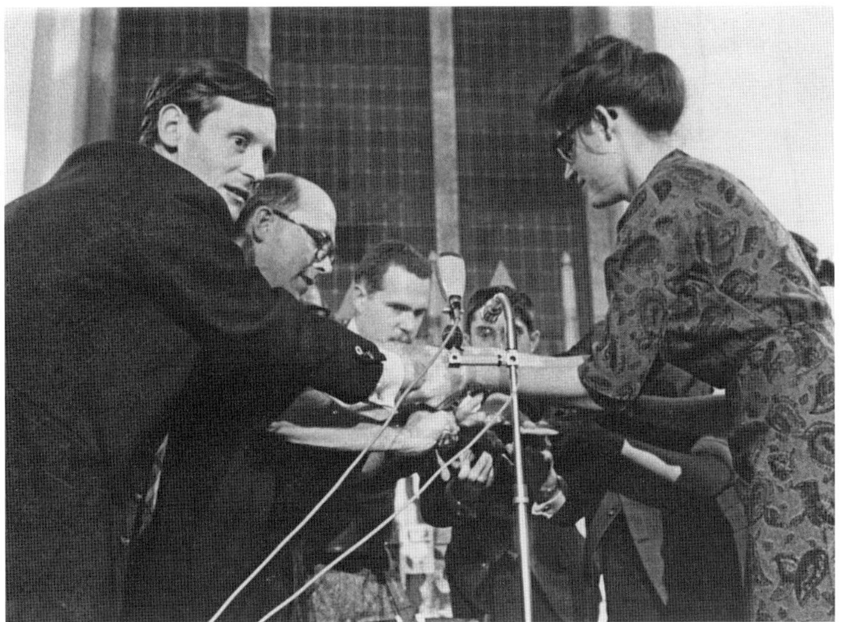

**Figure 2.9.** Alison Knowles performing *Proposition #3: Nivea Cream Piece (for Oscar Williams)*, accompanied by Eric Andersen, Emmett Williams, Dick Higgins, George Maciunas, et al., at Fluxus Musik og Anti-Musik Det Instrumentale Teater, Nikolaj Kirke, Copenhagen, November 23, 1962. Image © The Museum of Modern Art. Licensed by SCALA/Art Resource, NY.

as part of the Nordic Festum Fluxorum on November 23, 1962. The published score reads:

> First performer comes on stage with a bottle of hand cream, labeled "Nivea Cream" if none is available. He pours the cream onto his hands, and massages them in front of the microphone. Other performers enter, one by one, and do the same thing. Then they join together in front of the microphone to make a mass of massaging hands. They leave in the reverse of the order they entered, on a signal from the first performer.[61]

Nivea Cream was a commercial beauty product primarily marketed to women. In using male pronouns for the propositional subject—"*He* pours the cream onto *his* hands"—Knowles dislocates the "she" supposed by ad campaigns in favor of a more complex relationship to touch, image, body, and text.[62] "He" is later joined by other performers, neither number nor genders specified, who enter at intervals and repeat "his" actions, multiplying the sights, sounds, and smells of the originary moment. The openness of *Nivea Cream Piece* to interpretation and variation goes beyond this oscillation from a specific male body to a fluidly gendered cast, as evidenced by the score's evolution across its European iterations: notably, the increased quantity of the moisturizer—"at least one jar per person"—with which each participant would "lather up his arms and face, then his colleagues, in a fragrant pig pile."[63] Wherever the work is performed, in whichever version, a group of persons is directed to come together in front of the microphone in "a mass of massaging hands"—a chorus

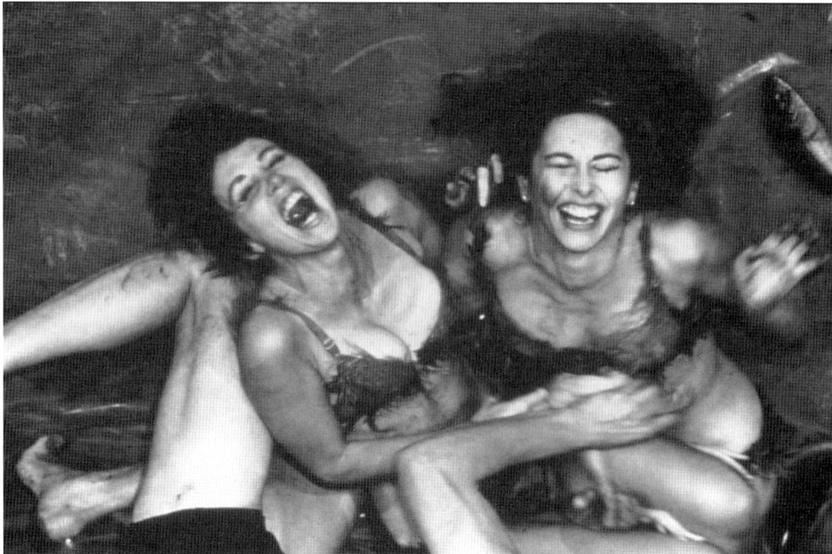

**Figure 2.10.** Dorothea Rockburne and Carolee Schneemann performing Schneemann's *Meat Joy*, with Stanley Gochenouer and James Tenney (not pictured), at the Judson Dance Theater, Judson Memorial Church, NY, 1964. © 2025 Carolee Schneemann Foundation/Artists Rights Society (ARS), New York. Courtesy Lisson Gallery and P•P•O•W, New York. Photo: Al Giese, © 2024 Mary Hottelet (Giese). Licensed by Artists Rights Society (ARS), NY.

of smacking heard and felt by the audience, suggestive of a sexual act. Calling attention to the lubrication of bodies, the aroma and eroticism of bodily touch, the work takes on added personal significance when we recall that it was written for Emmett Williams, whom aside from Higgins, was the artist's closest and most trusted interlocutor throughout the 1960s.

It is worthwhile to compare *Nivea Cream Piece* with contemporaneous works by Knowles's artist friends Carolee Schneemann and Shigeko Kubota. Schneemann was a lifelong confidant whom Knowles first met in her pre-Fluxus days when they were staging works (Schneemann) and designing sets (Knowles) for The Living Theater in New York. Knowles was introduced to Kubota by Maciunas and Nam June Paik in New York, after the European Fluxus tours. Like Knowles's *Nivea Cream Piece*, Schneemann's wildly influential *Meat Joy* (1964) coupled the erotics of skin-on-skin contact with live performance, producing another pig pile of sorts (fig. 2.10). First performed in Paris on May 29, 1964, as part of Jean-Jacques Lebel's Festival of Free Expression at the Centre Américain des Artistes, *Meat Joy* was performed twice more that year, in London's Denison Hall and at Judson Memorial Church in New York, each iteration bringing together human bodies with material substrates (paper, paint, plastic, raw meat, etc.) against a collaged sound track of pop music and street noises.[64] Unlike *Nivea Cream Piece*, however, Schneemann's piece is heavily scripted, instructing a defined group of players (four men, five women) in meticulous detail to perform actions more explicitly sexual in nature. The half-

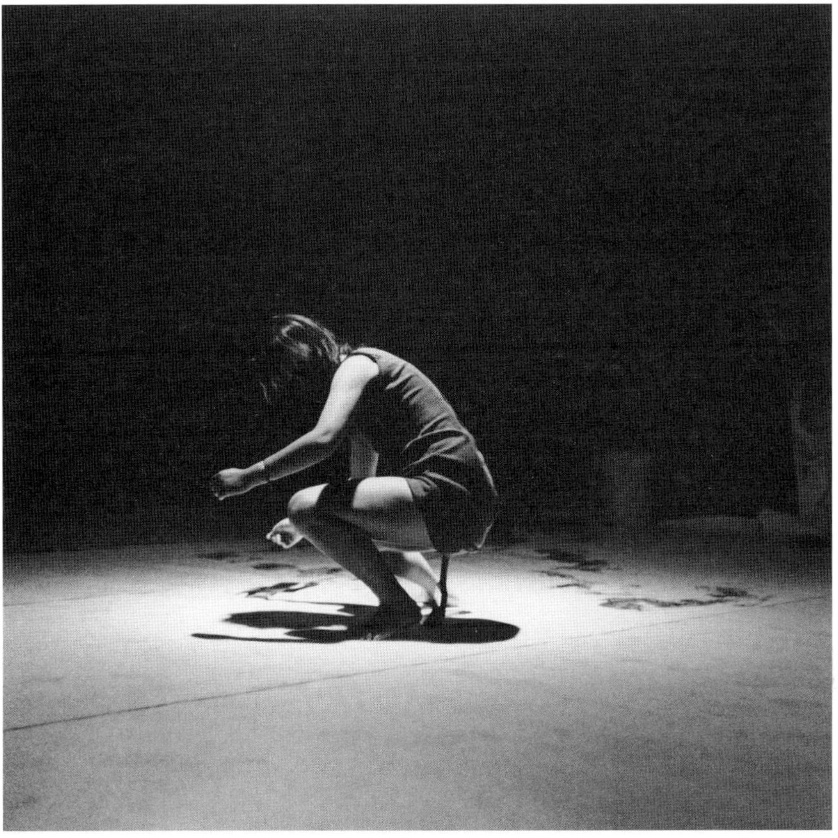

**Figure 2.11.** Shigeko Kubota, *Vagina Painting*, performed during *Perpetual Fluxfest*, Cinematheque, New York, July 4, 1965, 1965. Gelatin silver print, 35.6 × 35.5 cm. Photo: George Maciunas, © 2024 Estate of Shigeko Kubota. Licensed by VAGA at Artists Rights Society (ARS), NY. Image © The Museum of Modern Art. Licensed by SCALA/Art Resource, NY.

nude performers roll around playfully in a slick and slippery environment of imitation blood (red paint), rubber chickens, and raw butchered chicken and fish, in a choreographed game of sensual amusement. Schneemann's explicit direction and her presence are critical (she plays the star) to *Meat Joy*, whereas with *Nivea Cream Piece*, Knowles instigates an action, or sequence of actions, but need never directly participate. That Knowles's propositions refused nudity and overtly sexual imagery announces an aesthetic distance from the more exuberant and expressionistic tendencies seen in Schneemann's *Meat Joy*, or even Nam June Paik's notorious performances with Charlotte Moorman, which Knowles declined to participate in. Knowles's more minimal, nuanced approach may account for why she has been, until very recently, less well known than Schneemann, Paik, and other Happenings and Fluxus peers as a pioneer of live-art practice.

The photograph documenting Shigeko Kubota's *Vagina Painting*, performed at the Perpetual Fluxfest in New York City (1965; fig. 2.11), shows the artist squatting on a large sheet of paper with a paintbrush seemingly inserted in her vagina.[65] Knowles reportedly recoiled from the performance, declining to watch for its entire duration. Offering a generous interpretation of this refusal, Midori Yoshimoto has suggested that, as a woman, "Knowles could

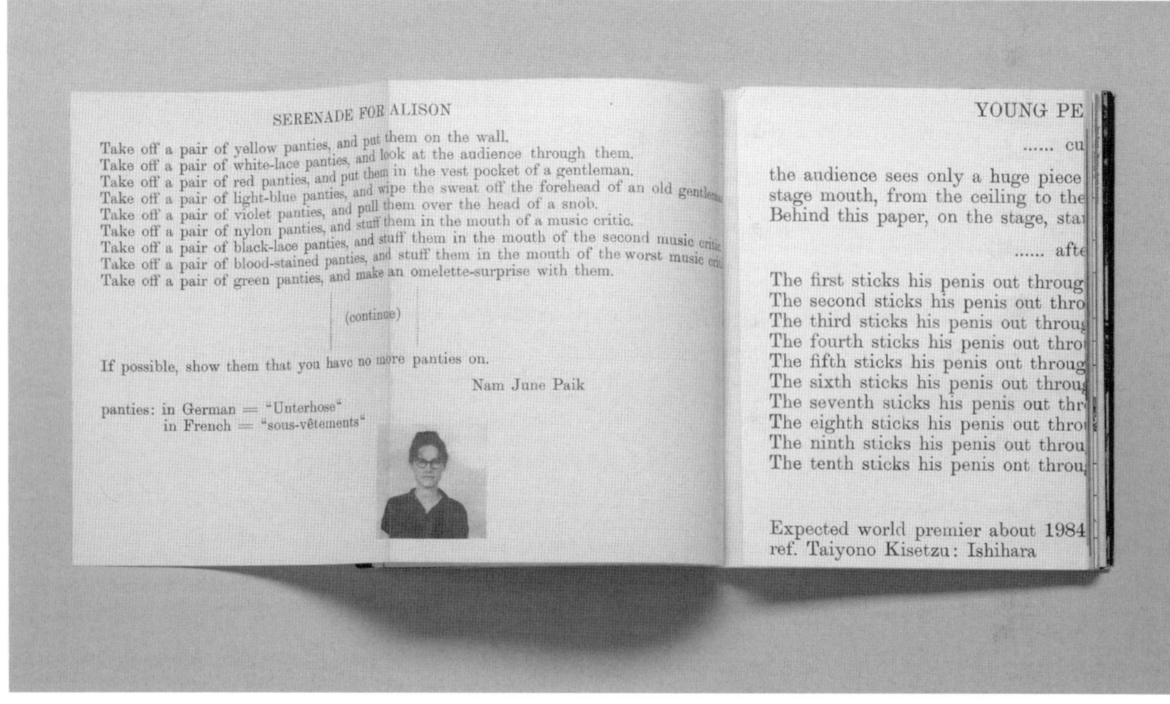

SERENADE FOR ALISON

Take off a pair of yellow panties, and put them on the wall.
Take off a pair of white-lace panties, and look at the audience through them.
Take off a pair of red panties, and put them in the vest pocket of a gentleman.
Take off a pair of light-blue panties, and wipe the sweat off the forehead of an old gentleman.
Take off a pair of violet panties, and pull them over the head of a snob.
Take off a pair of nylon panties, and stuff them in the mouth of a music critic.
Take off a pair of black-lace panties, and stuff them in the mouth of the second music critic.
Take off a pair of blood-stained panties, and stuff them in the mouth of the worst music critic.
Take off a pair of green panties, and make an omelette-surprise with them.

(continue)

If possible, show them that you have no more panties on.

Nam June Paik

panties: in German = "Unterhose"
in French = "sous-vêtements"

YOUNG PE

...... cu

the audience sees only a huge piece
stage mouth, from the ceiling to the
Behind this paper, on the stage, sta

...... afte

The first sticks his penis out throug
The second sticks his penis out thro
The third sticks his penis out throu
The fourth sticks his penis out thro
The fifth sticks his penis out throug
The sixth sticks his penis out throu
The seventh sticks his penis out thr
The eighth sticks his penis out thro
The ninth sticks his penis out throu
The tenth sticks his penis ont throu

Expected world premier about 1984
ref. Taiyono Kisetzu: Ishihara

**Figure 2.12.** Nam June Paik, *Serenade for Alison*, reprinted in Wolf Vostell, *dé-coll/age*, no. 3 (1962), offset lithograph on paper. Rosemary Furtak Collection, Walker Art Center Library. © Nam June Paik Estate. Photo courtesy Walker Art Center.

identify with Kubota's body and imagine vividly the discomfort involved in painting with the sexual organ . . . [and thus] the impact of *Vagina Painting* was felt more corporeally than visually [because it] violated what was normally acceptable for a woman to do."[66] Given Knowles's close friendship with Kubota, I view the incident as having less to do with what was or was not acceptable than with aesthetic taste and preference.[67] Knowles's own unpretentious notational scores, while provocative, are stubbornly subtle, suggesting almost imperceptible movements that require a different kind of attentiveness and interpretive framework. Knowles's absence from the art historical literature contending with the complexities of feminist representation can thus be seen as less a deliberate scrubbing and more a misunderstanding of the contours of her practice seen alongside other artists' theatrical, seminude, painterly (even bloody) expositions of the body in creation or in crisis in the 1960s.

But Knowles's oeuvre does share some of the era's political concerns regarding power and control over female bodies and their representation. This includes performance scores written specifically for Knowles by other Fluxus artists. One such case was Paik's *Serenade for Alison* (1962), the score for which specifies a succession of explicit tasks, including "Take off a pair of nylon panties, and stuff them in the mouth of a music critic" (fig. 2.12).[68] Knowles's alteration of the directives in an October 1962 performance signals her refusal to play the exhibitionist for Paik. For this program of Fluxus work, organized by Wolf Vostell for the Parallele Aufführungen Neuster Musik (Parallel Performances of New Music) and held at the Kunsthandel Galerie Monet in Amster-

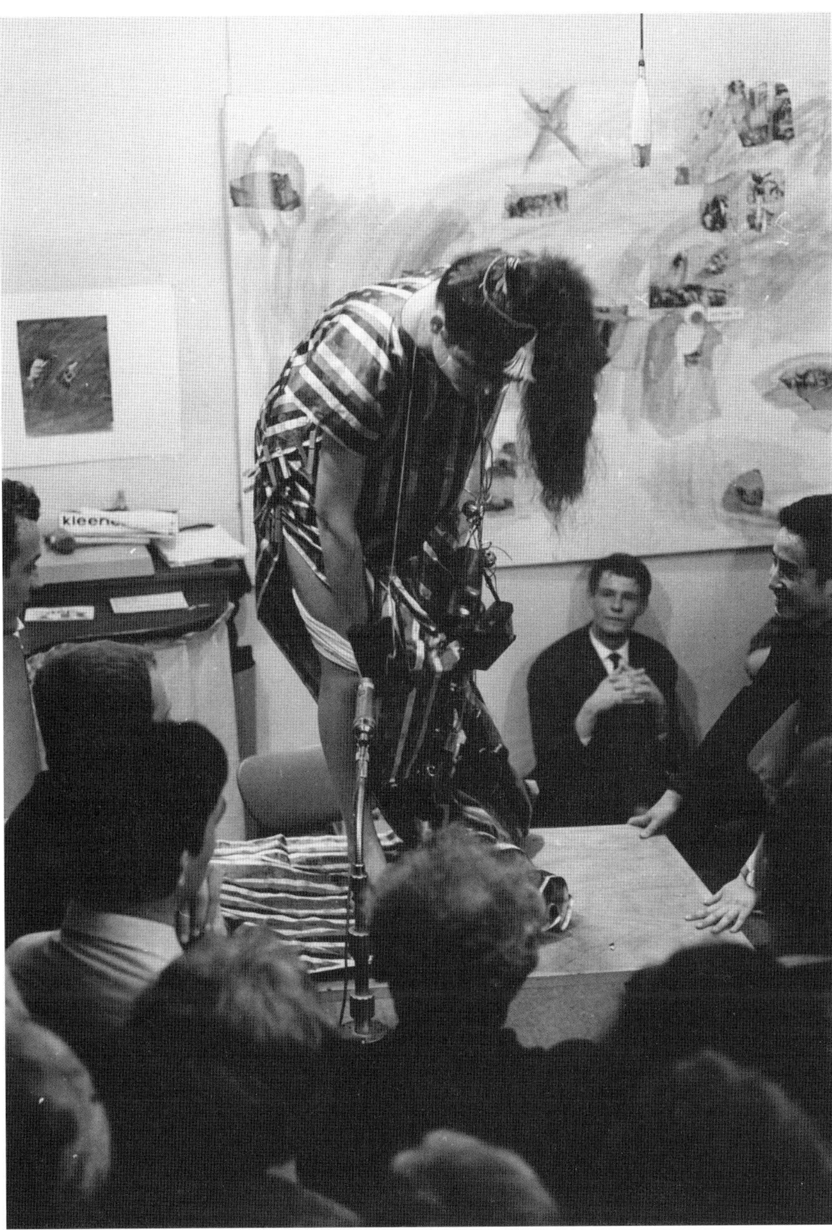


**Figure 2.13.** Alison Knowles performing Nam June Paik's *Serenade for Alison* at Parallel Performances of New Music (Paralelle Aufführungen Neuster Musik), Galerie Monet, Amsterdam, October 5, 1962. Gelatin silver print, 7⅜ × 9$^{15}/_{16}$ in. (18.8 × 25.3 cm). © Nam June Paik Estate. Photo © Hans de Boer/Nederlands Fotomuseum. Image © The Museum of Modern Art. Licensed by SCALA/Art Resource, NY.

dam, Paik had placed Knowles on a high-top table (fig. 2.13). But rather than following his script, she reclaimed her artistic and personal agency, neither removing her clothes during the performance nor stuffing underwear into the mouth of any critic. Moreover, she added an homage to Cage's 1951 composition *Imaginary Landscape No. 4 for 12 Radios*, hanging several found transistor radios, bells, and empty tape spools around her neck. Draping herself in a long, striped Korean robe given to her by Paik, held together by clothespins, Knowles put on, then slowly removed, several layers of shorts and underwear (some of them belonging to Higgins), periodically pausing to turn the various dials on the dangling radios. The underpants were thrown into the room to the delight of the predominately male audience.[69]

The changes from Paik's prescribed actions, which relegated her body to the contours of erotic fantasy and male objectification achieved both a rigorous rereading of the score and an accommodation to her sense of physical comfort and safety before the gathered spectators:

> My hair was down mostly (not in a bun on the top of my head as it often was). What I added was a transistor radio around my neck. [I] changed stations with each removal of panties, threw each pair to the audience from the table until the ritual no longer amused me, then stepped down and led the audience out of the Galerie Monet in Amsterdam over the dikes of the town with the radio blasting the news. The audience followed.[70]

In Knowles's radical remake of Paik's serenade, she effectively tore at the authority of masculine writing (the composer's score) and the libidinal economy of male desire that accompanies it.

Another work Paik dedicated to Knowles, *Chronicle of a Beautiful Paintress* (1962), called for "a woman to stain the flags of selected world nations 'with [her] own monthly blood' and . . . expose [herself] in a beautiful gallery."[71] Kristine Stiles writes that Knowles declined to participate, but the piece was purportedly realized at some point (she stopped after staining just four flags) and hung on the walls of Paik's 1963 solo exhibition *Exposition of Music—Electronic Television* in Wuppertal.[72] In a kind of counterinsurgent gesture to his provocative pieces, Knowles's 1963 score *Proposition #13: Composition for Paik* required him to sit at the center of a room on a raised platform for an indeterminate period (fig. 2.14).[73] In 1964, Knowles placed him on a phallic platform of stacked books and newspapers that not only rendered his patriarchal authority almost comically moot but erased his physical ability to dominate the scene: He could not move without falling from a great height. We can read this displacement of power as part of a larger social resistance against the confines of (artistic) male dominance coming to the surface in the budding feminist movement of the early 1960s.[74] The indeterminate nature and chance Knowles embraced in her propositional scores binds her work to notions of risk and the abandonment of author-as-master hierarchies.

Similarly, Knowles's *Proposition #4: Child Art Piece* (1962), which premiered at the Fluxus Festival in Düsseldorf in February 1963, calls for "a single child, two or three years old," assisted by their parents, to play onstage with a set of small objects (e.g., a banana, a pail of water) or their favorite toy. The performance concludes when the child, for whatever reason—stage fright, boredom, or anything else—retreats from the stage. This is the only event score by any Fluxus artist to risk this form of indeterminacy. Knowles could complete the work only with the direct presence of a quite young child—a "performer"

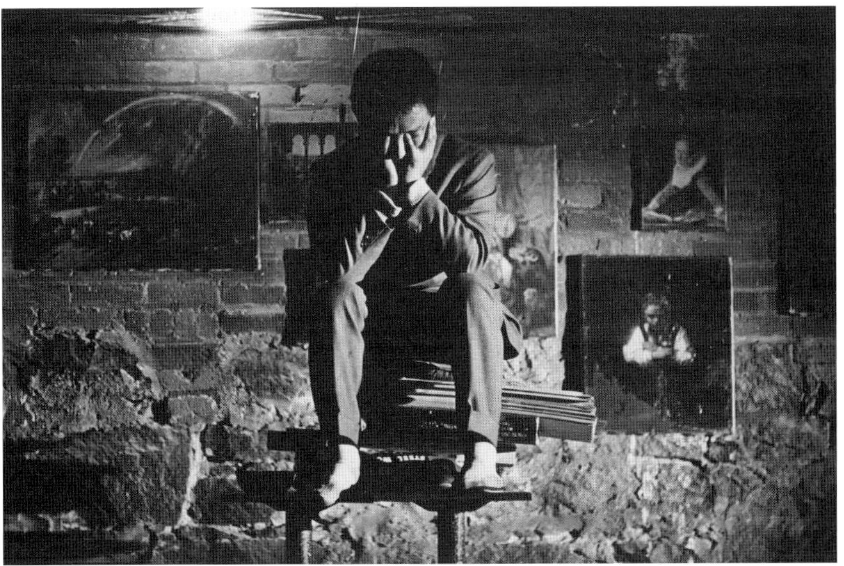

**Figure 2.14.** Nam June Paik performing Alison Knowles's *Proposition #13: Composition for Paik* (1963), Fluxhall, New York City, 1964. Photo: Peter Moore, © Northwestern University. Courtesy Peter Moore Photography Archive, Charles Deering McCormick Library of Special Collections, Northwestern University.

whose actions were largely unpredictable. For a 1963 performance in Stockholm, for instance, Knowles recounts, "I had to figure out how I would get a child to walk across a stage without his mother and just stand there for a few minutes. I put his toys on the stage, with his mother standing in the wings, he stands there for a minute and looks around wondering where the hell he is, and then he walks off the stage."[75] Her score changed over time; the published version was more succinct than the original and had the child's parents choosing the onstage activity: "Two parents enter with their child, and they decide a procedure which they will do with the child, such as bathing, eating, playing with toys, and they continue until the procedure is finished."[76] The score was featured prominently by Maciunas in posters and concert announcements as the Fluxus retinue traveled across Western Europe, but back in New York, the Society for Prevention of Cruelty to Children forbade the performance as originally specified—what troubled them is unclear. Knowles responded by composing a modified score, *Variation #1*, that gives the simple instruction: "Exit in a new suit."[77]

As independent texts, *Nivea Cream Piece* and *Child Art Piece* both specify performers with the pronouns "he" and "they." The same is true of *Proposition #6: Shoes of Your Choice*. Conceived during Knowles's travels with the Western European Fluxus group, its US premiere was scheduled in early April 1963 (she considered the staging "a failing piece"), during a series of activities at Douglass College in New Jersey, in which Happenings artists were also represented.[78] The event score reads, "A member of the audience is invited to come forward to a microphone if one is available and describe a pair of shoes, the one he is wearing or another pair. He is encouraged to tell where he got them, the size, color, why he likes them, etc."[79] The score is open to any content.

Storytellers can can omit or misremember details; they can choose their mode of address, their narrative tone—celebratory, elegiac, humorous, tragic, ironic. Memories become the storehouse and projection of materiality; the human voice, its manifestation.

Julia Robinson, in one of the most perceptive interpretations of Knowles's work, has argued that the propositional score, conceived as a musical notation, relates to Claes Oldenburg's sculptural representation of shoes but goes well beyond those drippy plaster casts of everyday wares. "Unlike the consumer items that appear as painting or sculpture in Pop art . . . the shoes Knowles represents do not parrot reified object relations," she writes. "Knowles's shoes take shape in unfolding time: they are performed into being, continually defined and redefined according to the idiosyncrasies of successive personal accounts."[80] This point is vital. Knowles was committed to the contingencies of language, text, music, and object as multiple vehicles of expression, but the proposition's deliberately neutral, memorandum-like format belies the radicality of her program. Robinson's observation about "unfolding time" recognizes the immediacy and *presentness* of a narration that is unrehearsed and, directed only by Knowles's minimal, open-ended proposition, "draws on the personality of the individual performing the event."[81] The temporality of this and other scores, I contend, relies not only on the expressionistic tics or talents of each successive performer but on the translation of the enigmatic propositions (textually and culturally) in every iteration.

A version of *Proposition #6: Shoes of Your Choice* was presented by Knowles in Madrid in November 1966 at Events y New Music, organized by experimental musicians and composers performing as the Zaj Group.[82] On a stage in the auditorium at the Escuela Técnica Superior de Arquitectura, Knowles displayed two pairs of her own shoes on a small table (fig. 2.15). Holding up, in turn, a single shoe from each pair, and from the pair she had been wearing, she offered lengthy and meticulous descriptions, as if analyzing lab specimens, including a narrative history of how she felt about her selections. Once Knowles had concluded her story, audience members were invited to participate, in keeping with the score's instructions. Knowles watched from the background as one man came on stage, silently placed his foot on the table, and tied his shoe (fig. 2.16); another sat on the edge of the platform and flicked ashes from his lit cigarette into his loafer.[83]

In a rather more dramatic performance of *Shoes of Your Choice* for an October 1966 Fluxus Concert at Galerie René Block in Berlin, Knowles reportedly offered a "long recital" of silence followed by a lengthy shoe meditation: "While polishing her shoe with a cloth, she gave the listeners different pieces of information, regarding the process of shoe fabrication, the different materials from which shoes can be made . . . [and] different English figures of speech that involved the word 'shoe.'"[84] An audience member was apparently so annoyed by the performance, loudly and aggressively mocking Knowles, that

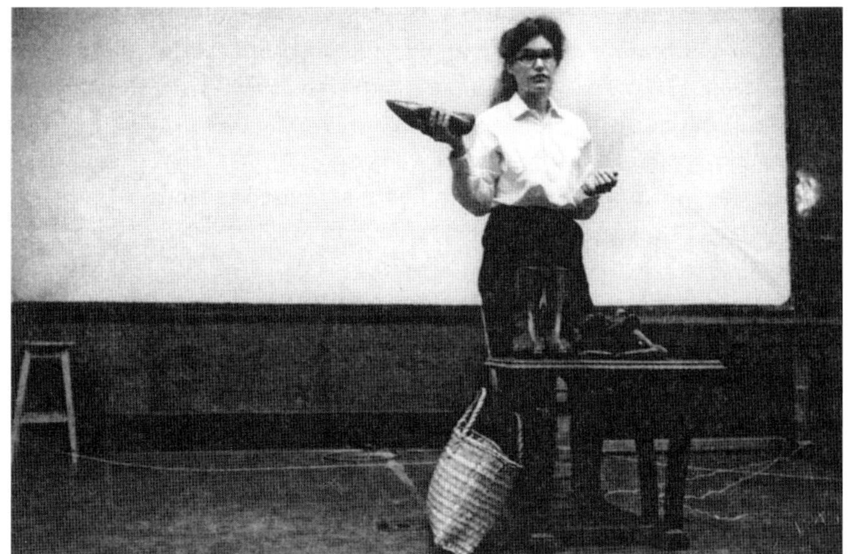

**Figure 2.15.** Alison Knowles performing *Proposition #6: Shoes of Your Choice*, Events y New Music, Escuela Técnica Superior de Arquitectura, Madrid, November 12, 1966. Photo: Alberto Schommer García, © 2025 Artists Rights Society (ARS), New York/VEGAP, Madrid.

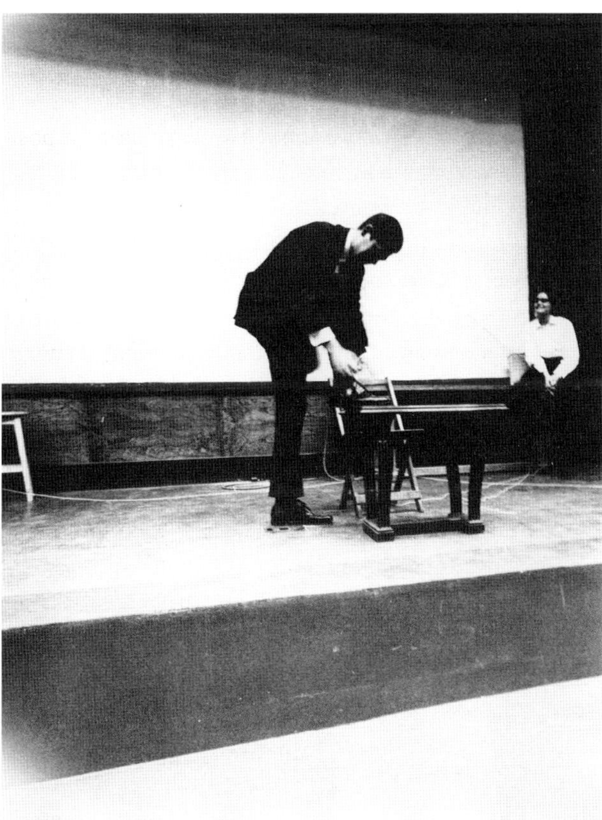

**Figure 2.16.** Audience member performing Alison Knowles, *Proposition #6: Shoes of Your Choice*, Events y New Music, Escuela Técnica Superior de Arquitectura, Madrid, November 12, 1966. Courtesy Archiv Sohm, Staatsgalerie Stuttgart/Art Resource, NY. Photo: Alberto Schommer García, © 2025 Artists Rights Society (ARS), New York/VEGAP, Madrid.

Higgins rolled up his sleeves and ordered the man onstage. A tussle ensued, and Higgins emerged the victor after he "pinned, clearly visible in the flashlight of the photographer, the Fluxus-adversary with both shoulders to the floor quite like in a ring."[85] A less histrionic ending had occurred a month earlier at Moorman's 4th Annual Avant Garde Festival, held in New York's Central Park. As reported by a reviewer for the *New York Times*, a young man came up to the microphone and thoughtfully stated, "These shoes I'm wearing are not sneakers. They are athletic shoes, and most of the greatest basketball players wear them, and I am a credit to them. Thank you."[86]

Again and again, in the context of Fluxus, Knowles's scores enact an indeterminate, temporally fluid generosity that extends the immediacy of the live experience into speculative futures. In a 1963 article, Paik argues for a fresh musical paradigm based on "action," a kind of structured unknowability in which a composition progresses or halts according to a kind of site-specific program. The street, for example, is a "moving theatre" where sights and sounds are encountered unexpectedly. "The beauty of moving theatre lies in this 'surprise a priori,' because almost all of the audience is uninvited, not knowing what it is, why it is, who is the composer, the player, organizer—or better speaking—organizer, composer, player."[87] To illustrate, he cites two furtive works by Knowles; in the first, "Alison Knowles notifying no one escaped secretly from the hotel and saying nothing unrolled 1000 meter sound tape in a street of Copenhagen. There was not one invited 'audience,' not one photographer; only the program was due to be printed, announcing 'Time indeterminate, date indeterminate, place somewhere in Copenhagen and Paris."[88]

Knowles's propositional format demonstrated a consistent preference for concrete action and direct language over the abstraction of her painterly training. Her invitational scores both negated and playfully celebrated the artificial vectors of social and artistic mores. By actively engaging with both real-time and future audiences—and reaffirming, rather than transgressing or undermining, the artist's traditional role as producer of advanced knowledge—Knowles makes us acutely aware of our limited yet aspirational capacities for communication and empowering communion with others.

Nearly all of Knowles's propositional Fluxus scores explore the dimensions between private experience and public expression. They advance, too, some of the ideas around reception voiced by Italian critic Umberto Eco in *Opera Aperta* (The Open Work), published in 1962, the same year as *Make a Salad*. In this now famous treatise, Eco argues, "Every reception of a work of art is both an *interpretation* and a *performance* of it, because in every reception the work takes on a fresh perspective for itself."[89] Knowles's propositional scores might be productively understood, then, as an ensemble of possibilities, an overture toward an individual or group action that generates provisional conditions for reception that are infinitely open to the contingencies of time and place. The artist's own definition of event scores affirms this:

> Simple actions, ideas, and objects from everyday life recontextualized as performance. Event Scores are texts that can be seen as proposal pieces or instructions for actions. The idea of the score suggests musicality. Like a musical score, Event Scores can be realized by artists other than the original creator and are open to variation and interpretation.[90]

Unlike other conceptually oriented artists of the era who often privileged ideas as such over their material realization, Knowles instigated a career-long investigation of the dialectics of chance, making time-based work using language and text, speech and action, body and sustenance, rituals and reflection, as coequal thematic and structural devices.[91]

Returning to *Make a Salad*, we might recall that the score is purposefully modest, its realization multifariously sensual. Its first performance in London and its later iterations stage the often disregarded ritual of making and serving food. The convivial experience of preparing and eating the salad adds an extra-acoustical materiality that provides an audience with an entrée toward radical nonintentionality.[92] Moreover, the pithiness of the proposition, stated as an imperative, suggests less a one-off performance than a recurring visual activity. Asked in a 1977 interview about her ongoing interest in food and the structures she provides for audience interaction, she noted, "I always work with images really. Even in the performance pieces. What an elegant image, a huge salad! Let's do it at Grand Central Plaza and feed all the passersby!"[93]

Indeed, there would be large-scale iterations. In the decades since its first realization, Knowles has been regularly summoned to reenact *Make a Salad* in august museums and other cultural settings. In 2003, she was invited to execute the score (accompanied by a string duo) for the opening of the exhibition *Work Ethic* at the Baltimore Museum of Art. The piece has also been restaged at the Tate Modern, London (2008); the High Line, New York (2012); the Walker Art Center, Minneapolis (2014); MoMA PS1, New York (2014); Beijing Live (2016); the Aspen Art Museum (2018); and the Los Angeles Philharmonic (2019). With each reprise, Knowles's artistic status and attendant meal becomes more widely visible.

The desire for these performances acknowledges Knowles's enduring influence and her works' continued relevance, but also shifts in the nature of art making since the 1960s—the prevalence, for example, of contingent, time-based, post-studio, and site-specific work. It reveals as well the complexities of museum collecting and programming practices and a greater institutional commitment, since the late 1990s, to historicizing and reanimating ephemeral works.[94] Knowles has expressed both delight and consternation over museological regenerations of her scores but accepts most requests on the condition that she retains the role of a "major conductor" directing assistants. Knowles has created a basic kit that invitees are encouraged to follow when she (or others) reperform the score.[95] Its guidelines reflect her personal preference for locally sourced, preferably organic salad composed of leafy green lettuces, fresh carrots, onions, and tomatoes, all tossed in a simple vinaigrette. Ever attentive to the conditions of the presentation space and coperformers (e.g., sometimes regional chefs, as in the rooftop performance in Aspen), Knowles is keen to anchor the conceptual breadth of *Make a Salad* within the limits of exhibition and institutional contexts.[96]

By drawing our attention to the biological, social, and aesthetic activities of daily life, Knowles's early Fluxus scores formally and thematically manifest an openness that engages and multiplies Cage's model of indeterminate outcomes and sonic perceptivity; at the same time, such openness dialectically signals a dimension of art making heretofore underexplored in the grand narratives of late modernist art—seemingly imagining site and site-specificity as also involving intersubjective, political relations.

As scholars have noted, expanded fields of production—visual, aural, theatrical, environmental—are central to art of the postwar period. The dislodging of traditional terms and procedures inspired Knowles to forswear abstract painting for the textual mash-up of visual and sonic material in a career-long investigation of embodied experience. For Knowles, Cage's acceptance of everyday sounds and chance methods "made a lot of other things possible . . . something about how his life and art all fit together [was] so inspiring."[97] In her hands, Cagean aesthetics unfolds into a protofeminist dialectic framed by durational structures that was fundamental to the convergence of language, ritual, and everyday materials in several groundbreaking performance works of the mid- to late 1960s. As this chapter has shown, Knowles was among the original progenitors of chance-based experimental art. The next chapter looks closely at Knowles's singular role in the (re)formation of Fluxus in New York after her return from Europe.

# 3 THE PROVISIONAL

At that time, I was cooking for people at our house, and I usually had bean dishes going for many meals. I said to George [Maciunas], "I'll do recipes about beans." It was an artist's book, a canned book in fact.
**Alison Knowles**[1]

Returning to New York in the spring of 1963, Alison Knowles and her Fluxus peers found the environment for collective practices markedly different from what they had experienced during their tour of "newest music" concerts in Western Europe. Pop art was ascendant, and they perceived the dearth of viable performance or exhibition spaces as a sign of institutional hostility toward their artistic concerns and sensibilities. Nevertheless, Fluxus artists and like-minded practitioners remained visible within the neo-avant-garde scene, organizing festivals, environments, and art shows wherever they could. Charlotte Moorman's chaotic but groundbreaking Annual Avant Garde Festivals, held throughout the city beginning in 1963, became sites of Fluxus activity, as did mainstream and alternative spaces like Carnegie Recital Hall, Thibaut and Kornblee galleries at Fifty-Seventh Street and Madison Avenue, the Hardware Poets' Playhouse (housed in a midtown loft above a hardware store on West Fifty-Fourth Street), Washington Square Gallery and Judson Memorial Church in the West Village, artist George Segal's farm, and Douglass College at Rutgers University in New Jersey.[2]

The reception of Fluxus in the United States was complicated by numerous factors—the relative poverty of many of the group's participants, their competing ambitions, contention over what kind of work counted as Fluxus, interpersonal bickering—yet the artists sustained a remarkably productive, albeit tense, creative milieu. Despite small and, at times, perplexed audiences, their practice remained predicated on collaborative interaction. Fluxus artists returned, in several early to mid-1960s programs, to scores first performed abroad, including Emmett Williams's roll-call score *Voice Piece for La Monte Young* (1962), which wryly asks if the experimental musician and composer is present or listening via telephonic mediation, and Youngs's own ambient and elemental scores, such as *Composition 1960 No. 2* (1960), which directs performers to "Build a fire in front of the Audience" and calls for its sounds to be

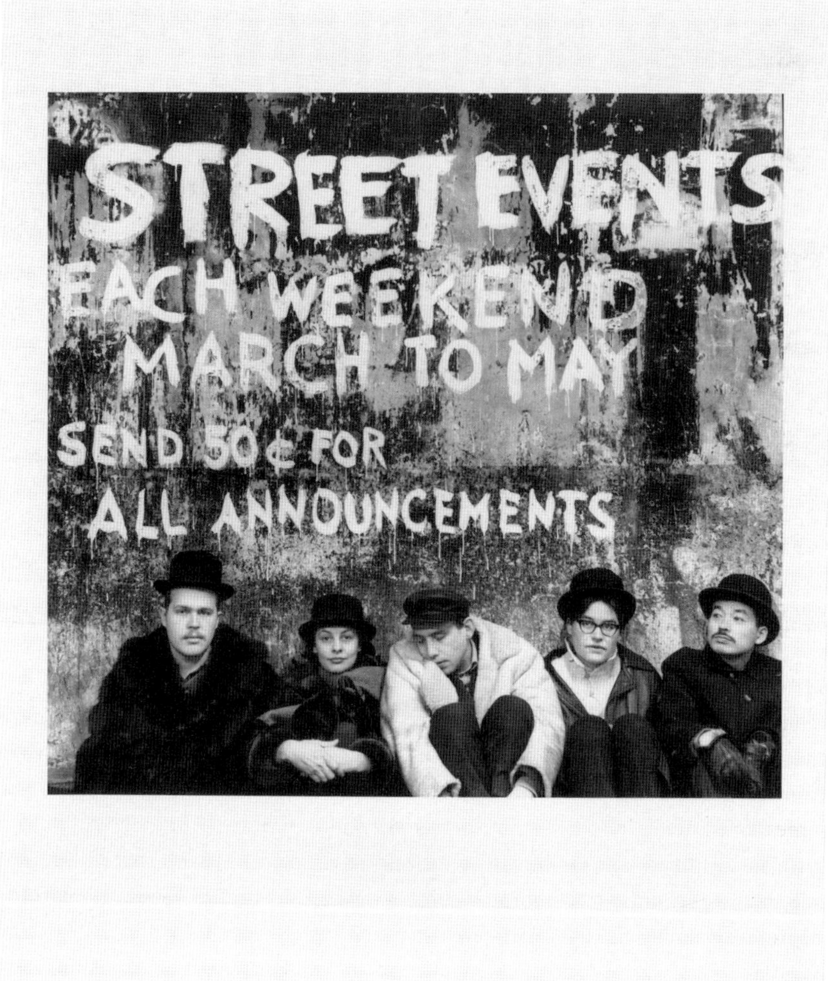


**Figure 3.1.** Dick Higgins, Lette Lou Eisenhauer, Daniel Spoerri, Alison Knowles, and Ay-O. Announcement for *Fully Guaranteed 12 Fluxus Concerts: Street Events*, Fluxhall, 359 Canal Street, New York, March–May 1964. Gilbert and Lila Silverman Fluxus Collection Gift, Museum of Modern Art, New York. Photo: George Maciunas. Courtesy Billie Maciunas. Image © The Museum of Modern Art. Licensed by SCALA/Art Resource, NY.

amplified.[3] In their conceptualist nullification of the conventions of musical notation, and with an eye and ear open to direct experience of seemingly banal information and sonic texture, Williams and Young's concise instructions parallel Knowles's propositional scores of the era, introduced in chapter 2.

Knowles, too, remained engaged with performance and notational scores, not returning to the visually dynamic collaged and screen-printed canvases that preoccupied her before the tour—many of which might more readily have fit within the prevailing Pop vernacular. Photographs, personal letters, artworks, and public broadsides from 1963 to 1966 record her partnering with Ay-O, George Brecht, Lette Lou Eisenhauer, Robert Filliou, Dick Higgins, George Maciunas, Nam June Paik, Ben Patterson, Mieko Shiomi, Daniel Spoerri, Robert Watts, and others to enact her own scores or theirs (fig. 3.1; plate 4). A memorable series of live actions that took place in Lower Manhattan was faithfully documented by Maciunas. One photograph of a 1964 event

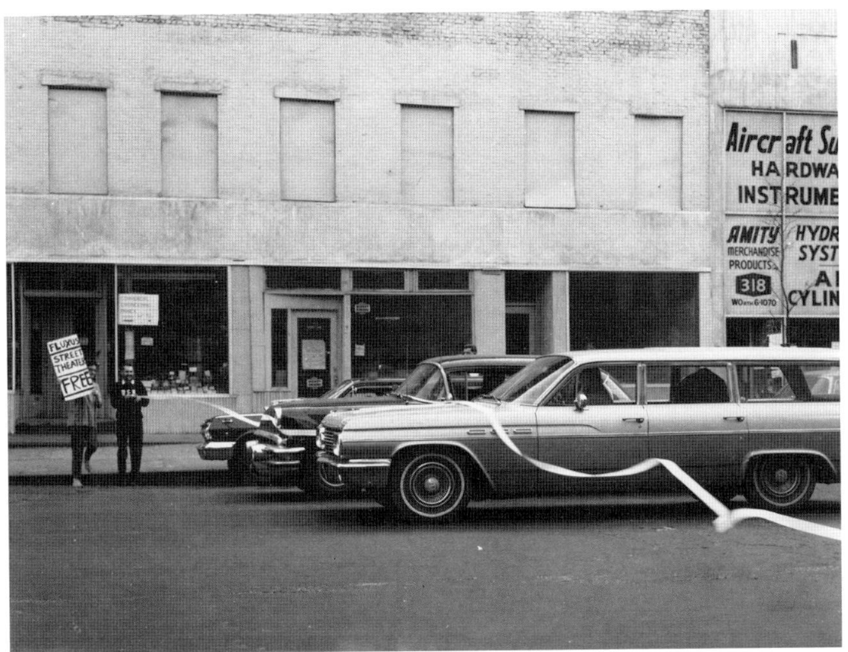


**Figure 3.2.** Alison Knowles and Ben Vautier performing Robert Watts's *Two Inches*, New York, 1964. Photo: George Maciunas. Courtesy Billie Maciunas. Image © The Museum of Modern Art. Licensed by SCALA/ Art Resource, NY.

shows Knowles wearing slacks and a maternity shirt (she was by then pregnant with twin daughters), walking back and forth across Canal Street with French Fluxus artist Ben Vautier (fig. 3.2). Knowles holds up a hand-painted street sign announcing their actions as free "Fluxus Street Theater," as Vautier unfurls a long ribbon across parked and moving cars in an interpretation of Watts's *Two Inches* (1962), whose original score instructs performers to stretch white tape across a stage.[4] Shifting the score's location, and keeping the ribbon stretched across the street for as long as traffic allows, held by an artist on either side, Knowles redrew urban lines, suggesting a kind of protest barrier or even sport. Other photos show Knowles performing her own *Music by Alison* (1962), which involved whipping yards of fabric of varying weights and lengths through the air for their acoustic effects (Vautier stands nearby holding a small, chalked sign announcing the sound work; fig. 3.3), and Knowles carrying out composer Takehisa Kosugi's *Anima I* (1961), binding Vautier with string to a chair (fig. 3.4). She revisited the latter work a year later; both Knowles and Ay-O were tied to chairs in a Higgins-directed rendition of Erik Satie's *Relâche* for Moorman's 3rd Annual Avant Garde Festival (1965; fig. 3.5). Vautier would aid in a related performance, of Knowles's *Proposition #10a, Variation #1 on #10 (String Piece)* (1962), which instructs a performer to "tie up the audience" using as many balls of string as there are performers. The piece was enlivened by the artists' reciprocal play and the audience's pulling at the string with which Vautier linked all present bodies, including Knowles's, into a communal web (fig. 3.6).

Through such cooperative, corporeal artistic labor, Knowles was forging

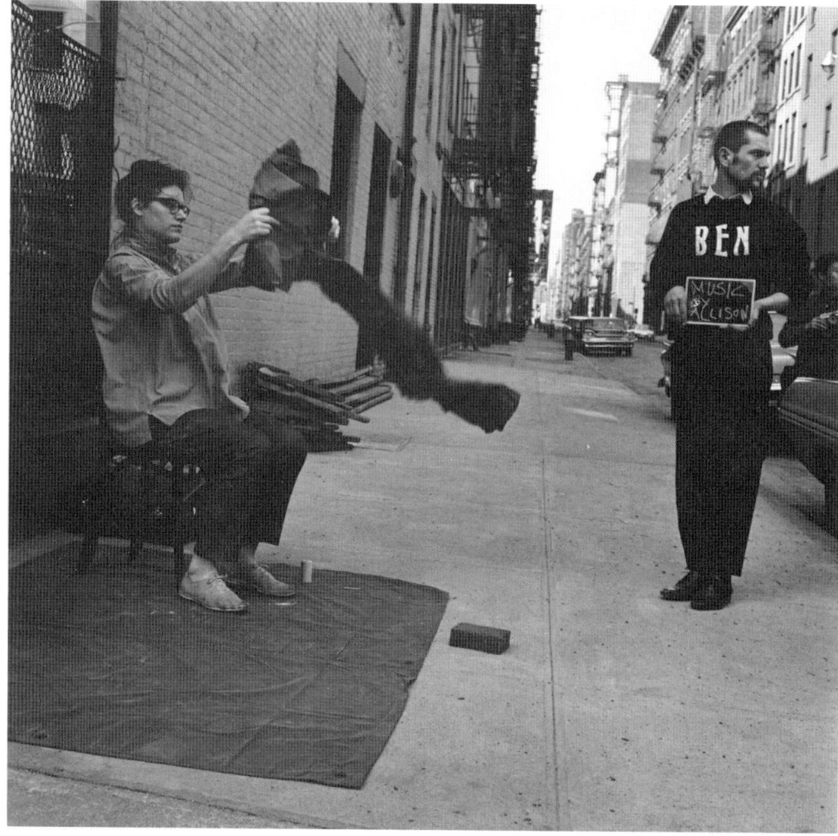


**Figure 3.3.** Alison Knowles, *Music by Alison*, performed during *Fully Guaranteed 12 Fluxus Concerts: Street Events*, Canal Street, New York, May 23, 1964. Gelatin silver print, $9\frac{15}{16} \times 7\frac{15}{16}$ in. (25.3 × 20.2 cm). Photo: George Maciunas. Courtesy Billie Maciunas. Image © The Museum of Modern Art. Licensed by SCALA/Art Resource, NY.

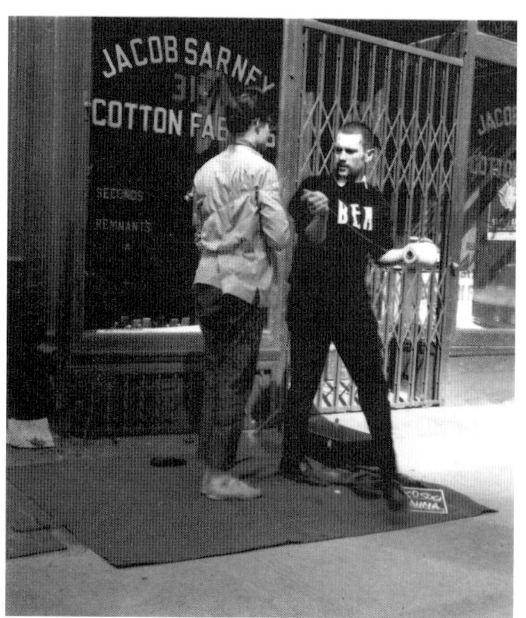


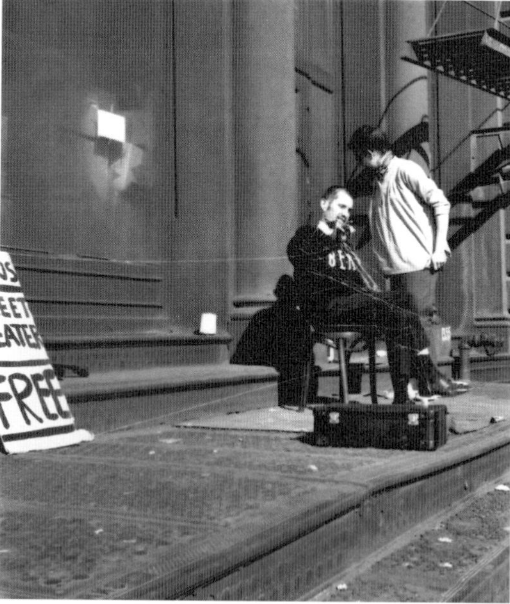


**Figure 3.4.** Alison Knowles and Ben Vautier performing Takehisa Kosugi's *Anima I* (1961), Canal Street, New York, 1964. Photo: George Maciunas. Courtesy Billie Maciunas. Image © The Museum of Modern Art. Licensed by SCALA/Art Resource, NY.

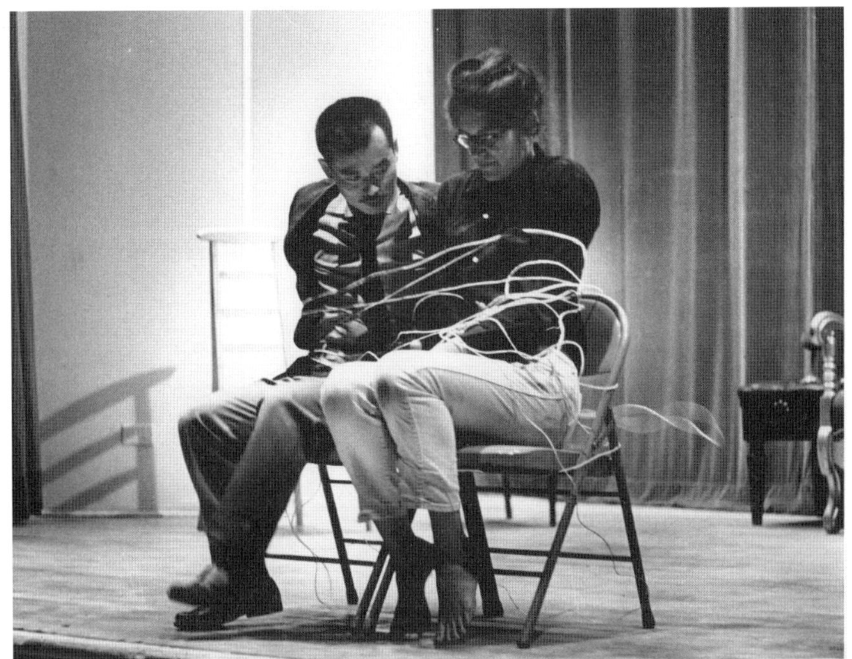

**Figure 3.5.** Ay-O and Alison Knowles performing in a rendition of Erik Satie's *Relâche*, 3rd Annual New York Avant Garde Festival, Judson Hall, 165 West 57th Street, New York, 1965. Photo: Peter Moore, © Northwestern University. Courtesy Peter Moore Photography Archive, Charles Deering McCormick Library of Special Collections, Northwestern University.

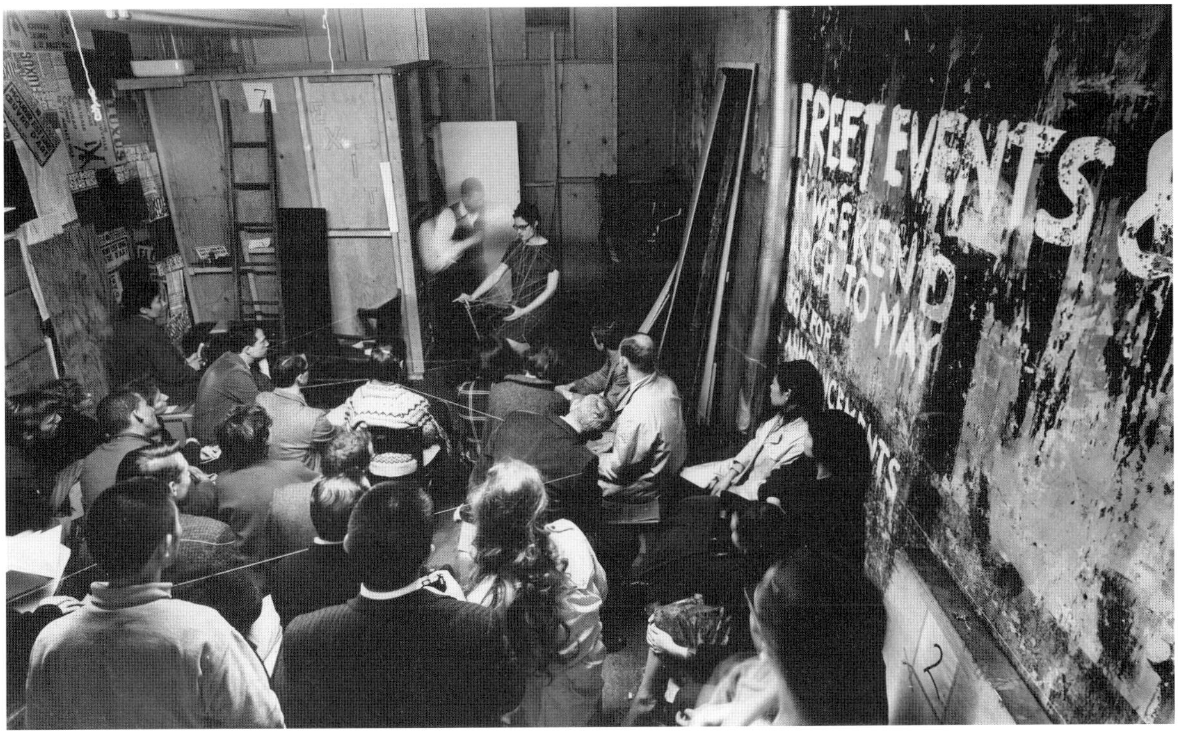

**Figure 3.6.** Alison Knowles and Ben Vautier performing Takehisa Kosugi's *Anima I* (1961), Fluxhall, 359 Canal Street, New York, 1964. Photo: Peter Moore, © Northwestern University. Courtesy bpk Bildagentur/Archiv Sohm, Staatsgalerie Stuttgart/Peter Moore/Art Resource, NY.

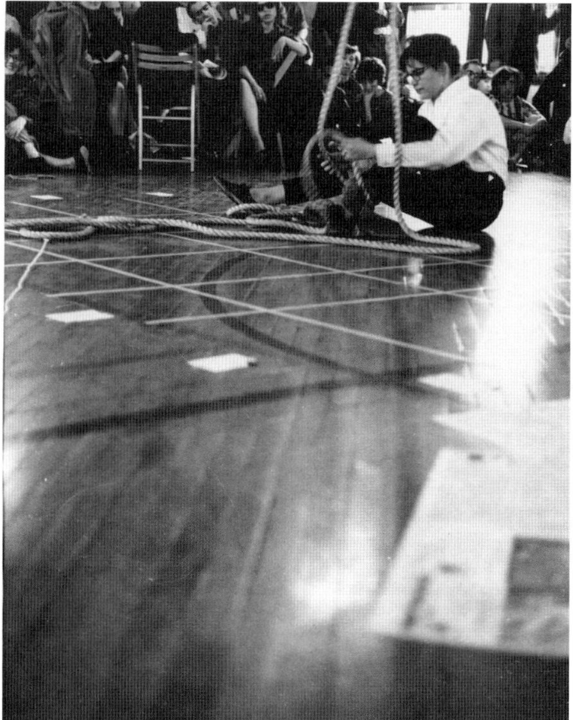

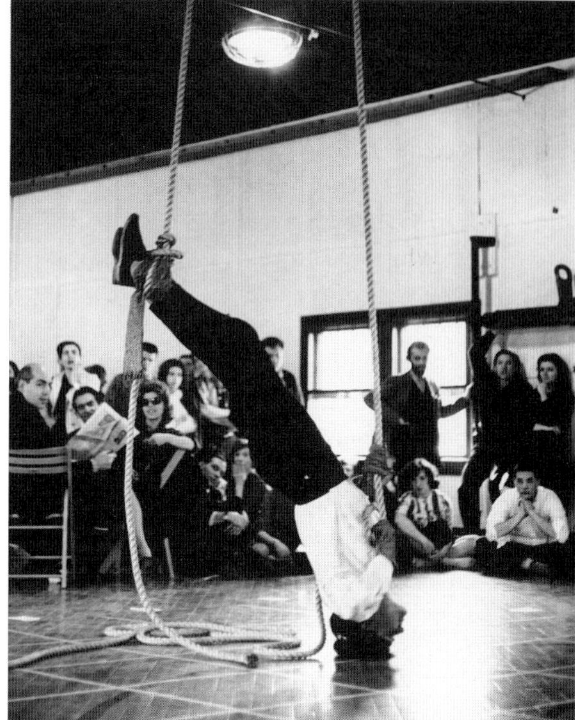

**Figure 3.7.** Alison Knowles performing Benjamin Patterson's *Solo for Dancer* (1962), Rutgers University, New Jersey, 1964. Photo: Peter Moore, © Northwestern University. Courtesy bpk Bildagentur/Archiv Sohm, Staatsgalerie Stuttgart/Peter Moore/Art Resource, NY.

**Figure 3.8.** Alison Knowles performing Benjamin Patterson's *Solo for Dancer* (1962), Rutgers University, New Jersey, 1964. Photo: Peter Moore, © Northwestern University. Courtesy bpk Bildagentur/Archiv Sohm, Staatsgalerie Stuttgart/Peter Moore/Art Resource, NY.

an awareness of her body as it related to varying publics. Her willingness to perform anywhere, for friends or an open-minded audience, is evidenced memorably in her 1963 role (before her pregnancy) in the US premiere of Ben Patterson's *Solo for Dancer* (figs. 3.7–3.8), a piece she had first attempted the previous year at the Festum Fluxorum in Copenhagen.[5] In Germany, Knowles had grown close to Patterson, whose indefinite score instructed the "dancer" to pull their own body up from the floor using a rope pulley suspended from the ceiling. Knowles's US iteration took place at Douglass College in New Jersey, among students and fellow Happenings and Fluxus artists, and exemplified her improvisatory explorations of space, time, and physicality in public events.[6] Throughout this period, Knowles focused on the inherently contingent nature of the aesthetic process, creating permutations of works sensitively attuned to the specifics of site and context. This contribution to Fluxus's post-European, US-based performances was integral to the group's pursuit of new modes of representation that would fundamentally question what an artwork could do—and mean.

This chapter considers the shift in Knowles's practice, in the mid- to late 1960s, toward investigating daily rituals and readymade provisions for their visual and acoustic potential. Through a rigorous exploration of quotidian materials and embodied experiences (eating, listening, feeling), and nuanced recourse to language, Knowles moved beyond her initial foray into performative intermedia, in the context of Fluxus, helping to initiate a variety of historical, theoretical, and artistic leitmotifs of the period.[7]

While dozens of examples from Knowles's oeuvre could be marshaled, I focus here on two foundational works, *Bean Rolls* (1963) and *The Identical Lunch* (1967–1973). Although distinct in form and intentionality—the former, a "canned book," the latter, a performance score—both exemplify another, related shift in her artistic development: the extension of notational scores to object-making and its intersection with corporeality (literal, figural, analogical) as a transformative, collective medium. And both tacitly expose gendered labor in the public and private spheres, deploying edible material as a substrate for the commodified organism of visual art—marking Knowles as a pioneering figure in the emergence of user-generated artistic practices. In both, Knowles's embrace of the *provisional*—or indeterminate outcomes, objects, and experiences related to food—contributes to her redefinition of the conditions of artistic and domestic labor.[8] Indeed, I argue that Knowles, using beans, sandwiches, and the sociobiological processes of daily life, proposes an alternative model for understanding exchange value, materialism, and the limits of commodity culture.

## Bean Networks

Two years post-Europe, the unconventional character of Fluxus scores, performances, and multiples required explication, if not defense, when presented to an art audience primed to embrace Pop, Op, color-field painting, and minimalism. In May 1964, George Brecht, Knowles's Fluxus colleague and close friend, wishing to maintain the group's experimental activities and avert potential "misunderstandings" regarding their cooperative mode of working, noted that, in contradistinction to earlier avant-gardists like the Futurists and the Bauhaus, "there has never been any attempt to agree on aims or methods."[9] Reasoning that viewers could achieve artistic knowledge and apperception outside of a formalized art context, Brecht pointed to small multiples issued under the Fluxus signature—Knowles's *Bean Rolls* (fig. 3.9), Ay-O's *Tactile Finger Box* (1963), Robert Watts's *Rocks Marked by Weight in Grams* (1964)—as evidence of a shift from the European festivals' nearly exclusive emphasis on live events and notational scoring to more durable, object-based (perhaps even salable) production. Knowles, Ay-O, and Watts, he wrote, deployed strategies of visual and tactile engagement that radically reconsidered the notion of sculpture (as found in the readymade, for instance), without succumbing to any officially sanctioned, universalizing aesthetic agenda. The three artists'

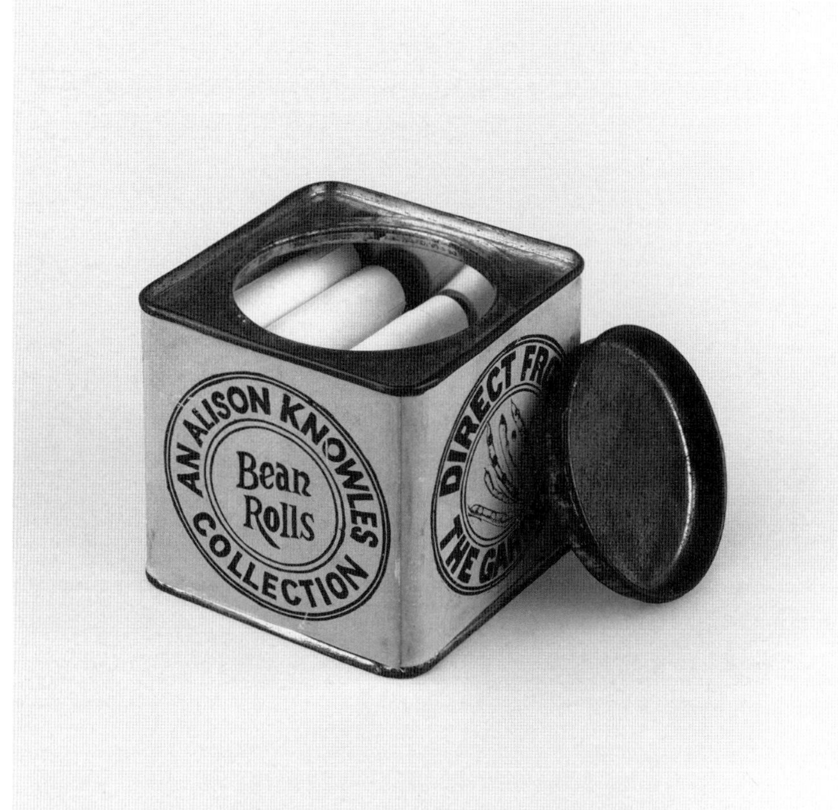


**Figure 3.9.** Alison Knowles, *Bean Rolls* (1963) from *Fluxkit*, 1965. Metal tin with offset label, containing dried beans and sixteen offset scrolls; 8.3 × 8.3 × 7.9 cm. Jean Brown papers, 1916–1995 (bulk 1958–1985), Getty Research Institute, Los Angeles (890164).

disparate multiples, in his view, shared "something unnamable in common" that promised a "nourishing" effect on the development of "original, and often uncategorizable" objects.

This development, Brecht said, would transpire in a "strange new way." Given the uneven reception of Fluxus performances in the US, compared to Europe, the number of such events waned; simultaneously, Fluxus publishing and object-making activities surged. In 1963, Maciunas moved into a shabby warehouse at 359 Canal Street; Dick Higgins, whose studio was directly above in the same building, helped Maciunas secure the space, where he established Fluxhall/Fluxshop, a storefront, concert space, and mail-order business that would serve, from 1964 to 1966, as the center of Fluxus operations. Here Maciunas designed, manufactured, and promoted *Fluxboxes*, *Fluxyearbooks*, and the occasional Fluxus newspaper, giving a professional gloss to ordinary objects often meant as elaborate gags.

Also in 1963, Higgins (with Knowles) founded Something Else Press (SEP), initially operating from an office at 106 Fifth Avenue.[10] True to the artists' aleatory inclinations, the name of the publishing house was purportedly settled on by chance: Knowles dismissed Higgins's first, cheeky proposals—Fluxus Annex, Original Fluxus, Shirtsleeves Press—as unsuitable and advised him to

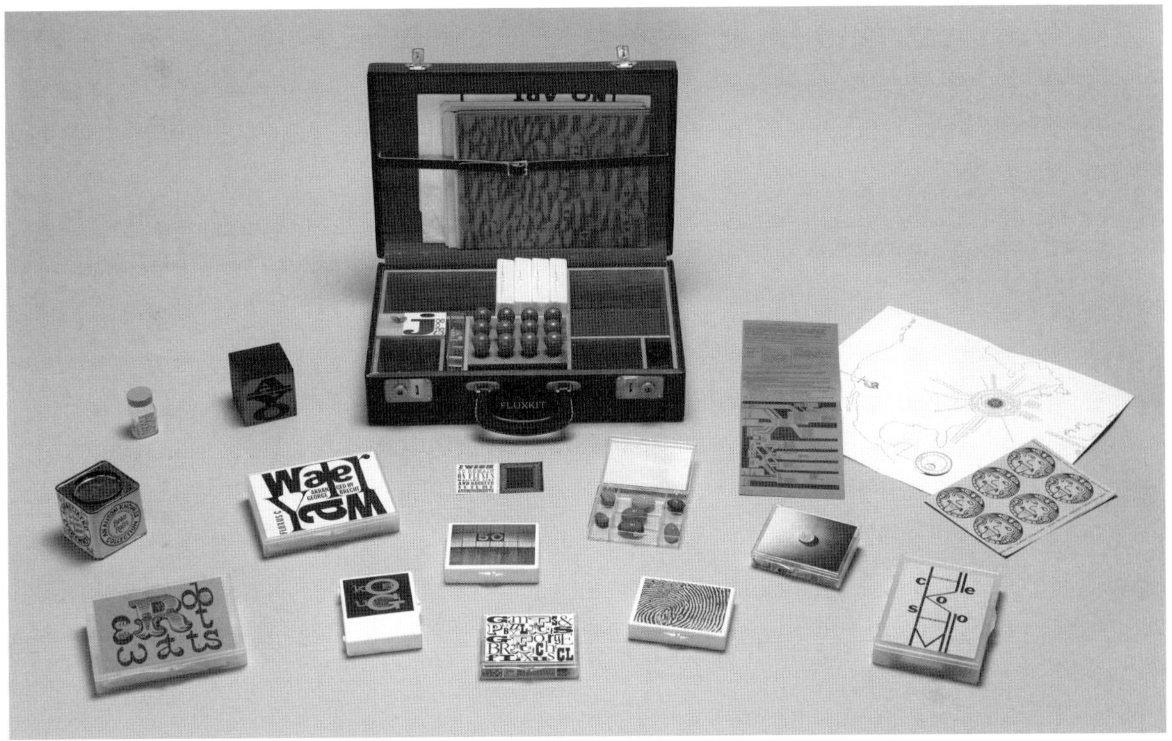

Figure 3.10. Various artists, *Fluxkit*, 1965–1966. Vinyl-covered attaché case, containing objects in various media, 24 × 44.5 × 12.5 cm (closed). Image © The Museum of Modern Art. Licensed by SCALA/Art Resource, NY.

name it "something else."[11] For over a decade, Higgins, who had extensive training in printmaking and book crafting, edited and published some of the most important historical and neo-avant-garde texts, manifestos, novels, and anthologies of poetry of the half century, including 1966 reissues of Gertrude Stein's *The Making of Americans* (1925) and Richard Huelsenbeck's *Dada Almanach* (1920), his own landmark essay "Intermedia" (1965), Claes Oldenburg's *Store Days* (1968), John Cage and Alison Knowles's *Notations* (1969), and the influential Great Bear Pamphlets. For Knowles, the physical and conceptual presence of SEP in her home—coupled with her work on its editorial board and her training at the Manhattan School of Printing—fostered an interest in developing alternative outlets for her own artistic development, especially the idea of synthesizing text, object, and performance genres into a critical practice. Within this fertile environment, Knowles created one of her first object-based Fluxus works, *Bean Rolls*.

*Bean Rolls* was commissioned by Maciunas for an early iteration of *Fluxkits* (fig. 3.10). *Fluxkits*, issued between 1963 and 1965, were collections of small Fluxus multiples housed in found vinyl cases or wooden crates and designated as boxed treasures (or even migratory museums) in an explicit homage to Marcel Duchamp's *Boîte-en-Valise* works (1935–1941). Each attaché, meticulously assembled by Maciunas, held multiples by at least thirty-nine artists, most encased in smaller plastic, cardboard, or metal containers or paper folders.[12] Individual objects could also be purchased separately. As her contribution, Knowles proposed a can containing dried beans and scrolls printed with poetic fragments of stories, myths, and recipes, unyoked from their original textual context and effectively randomized.[13]

Humorous, ironic, playful, and irreverent, *Bean Rolls* and other *Fluxkit* enclosures nevertheless alluded to contemporary anxieties regarding the authenticity of cultural labor. Maciunas himself intended to advance a more radical political agenda than most of the artists were then comfortable with. In a letter to German artist Tomas Schmit, he posited the *Fluxkits* as promoting the eventual "destruction of the authorship of pieces . . . mak[ing] them totally anonymous—thus eliminating artists' ego."[14] Yet he designed special branding labels around each artist's name (fig. 3.11), and the individual contributors were credited and retained copyright. Like the others, Knowles could not control how viewers would handle (or reject) her offering—the contingent and ephemeral being prized over the timeless and precious. Nonetheless, in *Bean Rolls*, the artist's (literal) skilled hand asserts its authority to *transform* banal materials into works of art.

To the extent that *Fluxkit* contributors subordinated individuality to collective accumulation and dispersed authorship, Brecht aligns Knowles's *Bean Rolls* with the radical "professional anti-culture and down-withs (paying culture a sort of inverse compliment)" events staged by concept artist Henry Flynt (such as protesting a performance of Karlheinz Stockhausen's *Originale* at New York's Town Hall in late April 1964).[15] Flynt's political activism, he suggests, could result in "making [Knowles's] bean-sprouts seem even lovelier." Brecht tries here, notably, to understand Knowles's turn toward object-based (sproutable, edible) artwork as a reexamination of making itself, consistent with a broader critique of capital—a communally based art-sharing practice micro-focused on her immediate artistic circle and intimates. Indeed, as Knowles has noted, by the time of her new "voyage" in the world of beans, the impetus "had gone out of cooking and into reviewing the culture and how beans would affect anything, whether it was an artwork, a song, or a proverb, something that would reflect onto the culture of beans."[16]

Formally, *Bean Rolls* consists of a dozen or more printed scrolls and assorted dried beans in a repurposed tea tin, roughly a three-inch cube, with a wrap-around printed label (plate 5). The scrolls present texts culled from extensive digging at the main branch of the New York Public Library, all regarding beans—their history, etymology, myths, rituals, songs, proverbs, and preparation as foodstuffs. Knowles discovered, for example, a panoply of bean names: Early Red Valentines, Early Mohawks, Long Yellow Six Weeks, English Canterburys. The phrase "Ich bin ein . . . ," printed on several scrolls, makes clever reference to the uncertain political moment in which the *Bean Rolls* were conceived and produced, recalling President John F. Kennedy's June 1963 expression of solidarity, "Ich bin ein Berliner," uttered to a West German audience at the height of the Cold War.

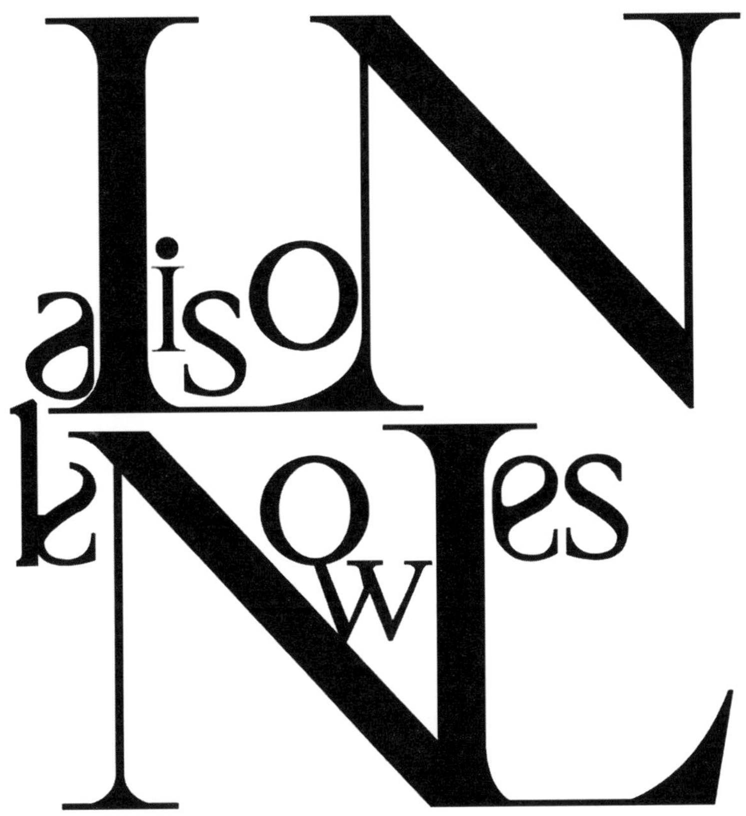

**Figure 3.11.** Fluxus Artist Name Card for Alison Knowles, designed by George Maciunas, New York, 1964. Offset card, 6.6 x 6.5 cm; part of *Fluxus 1* (version book). Courtesy Billie Maciunas.

Judith F. Rodenbeck astutely argues that Fluxus multiples like *Bean Rolls* "transvalue[d] the production and consumption of food into art activities" through a positioning of "material simplicity."[17] Indeed, Knowles categorically expanded art's conceptual and material borders, exploring the multidimensional pleasures of found objects packaged in cheap, mass-produced containers as well as performances around the subject of food. In pushing the linguistic, conceptual, and material limits of the "event score" to include processes of the domestic everyday, Knowles's practice would develop into a sustained exploration of different dissemination systems and economies of exchange—biological, political, historical, literary.

*Bean Rolls* is a complex repository activated by the reader. Rolled and unrolled, the scrolls engage the hands. Seen, or not; read, or not; heard, or not; understood, or not—the canned books implicate the visual, the auditory, the cognitive. The sheer mass of bean data, assiduously collected and edited down to a series of textual remains, affords the viewer-reader so many means of consumption as to arrest all temporal flow. Knowles synthesizes multiple information technologies: the ancient scroll form, associated with religious observance, ritual, and social gathering; the modern printing press, which renders her fragments infinitely reproducible; and the alphanumeric ordering of the library or archive's hidden holdings, subverted here by the absence of context or citation.

The artist/reader can reorder the contents as she pleases: recipes overlap proverbs, myths nestle songs, dried beans rattle in the tin. This clattering links *Bean Rolls* to Cage's lessons on percussive instrumentation.[18] It reaffirms, too, Knowles's growing interest in the extra-acoustical elements of sound, evident as well in her whipping of fabric in the street performance with Vautier. The preserved legumes suggest scarcity or plenty, or oscillate between readings, while the recipes declare their vast gustatory-culinary potential. It is important to recall that Knowles conceived *Bean Rolls* as a book—a text to be consumed, albeit not read in any traditional way. The reader-viewer is meant to attain, not infinite knowledge of beans but, rather, the potential to learn and experience *something* about them. Total knowledge of any subject is revealed as impossible.

Enabling a directly tactile encounter with a work of art, *Bean Rolls* invites an operational manipulation of its materials at hand: the shaking of the tin; the spill of objects; the unfurling of the scrolls. In this way, it suggests a conceptual affinity to Duchamp's *Box with Hidden Noise* (1917), a small sculpture Knowles observed in the 1961 Museum of Modern Art exhibition *Art of Assemblage*. Duchamp's indeterminate sound box was first fabricated in 1916 with the help of friend and benefactor Walter Arensberg and remade in 1964 by Arturo Schwarz: An unspecified object is placed within a ball of twine, pressed between two copper plates (inscribed with an enigmatic text in French and English), and secured by thick bolts. Evoking classified information, accessible to only a privileged few, Duchamp instructs lucky handlers simply to "listen to it."[19] While Knowles's assemblage was intended to be read, it was also, like Duchamp's assisted readymade, meant to be heard ("hard little pellets making music inside the sealed can").[20]

Knowles accentuated this auditory component by composing a score to accompany the physical object. *Proposition #12: Simultaneous Bean Reading* (1965) calls for six to eight performers to open the *Bean Rolls* can and carefully unroll the scrolls, reciting them aloud to any available audience. When it debuted at the Café au Go Go in Greenwich Village, a single performer determined both the overall duration and the length of each reading by "cutting out large sections of the rolls" with scissors.[21] Rerolling and returning the fragments to the can, or creating a new performance of the texts via the cuts and throwing them away, creates a perpetually chance-derived series of options. The score, Hannah Higgins observes, "engage[s] a person in exploration without awareness of time or place," resulting in action that is "simultaneously conceptual and Event-like."[22] This was also true a decade later, when Knowles first performed her sonic sculpture *The Bean Garden* (1971) at Floyd Bennett Field for Moorman's 12th Annual Avant Garde Festival in 1975: Participants were invited to shuffle their feet in the "garden," a wooden box filled with hundreds of pounds of navy beans and fitted with contact microphones amplified by bell jars. The score for the piece, *Proposition X: Build a Bean Garden*, was originally based on Ryōan-ji, a dry rock Zen temple garden located in Kyoto, Japan, that she had long admired.[23] With white navy beans replacing the white pebbles and rocks at Ryōan-ji (among other substitutions), *The Bean Garden* becomes a tactile encounter where participants can not only awaken the sound underneath their feet, but also rake the beans "in waves" to hear the bells chime.[24]

The earlier *Bean Rolls*, in my view, typifies Knowles's practice, after the European Fluxus concerts, of merging concept and event into multisensorial projects predicated on chance. It operates on three competing archival registers: as *text* (containing printed words, supplemented by a written score), as *object* (a mass-produced tin can and potential percussive instrument), and as *performance*, of the score or of social rituals evoked by the contents. Art-as-event visualizes these rituals: the daily labor of the living artist, the activities and conditions that make her work possible—in this case, the biological necessity of eating. *Bean Rolls* considers food within both organic and inorganic exchange systems, through the circuits of both public (use) and private (art) economies. The global body politic referenced in Knowles's Fluxus objects, not least through her inclusion or regional/national varieties of legumes, relates to her understanding of the post-Duchampian readymade. Her canned food object, that is, elevates the readymade's inherent radicality toward the private operations of biological vitality and nourishment and, thus, labor and expenditure.[25]

By the later 1960s, Knowles had become so associated with beans as the stuff of art that other artists, including Jackson Mac Low and John Cage, began to compose bean works for her.[26] Knowles's own blending of culinary and art language continues in later works such as *Bean–See Also Bein for George Maciunas*, a text extracted from a 1965 New York City telephone book, consisting of entries with "Bean" surnames, to be performed as a memorial to Maciunas after his death in 1978. It is, the score explains, "A poem for two voices, one reading the name preceded by the other reading the number. An audience can be substituted for the second reader."[27]

In later decades, Knowles voyaged further into language systems and the world of books and beans, constructing a room-sized installation. *The Book of Bean* (1981), like *The Big Book* twenty years prior, is a large-scale book with walk-in pages and a variety of stimuli. First exhibited at Franklin Furnace in Brooklyn as the culmination of an artist residency, it subsequently traveled to New Jersey, Philadelphia, and eventually the Venice Biennale (fig. 3.12).[28] *Loose Pages* (1983) continued her exploration of beans, sounds, and textures. A multiple made of cotton and flax paper embedded with red lentils, *Loose Pages* is donned by a performer as a novel to be worn ("a human book with human appendages.")[29] *The Giant Bean Turner* (1995–2000), as well as smaller bean sculptures, is an irregular vertical tube made of air-dried paper pulp and flax fiber, containing unspecified quantities of beans whose motion, when the

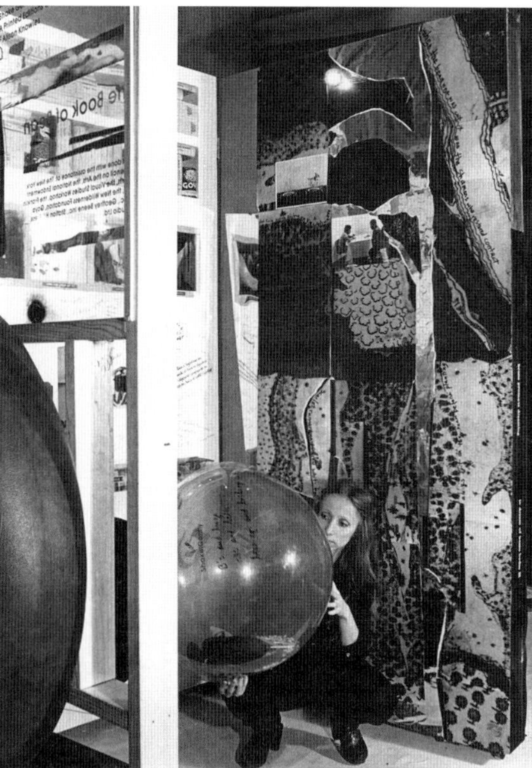
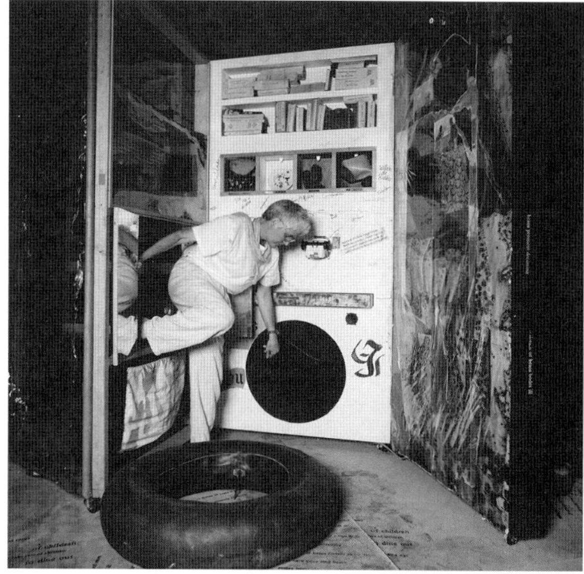
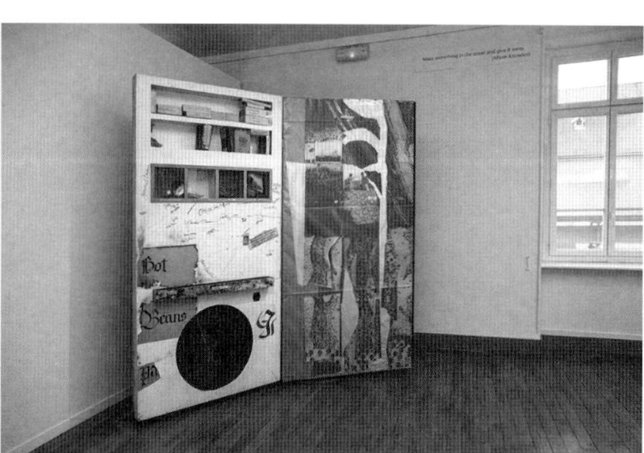
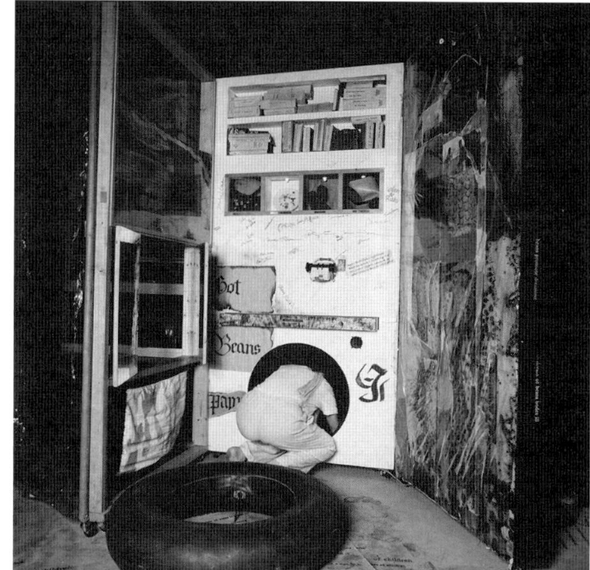

**Figure 3.12.** Alison Knowles, *The Book of Bean*, 1981. *Clockwise from upper left:* Installation view, Franklin Furnace, New York (courtesy Franklin Furnace Archive); Knowles activating installation, Venice Biennale, 1990 (photos: Caspari de Geus); at Collection Gino Di Maggio (© Fondation du doute–Ville de Blois, France).

column is inverted, creates a rush of sound that is amplified by the structure. Hand-held, portable versions of the bean instruments are found in her *Time Samples* (2006), a series of found, repurposed objects with plastic tags linking them to fiction writers, poets, composers, and others. In each of these iterations, we might ask what kind of audience, reader, and viewer these thematic bean works, installations, and boxes are intended for. What kind of *public* does Knowles imagine beyond Fluxus?

In terms of spectatorship, the heterogenous bean works allow Knowles to both liberate and obligate her audience. The position of the viewer, given hands-on access to the *Bean Rolls*, for example, shifts from passive to active; its handling is a temporal, tactile experience. At the same time, engagement with its archive of bean lore requires not only the concentration demanded by reading but manipulation of the tiny scrolls and decisions as to their order. The time and energy expended in producing these objects becomes apparent and is crucial to their meaning. Though housed in cheap, surplus tins purchased by the dozen, the scrolls entailed the artist's efforts in the library, skillful design and printing, and literally painstaking hand-rolling—Knowles and her mother labored at the task until their hands became clawed and cramped.[30] As in the early participatory scores, Knowles's reframing of banal experience *as art* anticipated an audience that could go beyond its conventional spaces of viewership and reception and into a more general economy of shared knowledge and experience. In her hands, beans become provisional (art) objects intimately related to processes of biological life (nourishment), social praxis (ritual), and communication (reading)—all of which could be manifested both privately and publicly.[31]

I view Knowles as pursuing aesthetic and social ends in common with emerging discourses of feminism and liberation politics, and sharing too their anxieties around artistic and domestic labor. Indeed, what is most interesting about her use of beans—beyond their seeming ubiquity and infinitude of forms and uses—is their relation to political and social inequity. "The bean is an everyman food," Knowles has noted. "One thinks of the famine in medieval Europe when poor people survived on beans alone . . . My concern with the physical stuffs came from growing up in a frugal family."[32] Elsewhere, she has written:

> Beans are the first food associated with the poor. Documents in tablet form with recipes have been discovered, but most recently in a rock crevice on cliffs off the Pacific coast what may be an ancient vestment has appeared. Its origins are completely unknown. It is made of paper melded with muslin containing red lentils . . . Egyptians imagined it was sufficient to eat lentils to enlighten the mind and open the heart, and perhaps as well to make music![33]

Encouraging attentiveness to the humble bean and its presence in agriculture, economies, and regional diets, Knowles's formal, material choices situate her within a postwar context concerned with social engagement. Eschewing any explicitly political program, Knowles was yet conscious of heteronormative modes of sexism and sociocultural conditioning. As critic Jill Johnston observes, "Alison Knowles is quite aware at this point that *only* a woman would have made a public salad in 1962, and that *only* a woman would be so identified with food—beans, of all kinds, which have featured in so much of her work."[34]

Knowles was not, however the only conceptually oriented artist deploying the language and materiality of food or eating in the 1960s. Vautier produced *Flux Mystery Food* (1967); Daniel Spoerri (at times associated with Fluxus) created assemblages of dishes on tabletops (1960). In Maciunas's large-scale installation *One Year* (1973–1974), food packaging, appropriated as a readymade, foregrounds graphic postwar techniques of market representation. And Marcel Broodthaers constructed paintings with *coquilles d'oeufs*, egg shells (1965), while Piero Manzoni, in *Achrome* (1962), affixed buns coated in kaolin to a canvas support.[35] Knowles's bean projects gesture toward a more radical choice: removing the pristine modernist canvas (or vertical tabletop) altogether, letting her accumulated beans and bean data generate multiple readings and experiences outside the frame of art. The food objects are contained but remain uncontainable.

The assorted dried beans in Knowles's *Bean Rolls* associate the artwork with sustenance and creativity. They are also unruly, prone to spilling, scattering and clattering into, potentially, an infinite number of configurations and sound events. The work is a curious counterpoint to Manzoni's *Merda d'artista (Artist's Shit)* (1961; fig. 3.13), a multiple that recovers a past spilling out; each of the small circular cans purportedly contains thirty grams of the artist's bodily waste. The work's materiality speaks to the physical residue of eaten objects and commodities; indeed, the product's nominal price, initially equivalent to thirty grams of gold, fluctuates according to market contingencies. Knowles's objects also allude to market exchange—beans, we learn, have served as currency in various cultures (cocoa beans, for example, in pre-Columbian Mesoamerica). And in recasting the value of beans within the currency of art,

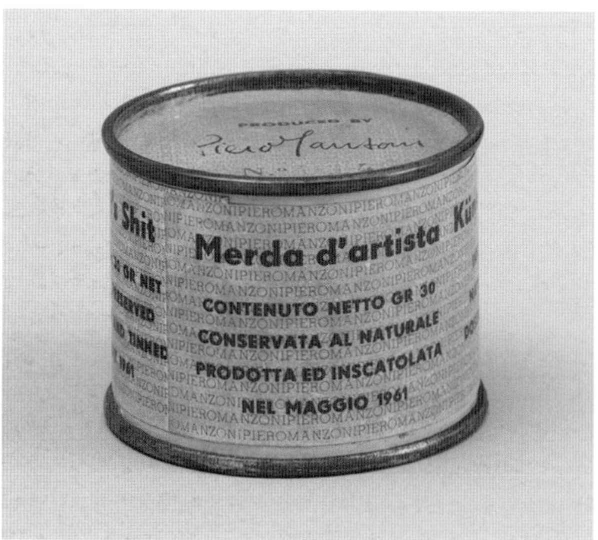


**Figure 3.13.** Piero Manzoni, *Merda d'artiste (Artist's Shit) No. 014*, 1961. Tin can, printed paper, and excrement, 1⅞ × 2½ in. (4.8 × 6.5 cm). © 2024 Artists Rights Society (ARS), New York/SIAE, Rome. Image © The Museum of Modern Art. Licensed by SCALA/Art Resource, NY.

Knowles hints at both ancient and modern rituals of conviviality and social exchange. Moreover, unlike Broodthaers's foodstuffs, which Rachel Haidu relates specifically to his Belgianness, Knowles's beans do not signify (ironically or otherwise) a particular national diet or identity.[36]

In works like *Bean Rolls*, Knowles addresses the corporeal, provisional, and political conditions of living—the phenomena of global poverty, the conditions of domestic labor—through a sustained meditation on the economic and circulatory systems of the literal body and the body politic. Using food or food service as a subject and object of *artistic* labor, rather than a means of affirming prescribed gender norms—the "happy housewife" role, its ideological aspect evident in the proliferation of cookbooks pitched to nationalist ideals in postwar North America—Knowles's "canned book" with bean recipes subverts the expectations both of culinary tastes and of art as a discrete, authentic object.[37] Throughout the late 1960s and early 1970s, Knowles's art practice reflects on eating as not only a process of the body but a procedure of art, and aims to reexamine art as itself as a social relation.

## Performance and the Eating Subject

In late 1967, Alison Knowles began eating the same lunch, in the same place, at roughly the same time, nearly every day. For two years, her noontime meal consisted of a tuna fish sandwich on wheat toast with a large glass of buttermilk, which she consumed at Riss Foods Diner, on Eighth Avenue between Twenty-Second and Twenty-Third Streets in her Chelsea neighborhood.[38] Close to home, cheap, and with quick service, the diner was a boon to a working artist and mother. A few months into the habit, Knowles began documenting her experiences in abbreviated journal entries, noting interactions with food servers, variations in quality of the sandwiches made by the rotating chefs, sartorial notes and other observations about her fellow patrons, and miscellaneous mundane experiences. She first published excerpts from the journal in 1968.[39]

Philip Corner, an experimental composer and close friend who shared a studio loft with Knowles, observed the regularity of her meal and, according to Knowles, practically "midwifed if not actually preconceived" its formalization as a ritual they could investigate together.[40] By 1969, the routine turned into a recipe, an event score known as *The Identical Lunch*: "tuna fish sandwich on wheat toast with lettuce and butter, no mayo, and a large glass of buttermilk or a cup of soup" (fig. 3.14). As with earlier Fluxus propositions that privileged making and sharing, *The Identical Lunch* became an enduring work within Knowles's oeuvre, performed for Charlotte Moorman's 9th and 11th Annual Avant Garde Festivals—in 1972, aboard the riverboat *Alexander Hamilton*, and 1974, at Shea Stadium—and in countless private iterations and museum reenactments in recent years.[41]

Corner's and Knowles's initial proposal was modest. Each would reenact

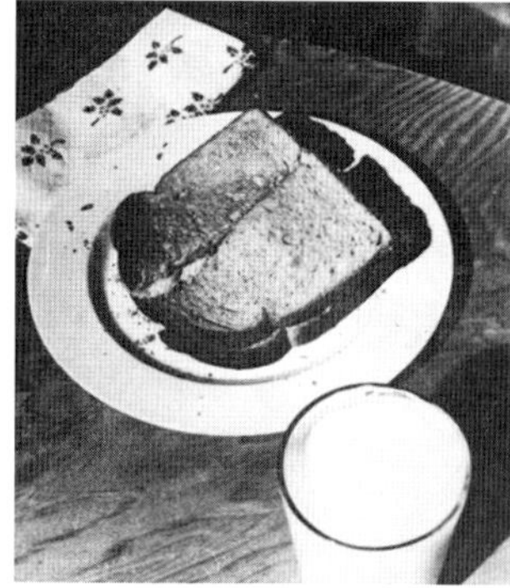

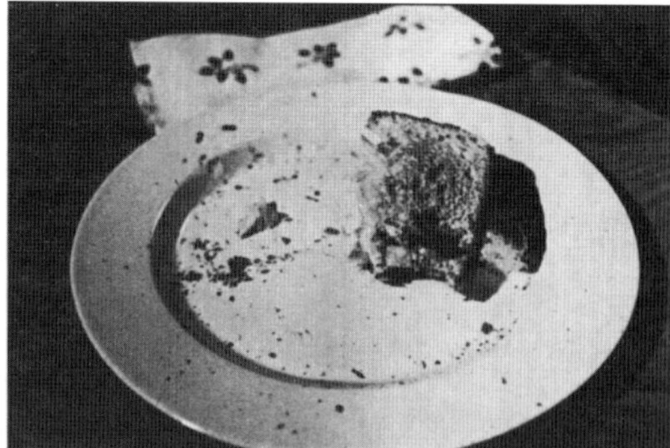

**Figure 3.14.** Residual object from Alison Knowles's *The Identical Lunch*, 1967–1973. Photographer unknown.

*The Identical Lunch* at Riss Foods or any establishment (or domestic space) that offered the same combination of available ingredients on its daily menu for a year or until they tired of the venues or the rather dull cuisine.[42] While the score indicates what is to be eaten, it does not specify the place, time, or duration of the meal, or the number of days it should be repeated, or even if the tuna should be canned or bought fresh from a local fish market.

Like *Proposition #2: Make a Salad*, the *Identical Lunch* score frames a condition of possibility in straightforward, unpretentious terms. As Knowles told an audience of art students in 1973, "*The Identical Lunch* is my effort to find an ingredient in my experience that we all share, and to put into all of my life experience and to get out from it, my art."[43]

The practice was, initially, meditative, a break in the day to gather her thoughts and revive her creative energies while her young daughters played at home or went to daycare. As a studio strategy and parental coping mechanism—establishing a reliable time and space for somatic *and* psychic nourishment—*The Identical Lunch* instituted a space for negotiation between artistic labor and the demands of motherhood, with evident feminist implications. When Knowles eventually tired of the lunch, she recognized how radically these circumstances had changed. Corner, she says, became "obsessed" with its repetition, and repetition became its impetus. At that point Knowles decided *The Identical Lunch* worked better as a serial event score for others to enact on their own terms: "From that day on, I was able to name it, claim it, detach from it myself, look at it, write it up or leave it alone."[44]

Before abandoning her own habit completely, Knowles invited several poets and artist friends to execute the score and its variations at their leisure for the next two years. From Corner, Higgins, John Giorno, Susan Hartung, Vernon Hinkle, Emmett Williams, and others, she solicited materials documenting their wildly divergent victual performances—receipts, notes, drawings, letters, photographs, and other ephemera—which she collaged under the rubric "encounters with tuna fish on wheat toast" and published in 1971 as *Journal of the Identical Lunch* (fig. 3.15).[45] With a motley mix of participants from New York and California, the *Journal of the Identical Lunch* exemplifies

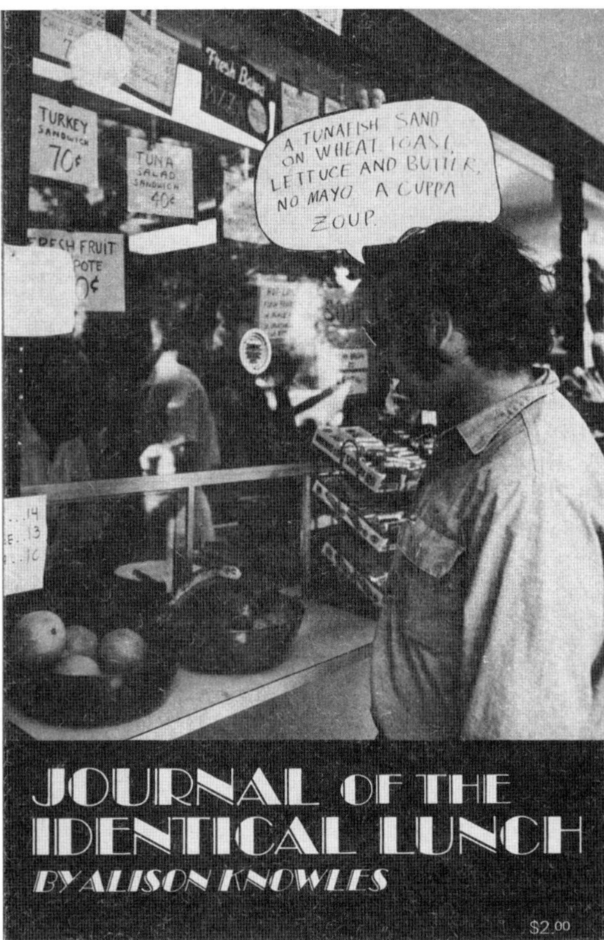


**Figure 3.15.** Alison Knowles, *Journal of the Identical Lunch* (Nova Broadcast Press, 1971), front cover.

Knowles's peripatetic status as she negotiated the tricky business of working and living on both coasts.

The *Journal*'s accounts of lunches consumed by the various performers are relayed to the reader to be consumed in an epistemological sense. Bound in soft brown paper, the publication presents a procession of entries, a mix of straightforward and meandering narratives. Between these are photographs taken by Peter Moore in 1969 of friends eating the lunch at Riss Foods.[46] Jeffrey (Jef) Raskin, a frequent collaborator whom Knowles first met in New York in the late 1960s, is pictured on the cover and throughout the *Journal*, ordering and ingesting the meal and discarding the resultant waste.

In a letter to the book's publisher, Jan Herman, Knowles characterized the voyeuristic quality of consciously performing the lunch *as a score* while also observing others performing it: "It's like looking through a keyhole and seeing the most extraordinary events, how much is revealed that is extraordinary, that people almost didn't realize they were saying."[47] While her thought drifts off, we may assume she was countenancing the transformation, even elevation,

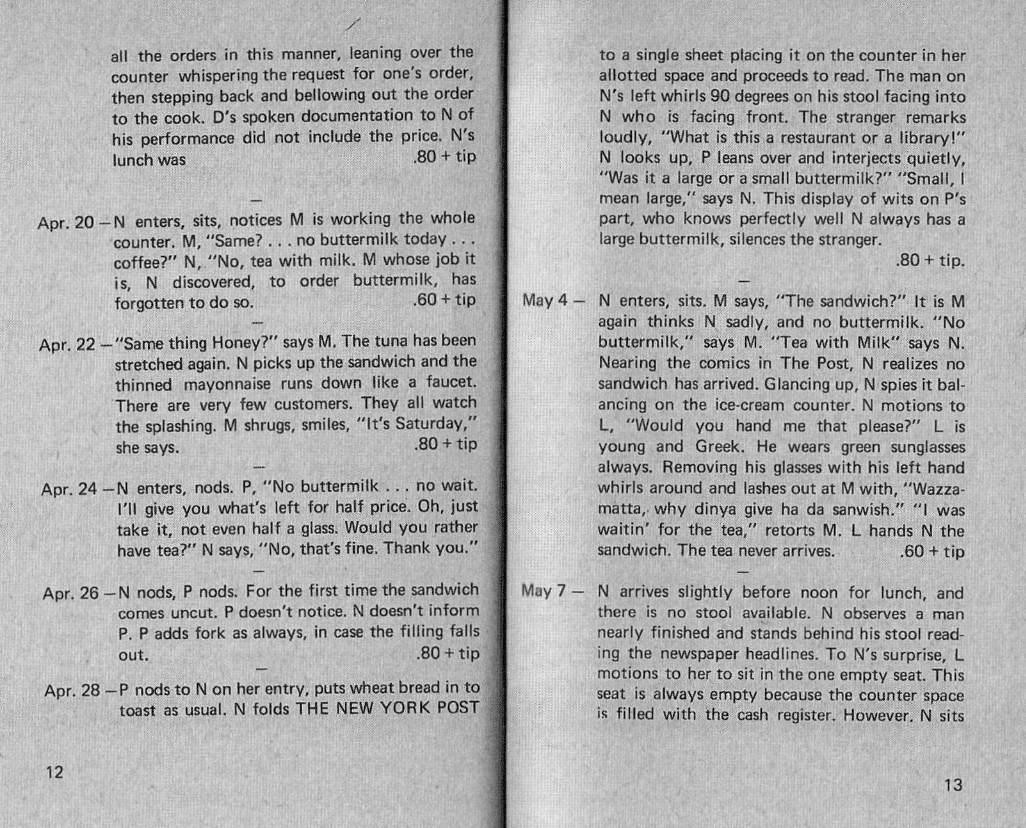

all the orders in this manner, leaning over the counter whispering the request for one's order, then stepping back and bellowing out the order to the cook. D's spoken documentation to N of his performance did not include the price. N's lunch was .80 + tip

—

Apr. 20 — N enters, sits, notices M is working the whole counter. M, "Same? . . . no buttermilk today . . . coffee?" N, "No, tea with milk. M whose job it is, N discovered, to order buttermilk, has forgotten to do so. .60 + tip

—

Apr. 22 — "Same thing Honey?" says M. The tuna has been stretched again. N picks up the sandwich and the thinned mayonnaise runs down like a faucet. There are very few customers. They all watch the splashing. M shrugs, smiles, "It's Saturday," she says. .80 + tip

—

Apr. 24 — N enters, nods. P, "No buttermilk . . . no wait. I'll give you what's left for half price. Oh, just take it, not even half a glass. Would you rather have tea?" N says, "No, that's fine. Thank you."

—

Apr. 26 — N nods, P nods. For the first time the sandwich comes uncut. P doesn't notice. N doesn't inform P. P adds fork as always, in case the filling falls out. .80 + tip

—

Apr. 28 — P nods to N on her entry, puts wheat bread in to toast as usual. N folds THE NEW YORK POST

12

to a single sheet placing it on the counter in her allotted space and proceeds to read. The man on N's left whirls 90 degrees on his stool facing into N who is facing front. The stranger remarks loudly, "What is this a restaurant or a library!" N looks up, P leans over and interjects quietly, "Was it a large or a small buttermilk?" "Small, I mean large," says N. This display of wits on P's part, who knows perfectly well N always has a large buttermilk, silences the stranger. .80 + tip.

—

May 4 — N enters, sits. M says, "The sandwich?" It is M again thinks N sadly, and no buttermilk. "No buttermilk," says M. "Tea with Milk" says N. Nearing the comics in The Post, N realizes no sandwich has arrived. Glancing up, N spies it balancing on the ice-cream counter. N motions to L, "Would you hand me that please?" L is young and Greek. He wears green sunglasses always. Removing his glasses with his left hand whirls around and lashes out at M with, "Wazzamatta, why dinya give ha da sanwish." "I was waitin' for the tea," retorts M. L hands N the sandwich. The tea never arrives. .60 + tip

—

May 7 — N arrives slightly before noon for lunch, and there is no stool available. N observes a man nearly finished and stands behind his stool reading the newspaper headlines. To N's surprise, L motions to her to sit in the one empty seat. This seat is always empty because the counter space is filled with the cash register. However, N sits

13

**Figure 3.16.** Alison Knowles, *Journal of the Identical Lunch* (1971), pages 12–13.

of a banal experience into an extraordinary one. Indeed, as Jessica Santone has noted, in this piece "we encounter an approach to spectatorship where the artist is both performer and spectator."[48] The highly personal nature of the endeavor (for Knowles or her friends) is among the "reasons for liking certain scores and performances" in *The Identical Lunch* and enacting them again and again.[49] Repetition, close observation, and the merging of public and private operations engendered the possibility for poignancy. Nye Ffarrabas (then Bici Hendricks) wrote with fondness to Knowles in summer 1969 that she craved *The Identical Lunch* every time she was in labor, thus inextricably associating the joy and terror of childbearing with a tuna fish sandwich.[50]

Knowles's own contributions to the *Journal* meticulously details her lunch routines over a period of months (figs. 3.16–3.18), reporting her experience "in a televised style," a legend clarifying for readers how names are abbreviated.[51] In a series of interactions with Pauline, a Riss Foods waitress, for example, Knowles becomes "N" and Pauline "P"; "C" is the counterman in the back, "L" the cashier, and "G" Philip Corner. One entry, strikingly, compresses both financial transaction and bodily interaction into a single line: "Jan. 10—N en-

Jan. 10 – N enters, sits . . . nod . . . smile nod. .80 + tip

–

Jan. 11 – N enters, sits. nod. N notes sadly that L has been replaced by B, the smiling pacer. B constantly walks the area near the register looking for tips, which he slips somewhere under the counter. He is abstracted and as unpresent as S. N has seen him on the street at night, at which time they exchange nods. Aside from pacing and watching the counter adjacent to the register, he rings up the checks, waiting for at least three people to pile up in the small space before he performs the cashier's service. N has moved into her third beverage change since the outset of this research. N also allows other performers considerable license with the beverage. The buttermilk is no longer stocked at Riss, perhaps because of N's summer absence, the tea with milk is unsatisfactory and N is compelled therefore to make a third choice of what to drink. It shall be soup. There is no choice of soup at Riss. It is a soup of the day. The possibilities are: yankee bean (very good, lentils and other things, split-pea, also good, vegetable, mostly potato, and chicken noodle, greasy and poor.) Riss also has clam chowder. N has another thought on B. He is a good bouncer and tough on those who don't pay, a common occurrence since many of the clients are on welfare and old. L is now a cook, and N can't imagine him bouncing anyone.

–

Jan 13 – N enters, sits. M speaks, "Cup a soup?" This is the first time in the new year M has taken the

18

initiative to speak before N repeats the identical lunch order. B has added to his pacing and cash register the operation of pushing water. It is indeed very crowded. .80 + tax

–

Jan. 17 – N enters, "Hi" says P. "Hi" says N. P repeats the Hi a second time and N turns to see another "regular" at her right. There are many "regulars" at Riss possibly having their own identical lunches, perhaps sometimes overlapping with N's own lunch. N speculates what a nice graph this would make. P, "cup a chowder?" "Yes," says N. P has never described a cup of chowder as soup. If there is chowder and P is the waitress, as opposed to M, N will know in advance what the soup will be. N has never looked to see if on the board they list the soup of the day. N knows that if P asks "cup of soup" chowder is ruled out, with the three other possibilities remaining, whereas if M is the waitress, the possibilities are widened to include chowder. The regular now speaks with annoyance, "Pie, lady, pie." N had not heard the regular order pie before. Perhaps N did not hear him, or perhaps this man always has pie. P, "The other girl doesn't move, you know." This is true, M is terribly slow. "I know" says N. "It don't pay" says P. The regular receives his pie. .80 + tip

–

Jan. 20 – N enters. M, "cup a soup?" N nods. M, "crackers, hm?" "Just the soup," says N. It occurred to N today that the reason M has never been noticed by the management in her price error is

19

ters, sits . . . nod . . . smile nod. .80 + tip" (fig. 3.17). Knowles recites the facts of her (almost) identical lunch ("no buttermilk today . . . coffee?"), recounting its fiscal, durational, gustatory, and even psychic aspects in monotonous, unornamented prose.

**Figure 3.17.** Alison Knowles, *Journal of the Identical Lunch* (1971), pages 18–19.

That Knowles considered *The Identical Lunch* to be a "concept art piece" mediated in a televisual style demonstrates her awareness of the nexus of site, performance, object, and presentation in the late 1960s and early 1970s—a crucible of production and reception that would set the terms of critically engaged art for decades. Indeed, *The Identical Lunch* stands as a forebear of what would come to be known as institutional critique. Knowles is distinctive, in a period when *information* was becoming a salient term within mainstream art institutions, in fusing with informational conceptual strategies the metabolically and aesthetically complex subject of food.[52] Aside from the "administration of aesthetics" implied in its instrumentalized entries, *Journal of the Identical Lunch* also reports, albeit out of temporal sequence, conceptual developments and setbacks related to Knowles's then-current installation projects, *The Big Book* and *The House of Dust* (fig. 3.18).[53]

silverware. With Riss in high gear, N's lunch is at its best — fast, hot, crisp and crunchy. .80 + tip

—

Feb. 12 — N enters Riss at precisely twelve noon. L is at the register! L, "Hello." N, "How are you." L, "Yeah." N, "Not in the kitchen today?" L, "Next week." P gives water to N, napkin and fork as usual. P says, "Hi." The biggest snow fall since 1961 has thrown New York into a state of emergency. There is no daily paper. L speaks, "So how are ya anyway, how da kids?" "They're fine. I work around the corner. printing . . . and a variety of things. "uh . . . huh. Ya got two boodiful eyes behind dem glasses." smiles L. "Yeah, well . . . You wear glasses all the time yourself?" "Yeah, well . . . " says L. From the second window table a loud female voice, "Neversuch, New York, that's the name it says, Neversuch!" .80 + tip

—

Feb. 13 — N enters takes seat (1). P nods, "cup a chowder" she shouts back. Split-pea arrives. .80 + tip

—

Feb. 17 — N sits in back section. S, having forgotten the buttermilk encounter months before (see May 23rd performance), gives N no particular acknowledgement. N, "Tunafish sandwich on wheat toast, lettuce and butter, no mayo and ca cup of soup?" S, "soup?" N, "what is the soup today?" Why did N ask. She doesn't know. "Yankee bean," says S. N leaves in high anticipation of the afternoon with just a backward glance at L's clean black head of curls. .80 + tip

22

Feb. 27 — N enters, orders tuna salad plate. P is not surprised. N requests double on the coleslaw, no potato salad. N sits in desirable seat (1). Reads paper. 1.20 + tip

—

March 6 — N's THE BIG BOOK having arrived from Copenhagen, N finds herself in La Jolla, California to perform it. N dines with Jeff Raskin and wife Karen at lunch stand near computer center. These three will fuss with some machines later. N speaks to waitress behind counter, "Tuna, wheat toast, lettuce and butter and a glass of buttermilk." "We don't have buttermilk or wheat bread, miss." N glances at the very dry pies and one sad danish in the case. N fears for the lunch. "Well then, rye toast and a cup of soup, please." "Would like the soup now?" says the girl. "Yes" says N. At this moment the girl hands N a number reading 29. N sees no one waiting, and is pondering the mysterious number game, when the soup arrives at the counter. N sits at table with friends who order turkey. The soup is thick and dimly vegetable. N attempts improvement with salt, pepper and a shot of ketsup. As N squeezes the ketsup container (plastic) she simultaneously gives the thing a forward thrust. The top flies into the soup accompanied immediately by the entire contents of the container. BLOP! N jumps up, soup mess is all over N's pants, table and floor. All is rapidly mopped up, and N is spared eating more of the soup. Jeff continues to discuss N's poem HOUSE OF

23

**Figure 3.18.** Alison Knowles, *Journal of the Identical Lunch* (1971), pages 22–23.

Importantly, the war raging in Vietnam cuts through the minutia of the lunch and its minor inconveniences ("thinned mayonnaise," "chicken noodle [soup], greasy and poor") by way of the newspapers Knowles reads at the diner. "March 10—N enters Riss. On entering N spies a friend but does not interrupt him. L comes alongside and she opens daily Post and together they read headlines: FIVE BATTLES RAGE IN VIET . . ." Another abbreviated headline, "2ND BATTLE OF COLUMBIA," can be sourced to a May 1968 *Washington Post* story reporting violent clashes between a phalanx of police officers and students at Columbia University who occupied Hamilton Hall in protest of the university's participation in war research.[54] Student protests erupted across the nation in 1968 as peace talks between US and North Vietnamese delegations broke down.[55] Domestic political violence was also on the rise, as evidenced by the assassinations of Dr. Martin Luther King Jr. in Memphis and Robert F. Kennedy in Los Angeles.

These abbreviated signals toward current events in *Journal of the Identical Lunch* create an indefinite effect akin to the semantic play seen in synthetic Cubist collage decades earlier.[56] As readers, we are left to ask if the allusions reflect Knowles's personal politics or mere flashes of history unfolding that signal (as Walter Benjamin might have it) both a sense of political urgency and a leveling of that tension by the dreary realities of everyday life. In casting the banal tuna fish sandwich as recurrent exemplar of quotidian US consumption, Knowles insinuates a sly rumination on the dietary choices deeply entrenched in the global matrix of broader social upheaval and change. Within two years, other artists in New York would undertake more direct activist responses to the grinding carnage in Vietnam.[57]

In Corner's submission to Knowles's *Journal*, and in his separate published account of meal performances, each iteration of the score carries associations and deploys discursive modes determined by where it occurred.[58] One allusive, colloquial entry evokes the stubborn persistence of segregation and an increasingly militant atmosphere across the US:

> The sign in front of this little place says Eat Brother Eat. What almost unavoidable conjunction that makes today with what we know is happening in the cities (Free breakfast on School Days by the Black Panthers? communal Digger stew?) That makes me think of 1 PM in Peekskill two summers ago, the summer of the riots, when we found open, the only place open, to have something to eat, a soul food place on an unlit street, a *good* place to eat . . .[59]

Corner, who had spent time in the American South as a Freedom Rider in the early 1960s, offhandedly references a recent "summer of riots"—violent responses, often by police, to civil rights activism in the later 1960s—and evokes indirectly the 1949 "Peekskill riots," a mob attack by white residents of the rural New York community on concertgoers at a benefit performance by African American actor and singer Paul Robeson. Robeson was a vocal civil rights advocate and member of the Communist Party, and the riots had both anti-Black and antisemitic overtones.[60]

The testimonies of friends who performed (or attempted to perform) *The Identical Lunch* reveal the impacts not only of mass politics, however, but of their own divergent tastes and sociocultural subjectivities.[61] It was in the late 1960s, after all, that "the personal is political" emerged as a rallying cry among student activists and second-wave feminists. Higgins, consuming a banal and soupless lunch, casts himself as a "suspect" pursued by an omniscient detective. Corner substitutes rye bread for wheat. Sue Hartung declares, "tunafish sandwiches are shitty," and much prefers "tuna raw, in thin slices, with Japanese horseradish"—while Knowles herself deems the buttery mix of lettuce and tuna fish particularly delicious.[62] Maciunas, a frequent performer of the lunch score, later proposed one of its most enduring variations: blending all of its ingredients into a super protein shake.[63]

The turn to "lousy tunafish sandwiches," as Corner's aunt Gertrude assessed them, was not unrelated to a sense of privation felt by many artists in this era. "In part as a response to their abject poverty," Hannah Higgins writes,

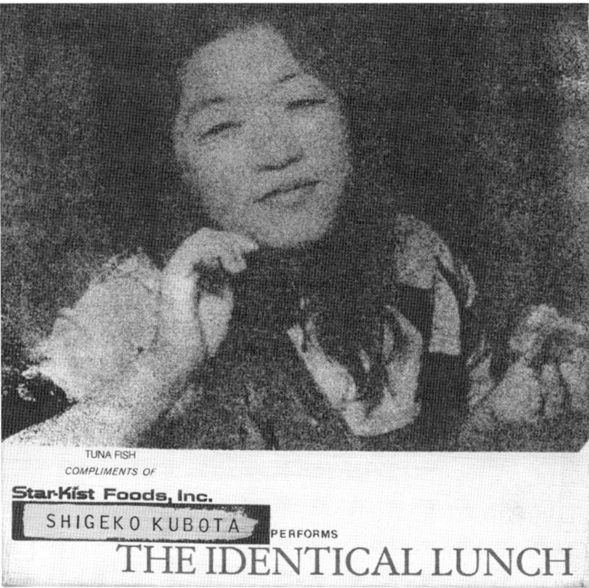


**Figure 3.19.** Alison Knowles, *Shigeko Kubota Performs The Identical Lunch*, 1969 (realized 1973). Screen print with hand additions on canvas. Image © The Museum of Modern Art. Licensed by SCALA/Art Resource, NY.

"Fluxus poets Robert Filliou and Emmett Williams co-invented the spaghetti sandwich, basically homemade spaghetti sauce on bread, for friends and (later) gallery visitors who sought conviviality and a community of shared food."[64] Retrospectively, we might conclude that Fluxus artists' poverty was exacerbated by their marginality as a group of performance/conceptual artists developing a space for experimental practices outside the traditional disciplinary boundaries and a market then dominated by Pop art.[65]

Extending the discursive frame of *The Identical Lunch* beyond live-action performance and its documentation, Knowles began in 1970 to create limited-edition screen-prints of friends performing the score. Black-and-white "poetic camera shots" of Maciunas, Jan Herman, Shigeko Kubota, Ay-O, and her daughters consuming the meal (some taken during the 1969 *New Year's Eve Flux-Feast* and some at the 1972 Avant Garde Festival) were later printed onto canvas over a yellow ground, or left as black-and-white canvases (figs. 3.19–3.20).[66] Each portrait captures an eater in the act of consumption and bears a similar transitive utterance (*Michael Cooper Performs The Identical Lunch*, *Shigeko Kubota Performs The Identical Lunch*, etc.).[67] In adopting a traditionally static image to preserve a temporal food performance, Knowles solidified its status as art (and gustatory pleasure) in a mannered memento mori. Each title/caption also includes the commercial trademark of StarKist Foods, Inc., in a Pop art gesture of ironic displacement (fig. 3.21).

Decades later, Knowles recalled how she came to appropriate the StarKist logo:

> In Piru, California, I lived on a commune far from CalArts, where I was teaching in the experimental program. A frequent visitor was a [film] student named

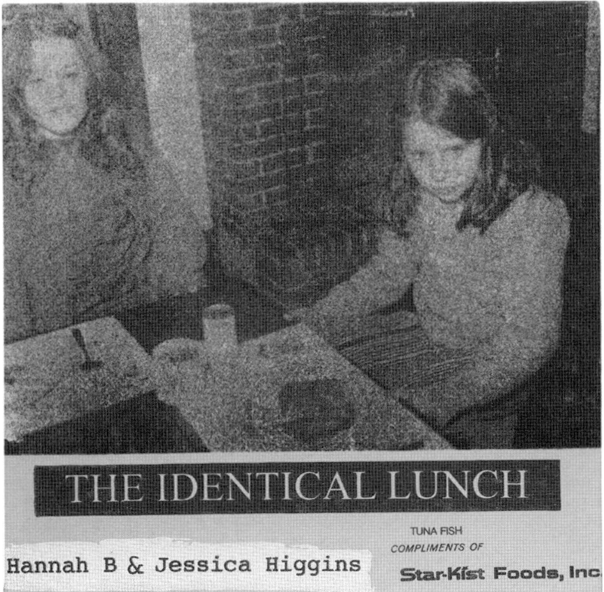


**Figure 3.20.** Alison Knowles, *The Identical Lunch with Hannah B and Jessica Higgins*, ca. 1973–1974 (realized 1992), Screen print on canvas, 48.3 × 49.5 cm. Courtesy Hannah Higgins.

> Josef Bogdanovich, whose grandfather, a Yugoslavian, had founded Starkist Tuna [*sic*]. I remember my excitement when I learned that there was a direct contact to the tuna industry itself, so Josef introduced me to the company. They sent a crate of tuna fish to the UC Irvine Duchamp Festival in 1972 . . . Later when I wanted to make a film at Starkist, it didn't work out because I was rumored to be a saboteur from Bumblebee![68]

The *DUCHAMP IS* . . . Festival, actually held in November 1971, saw the first gallery performance of *The Identical Lunch*. Organized by art historians Barbara Rose (also a critic) and Moira Roth, plus twenty art students, it grappled with Duchamp's outsized influence on art making at midcentury.[69] Roth, then working on her doctorate at UC Berkeley and an adjunct lecturer at Irvine, had originally proposed a dissertation on contemporary artists; having been denied "anything as fresh as that," she changed her topic to "The Artists of 1960 as Compared to Marcel Duchamp" and began teaching the influential French Dadaist in her classes. Roth also began contacting local artists to participate in the month-long celebration.

Rose curated a gallery exhibition featuring Duchampian art and artifacts, which was complemented by events all over campus. One student, according to Rose, evincing "a very theatrical interest in Duchamp" and his efforts "to say very serious things in a humorous way," planted his own name in seeds on a grassy hilltop.[70] Rose also spearheaded a symposia and lectures series, inviting, among others, critics Annette Michelson, Robert Pincus-Witten, Susi Bloch, Robert Hughes, David Antin, Walter Hopps (who in 1963 had curated the first Duchamp retrospective, at the Pasadena Art Museum), Nina Brenner, Peter Selz (Roth's dissertation advisor), and Richard Hamilton. Hamilton flew in from England for the occasion and gave a lengthy lecture on a history of Duchamp's *Large Glass*. Other talks considered Duchamp in the 1960s, his relation to Surrealism, and his "invention" of the readymade.[71] Conceptually, DUCHAMP IS . . . was organized around the idea that his artistic experimentations could serve as models for one's "own imaginative acts"—that is, as "a dialogue with Duchamp rather than a scholarly study of him."[72]

That the newly founded Irvine campus was the site of the Duchamp Festival seems remarkable amid Orange County's conservative politics but evinces the experimental ethos then evident on the West Coast. At the time, UCI's Art School boasted a faculty of artists and curators (Tony DeLap, Robert Irwin, Craig Kauffman, John Paul Jones, Alan Solomon), a "stream of influential visitors" (Rose, Frank Stella, Robert Morris, Joan Jonas), and notable teaching lecturers (Vija Celmins, Ed Bereal, John McCracken, Ed Moses, Larry Bell), all contributing to a new form of experimental pedagogy that had its roots in Los Angeles arts education.[73] John Coplans, a founding editor of *Artforum*, served as both first chairperson of the university's art department and first director of its Fine Arts Gallery. The first graduating class of MFAs—among them, Nancy Buchanan, Barbara T. Smith, Marcia Hafif, Robert Walker, and Chris Burden—established a now-famous student-centered gallery called F Space in a Santa Ana business park.[74]

Roth credits the Duchamp Festival's success to UCI's "collective spirit" and support from the Los Angeles arts community at large, particularly faculty and students from the also newly founded California Institute of the Arts.[75] Recruited by Happenings artist and friend Allan Kaprow, who was then associate dean and professor of studio art, Knowles had, by 1970, relocated to Southern California to chair CalArts' Graphics Print division and teach courses on "Intermedia" and technical media.[76]

Given their standing as pioneering neo-avant-garde artists, both Knowles and Kaprow were invited by Roth to participate in DUCHAMP IS . . . Knowles, a devoted advocate for Duchampian aesthetics, joined in eagerly, soliciting new versions of *The Identical Lunch* score from friends and contributing several versions of *Coeurs Volants*, the collaborative screen print she had created with Duchamp four years prior (figs. I.5–I.6), to the gallery exhibition. She also hung canvases from the series showing friends performing *The Identical Lunch* near a side gallery displaying a set of gridded holograms of performers eating the lunch, crafted by fellow CalArts teacher Peter Van Riper at a lab in San Francisco.[77] She planned to repeat the collaborative merging of live art and emergent technology as "A Dance Performance with Alison Knowles" at UC San Diego, this time with video tape recorder, monitor, speakers, microphones (for in situ feasting), and lasers to display the holograms.[78]

For the performance series at UCI, Knowles chose to reenact *The Identical Lunch* with Bogdanovich. In a letter to Jan Herman, she described a performance "inundated by 100 people or so," who sat eating the lunch while reading copies of *Journal of the Identical Lunch* (many of which, she reported, were

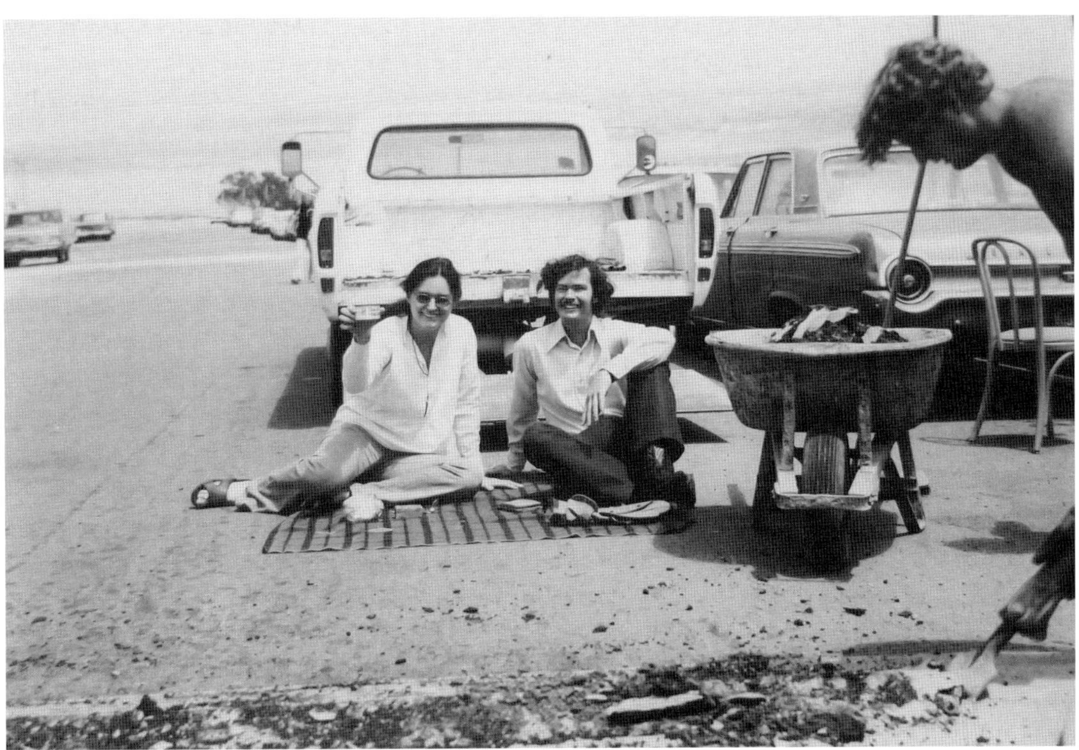

Figure 3.21. Alison Knowles holding a StarKist Tuna can at a performance of *The Identical Lunch*, Southern California, ca. 1971. Photographer unknown.

stolen).[79] The event recalled the original *Make a Salad* Fluxus performance in 1962, albeit with a documentary, multimedia overlay: The walls were covered with eight-foot sepia prints presenting, for example, "the statistics of the tunafish industry in 1946, photo studies of the founder of the Starkist [*sic*] industry, many studies of fish, albacore, blue-fin, etc., slides of situations and things having to do with the score."[80] She included Maciunas's blended lunch version, which she staged dramatically:

> Under a blue spotlight and up a theater step, I [ate] this, fully expecting it to return from my stomach all over the floor. No such. It is without a doubt the health food discovery of the year. Absolutely delicious! The folks were lining up to cream their sandwiches after one sip.[81]

In a 1973 proposal to translate the *Identical Lunch* score into a video piece, Knowles again recalled how the blended lunch iteration was received at the Duchamp Festival:

> Tables [were] outfitted with the mixed tunafish, lettuce, pitchers of buttermilk and toasters. Assistants began making up the sandwiches as the audience arrive[d] . . . The room [was] lighted by the single laser used to view the holograms. A tape [was] playing that was contributed to THE IDENTICAL LUNCH collection by Josef Bogdanovich. Second helpings [were whirring], blended

> into a creamy fish drink that is much enjoyed . . . two hologram anthologies [were] included and available to be read or purchased. Many people [sat] down with their second LUNCH and read to each other in small groups.[82]

If we read this performance of *The Identical Lunch* through the text-object-performance framework outlined for *Bean Rolls*, we find Knowles's use of provisional objects and experiences again codified into a conceptual matrix much like those of her colleagues in the late 1960s and early 1970s. Her own description sets the work firmly in line with strategies of interdisciplinary media that shifted to the subject of gender then emerging in the art world. In installations of the piece over the years, the sheer multiplicity of materials used (graphic prints, holograms, tape recordings), not to mention the groups of participants, calls out the complex conditions under which we experience language, knowledge, and sensory perception (fig. 3.22).[83]

The vitality of the lunch score shows how Knowles deftly reworked the conceptualist visual forms then available to her into an investigation expanding beyond the domestic lives of women. Documentary photo/text installations, for example, were not uncommon among performance and conceptual artists in the early 1970s.[84] While artists approached informational and appropriated media in disparate ways, Knowles deployed it most effectively, starting in the late 1950s, in chance operations, as when she gridded a canvas and placed colors based on the throw of a die. In *BLINK*, her 1963 collaboration with Brecht and Watts (fig. 1.13, plate 4), the grid multiplied into rearrangeable square panels that were alluded to, or even became, product packaging. Knowles's inclusion in the Duchamp Festival of not only gridded photographs but the appropriated StarKist logo and detailed data about industrial fisheries, mimics the codes of visual communication design in public service campaigns, their rationalized, didactic merging of statistics, journalism, and documentary photography.[85]

Knowles's conceptualist approach to the social performance inherent in the score—taking food and the human body as sites of investigation—thus entails a prolonged focus on the complexities of lived experience. Where does our food come from? What form do our food experiences take? How does one develop *taste*—for the gustatory and for the aesthetic? In the Irvine performance of *The Identical Lunch*, participants who consumed blended sandwich shakes were encouraged to question the nature of eating itself, as if it were a behavioral experiment. The intent was to instigate conversations about food production—from threats of ecological disaster to corrupt food industry practices to public health concerns to the pursuit of sustainability and environmental protection.[86]

Knowles's politics in the later 1960s and 1970s, such as they were, fit within the participatory model of making that she favored—a practice of spirited generosity predicated on engaging various publics. In the 1973 funding request, Knowles proposed using new media technologies to allow the *Identical Lunch*

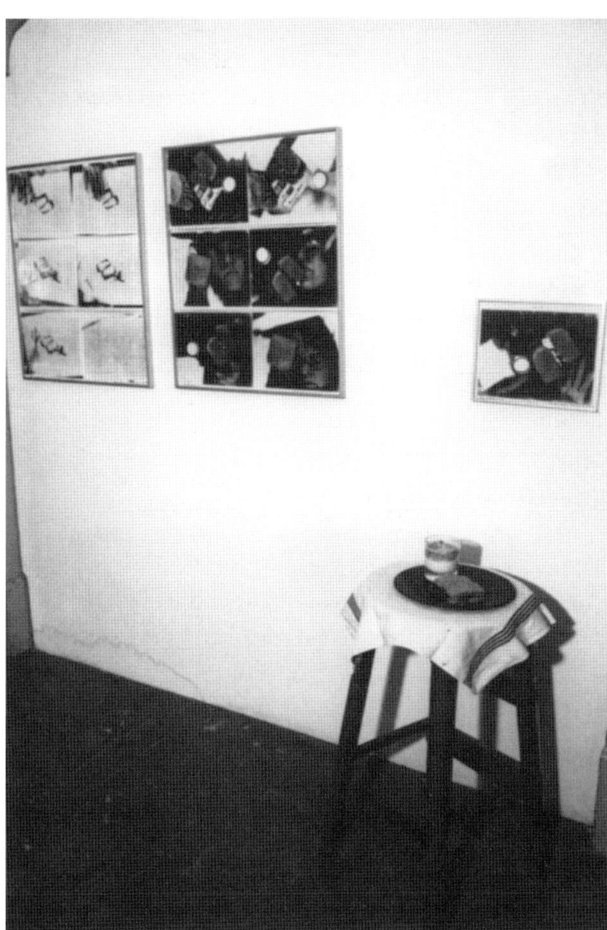

**Figure 3.22.** Alison Knowles, *The Identical Lunch*, ca. 1970s, installation photograph of edible tuna fish sandwich score plus works on holograms and colored copier paper. Exact date, location, and photographer unknown.

score to reach wider audiences. A collaborative video series would document, for example, the "blind-lunch," "step/on lunch," "drawn/out lunch," and "street lunch"; the score, she asserted, operates most successfully as a "centering device for live performance, graphics, and silkscreens."[87] These perceptually expansive lunch versions were intended to be recorded and visually patterned for video by interactive sound artist Liz Phillips in the Ted Estabrook Studio at 103 West Tenth Street.[88] In *The Identical Lunch (Drawn/out Lunch)*, a scripted set of actions combined with various elements allows chance to play a structuring role. A blindfolded performer (of unspecified gender or ableness) enters a semidarkened space and is guided to a large table. On the table are both expected and unusual "materials" related to prior performances of *The Identical Lunch*: "publications, the sandwich, a carton of buttermilk, the empty tuna can and some live cats."[89] Rather than simply consume the sandwich, the performer, taking pens and pencils from a nearby suitcase, is instructed to draw around the objects "with great concentration, separating the sandwiches and drawing around the parts," all the while, presumably, staving off curious (and possibly hungry) felines.[90] Here Knowles's experiments with *The Identical Lunch*'s original score shows its inherent pliancy, enacting her version of Cage's "composition as process," infinitely open yet rigorous in its articulations of multimediated forms.

Much like Cage's *4′33″* (1952), *The Identical Lunch* (in any of its variations) draws participants' attention to incidental sounds and other aspects of their environment within the temporal duration of the work's performance. As Jim Maya observed of his experience:

> An Identical Lunch is very different
> Than the other kind which is different
> From the rest.
> The identical food demands little or no thought:
> The surrounding activities take all your thought:
>
> The waitress, her hair, her lips, the napkins,
> Their embossments or lack of embossments.
> The stools, the chairs, the heat.
> When you've finished—
> You hardly know you've eaten.[91]

This heightened perceptiveness, this openness to indeterminate outcomes, is, of course, the point. When Higgins, evoking the "search for the perfect wave" in the 1966 surfing documentary *The Endless Summer*, posited that "the endless lunch" chases "either the ultimately abominable or the absolutely perfect tuna fish sandwich," Knowles pointedly clarified her intentions: "The Identical Lunch has nothing to do with the pursuit of perfection. . . . I am interested what [*sic*] various people do with the problem . . . of the lunch—the simplest and most accessible in their parts. I pursue no perfect wave. So, Dick, do it again. Eat the lunch again."[92] Knowles, calling out to contemporaneous and future publics via permutable, perpetually generative scores and recipes (do it again), never stopped finding the expressive value (and potential) of material experiences and social rituals.

Knowles's commitment to generative process unfolds opportunities for socialization both within and beyond the artist's control. *The Identical Lunch*'s potential seriousness is matched by its compulsive absurdity. The score speaks to eating as a chore, to food-related trauma and distress, and to habits and tastes—how they are formed and, often, rigidly fixed. But as always in Knowles's event scores, chance and humor, even an erotics, also play a role. We see this in one spontaneous performance, wherein the "identical" lunch became the "naked" lunch.

In the late 1970s, on a bitterly cold winter day in Barton, Vermont, where Knowles and Higgins (by then divorced but on friendly terms) owned a farmhouse, the artists, along with fellow New York Fluxer Geoffrey Hendricks, performed *The Identical Lunch* in the spirit of Édouard Manet's infamous painting *Le Déjeuner sur l'herbe* (1863). Except they queered the composition: Higgins and Hendricks sat naked in the snow, while Knowles, clothed, ate the tuna fish sandwich near a brook. During the lunch, Knowles too would strip down and pose à la Manet's central female figure. As Hendricks recalled, "Alison, with her camera, clicked us taking a bite out of the sandwich, and we quickly raced back up the hill into the farmhouse to warmth again."[93] The distinct sense of comfort and intimacy among the three artists had formed in the context of experimental happenings in New York in the early 1960s.[94] For decades the artists shared in each other's personal and professional lives, extending beyond personal dalliances and mutual sensibilities and including the difficulties of coparenting as divorced couples.[95]

In her own retrospective account of the naked lunch, Knowles tied the performance to larger conceptual goals:

> All you had was a recipe for action. You never had, as you do with theater work, a staging or a script. All you had was a direction. So that [in] something like The Identical Lunch in the snow, [the score] which simply gives the recipe a tunafish sandwich and a glass of buttermilk, can be taken anywhere, at any time, in anyplace. I can't emphasize enough how important this open form is to this mystery or beauty or ugliness that can creep in.[96]

Reflection on daily rituals in all their concreteness and mystery is the structure underlying much of Knowles's art practice, within Fluxus and beyond. Engaging the literal and metaphorical substances of everyday life, Knowles's work in the later 1960s and 1970s bridges divides of gender, public and private, high and low; it is intimate, playful, tactile and otherwise sensual, always referring to the body's desires.

Knowles's performance-based food work since *Make a Salad* turns on the notion of erasure; that is to say, it vanishes, often (as art historians have observed of other food-based practices), as the meal is prepared and eaten. Yet there has been an effort to record the experiences, through photographs, prints, texts, and other means. Knowles has been keenly attuned to the ways in which habit can ossify experience, commodify rituals, drain daily life of meaning (as in the clichéd self-help therapies developed under neoliberal models of subjective agency).[97] She counters that emptying out by composing works that rely on the direct engagement of an audience, by performing food-centered service—preparing a salad in a public space, packing beans in cans, repeating a tuna fish lunch in a diner, a gallery, a winter forest. Knowles thus recasts the relation of the body to larger consumptive forces. In calling our attention to the gender-coded and standardized conditions of certain domestic duties and, by extension, her post as a woman artist among mostly male colleagues, she vivifies her unique status in the historical reception of Fluxus along with her own individual interests and artistic investigations.

## Provisional Affects

Knowles's food-based objects, performances, and texts compose material encounters with lived experience, fostering a relational awareness of the body as it moves beyond the sensorial and into the space of objects that have meaning only when apprehended by sentient beings. Her work, foregrounding our desire to conjure the world by enacting correspondences, reverberations, and synchronizations of language and bodies, is therefore a visual, aural, and textual analogue of our daily world.

In positioning Knowles's objects and performances as inquiries into the fundamental nature of the *provisional*, I wish to make clear that this post-Fluxus work is ordered around the imperative of sensorial pleasure—the sensuousness of objects, texts, and sounds, motivated by the desire of thinking and feeling, in their material forms, a radical displacement of their context and character. The artist emphasizes, in her close investigation and repurposing of things (a broken shoe heel, whirring blenders, tea tins), their sonic possibilities:

> The objects used in my artworks are commonplace, often ephemeral and always change from use. Interactions with the working process happen automatically, the materials *speaking* for themselves. Useful or edited out, all random occurrences are of value. Fragments come together and take shape. It's the same with the physical objects in performances. Each object has its sound *already* existing when I find it.[98]

Among Knowles's later works exploring foodstuffs and sound as a readymade—an already existing aural materiality—is *Onion Skin Song* (1971/2003), a score derived from an earlier work, *Three Songs* (1971–1973; fig. 3.23).[99]

*Onion Skin Song*, also known as "Song #1," was conceived while Knowles was a faculty member at CalArts, living communally in Piru and frequenting local farmers markets. Red, purple, and dark yellow onion carapaces, distributed by chance, are sandwiched between two sheets of Saran Wrap, which volunteers may step on to flatten (crunch, crunch, crunch). The paper-based work involved running this construction through the blueprint machine in the school's Graphics Print Lab, which further pressed the skins, releasing their inky juices. Describing the process, Knowles notes the mechanisms for putting sound and image into contact:

> Once the dials are set the lights and darks of the skins are interpreted and printed by voltage. These change elements, the turning drum changing the position of the skins on the plastic and the crushing action, plus the differing electrical charge[,] I find preferable to the calligraphy I might draw by hand. Musical notation (notes) would not apply as useful here at all as the situation I

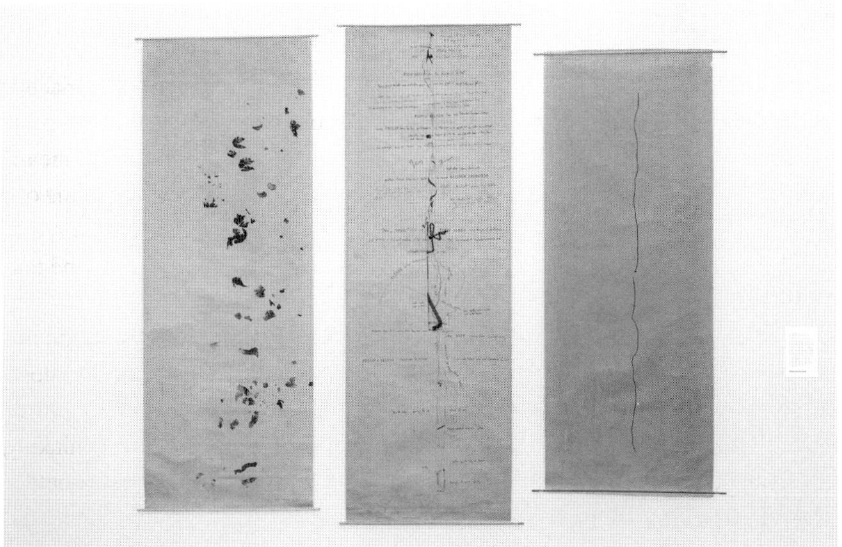

**Figure 3.23.** Alison Knowles, *Onion Skin Song* (1971), from *Three Songs*. Installation view, *Alison Knowles*, Carnegie Museum of Art, Pittsburgh, May 20–October 24, 2016. Photo © 2023 Carnegie Museum of Art, Pittsburgh.

> am interested in [is] this relation of the physical world (the onion skin and how it looks itself) and the world of physical sound derived from it. The interpreter or performer studies these skin patterns and in their lights and darks, breakings and spaces, . . . relates them to his/her own performance capabilities. The resulting performance makes one thing of the print and the sound of it.[100]

The temporal-durational score instructs performers, whatever their instruments, to examine the print or layered object, "mark off sections of time," and "play horizontally or vertically."[101] In the case of *Three Songs*, all can be played at once or in sequence, as Knowles did in 1978 at Franklin Furnace, accompanied by Malcolm Goldstein, who played *Onion Skin Song* on violin, facing a wall on which the sepia print on vellum was stretched horizontally, and allotting one minute of action per onion skin.

In its any of its variations, *Onion Skin Song* offers a meditation on the textures of sound, as the performer works through the "raw material" in order "to find patterns for organizing these 'collections' into life . . . chance always [being] at work in the metamorphosis."[102] Not unlike Marcel Broodthaers's mussels and eggshells, Knowles's onion skins are essentially molds of a formerly contained substance. Not attached to a fixed support, they shift about as the blueprint machine "crushes the skins as it makes the prints":

> The performer works out his own timing and sounding patterns. The attempt is to present the onion skins unobscured by overt literal meaning. His/her performance and my own is exemplary but not definitive. Anyone in the audience might be in the position of performing this piece, and therefore becomes an artist.[103]

I am intrigued by Knowles's rhetorical shift to direct relationality, a feature present in her work since the late 1950s but more pronounced as it relays form toward the (conditional, provisional) experiences of the body. In producing a residue-based graphic notation, the organic fragments in *Onion Skin Song* may act as placeholders for the delicate organ encasing us—human skin, too, flakes and sheds, is both transparent and opaque. This relay between the body's epidermal surface and the minimalist presentation of ambient sounds from the natural world is effectively represented via the body's ability to see, to hear, and to touch. By adding industrially produced polyethylene food wrap and specialized blueprint/vellum supports, Knowles further extends the metaphor to the casings both of meal preparation and preservation and of bodily sustenance and nourishment in capitalist consumption. This continues the conceptual thread first begun in *Make a Salad*, *Bean Rolls*, and *The Identical Lunch* in the 1960s—that is, a multimediated exploration of readymade objects, especially foodstuffs, within the domain of art.[104]

The acoustic realization of the work, consistent with Knowles's dedication to openness and site-contingency, depend on a given performer's manipulation or interpretation of the indeterminate object's chance-based configuration. The immediacy and elegance of this chance relay is discernable to viewing audiences. The speckled plastic assemblage, stretched across the available space, may itself be an instrument, to be handled as the participants choose, or may provide notation for other instruments. What remains of a performance is also uncertain. In addition to documentary photographs, there are residual objects—the onion skins themselves—which the artist often leaves to the spectators to dispense with. Many performances end with trashcans stuffed with erstwhile instruments, but some venues choose to exhibit the leavings as authentic relics.

Knowles fleshes out her critical art practice by incorporating readymade objects from everyday life, allowing for fresh takes by drawing on what is readily accessible in her immediate environment—anything she can find in a local library, on the street outside, in her own pantry, or in the organic distribution systems of the body. The aesthetic of the everyday, pursued by many postwar artists, offers Knowles an avenue of exploration via shared viewing and acting. As with her appropriation of branded corporate products—StarKist Tuna, Saran Wrap, Nivea Cream—repurposing the standardized commodities brings into being a more sensuous realm of consumption and the possibilities inherent in switching between linguistic and material signifiers.

Alternative delivery systems were central to the Fluxus enterprise, and the works Knowles made in its most productive years and since are no exception. *Bean Rolls*, *The Identical Lunch*, *Onion Skin Songs*—all are attuned to the sensorial, biological acts of everyday life and represent a major shift by the artist to an open-ended practice premised on the potential of the found environment and the complexity of objects and rituals that bind the social sphere. Knowles's receptiveness to provisional, unknowable outcomes, then, is no arbitrary formulation but, rather, a politics, a system, a stake in the reception and distribution of meaning. Broadly speaking, her modestly produced canned book of beans and eternally reconceived tuna fish sandwiches, her cataloging of meals and scrutinizing of movements, slow life down, illuminating its mundanities and its intimacies and engendering a rich examination of the institutional and social pressures one negotiates every day.

**BOOKS**

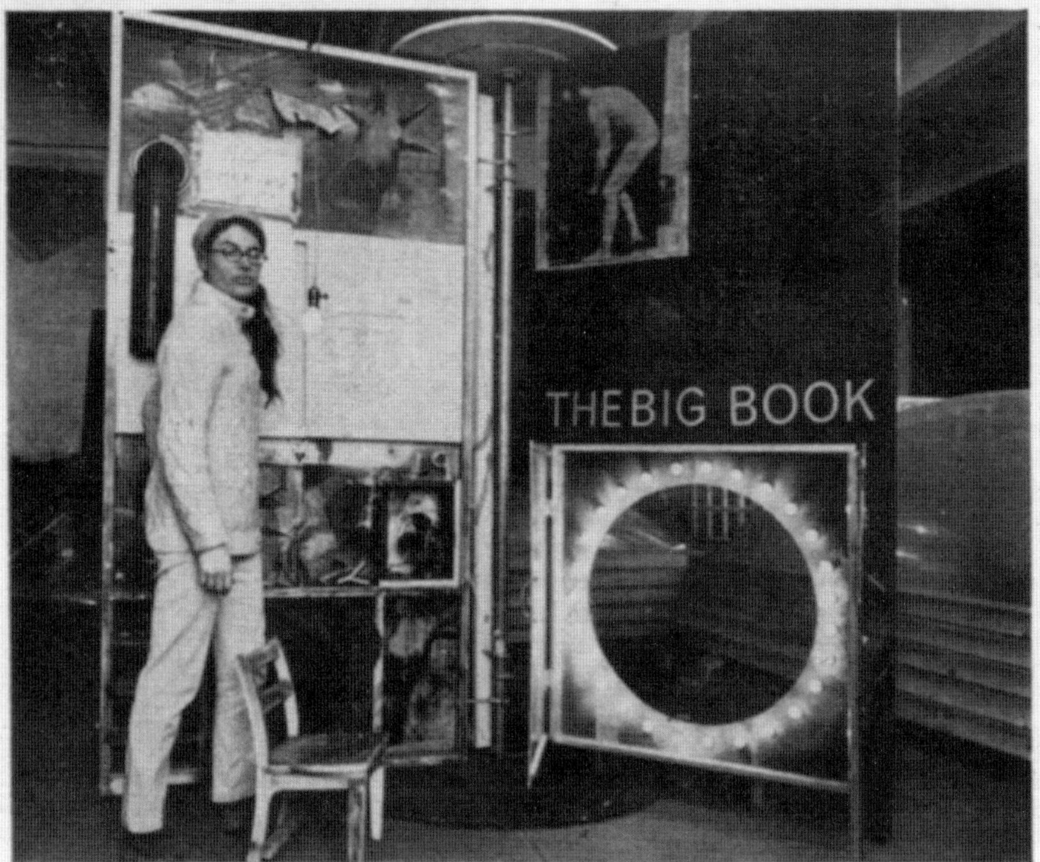


Newsweek—Robert R. McElroy

**Knowles: Reshaping the book for post-literate man**

**Figure 4.1.** Alison Knowles shown with *The Big Book*, *Newsweek*, April 29, 1968. Photo: Robert R. McElroy.

# 4 NOVEL ENVIRONMENTS

[*The Big Book*] is about my life . . . the things I enjoy, things other people enjoy.
**Alison Knowles**[1]

"It's the book we've all been waiting for," declared art critic Howard Junker in 1968, appraising recent artists' publications in the pages of *Newsweek*. The book in question? Alison Knowles's large-scale, mixed-media installation *The Big Book* (1966–1969; fig. 4.1). Tracing a loosely defined trajectory from Marcel Duchamp's *Boîte-en-Valise* (1935–1941) to George Maciunas's compilation of texts and objects for *Fluxkits* (1965–1966; fig. 3.10) to the customized art boxes of conceptually engineered *Aspen* magazine (1965–1971)—Junker extrapolated the century's productive mixing of found objects and multiples into an expanded vision of containment and interactivity. His largely positive review privileged Knowles's work for its material and spatial dislocations, and he approvingly compared her with the high priests of literary modernism: "[Her] radical reshaping of the book format is only the latest effort in an iconoclastic tradition dating back to the century-old suggestion by French symbolist Stéphane Mallarmé that a book-in-a-box could have parts as well as lines."[2]

Noting the imagination undergirding *The Big Book*'s conception and construction, he concluded that the "permissiveness" inherent in the discursive space it opened up was "just what Marshall McLuhan's post-literate man needs to revive his interest in printed matter."[3] Magnifying McLuhan's futurist projection and Mallarmé's liberation of the book from its bindings—in particular, its reliance on conventional page turning, linear narrative, and fixed type—Junker championed Knowles's three-dimensional novel for revivifying the book as a *contemporary* medium. Which is to say, Knowles anticipated the need for new forms of social objects and experiences and so reoriented bookmaking under the vexed conditions of late modernism.

Yet, what was so radical about *The Big Book*? Junker's jaunty description provides a hint:

> 8 feet tall, weight about a ton . . . a 4-foot sleeping tunnel lined with artificial grass. Blinking lights, a tape collage and a film complete the visual impact of this eight-page volume . . . *The Big Book* is, of course, not really a book. It is something else, literally a book-world.[4]

Knowles's multimedia environment was more than a "subversive" redesign of a conventional format; it met, in Junker's view, an urgent need.

The possibility of inhabiting the spatial-temporal conditions of both reading and living, implied in the construction of a "book-world," is this chapter's focus. In shifting to large-scale installations in the later 1960s—a second example, *The House of Dust* (1967–1975; plate 8), is discussed in chapter 5—Knowles modeled a novel form of art making, using the concept of the book and other poetic systems precisely for their pertinence to private, everyday domestic spheres.[5] The methods and activities directing Knowles's earlier works (e.g., chance aesthetics, the notational propositional score, live performance, daily rituals, and foodstuffs) are here expanded to include a consideration of the physical and metaphorical use of the built environment, including the ways in which post–World War II ideas about the home were tacitly gendered and critiqued.

Previous chapters have considered several key works; here, I focus on *The Big Book*, charting the history of its construction and its relation to the demands of Knowles's personal and professional life through meticulous archival research. The first major project that developed her own artistic identity apart from Fluxus, *The Big Book* bridges performance and intermedia with the expansive environment of language. It thus plays on several visual, physical, and phenomenological registers at once: text and texture; use and function; epic literary fantasy and mundane lived reality; corporeal agility and indeterminacy. Adjacent projects and collaborations with John Cage and others from the mid- to late 1960s that fostered an experimental approach to design, notation, and ritual are addressed here, too. One aim in revisiting Knowles's novel environment decades later is to broaden our understanding of the experimentalist spirit during the 1960s and 1970s, while complicating the history, within that narrative, of women's artists' books, especially as they relate to the emerging genres of installation art and post-studio practices. Highlighting Knowles's sustained investigation of the book as an art form and her diverse experiments in language, I conclude by emphasizing how *The Big Book* underscores the cultural anxieties felt, politically and otherwise, in and around the subject of domesticity.

## The Book and the Lived Body

In 1967 Knowles was photographed on the first floor of her Chelsea brownstone, standing next to three opened, oversize "pages" of *The Big Book* (fig. 4.2).[6] Conceptually, *The Big Book* was a material, spatiotemporal manifesta-

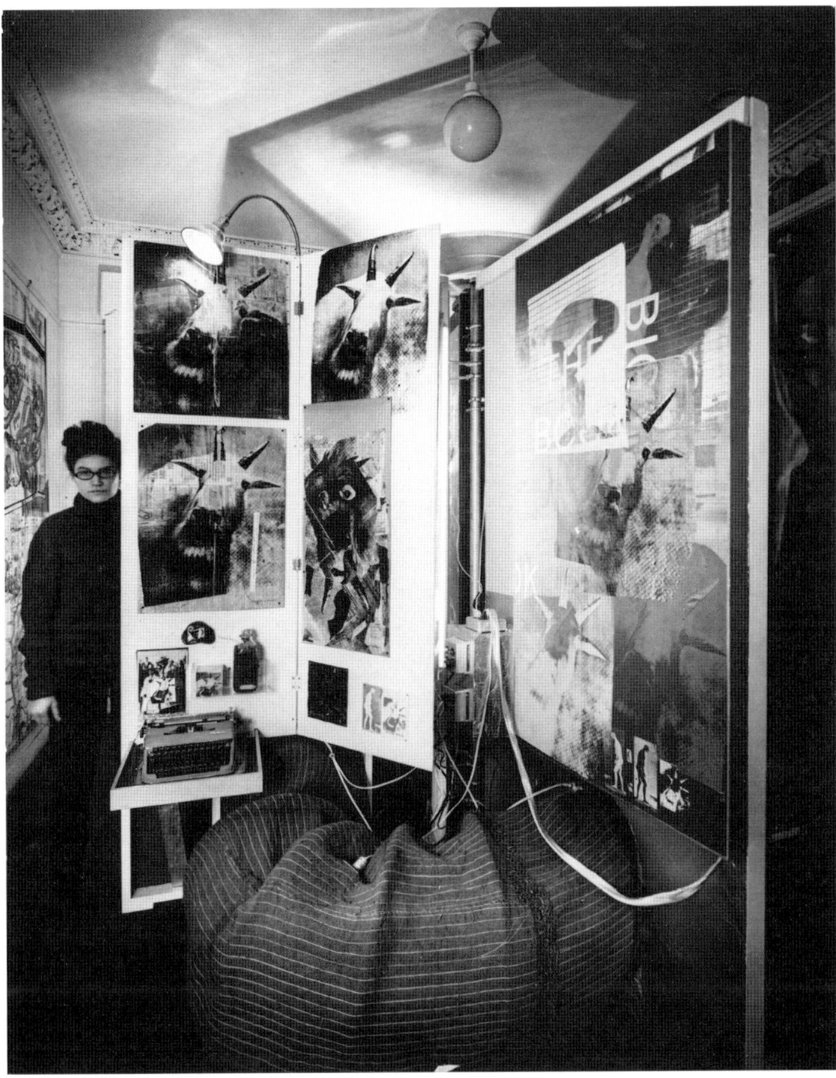

**Figure 4.2.** Alison Knowles activating *The Big Book*, 1966–1969, New York. Photo: Peter Moore, © Northwestern University. Courtesy Staatsgalerie Stuttgart.

tion of what Dick Higgins first described in 1965 as *intermedia*—uncategorized work that occupies the "uncharted land that lies between" recognized artistic mediums.[7] Among the examples he compiled are Cage's experimental compositions, Robert Rauschenberg's Combines, Robert Filliou's assemblages, and Al Hansen's collages and graphic notations.

Knowles issued *The Big Book* as an edition of one, a logical extension of the intermedia concept, under the imprint of her and Higgins's publishing house, Something Else Press (SEP).[8] SEP publications were widely available in Manhattan bookstores, due in no small part to the "mimeograph revolution" instigated by Beat poets and writers in the late 1950s, and Knowles, after *Bean Rolls*, was keen to expand her foray into book-inspired works.[9] As she told Emmett Williams:

> I'd been doing small things for a long time—performance pieces, Fluxus things, small statements, the things collected in *by Alison Knowles*, and I suppose I was looking for something bigger. Bigger, but still impersonal, like my performance pieces. And I got the idea for a big book that would not only incorporate performance pieces but involved everyone who enters it as a performer.[10]

The monumental work, which consumed the artist for almost a year, can be considered a continuation and synthesis of her Fluxus pieces of the early 1960s. Scores such as *Proposition #2: Make a Salad* and *Proposition #3: Nivea Cream Piece* (figs. 2.1, 2.9) offered simple, conceptually flexible "recipes" that could be enacted by anyone at any time; performances, often collaborative, were presented to public audiences but invoked domestic space. Knowles's three-dimensional work went further, creating environmental conditions within which spectators were invited to act. *The Big Book* afforded opportunity for a performance of potentiality—a chance to reread our abilities, our bodies, spaces, and narratives, in (literal) concrete prose.

As she moved from linguistic operations to spatial ones in the 1960s, Knowles remained active in New York's neo-avant-garde, performing, for example, on Canal Street with Ben Vautier (figs. 3.2, 3.3, 3.4, 3.6), and at the Café au Go Go, where she made soup for a sold-out audience (fig. 2.5). For George Brecht and Robert Watts's Yam Day festival at the Smolin Gallery in May 1963, she designed fantastical caps; gamely sported by family and friends (figs. 4.3–4.4), they incorporated "fabulous, whimsical, fairylike materials ranging from found objects to glass. Something to see; something to wear; something to use in your house as sculpture."[11] Her millinery contribution included arranging for multiple artists to make hats, which she suspended from the ceiling using picture wire, as well as a "hat bulletin board" for trying them on—another in-

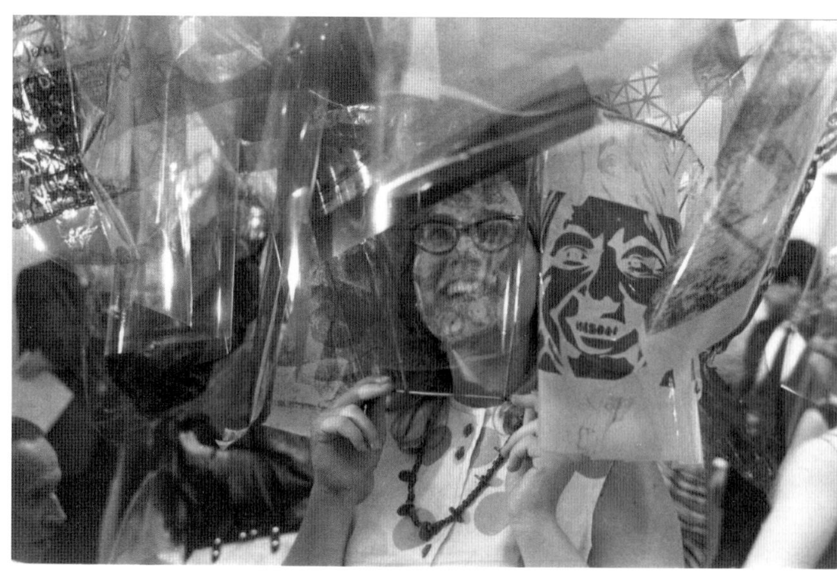

**Figure 4.3.** Dick Higgins's sister Lisa Higgins Null wearing one of Alison Knowles's imaginative hats for the Yam Hat Sale, Smolin Gallery, Yam Festival, New York, May 1963. Photo: Peter Moore, © Northwestern University.

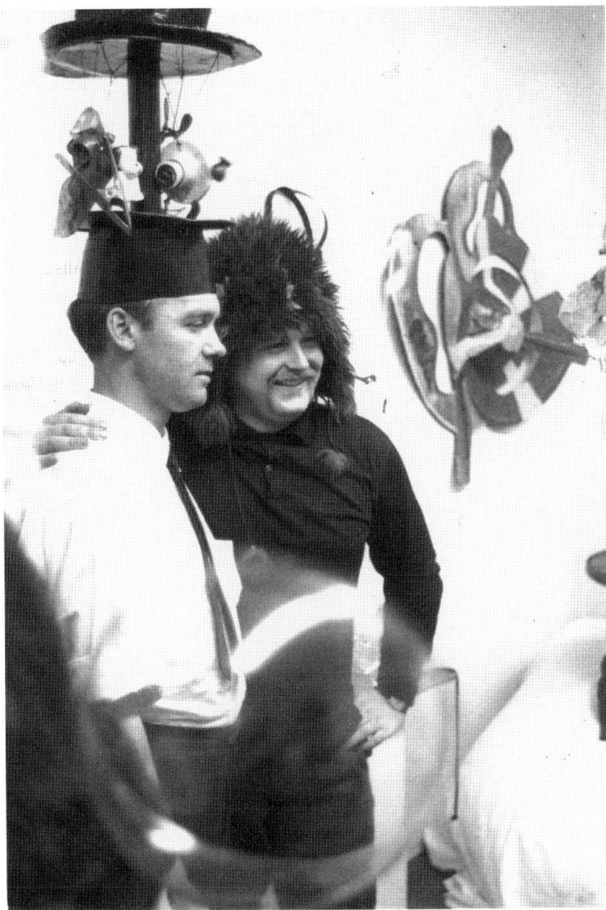

**Figure 4.4.** Al Hansen and Wolf Vostell wearing Alison Knowles's imaginative hats for the Yam Hat Sale, Smolin Gallery, Yam Festival, New York, May 1963. Photo: Peter Moore, © Northwestern University.

stance of playful artworks installed with sensitivity to specific environmental considerations.[12]

It was in this richly collaborative context that Knowles initiated *The Big Book*. As noted by Junker, the installation was a veritable world, replete with text and all manner of material: silk-screen prints, a chalkboard, a guest book that accumulated entries in a dozen languages, found images and objects, mirrors, a blueprint of a ship.[13] Framed in wood, mounted on casters, and bound to a steel spine, each page could be removed and freestanding, although Knowles's intention was always that viewers be "part of a total experience," going through the assembled environment.[14] Upon first seeing the work—in the artist's living room (fig. 4.5)—Jan van der Marck, director and chief curator of Chicago's Museum of Contemporary Art, discerned its corporeal lived-inness: "the door-size pages create compartments which function, literally, as rooms of a house, metaphorically as 'stills' of everyday existence, and metaphysically as nooks and crannies of the mind."[15] Friend and art historian William (Bill) Wilson viewed *The Big Book* as presenting "the processes of life nonchalantly," noting a visual parallel to unpretentious Manhattan loft living

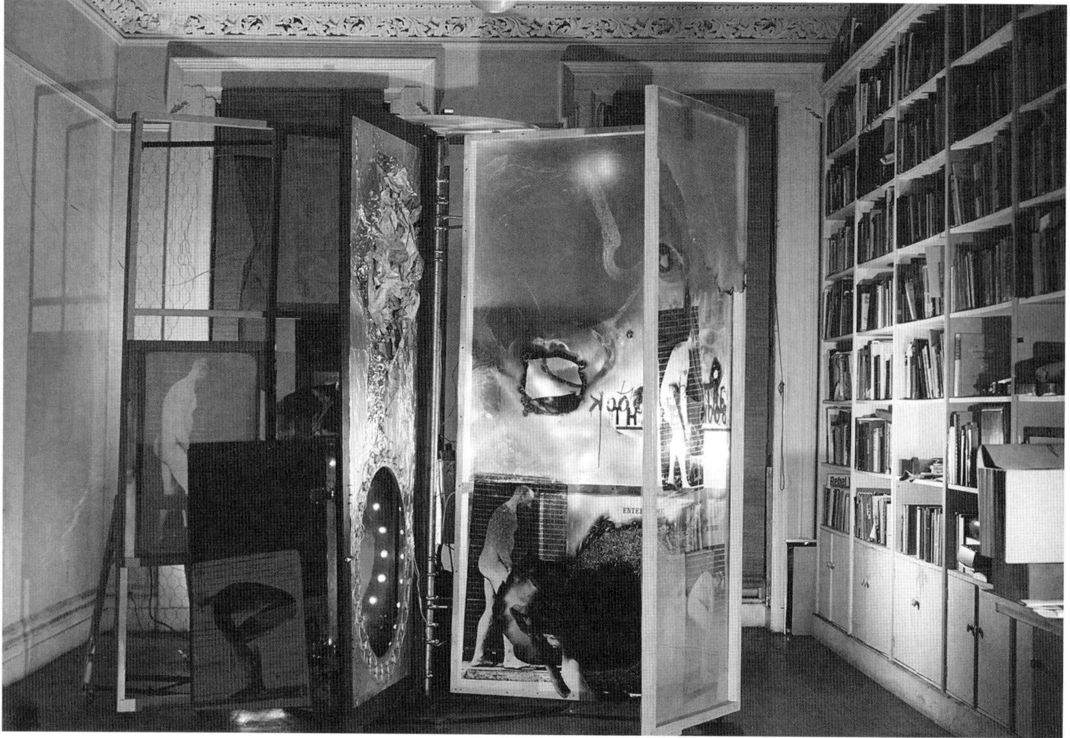

**Figure 4.5.** Alison Knowles, *The Big Book*, 1966–1969, New York. Photographer unknown.

of the late 1950s that in accepting "this mundane, workaday underworld has the effect of elevating it."[16] Knowles had anticipated such a reading in her explanation of the environment: "I don't want to drag the reader through the book simply on my own terms. I want [everyone] to see and hear enough of the pages and their background to know what it's really all about . . . Maybe having done *The Big Book* is better than going through it but offering it to others as a performance piece is the best I can do."[17]

Mixing up traditional forms was precisely Van der Marck's intention. He included *The Big Book* among the sixty-eight works by twelve artists in *Pictures to Be Read/Poetry to Be Seen* and claimed as their antecedent Marcel Duchamp's confounding of the boundaries of painting and sculpture with *The Bride Stripped Bare by Her Bachelors, Even* (1915–1923).[18] He thus sketched a formal and conceptual lineage linking innovative art of the later 1960s—with all its seemingly illegible forms and "far out" provocations—to the historical avant-garde.[19] Within the show, Van der Marck proclaimed, you could find "the same attitude of combined attachment and detachment on the part of the artist, the same irreverent attitude toward the idea of art as precious and unique, the same delight in destroying conventional meanings and substituting new or counter meanings for them, and the same attack on our intellectual and perceptual faculties."[20]

In fact, Knowles's installation was specifically situated between readymade

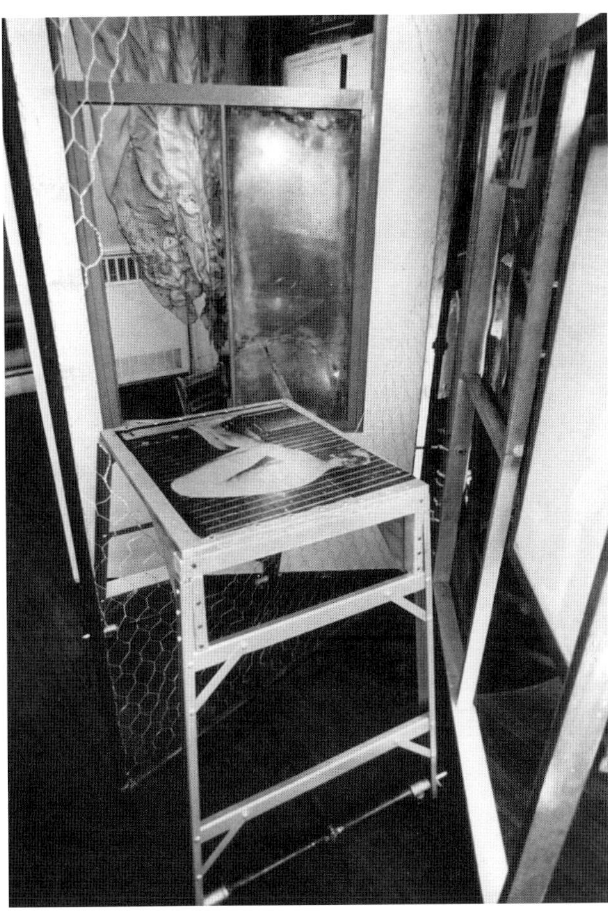

**Figure 4.6.** Alison Knowles, *The Big Book*, 1966–1969, New York (detail of stepladder). Photo: Peter Moore, © Northwestern University.

objects and the performances (and architectures) of everyday life. We see this in the wheeled stepladder affixed to the structure, which supplied the viewer-reader with a precarious tool for climbing in and out of doors, windows, and tunnels (fig. 4.6). Knowles mailed copies of a mountain-goat print she found in the New York Public Library photo collection to artist friends, who "collaged it, cut it up, bottled it, etc., and sent it back to make up the goat gallery"— one of *The Big Book*'s pages (plate 1).[21] The book also included functional items and spaces for living: a working kitchen, a telephone, an electrical system, a library with books and a typewriter, a medicine cabinet, and an artificial-grass burrow, lit by twinkle lights, that could double as a garden or a bed (fig. 4.7).[22] As art critic Harold Rosenberg wrote after the installation's MCA premiere, "It is practical: to make sure that art does not cut one off from life, there is a telephone in it on which one can call the office or the babysitter."[23] *The Big Book* also contained a chemical toilet but no formalized waste or disposal system—a slightly anarchic gesture that hinted at the ultimately utopian impossibility of dwelling in the space for long.

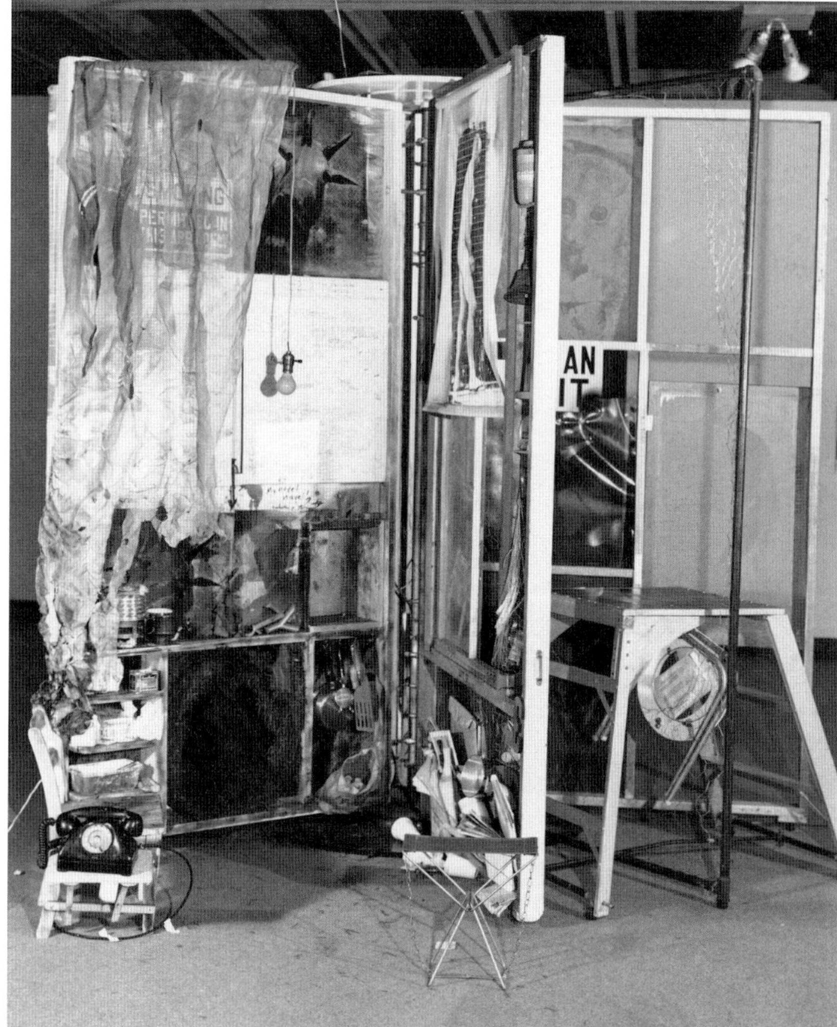

**Figure 4.7.** Alison Knowles, *The Big Book*, 1966–1969. Installation view, *Fluxus/The Big Book*, University Art Gallery (UCSD), February 12–March 22, 1969. Photo: John F. Waggaman. Courtesy Special Collections & Archives, UC San Diego Library.

*The Big Book*'s cover offered a literal portal—a circular hole surrounded by lights (fig. 4.8)—and throughout the book, signs and arrows directed the reader toward points for entry and egress. Navigating the environment—climbing or crawling through the moving vertical frames that served as doors and windows—required some flexibility and dexterity. The unperforated portions of the pages were made of vinyl sheeting, some transparent, some opaque, which, like the partitions in Allan Kaprow's *18 Happenings in 6 Parts* (1959), allowed only hints of what would be revealed on the other side. The pages were variously covered with painted and penciled murals, collages, scraps of paper, and, most intriguingly, frames from one of Eadweard Muybridge's chronophotographic studies of human and animal motion, silk-screened by Knowles as negative and positive images.

To make his now-iconic images, Muybridge developed a complex system of

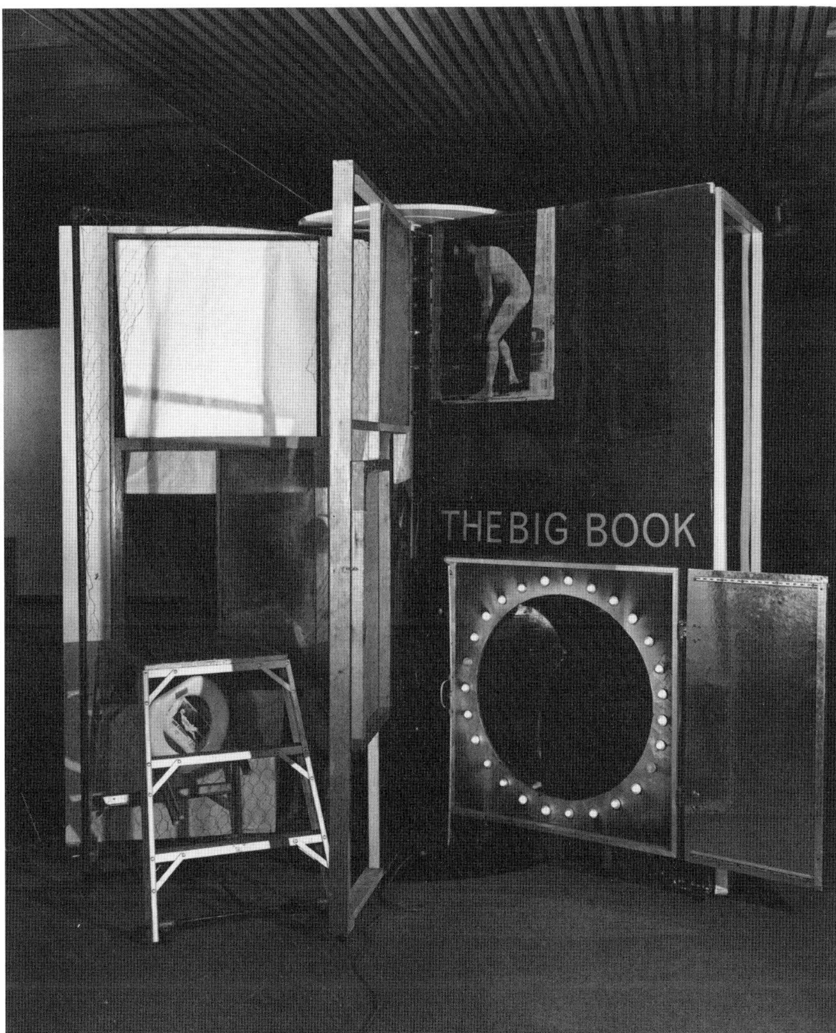


**Figure 4.8.** Alison Knowles, *The Big Book*, 1966–1969. Installation view, Pollock Gallery, Toronto, 1967. Photo: John F. Waggaman. Courtesy Special Collections & Archives, UC San Diego Library.

electromagnetic shutters that, triggered in sequence, captured freeze frames simultaneously from three perspectives (profile, front three-quarter, and rear three-quarter).[24] The human studies depict nude figures carrying out a specified action: men are typically pictured at work (as blacksmiths, bricklayers, etc.) or in sporting activities (baseball, cricket); women, performing domestic tasks (cleaning, washing) or self-presenting in passive or erotic poses. Many of Muybridge's models were, indeed, known for their depicted activity.

From Muybridge's hundreds of studies, undertaken at the University of Pennsylvania between 1884 and 1887, Knowles selected plate 382, which depicts a nude male figure lifting a log (fig. 4.9), and specifically the first five frames of the profile sequence. Including these images in *The Big Book* invokes the role photographic technologies played in visualizing and reorganizing notions of time, duration, and the body in the late nineteenth century. But

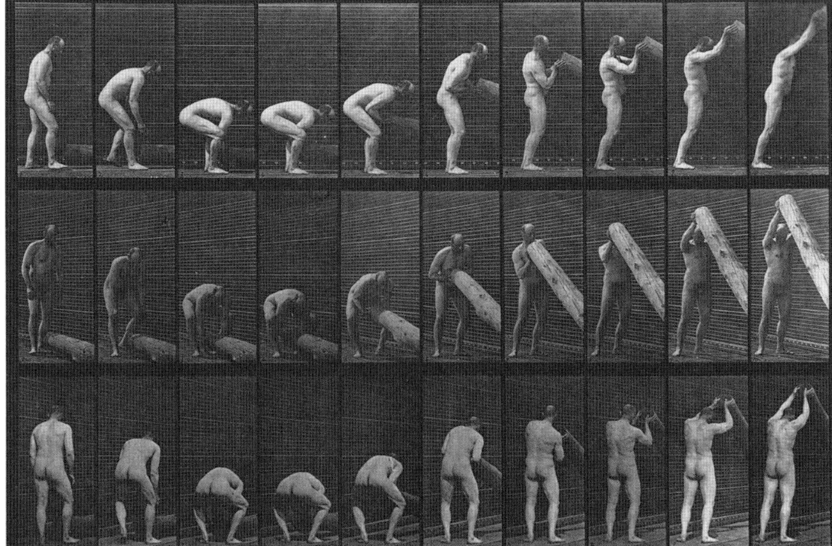

**Figure 4.9.** Eadweard Muybridge, *Lifting a log on end*, plate 382 from *Animal Locomotion: An Electro-Photographic Investigation of Consecutive Phases of Animal Movements* (1887).

Knowles also arranged them to mimic the body of the reader as they traveled through the installation: "continuing by beginning again . . . standing, bending down in different sizes for different occasions . . . one at a time, lighting your own way through."[25] Emmett Williams, Knowles's close friend and fellow Fluxus member, recalls the "ever-present naked gentlemen whose changing gestures ape one's own" (fig. 4.10).[26] Extending the droll cross-referencing of items in and around *The Big Book*, Muybridge's naked gentlemen appeared as well in the shape of the cookies Knowles placed in the kitchen next to coffee, headache remedies, and cigarettes.[27]

Reviewing the installation in *Art in America*, Bill Wilson cited Muybridge's man as exemplary of the "extended metaphors that, through repetition and metamorphosis from page to page, optically parallel the activities of the viewer-reader-performer."[28] Williams attested to Knowles's plan for a *Big Book* trilogy. Volume 2, *The Big BIG Book*, would be a monumental outdoor sculpture, ten times the size of the first installation, with a towering forty-foot ladder, "a real waterfall on page 2," and "an elevator running up the edge of another page."[29] Volume 3, an eighty-foot cast bronze. A vision merging environmental sculpture and post-studio practice, among other conceptual innovations, *The Big BIG Book* presciently anticipates the monumentalized activities of Land artists to come.

Wilson, Van der Marck, Marshall McLuhan, and others first saw *The Big Book* in situ on the first floor of Knowles and Higgins's New York home (figs. 4.2, 4.5).[30] Some of its precursors, including a found-object sculpture and the paintings *Mother, or the Great Train Robbery* (fig. 1.8) and *Untitled* (fig. 1.9), reappeared in spring 1966 in *Object Poems*, the first of three exhibitions organized by Higgins in that very space, under the name Something Else Gallery

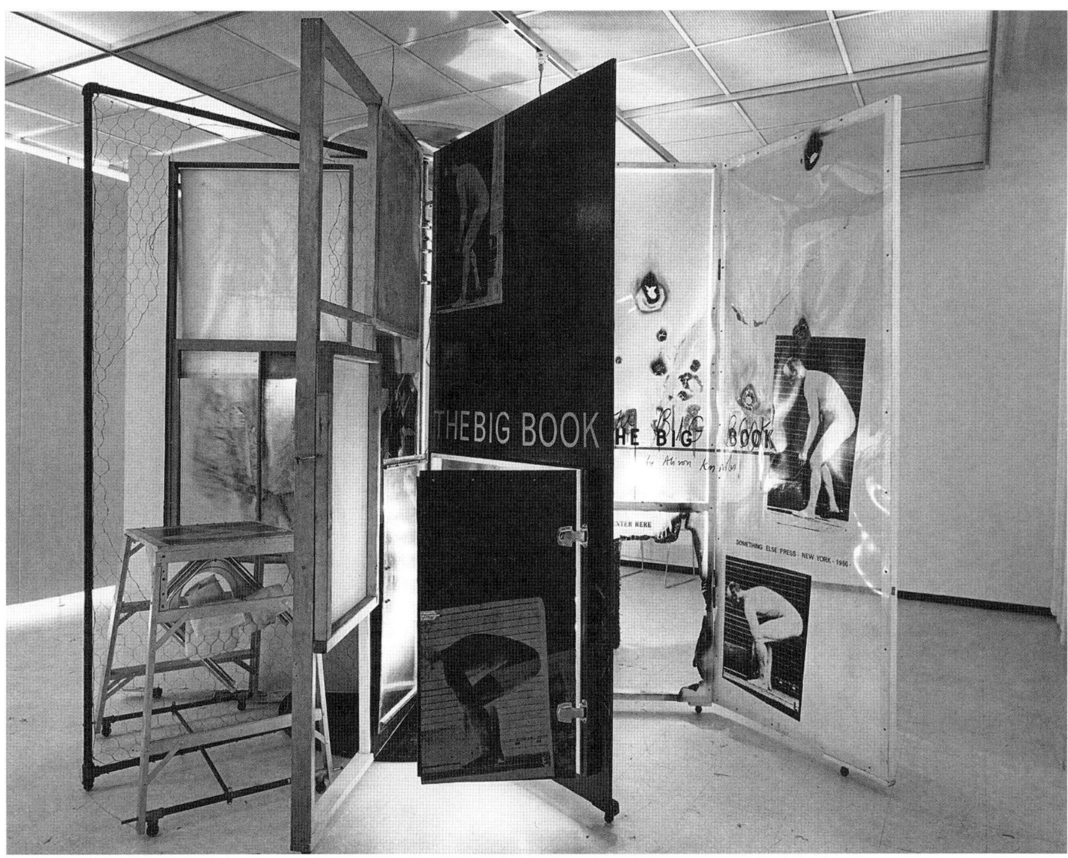


**Figure 4.10.** Alison Knowles, *The Big Book*, 1966–1969. Installation view, *Pictures to Be Read/ Poetry to Be Seen*, Museum of Contemporary Art, Chicago, 1967. Photo: Dan Van Riper, © MCA Chicago.

(SEG). *New York Times* art critic Grace Glueck reviewed the show, along with Something Else Press's publishing list, deeming the efforts among the "farthest out" at that time.[31] It is unsurprising that exhibitions of unusual work in a private residence might arouse some suspicion. Viewers encountered, for example, small kinetic objects they could interact with, self-playing mechanical instruments/sculptures (by electronic composer Joe Jones), screen-printed shirts, and large paintings that may or may not be part of the shows (both produced by Knowles).[32] Other visual artists, designers, and architects were also, in the mid- to late 1960s, positing affinities between their own unorthodox works and the activities and aesthetics of radical and psychedelic countercultural groups—including the antiwar and environmental movements. Glueck's astute but caustic reaction acknowledges an anxiety (and excitement) tied not just to the transdisciplinary forms emerging at SEG but contemporaneous manifestations like the art collective USCO's use of stroboscopes in its mid-1960s mixed-media performances, or Andy Warhol's psychedelic Exploding Plastic Inevitable.[33]

This (small) book opened with a journalist's photograph of Knowles working her way through *The Big Book* at a press preview for its showing in Chicago (fig. I.1). "She's close in something that's far out," the caption read. "Contemporary art such as 'The Big Book' here has creator, Alison Knowles, very much a part of it today at museum given over to display of controversial exhibits." It's almost comical. Colored lights and audio loops notwithstanding, Knowles's book environment could scarcely be called psychedelic. That it's nevertheless termed "far out" and "controversial" speaks to unease with the artist's reimagining the handheld book as large-scale sculpture, so defying the norms of each form.[34] Not to mention explicitly inducing her audience into theatrical modes of passage. As she artfully told Rosenberg, "No two people enjoy a hole in the same way."[35]

We can imagine *The Big Book* striking a nerve with formalist critics like Michael Fried, who in 1967 railed in the pages of *Artforum* against the increasingly theatrical nature of minimalist works, or what he pejoratively called simple "objects" that abandoned "presentness" and "grace," affecting nothing more than "objecthood."[36] In its blunt, interactive presentation of readymade domestic objects, *The Big Book* carried out (intentionally or not) rhetorical and formal shifts then being realized in three-dimensional art making. It echoed, as well, another contemporaneous model: the commune—low-tech, crafty, post-studio, "live-in work[s] of art" like Drop City.[37]

The experimental, intermedia quality of Knowles's installation may, however, be most emphatic in its extensive use of *electronic* media. *The Big Book* was wired for sound, an accompaniment that adds to the sense of real-world familiarity and brings to the fore studio and domestic labors that would otherwise not be registered. A two-channel audio collage made during the work's construction includes sounds of hammering and sawing and stretching silk screens, plus pop songs that were playing on the radio. On one track, muffled voices of the artist's twin daughters, Hannah and Jessica, can be heard, asking if they can come in and play.[38] On another, Knowles gives a detailed lesson on silk-screen printing and the "four basic types of graphic production."[39] In a contemporaneous interview with Wilson, Knowles affirmed that the tape juxtaposes, on separate channels, the sounds of rain from a spring thunderstorm hitting her studio windows and of silk screens being washed in the stainless-steel sink as her twins played nearby.[40]

Collaborating on the "big book music" with her friend the minimalist composer Steve Reich, Knowles imagined an endless tape loop that would play on a specialized device, with no need for rewinding, for each gallery presentation.[41] This sound track goes beyond the often hermetic and self-referential conceptualist strategies current in the early 1960s art world—as in Robert Morris's *Box with the Sound of Its Own Making* (1961). Capturing scenes from her life to be exhibited publicly served less to elevate domestic care or necessary studio labors to the status of fine art, as other artists of the era had sought to do, but—in an inventive lateral move that related directly to her interest in chance and indeterminacy—to acknowledge quotidian source material as already of equal value.

To move through the pages of *The Big Book* is to enter a visual, spatial, and sonic adventure, wherein the reader become one of the book's characters and coauthors. As Knowles puts it, "Going from page to page is very much like character development in the novel, only in this case . . . anyone who enters the book becomes part of the table of contents, just like the tunnel of grass, the electric fan and the bed." As with *Bean Rolls*, albeit on a larger scale, "each entrant participates by selecting his or her own experience."[42] To live and read among its pages—negotiating its ladder, tunnel, and windows was difficult, almost torturous. Nevertheless, the work's signal aesthetic achievement is the imaginative dwelling space it creates for its viewer-reader-inhabitants. We see this vividly in another of Wilson's descriptions of his encounter with *The Big Book*:

> This underworld, such as an epic hero usually enters, presents the processes of life nonchalantly, without varnish, for acceptance. The acceptance leads (led me) through the window of the apartment and up a short ladder, which I read to mean that when the apartment was felt to be sufficient, it ceased to be an underworld and became a means toward elevation. Others who read the *Big Book*, who take this journey through metaphors, will be on a different quest and will arrive at different goals, but necessarily while they are in the *Big Book* they will be as mobile, kinetic, audial, visual energetic, and beautiful as it is.[43]

Wilson's language is wonderfully expressive and specific: the "journey of metaphors," resulting in a "different quest" and "different goals" for each user, encapsulates the chance-based, site-specific, multimediated, visionary world Knowles wanted her readers to occupy. As an act of architectural displacement, *The Big Book* reformatted and unfolded lived domestic space into an exteriorized view. The interior was turned out, its daily, private operations publicly revealed. That the environment was mobile and adaptable (the pages/doors/walls could be moved and re-moved) proposed a new sense of the design of the home *as book*—perhaps even an advertisement or text of a person's life to be openly read and consumed by others.

In another way, *The Big Book* presents a literary and material reconsideration of Lewis Carroll's *Alice's Adventures in Wonderland* (1865), which imagines the exploits of a protagonist who enters through a mysterious hole. As installed in Chicago, each of *The Big Book*'s eight vinyl pages (some with additional layered sections) offered horizontal and vertical passageways that portended descent or ascent, including the ladder to access the library of books. The structure, with each page, on casters, turning on a galvanized-steel spine, represented a mode of thinking and living, much as language itself (including narratives, stories, and tall tales) acts through the constancy of change. Like *Alice's Adventures in Wonderland*, Knowles's book-world implies contingencies of place and structure, open to a critique of the routines of life (teatime, chores, etc.), and to furtive pursuits.

Knowles expressly conceived of *The Big Book* as a literary form—a three-dimensional novel-environment—that activates a definitive structure of experience: a set of characters, in the guise of agile readers, prompted by a sequence of events to negotiate the pages of the book, reaches a climax (coming out the other side) that resolves a plot specific to each individual performer. The installation, as an unfolding, fragmentary story of domestic living, can never be fully ascertained, as with Jorge Luis Borges's enigmatic story "The Library of Babel" (1962), where the library is the universe disguised and life and death, time and space, collide: "Everything: the minutely detailed history of the future . . . the true story of your death, the translation of every book in all languages, the interpolations of every book in all books . . . the library is unlimited and cyclical."[44] *The Big Book* shares with Borges's story a systematic rejection of linearity in favor of multiple temporalities, viewpoints, experiences, and epistemologies. This was not a place to elicit one specific author's textual meaning; rather, author-reader nexus is displaced in favor of unforeseen, indeterminate relationships. Again, Knowles sought to make, not just "something bigger," but an experience for "everybody who enters it as a performer."[45] As such, *The Big Book* is unlimited.

*The Big Book*'s construction contained a central paradox: the structure was so heavy that the book, for all its moving parts, could not readily be closed. Unlike, for example, Duchamp's *Boîte-en-Valise* editions, mobile collections of artworks recast as miniatures, Knowles's object-installation-environment-text needed to be physically stationary—whether experienced at home as a private playground for the artist's daughters or in a gallery, book fair, or other public site. *The Big Book* might be "far out" in terms of the formal expectations for three-dimensional artworks or books, but it could never fully "drop out" of the determinative experiences of reception and activation.

*The Big Book* thus exemplifies the experimentalist preoccupations and tendencies of its time, often referred to as "hippie modernism," wherein ecology, new media, communal living, sensorial aesthetics, and more, offered a novel way to navigate and negotiate the social body through participatory architecture.[46] Now-canonical projects fitting this profile include Buckminster Fuller–inspired DIY domes, the work of Reyner Banham and Archigram, Ant Farm's pneumatic structures, and Barry Shapiro's handmade "woodbutchers houses."[47] In Knowles's *The Big Book*, I want to suggest, this play between mobility and structural fixity might be understood as an implicit critique of domestic space that proposes more than the material conditions of living; that is, more than an apparatus of provisions for the necessities of pure survival.

## Feminist Spaces

In 1963, the year Knowles created *Bean Rolls* (plate 5), her first book-object, and three years before she began constructing *The Big Book*, the feminist-activist writer Betty Friedan published *The Feminine Mystique*, a critique of the repressive conditions of the post–World War II North American home. Urging readers to speak out against the "problem that has no name," Friedan rejected patriarchal social laws that restricted (predominantly white) women to the domestic sphere, analyzed notions of patriarchal authority in terms of Freudian "family romances," and set the home as *the* rhetorical and spatial site in which those conventions could be challenged by second-wave feminists.[48] The purportedly "happy housewife," Friedan and others argued, was in fact imprisoned by her home and family obligations, denied speech, economic independence, and political agency.

Extending Friedan's articulation of women's repression from the private to the geopolitical sphere, architectural historian Beatriz Colomina has shown how, after World War II, "expertly designed images of domestic bliss" were grounded in new forms of domestic architecture. "Launched to the entire world as part of a carefully orchestrated propaganda campaign," it proved powerful, explicitly nationalist visual weapons, ostensibly in support of democracy.[49] In the context of homemade nuclear fallout shelters and feminist reevaluations of the domestic sphere, Knowles's *Big Book* environment seemed to insinuate the need, in a moment of personal and political crisis, for self-sufficiency and an abundance of supplies. Knowles's shift from small, handheld objects and isolated performances to large-scale environments required viewers' active participation and attention to anxieties surrounding the home, and enacted these realities in an elaborate performance of the imaginary book-as-world.

Accordingly, we may envision *The Big Book* as an invitation to a complex multimedia adventure in the artist's own private space. As Philippa Tristram notes in her study correlating the rise of the novel with the English manor in the eighteenth century, "Novels *and* houses furnish a dwelling place—a spatial construct—that invites the exploration and expression of private and intimate relations and thoughts."[50] Knowles's installation is less an homage to some perceived feminine role as steward or protectress of the home than an analogue of Virginia Woolf's "room of one's own." The objects Knowles assembled speak to a way of living (her books, her tools, her curatorial bent) that would enable one to survive (at least symbolically) in the makeshift home without the support of a man or the structure of a heteronormative family. Shortly after completing the book's first iteration, she was asked about its deeply personal nature. Knowles responded thoughtfully:

> [*The Big Book*] is about my life . . . the things I enjoy, things other people enjoy. It's about grass, for instance. The tunnel you just crawled through was covered with grass and you still got some on you. So it's about grass and *psychological* activity. It's about lighting your way through the book, one person at a time. It's about settling down comfortably inside these pages for a while, disturbing the dust, breathing deeply on the Vick's inhaler, taking an aspirin, writing a letter, pulling down the shade and dozing. It's about going through the holes. . . . There's more than one way to eat an onion. These things are not merely represented, the things themselves are there, and the book is about

> these things and getting *involved* in them. Reading about coffee is different from crawling into a book and heating yourself a cup. The things in the book are one for one relationships.[51]

The experiential component of lived experience (in the form of reading) is here monumentalized as an all-encompassing phenomenon. The power of books, Knowles seems to imply, lies in their encouraging not merely literary explorations of time and space but also self-discovery. The scenes and zones of living staged in *The Big Book* were thus potential sites for an acquisition of self-knowledge predicated on a kind of experience that was felt not only spatially but in relation to the desires, habits, and capacities of one's body.

We might compare Knowles's invocation of the book as site of artistic and personal transformation with an earlier vanguard effort, Russian Constructivist Varvara Stepanova's play *An Evening of the Book* (1924). Stepanova's interest in graphic advertising and narrative publication design was cultivated in collaborations with her partner Aleksandr Rodchenko, including a suite of woodcut engravings depicting the film star and director Charlie Chaplin and over a hundred book and journal projects.[52] *An Evening of the Book in the Clubs of Youth (An Experiment in the Mass Artistic Agitation for the Book)*, part of a multimedia campaign promoting visual and textual literacy among everyday Russians, featured a script by filmmaker Vitalii Zhemchuzhnyi that "presented a conflict between heroes of old pre-Revolutionary and new revolutionary [eras]"—with characters stepping in and out of Stepanova's bold set design, "a spatial image of the book" that, in effect, presented literacy itself as "a tangible material object."[53] Black-and-white photographs documenting the performance show "the hero of each book" (costumed variously in a gingham hat, a long white beard, a moss-covered cloak) standing between the gigantic book's spread pages. Other, more widely published pictures show a line of female students, uniformed in Stepanova's geometrically designed sports clothing, engaged in synchronized maneuvers during the play's intermission.[54]

While Stepanova's installation appears minimalist in comparison with Knowles's object-filled assemblage, and Knowles's was less theatrical, and certainly less overtly political, than Stepanova's, the artists shared the idea that in monumentalizing the book's very architecture one might conjure both a public world where revolutionary forces triumph over the status quo and a private, domestically scaled space where disparate fictions cohabit. Reorienting familial space as an object and experience to be read and considered outside the home, Knowles's *Big Book* is, to me, clearly protofeminist in at least one concrete sense: It excavates and affords attention and value to the private sphere while magnifying the intimate rituals of reading/living in all its material and aesthetic potential. The readymade-filled environment of *The Big Book* destabilizes traditional boundaries of domesticity by providing a real space to be lived in but also mobilizing a "different kind of space"—a space for the female body and her discursive interaction between body and house.[55]

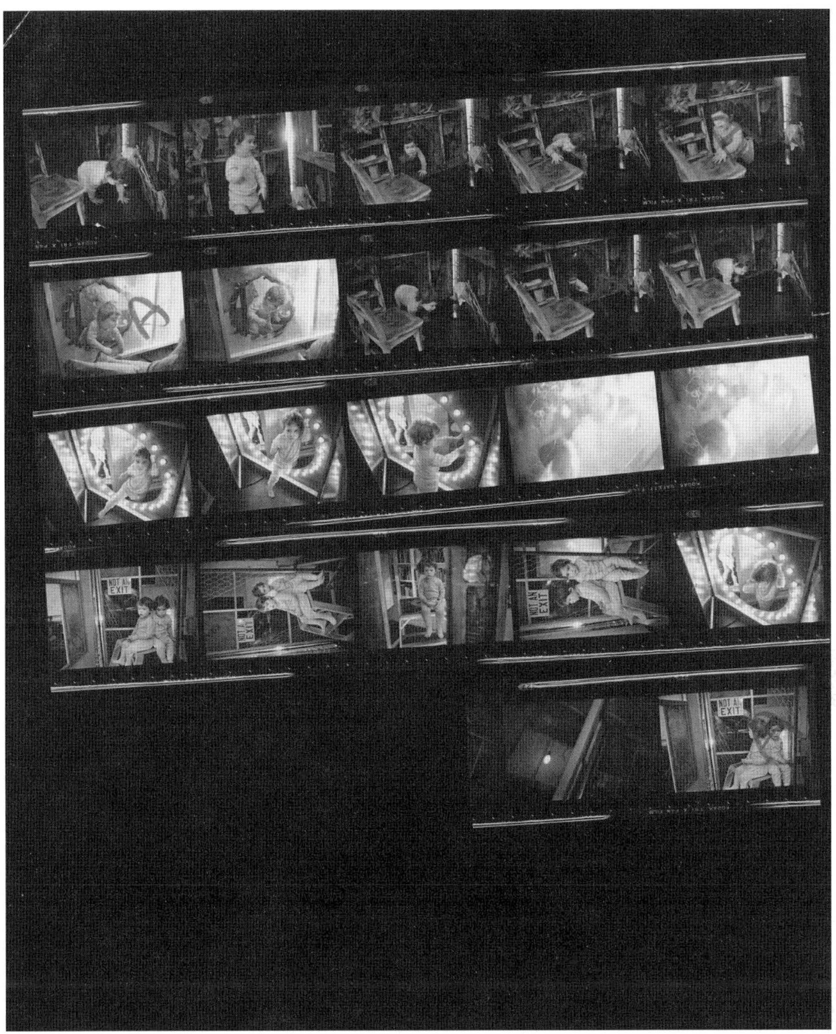

**Figure 4.11.** Photographic contact sheet by Peter Moore, ca. 1967–1968, showing Alison Knowles, *The Big Book*, and Jessica and Hannah Higgins playing. Photos: Peter Moore, © Northwestern University. Courtesy Dick Higgins Archive, Charles Deering McCormick Library of Special Collections, Northwestern University.

Indeed, Knowles collaborated with Higgins on a short 16mm film of *The Big Book* soon after its initial conceptualization, as she was in the midst of assembling it in their home.[56] The two artists are shown (separately) walking and working among its pages, seen from a variety of perspectives in framings from extreme close-up to wide-angle. A later filmed version shows one of their twins, Jessica, gleefully "reading" the book (fig. 4.11). As Rosenberg perceptively notes, "Here art has become so thoroughly entwined with life that one wonders whether life has anything left for itself. And, too, whether a work so personally *lived* is to any degree accessible to strangers, even if one should move in."[57] The merging of built space with zones of private interiority and public exhibition links biological and social concerns within dense webs of signification. At their densest, these become the *graph* or signature of the body and her labor in the architectures of house and body. Knowles's material expression of dwelling implores the reader to attend to the ways the space itself is inherently gendered. What she stages for her audience is a reconfiguration of hearth and home, of public and private, revealing not only the blandly familiar but the utterly strange in reconsideration of the reading experience.

These encounters were also possible because *The Big Book*, as a book, and unlike some other immersive installations, was portable, or at least itinerant. From Knowles's New York home/studio it traveled in 1967 to the Jack Pollock Gallery in Toronto, the Museum of Contemporary Art in Chicago, and the Art Library in the Nikolaj Kirke in Copenhagen; in 1968, to the Frankfurter Buchmesse, at the invitation of publishers Walther and Kasper König; and in 1969 to the University of California, San Diego, where it was presented as a solo installation in conjunction with a Fluxus group show (organized by David Antin with Pat Baxter) and Flux-Concert by Pauline Oliveros; and, finally, back to New York, where it was included in *Superlimited: Books, Boxes and Things* at the Jewish Museum (fig. 4.12).[58] With each change of venue, *The Big Book* materially transformed—parts were purloined, broken, left behind, discarded, added, or substituted. "You were clearly involved when there was still some grass in the tunnel," Knowles wrote to Ken Friedman in July 1967. "As objects are stolen and hot plates no longer heat, we will have here a one-hoss-shay. I contemplate a book burning."[59] Some, but not all, iterations of *The Big Book* showcased Knowles's collaged sound track, the "big book music." Through it all, the installation remained materially active and dynamic; indeed, its changeability foregrounded the possibility for narrative mutability and destruction. Shortly after its last public presentation at The Jewish Museum, the multipart work collapsed under its own weight, undone by the ravages of travel and poorly packed shipping crates.[60] Subsequent displays were limited to a few resilient pages. Knowles did not have space to store *The Big Book*. And when she moved to California in 1970, she signaled, as with her paintings in the early 1960s, that she was "finished" with it.[61] She allowed the work to be stripped down, and set many of its components out on a street in NYC to be taken away by passersby or trash collectors.

Knowles's disregard of the barriers that separate art, literature, and life led to her inclusion in *Pictures to Be Read/Poems to Be Seen* at the MCA in Chicago. In his catalog essay, curator Jan van der Marck argued that the works he'd selected document "the fusion between the literary, pictorial and performing arts."[62] Accordingly, the poetry on view, consisting mainly of "found words," was conceptually similar to the collaged pictures and found-object assemblage. Two of the artists, Knowles and Allan Kaprow, installed works to be performed (or, in Duchamp's formulation, "completed") by spectators' active participation.[63] Kaprow's environment, *Words* (fig. 4.13), first presented in 1962 in New York City, was divided at the MCA into two square rooms. The walls of one were plastered with dissociated words, while others, barely audible, played on phonographs. Visitors were provided strips of paper on which to write what they liked and staple guns to add them to the installation. In the other room, they could paperclip messages to paper streamers hanging from

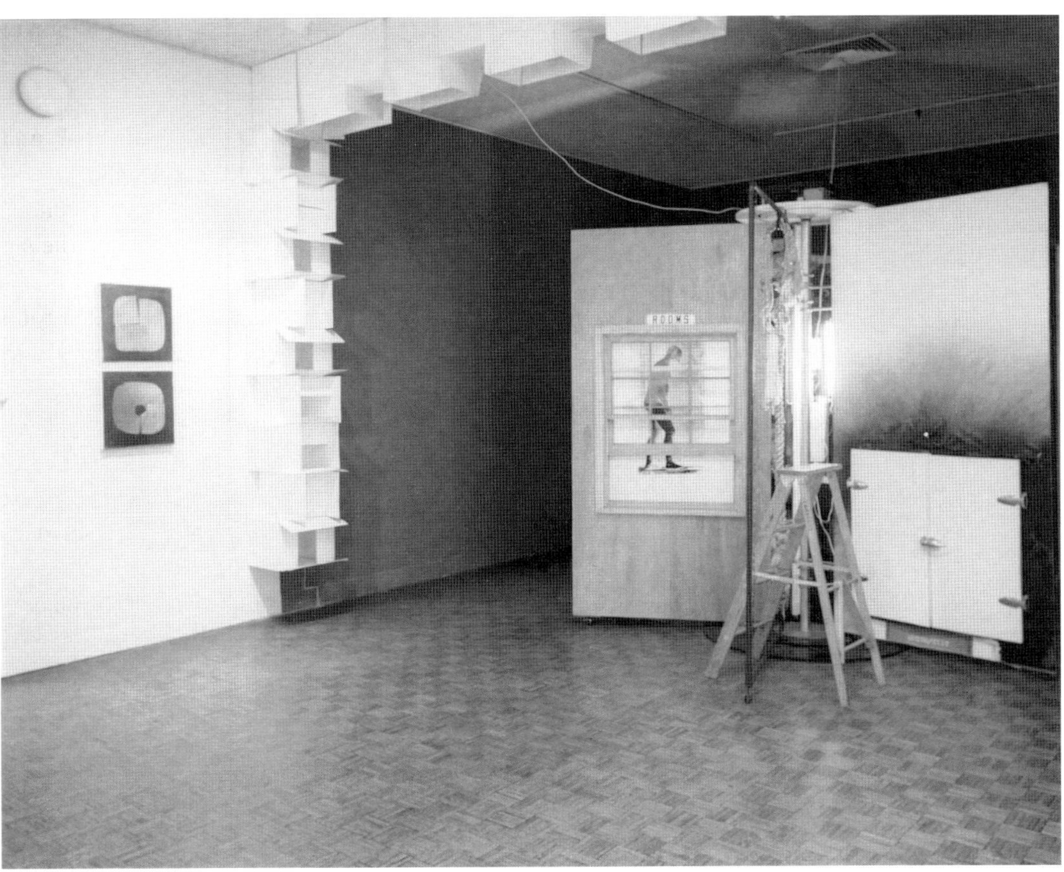


**Figure 4.12.** Alison Knowles, *The Big Book*, 1966–1969. Installation view, *Superlimited: Books, Boxes and Things*, Jewish Museum, New York, April 16–June 29, 1969. Art Resource, NY.

the ceiling. In his review of the show, Harold Rosenberg sarcastically quipped, "The public as a collective collaborator of works of art is notoriously lacking in talent, and it is unlikely that Kaprow's booth will be any more interesting by the end of its engagement than it was at the start."[64]

Rosenberg's reaction to *The Big Book* was decidedly more positive. In his final published review, and in handwritten notes now housed at the Getty Research Library, he described Knowles's installation as virtuosic: an "audio, visual, kinetic, mobile, structural, electrified landscape."[65] Knowles offers the reader "a physical metaphor that literally contains everything," he writes—"the story of the artist's life presented through copious examples of her domestic and cultural surroundings; it is both individual and collective."[66] The original exhibition venue—Something Else Gallery, in Knowles's home—perfectly matched the intimacy of the work's making. The expansive spaces of public galleries and museums provided a slightly awkward fit, yet even there, *The Big Book* opened up the site of domesticity to a view that was collective but still individuated, as each entrant experienced a distinct personal encounter with its text alongside others.

Knowles's personal motivations were further displaced and her public ad-

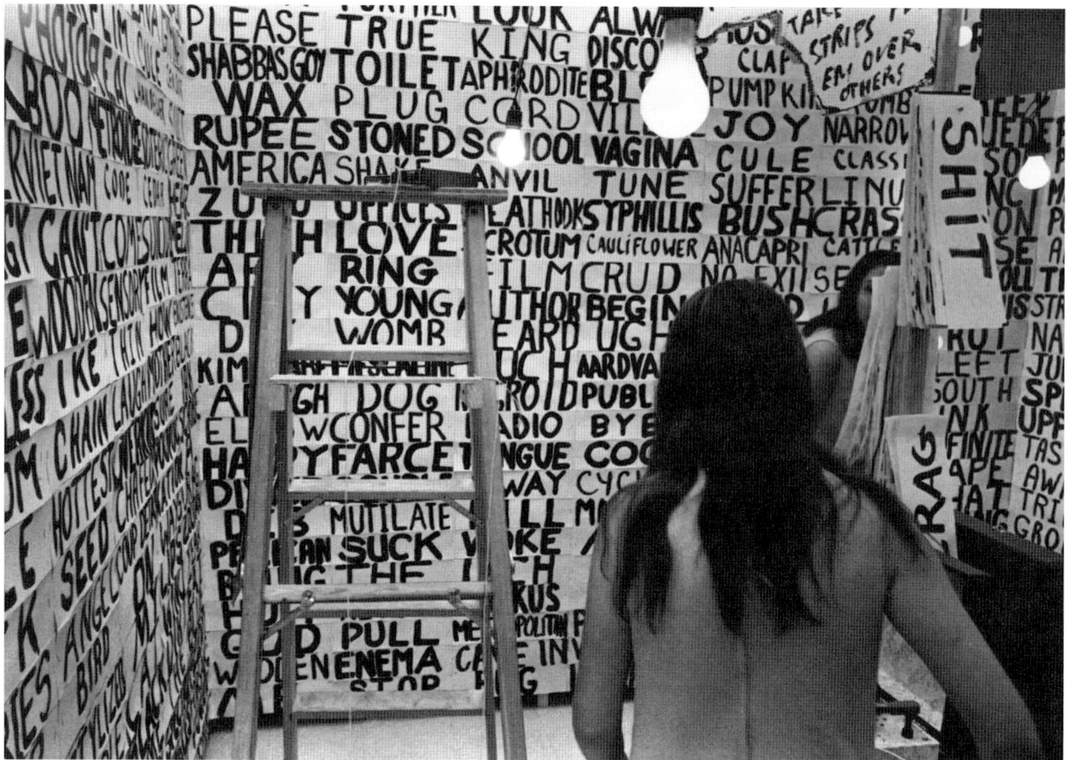


Figure 4.13. Allan Kaprow, *Words* (1962). Installation view, *Pictures to Be Read/Poetry to Be Seen*, Museum of Contemporary Art, Chicago, 1967. Courtesy the Estate of Allan Kaprow. Photo: Dan Van Riper, © MCA Chicago.

dress complicated by Van der Marck's request for an intermedia performance to celebrate the opening of the museum. The resulting "invitational event," an art experience/membership drive underwritten by the museum trustees and women's board, was staged by Knowles with three primary collaborators, Higgins, Kaprow, and John Cage, under the title *"What Did You Bring?"*[67] A playbill designed by Higgins listed scores to be performed, including Cage's *Variations VIII* (in which he intended to cook mushrooms), Knowles's *Bean Roll Readings*, and a reprisal of the string piece she had performed with Ben Vautier at Fluxhall/Fluxshop in 1964 (fig. 3.6).[68] As Knowles recounted later:

> John sat on the stage tracing and cutting out mushroom silhouettes, and then pinned them against the back wall. While John was doing that, I was doing *String Piece* within the audience, which was to tie a single figure on the stage—John was over to the side doing the tracing—and one of the people who had driven the *Big Book* . . . from Canada was placed in the center of the stage, and I tied him with the environment for, I'd say, about half an hour.[69]

The two-channel audio collage of labor and daily life that documented construction of *The Big Book* and served as its sound track was also played during the opening performance.

*"What Did You Bring?"* included time for Knowles to conduct *Proposition*

*#2: Make a Salad* ("a one-woman picnic for the 300 guests") with assistance from Cage, Higgins, and Kaprow (plate 6).[70] In this iteration, Knowles, as head chef, once again fully in command of her male collaborators, inverts the typical domestic gender hierarchy, instructing the men in preparing the ingredients, making the salad itself, and serving it to the audience. Knowles's selective restaging of her by-then well-known proposition works from the early to mid-1960s suggests a desire to flex that material and its aesthetic potential in varied private and public settings. Nonetheless, we may surmise from all the activity surrounding the physical presentation of *The Big Book*, that her challenging of traditional narratives, forms, and expectations is but part of a broader effort to make art and language track "a total experience" unmediated by conventional ways of seeing and perceiving. Jan van der Marck grasped this sensibility early on and noted of Knowles's *Big Book*, "It comes closer than any other work in the exhibition to a radical dissolution of the barriers that separate art and life."[71]

## Expanded Language Forms

As keen as Knowles was, throughout the 1960s, to dissolve (or at least complicate) the barriers separating art and life, a survey of her practice reveals an equal fascination with using the elasticity of linguistic operations and their spatialization to defamiliarize the categories of other media—graphics, celluloid, computation, sculpture.[72] This innovative fusion of art and visual poetry would be evident in various book and book-design projects she took on over the next decade.

*Notations*, a compendium of graphic musical manuscripts coedited by Knowles and Cage, built upon a collection of notational scores dating from 1884 through 1968 that Cage had been assembling for years. The pair initiated the book project in 1967 as a benefit for the Foundation of Contemporary Performance Arts, and the completed volume, presenting excerpts of compositions laid out in staves and measures, idiosyncratic shorthand, or combinations thereof, was published in 1969 through Something Else Press.[73]

The scores were ordered alphabetically by composer's name—from Murray Adaskin to Gerd Zacher—with names, titles, and (sometimes) dates set in a consistent style. (Reproduction permissions were also uniformly formatted, as slim lines of type running vertically along the sides of pages.) But other aspects of both content and layout, Cage explains in his brief preface, were determined by "I-Ching chance operations," including which of the contributing composers would be invited "to write about notation or something relevant to it"—"(never more than sixty-four words, sometimes only one)"—for which of their fellow composers' pages. "Other remarks were chosen or written by the editors—John Cage and Alison Knowles," and some entries had no such note. No other commentary or explanation was provided. The terse texts range in content and tone—from specific to general, profound to trivial, self-important to wryly self-effacing—and, notably, in visual form:

> Not only the number of words and the author, but the typography too—letter size, intensity, and typeface—were all determined by chance operations. This process was followed in order to lessen the difference between text and illustrations. The composition of the pages is the work of Alison Knowles.
>
> . . . A precedent for the absence of information which characterizes this book is the contemporary aquarium (no longer a dark hallway with each species in its own illuminated tank separated from the others and named in Latin): a large glass house with all the fish in it swimming as in an ocean.[74]

In her innovative layout—rarely, if ever, analyzed in the critical discourse on *Notations*—Knowles deployed rapid, random shifts in typeface and style. Jumps from small to large, serif to sans serif, small cap to bold italic—within a single word—are not uncommon, and many layouts dance diagrammatically across the page.

Affirming Cage's valuation of Alphabetical ordering sometimes creates analogical juxtapositions that affirm Cage's valuation of the aleatory, placing, for example, Milton Babbitt's duration measurement for electronic sound next to Ay-O's verbal arrangement, and Max Matthews's computer printout opposite an account of a dream by Richard Maxfield.

Knowles's dynamic approach to orchestrating images, words, charts, graphs, and notes in *Notations* parallels the process of composing her first silkscreen paintings in the late 1950s (plate 2; fig.1.7). In both, chance, as a philosophical framework and a tool for compositional choices, is deployed at every stage. The style and placement of letters and punctuation marks in the book design were, like the arrangement of collage elements and aspects of her notational scores, randomized. It was, she explained, "a metamorphosis that takes me a long time, and rather complicated and circuitous structures—a throw of the dice, opening of the dictionary, etc.—in order to find patterns for organizing these 'collections' into life (art)."[75]

*The Four Suits* (1965), an earlier collaborative book, edited by Higgins and also published by Something Else Press, included sections by Knowles and fellow Fluxus (and Flux-adjacent) artists Benjamin Patterson, Tomas Schmit, and Philip Corner.[76] Knowles's contribution, *The "T" Dictionary* (fig. 4.14), opens the volume and itself opens with three pages with the look of a conventional dictionary that cover the title letter in sixty-one entries, from "T,t" to "typewriter" by way of "tag" (cross-referenced to "thief"), "Tarwell Gibbs" ("A young man, as in 'my friend, Tarwell Gibbs'"), "tooth," and "tourist." The bland definition of "tacos" as "A Mexican dish consisting of meat and cheese wrapped up in a tortilla" is supplemented by a personal recommendation: "Try soft pork tacos at the Xochitl Restaurant, 146 W. 46th St., New York. The tacos are delicious with guacamole salad (avocado) and Carta Blanca beer."[77] "Talent" is drolly passed over as "an ancient unit of weight," and the second meaning for "trove"—"A Ray Johnson mailing"—is followed by a parenthetical cross-reference: "(See TAMPER, TITTER and TYPEWRITER)"—three terms

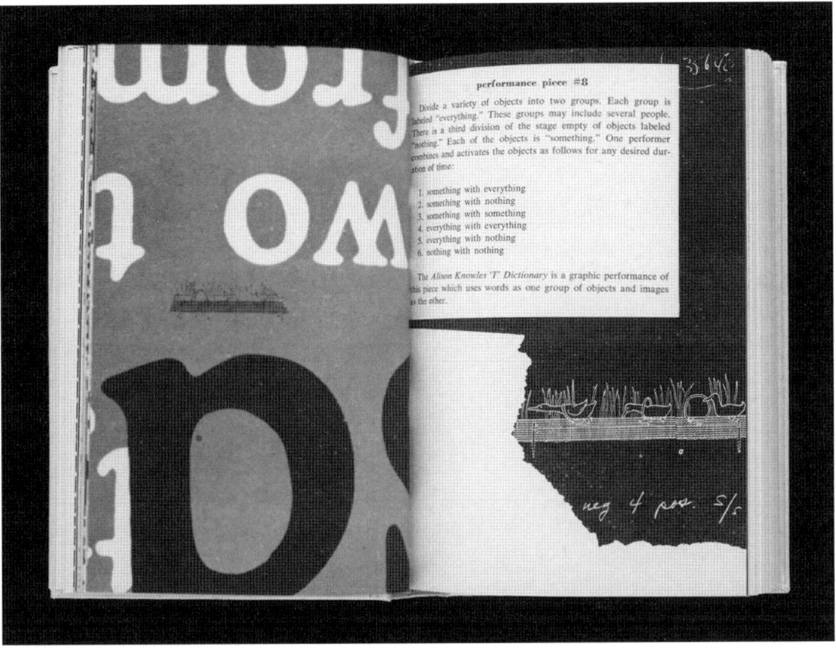


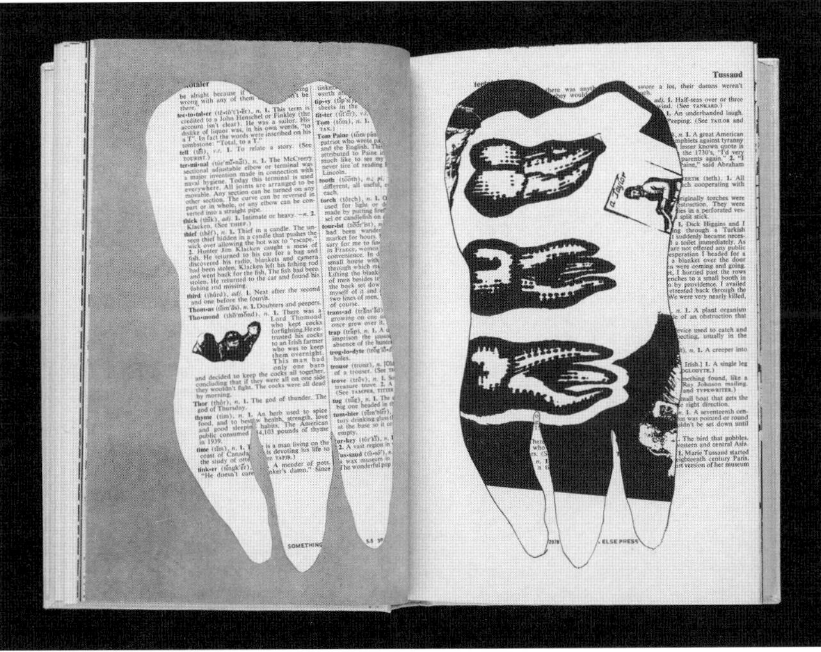


**Figure 4.14.** Alison Knowles, selections from *The "T" Dictionary*, in *The Four Suits* (Something Else Press, 1965). Book (offset lithograph on paper, cloth), 9 9/16 × 6 3/8 × 1 1/16 in. Collection Walker Art Center, Minneapolis Walker Special Purchase Fund, 1989. Photos courtesy Walker Art Center.

skillfully related to Johnson's furtive mail art practice. A few entries sit aside cryptic illustrations, a couple include etymological notes, and many offer more intimate insights into Knowles's culinary and aesthetic preferences—for example, "**taste** (tāst), *n.* **1.** 'The people I like best just do the best work' (an original Alison Knowles statement overheard by Mrs. Higgins)." Others relate also specific memories: "tourist" recounts an experience Knowles and Higgins had in a Turkish market; "technique" reports an overheard conversation between Philip Corner and a young piano student.

The next forty pages reconfigure details from the dictionary pages and other images—notably, of teeth and trunks. And seven pages from the end is a text relating *The "T" Dictionary* to one of Knowles's linguistic scores, *Proposition #8: Performance Piece #8* (1965):

> Divide a variety of objects into two groups. Each group is labeled "everything." These groups may include several people. There is a third division of the stage empty of objects labeled "nothing." Each of the objects is "something." One performer combines and activates the objects as follows for any desired duration of time:
> 1. something into everything
> 2. something with nothing
> 3. something with something
> 4. everything with everything
> 5. everything with nothing
> 6. nothing with nothing
>
> The *Alison Knowles "T" Dictionary* is a graphic performance of this piece which uses words as one group of objects and images as the other.[78]

As a "graphic performance," *The "T" Dictionary*, is a legible insertion into the activities of montage ("uses words as one group of objects and images as the other"), proffering a multiplicity of semantic values—metaphorical, philosophical, private. The repeated image of a single large tooth (as line art, silhouette, or halftone; alone or collaged with other material; paired across verso-recto spreads or multiplied within a single page) speaks to this directly, as it also appears in Knowles's *Blue Ram* page entry in *Notations* (a score she performed at "*What Did You Bring?*") and, screen-printed onto baby onesies, in an earlier work commemorating the birth of her fraternal twin daughters.[79]

Beyond these formative works, Knowles dedicated much of her speculative energies, throughout the late 1960s and 1970s, to literature more broadly, engaging with Cage's writings, Native American poetics, and the works of Henry David Thoreau, James Joyce, and Gertrude Stein (whose *The Making of Americans* was reissued by Something Else Press in 1966). She again collaborated with Cage on *Writing Through Finnegans Wake* (1978), his compilation of ten-line mesostics extracted from that novel.[80] Words and phrases containing the letters J-A-M-E-S-J-O-Y-C-E are horizontally displaced such that the Irish author's name runs vertically, repetitively, down the center of the page (not the edge, as in acrostics). Matching the formal and lexical experimentation of Joyce's magnum opus, Knowles and Cage further annihilate grammar and syntax by removing all punctuation and then re-placing it, often askew, via chance operations. The wanton punctuation, Knowles later observed, "flies across the page like dust," animating the reader's gaze and inducing a performative visual dance between symbolic coding and cognitive apperception.[81]

Knowles and Cage's close friendship and consonant tastes were expressed not only in collaboration but in dedicating works to each other over the course of many decades. Knowles's offset lithograph *White Stripes for John Cage* (1967) paid visual tribute to his *4′33″*, and Cage would compose a mesostic poem centered on the letters of Knowles's name for a 1992 exhibition in Cologne.

Knowles and others in the late 1960s New York neo-avant-garde shared an expansive interest in concrete poetics and the mutability of language. Knowles viewed Joyce's innovations, for example, as Western European analogues to the esoteric poetics within Indigenous literary and cultural traditions, especially those of the Kwakiutl of the Pacific Northwest. So, too, did poet Jerome Rothenberg, who, in retrospect, too often romantically and prescriptively appropriated native texts, and who invited Knowles to participate in a spring 1967 adaptation of his *Gift Event III: A Celebration of Poets, Dancers & Musicians, Based on the Orders of the Seneca Indian Eagle Dance* at Judson Memorial Church; the large cast also included Carolee Schneemann, Malcolm Goldstein, Max Neuhaus, Steve Reich, and James Tenney. *Gift Event III* was bookended, in its two evening performances, by composer Philip Corner's percussive *Friendship Event* and a "slow-torque solo dance" by Carol Ritter.[82] Corner's "mass-like interaction" involved musicians making noises using bells, drums, sticks, and claps, and a group of poets, including Higgins, Jackson Mac Low, Eleanor and David Antin, and Clayton Eshleman, reading out their pieces to the improvisatory movement of four dancers. A critic for *Dance Magazine* interpreted the transdisciplinary pieces as answering a "conviction . . . that modern man is spiritually impoverished because he lacks rituals to solemnize his values" by seeking "to invent such rituals."[83] Rothenberg viewed the event as both akin to Seneca dance rituals and coherent with Cage's conceit of neutralizing the individual ego through chance-derived composition. As one of the featured "musicians" tasked with playing Corner's *PoorManMusic* (1966)—making simple sounds by breathing, clapping, slapping, rubbing, or scratching their bodies near contact microphones—Knowles reveled in *Gift Event III*'s translation of bodily language/instrumentation and ritual into group action.[84]

Knowles's own "gift event" score, *Proposition #16: Giveaway Construction* (1963), was admired by Rothenberg and republished in *Technicians of the Sacred* (1968) and referenced in *Shaking the Pumpkin: Traditional Poetry of the Indian North Americas* (1972), his compiled "reworkings" and "versions" of First Nations' poetic practices. In his introduction to the latter, Rothenberg suggests that the translations operate "by analogy to contemporary, limit-smashing experiments (as with concrete poetry, sound poetry, intermedia, happenings, etc.)."[85] *Shaking the Pumpkin* thus includes contextual histories and commentaries, which cite Knowles's *Giveaway Construction* as comparable in the spirit of potlatch evoked in Seneca dances and, crucially, in Kwakiutl giving traditions: "Find something you like in the street and give it away. Or find a variety of things, make something of them, & give it away."[86] This score was later repeated by Knowles as an explicit nod to the potlatch in a performance at the California Institute of the Arts (discussed further in chapter 5), where she directed the Graphics Print Lab in the early 1970s.

What Knowles and Rothenberg appear to share is an investment in the process of transportable textuality, whereby non-Western forms of making could be used to "shake" the canon and reconfigure institutional discourses of visual art, music, and literature. Their "gift event" scores and performances, and later works like Knowles's *The Identical Lunch*, produce aesthetic jolts by mixing vernacular forms of daily life and rituals—what Rothenberg theorized as "the symposium of the whole."[87] Knowles would continue to demonstrate an appreciation for Indigenous narratives, histories, folklore, and aesthetics in collaborations throughout her career, including *Quecha* (1987), an elegant cyanotype on canvas, and the related screen-print series *Seven Indian Moons* (1990).[88]

Knowles's engagement with the motility of language—spatially on the page, materially in the book, and in live action—was apparent as well in her *Newspaper Music* (1965) and in her investment in Gertrude Stein's experimentation with nonlinear narrativity and temporal-durational heuristics (as we see in *The Big Book*). In *Newspaper Music*, Knowles conducts the speed and tempo of performers' vocalizations as they read from international daily newspapers in five different languages.[89] Her orchestration of overlapping words and dialects, recalling the sonic flux of *Proposition #12: Simultaneous Bean Reading*, tracks with Stein's experimental methods, which deeply influenced many in the literary and visual avant-gardes of this era, including Cage and Higgins, who Knowles encouraged to republish important works by Stein, starting with *The Making of Americans* (1966).[90] Beginning in 1973, Knowles co-organized annual New Year's Eve readings of that reissue, first at the newly founded Artists Space and then for the next three years at Paula Cooper Gallery, both in SoHo (fig. 4.15).[91] A *New Yorker* article on one such marathon—completing the 925-page tome took some fifty hours—reported artists, poets, musicians, students, and local residents drifting in and out of the gallery, taking shelter for a time from the frigid cold and reciting passages from the family chronicle.[92] On view in the gallery during the 1976 event were working drawings by Robert Wilson that composer Philip Glass used to write the score of his opera *Einstein on the Beach* (1975). In 1977 dancers Meredith Monk and Lucinda Childs, composer Annea Lockwood, and seventy others all read, at various paces, until exhausted. In 1985 the cast included writer Samuel R. Delany, filmmaker Stuart Sherman, and composer Pauline Oliveros. Not everyone present chose to read, a right of refusal Knowles not only anticipated but welcomed.[93] These occasions, connected to her identification as a *visual poet*, fostered an almost pedagogical, even civic, aim to attend to the daily life of her lived community through public acts of literacy. They exemplify, too, the democratizing

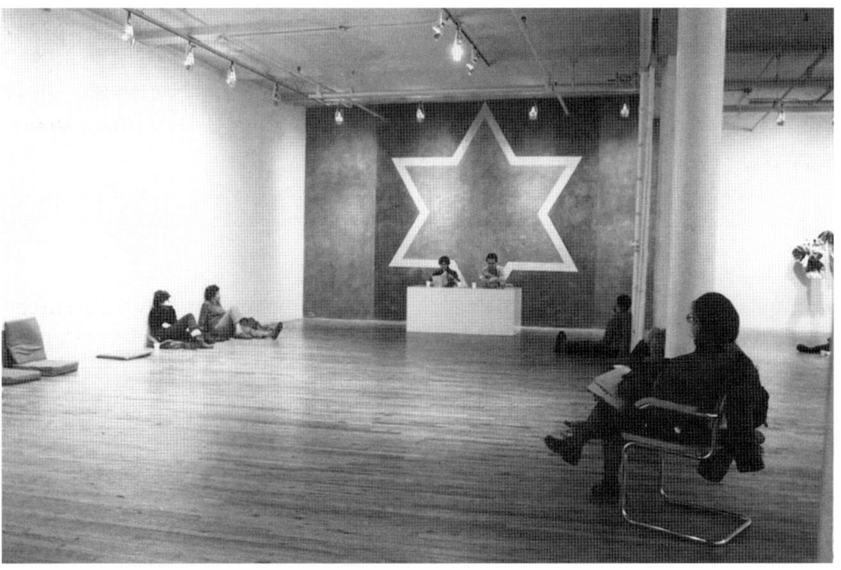

**Figure 4.15.** Annual reading of Gertrude Stein's *The Making of Americans*, organized by Alison Knowles and Annea Lockwood, Paula Cooper Gallery, 15 Wooster Street, New York, ca. 1973–1979. Photographer unknown.

gesture of the open work, a theme that goes beyond the bounds of traditional art making and persists in her practice over several decades. The endurance challenge posed by vocalizing Stein's complex text (or conducting newspaper readings of other voices) was a useful framework for Knowles's own interest in ritual, routine, and perceptual generosity, here expressed in the curation of narrative spaces, temporal and metaphorical, wherein viewer-readers could become participants and collectively mark the turning of the calendar via a "disorientation in time."[94]

Within the context of Knowles's art making and other activities throughout the 1960s and 1970s, we can read *The Big Book* as a protofeminist intervention where indeterminacy undermines hierarchy and, specifically, subjectivity as defined by space disrupts the boundaries of inside/outside and thus threatens patriarchal authority in both public and private spheres.[95] The large, methodically constructed installation undermined the categorical nature of art (and by extension, "woman's art") by crossing medium and aesthetic boundaries in an atypical ensemble that expanded architectural and perceptual space. It did not, as Helen Molesworth rightly says of Duchamp's readymades, oppose its "intended, mandated, standardized use" or "resist the working subject" but, rather, offered an extended experience of the working body through the physical exertion it took to interact with the book—squatting, twisting, standing, climbing, and turning its pages.[96] (Interestingly, *The Big Book* did not include objects that identified Knowles explicitly as a mother—even if her young daughters were invited to interact with the structure like an elaborate pedagogical pop-up book, activities Higgins filmed after the work's completion.[97]) *The Fingerbook of Ancient Language* (1986), another instance of Knowles's transdisciplinary exploration of books as expanded pedagogical forms, is a tactile, tabletop book for visually impaired audiences. Modeled on *The Big Book*, with scaled-down hinged wooden doors and cloth-draped openings, *The Fingerbook* presents, on stamped metal plates, text set in Braille, a sample of Incan quipu, and examples of Asante dialect, hieroglyphics, cuneiform, and "many texts which use pictograms to communicate."[98] Navigating its pages amplifies a uniquely percussive, sonic reading experience.

Crucially, in terms of her larger oeuvre, Knowles takes seriously, in *The Big Book* and conceptually adjacent projects, the nature of language: its texture, its granularity, its visual poetics; its social effects; its potential for mischief. In transforming the ideologically defined domestic space into a book-world of destabilized desires and priorities favoring the self over the familial, I contend, Knowles undermined the spatial integrity of the nuclear home and effectively collapsed the complex social rituals that inhabit and are reaffirmed in its kitchens, bedrooms, and other spaces. What is unique about her projects during this time, small-scale or large, is their use of the experiential book form to dramatize the act of reading daily life as a social text and space of self-reflection and chance operations.

As the first of two case studies of environmentally scaled works, *The Big Book* asks us to reconsider Knowles's work within the post–World War II moment, especially as it encourages a critical examination of the status of the art object. In this project, *labor* is characterized by a set of shifting terms and dialectical procedures: immediate and measured; public and private; literal and metaphorical; practical and imaginative; modest and grandiose; incisive and obscurantist; minimal and baroque. The logic of her book installation—its scale, sensations, textures, and affects—demonstrates how objects perceive and are perceived in that delicate residue of human experience that seeks to make them meaningful. Knowles's art practice, then, is one that carefully reexamines art as itself a social relation, an occasion of possibility. It is in these infinitely visual, sonic, and textured contexts that her work reactivates perception at the locus of sensorial experience. As with her propositional scores of the early 1960s, the artist is not central to the work's use and application: "I just give the game plan."[99] "To use these methods slackens the hold of the ego of the artist on the work," she continues. "These objects [I make] do not so much impose a vision [as] liberate processes for other people *to do*." We see this in *The Big Book*'s materialization, history, and reception, and in another novel, audience-activated environment she designed during the late 1960s: the object/poem *The House of Dust*.

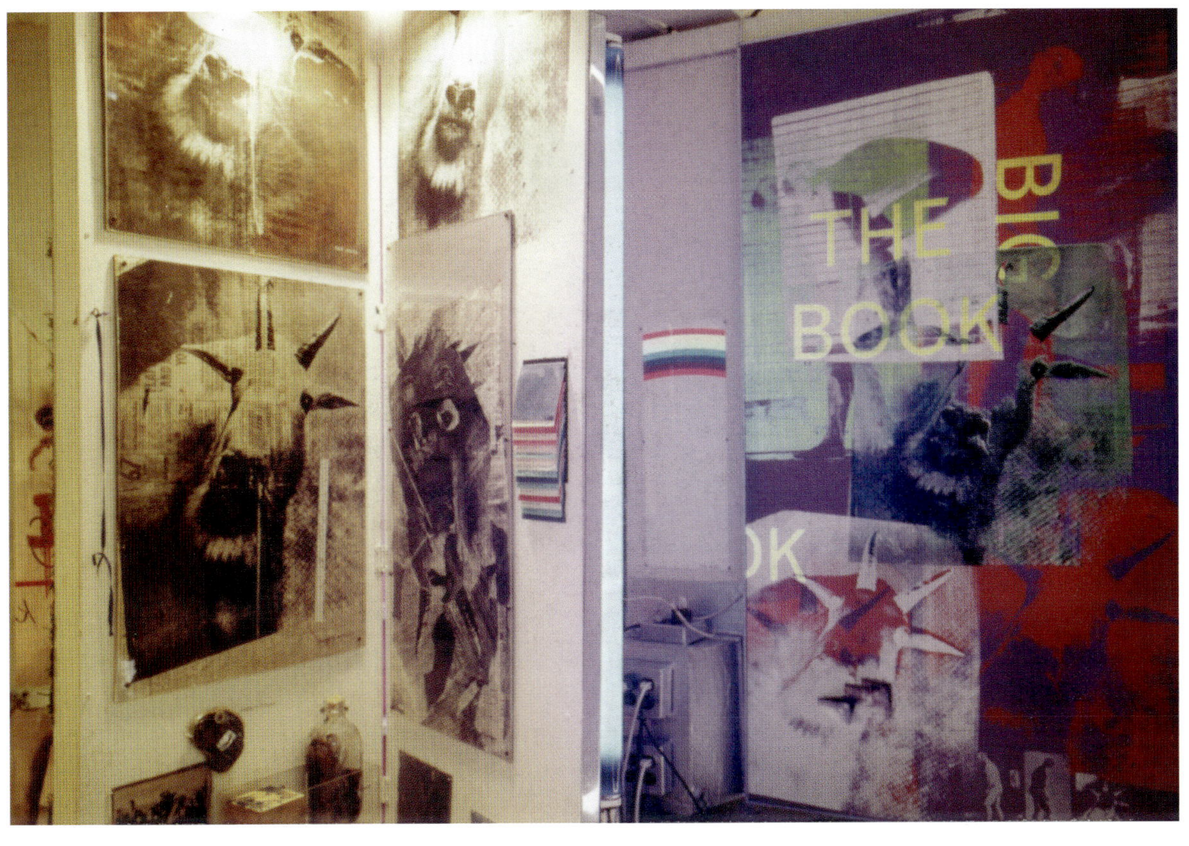


**Plate 1.** Alison Knowles, *The Big Book*, 1967. Installation view showing "Goat Gallery," Museum of Contemporary Art, Chicago. Photo: Dan Van Riper, © MCA Chicago.

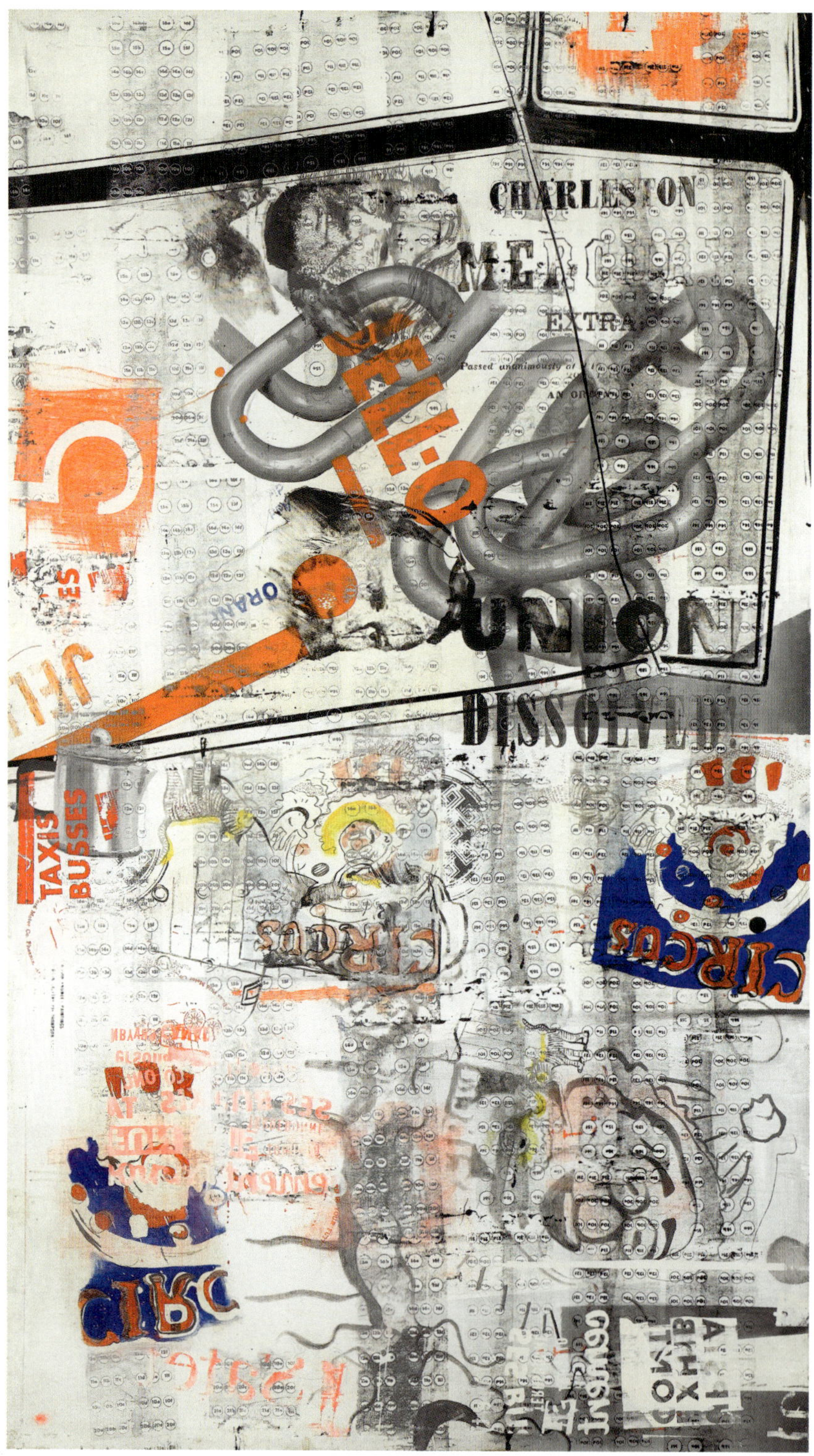


**Plate 2.** Alison Knowles, *Taxis and Busses*, ca. 1959–1960. Oil and screen print on canvas, 245.5 × 137.5 cm. Archiv Sohm, Staatsgalerie Stuttgart. Photo © Staatsgalerie Stuttgart.

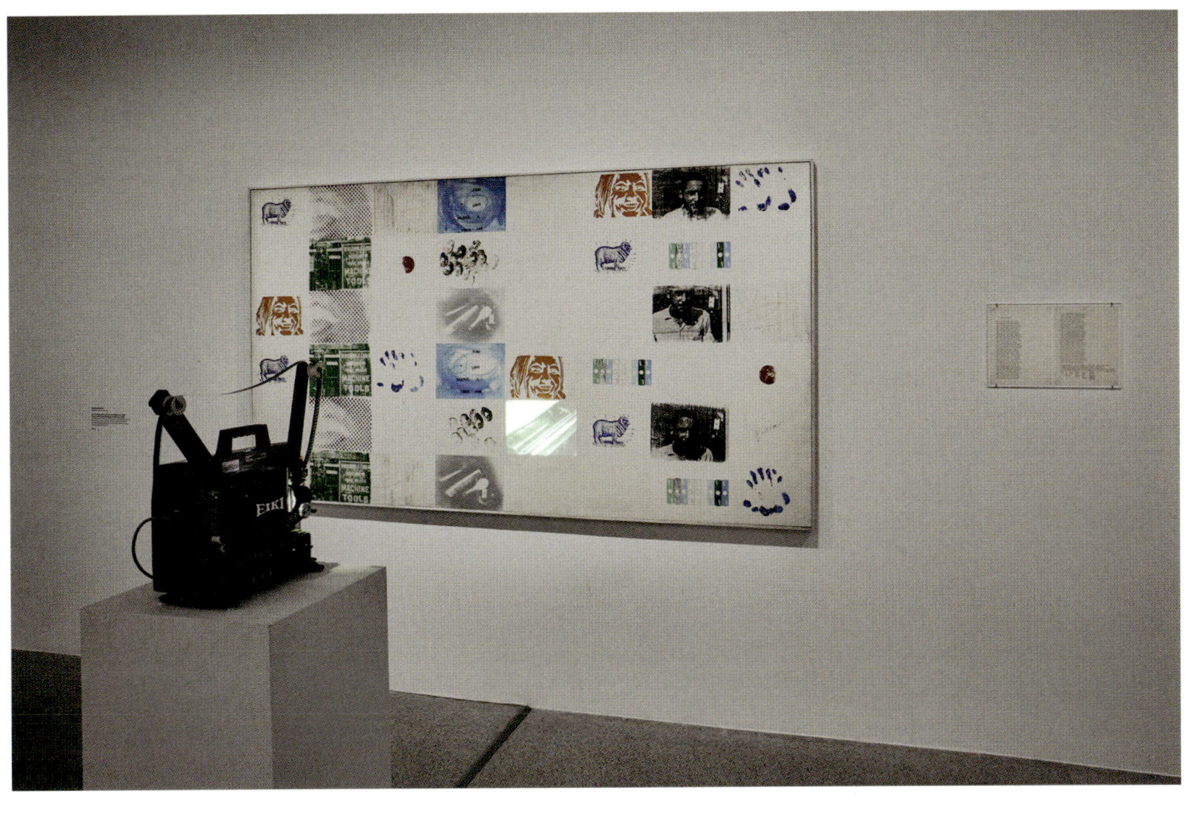


**Plate 3.** Alison Knowles, *Do You Remember (für Emmett Williams)*, 1968. Film projector, mixed media on canvas (137 × 242 cm), two pages of typescript on paper. Photo © mumok–Museum moderner Kunst Stiftung Ludwig Wien/Deinhardstein.

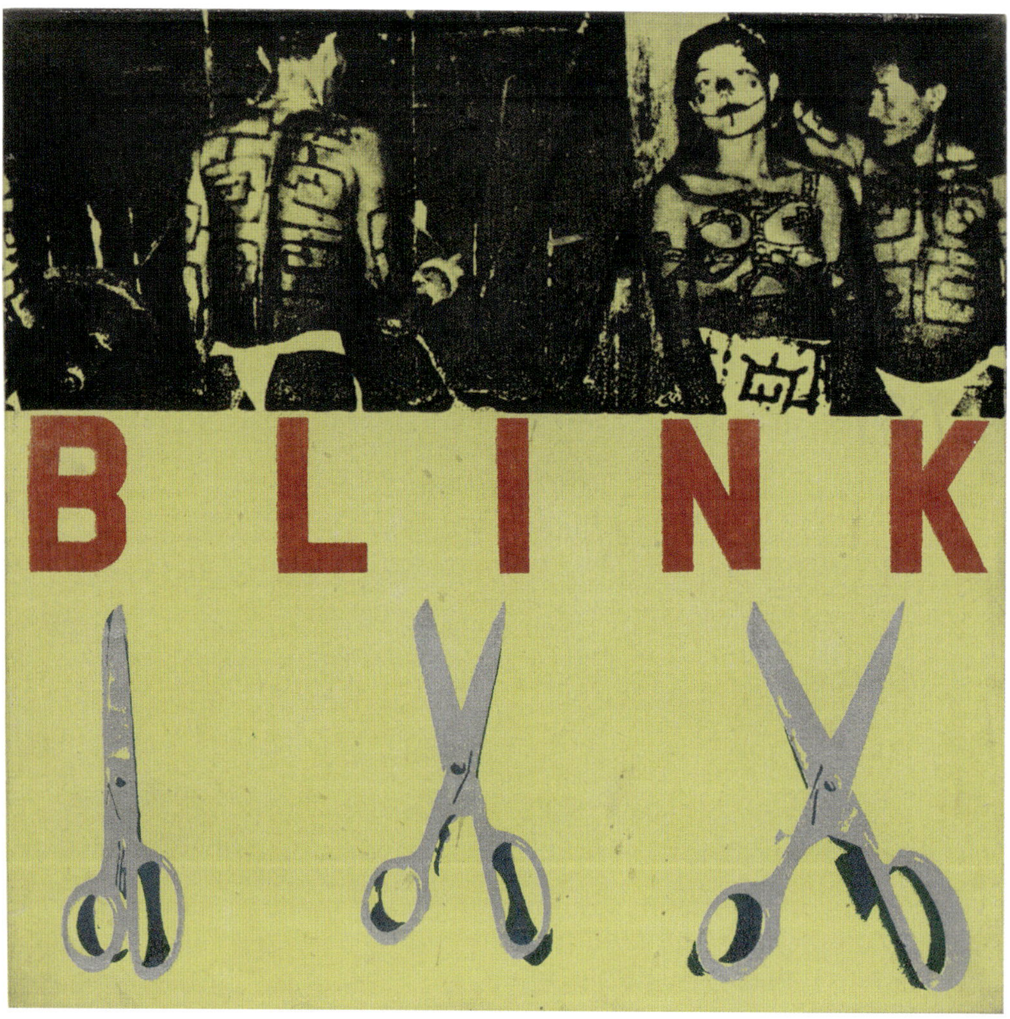


**Plate 4.** Alison Knowles, George Brecht, and Robert Watts, *BLINK*, 1963. Screen print and synthetic polymer paint on canvas. From *Blink Works*, exhibited by Sissor Bros. Warehouse (Knowles, Brecht, and Watts), at Rolf Nelson Gallery, Los Angeles, 1963. Edition size unknown. © 1963/2024 Alison Knowles, Robert Watts, and George Brecht. © 2024 Artists Rights Society (ARS), New York/VG Bild-Kunst, Bonn. Image © The Museum of Modern Art. Licensed by SCALA/Art Resource, NY.

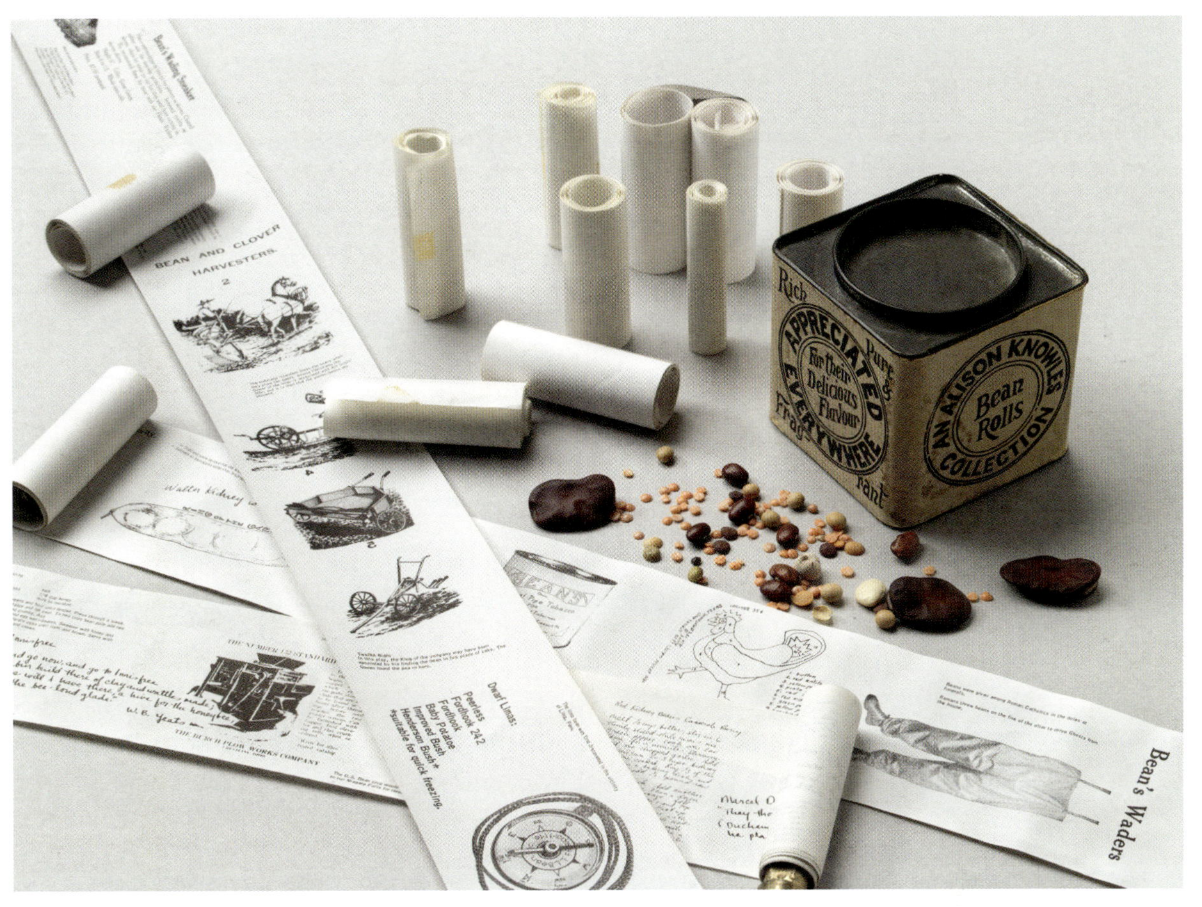


**Plate 5.** Alison Knowles, *Bean Rolls*, 1963. Metal tin with offset label, containing dried beans and sixteen offset scrolls; multiple, distributed as part of *Fluxkit*, 1963–1965. Bonotto Collection (Colceresa, Italy). Courtesy Fondazione Bonotto.

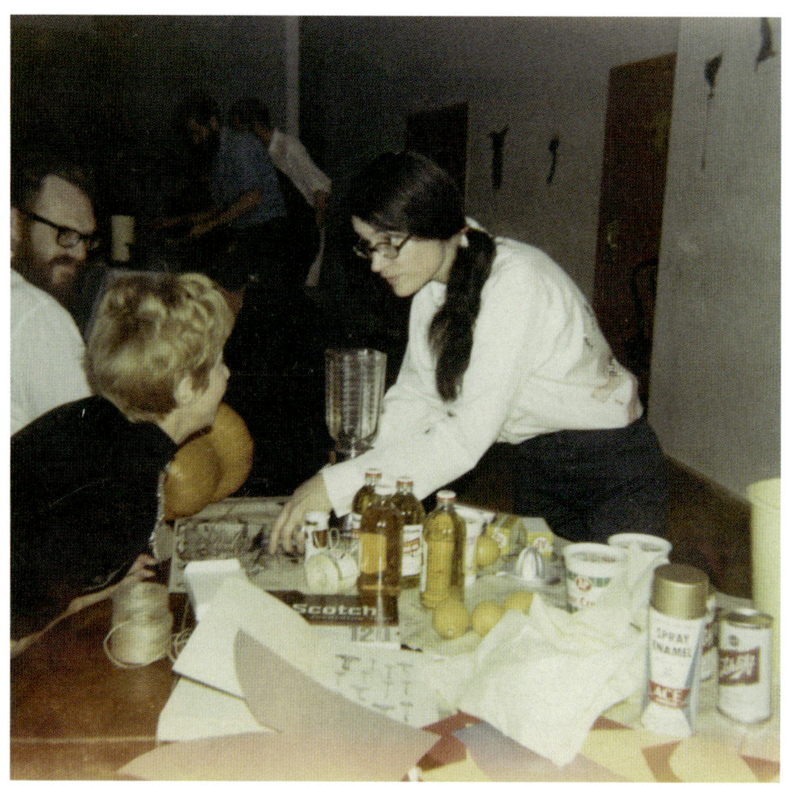


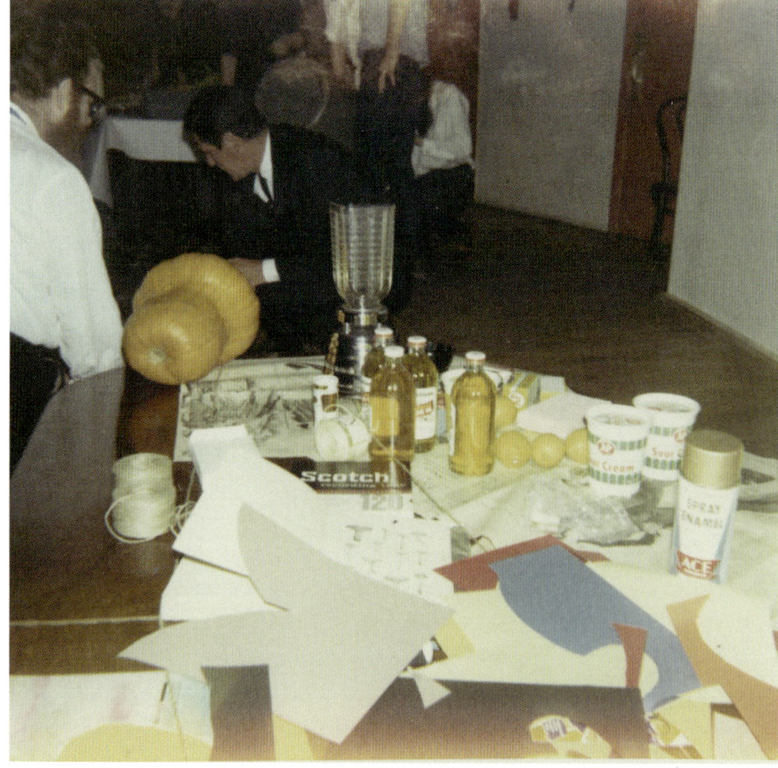


**Plate 6.** Alison Knowles, John Cage, Dick Higgins, and Allan Kaprow performing Knowles's *Proposition #2: Make a Salad* as part of *"What Did You Bring?,"* staged at Second City, Chicago, 1967. Dick Higgins papers, Getty Research Institute, Los Angeles (870613). Photos: Dan Van Riper, © MCA Chicago.

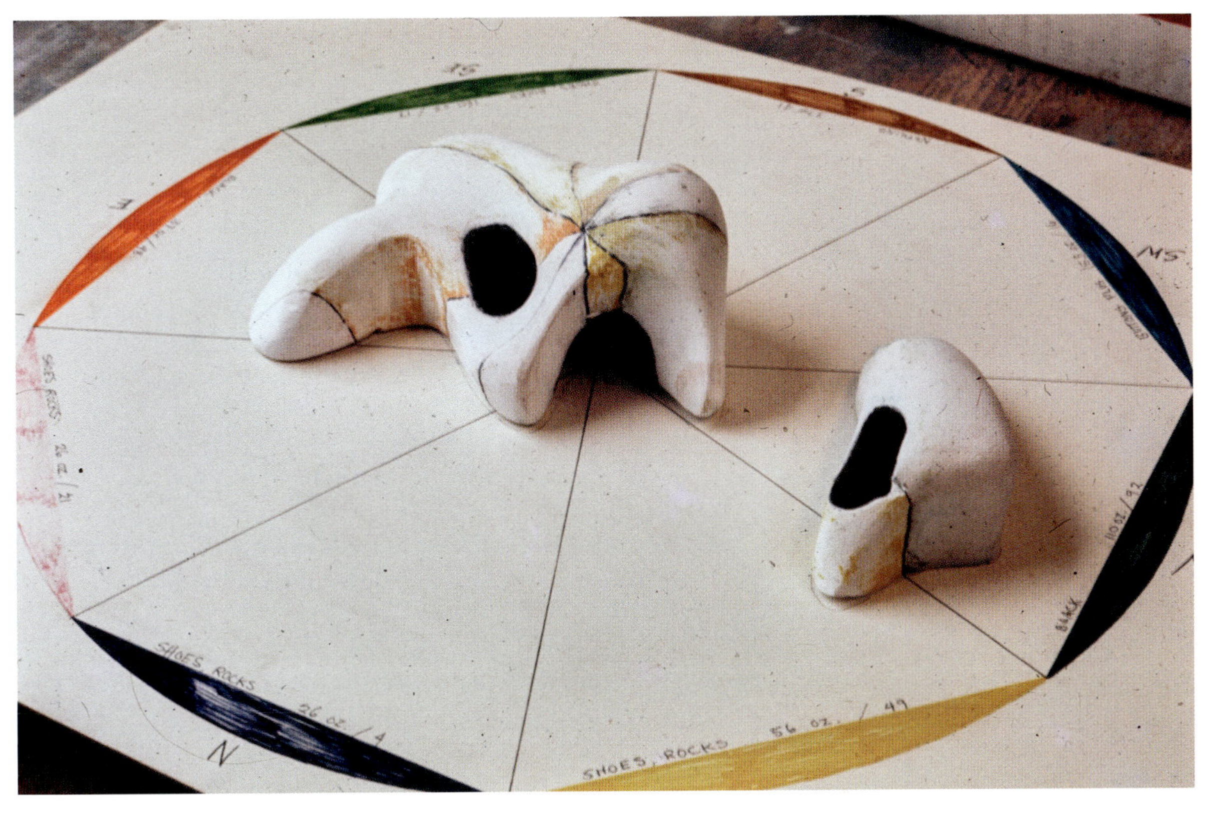


**Plate 7.** Alison Knowles, plaster models of *The House of Dust*, 1968. Photographic color slide. Experiments in Art and Technology records, Getty Research Institute, Los Angeles (940003).

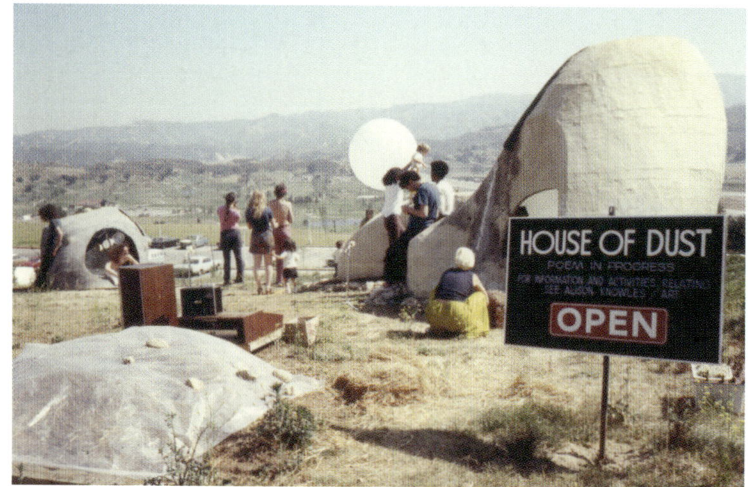


**Plate 8.** Alison Knowles, *The House of Dust*, 1969–1975. Two structures (since destroyed). California Institute of the Arts, Valencia, CA. Photographer unknown. Courtesy California Institute of the Arts Library & Institute Archives.

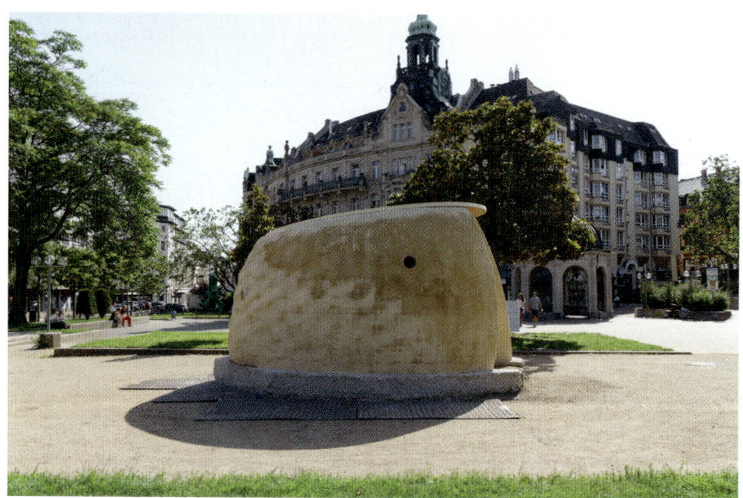

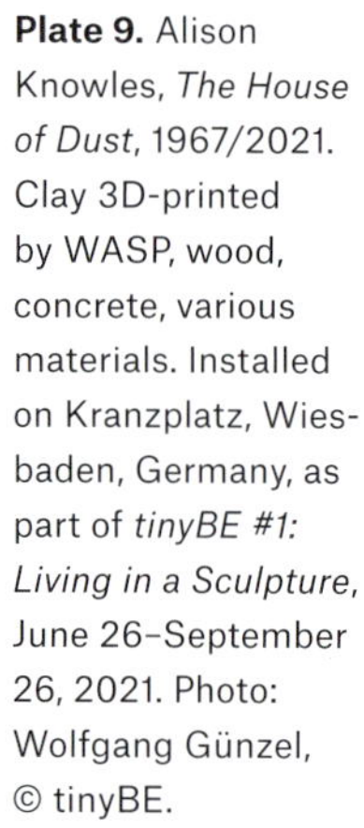

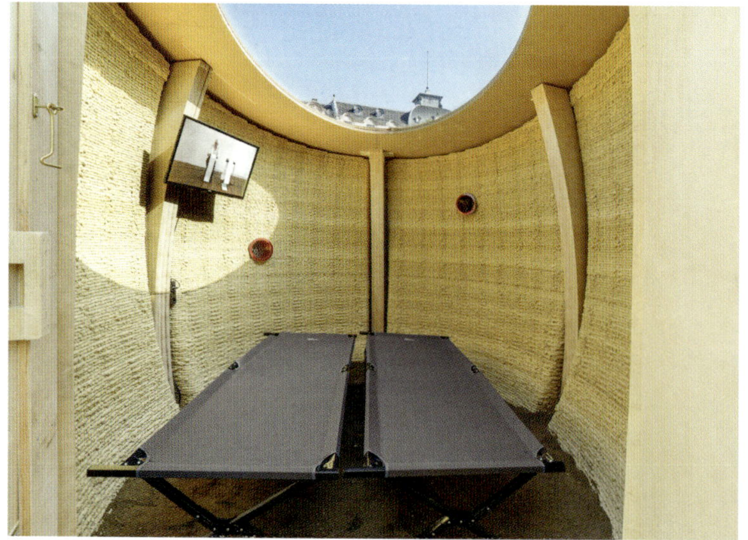

**Plate 9.** Alison Knowles, *The House of Dust*, 1967/2021. Clay 3D-printed by WASP, wood, concrete, various materials. Installed on Kranzplatz, Wiesbaden, Germany, as part of *tinyBE #1: Living in a Sculpture*, June 26–September 26, 2021. Photo: Wolfgang Günzel, © tinyBE.

# 5 OBJECT/POEM

> The most important thing to emphasize is the changing nature of the poem. . . . [It] is about dwellings, types of people and situations that sometimes do and sometimes don't get together.
> **Alison Knowles**[1]

In summer 1967, while assembling objects for *The Big Book* (fig. 4.2) and formalizing her score *The Identical Lunch* (fig. 3.14), Alison Knowles participated in an informal workshop on computer-assisted composition and information theory organized by her friend the experimental composer James Tenney. Tenney, an artist-in-residence at Bell Telephone Laboratories in New Jersey and an expert on the IBM programming language known as FORTRAN, introduced Knowles, John Cage, Philip Corner, Dick Higgins, Jackson Mac Low, Max Neuhaus, Nam June Paik, and Steve Reich to the rich potential of mixing visual art and music with electronic data processing.[2] The goals of the lessons were modest: to demystify the technology and show the artists and composers that their previous experimentation with "formulating indeterminacy" often resembled programmers' approaches to statistical information.[3]

During the weekly lessons, held on Tuesday evenings in Knowles and Higgins's Chelsea home, Knowles sketched ideas for individual performance-based pieces and, presciently, worked out a new approach to her artistic practice. In the late 1950s, after rejecting expressionism, she had used the *I Ching* or dice to randomize the placement and appearance of elements in her large silk-screen paintings; by the end of Tenney's workshop, she realized she could use the computer mainframe to streamline that compositional process.[4] While not yet a direct stand-in for a physical artwork, the computational formulae Knowles developed with Tenney proved an efficient apparatus with which to express her ideas, a practical and conceptually expansive shortcut that solved two problems at once, helping her to maintain productive studio time while caring for her young daughters. The fortuitous result was one of the first ever computer poems, "A House of Dust" (fig. 5.1).[5]

Since the 1950s, artists, mathematicians, engineers, and philosophers had been experimenting with computer-generated content, including poetry, music, design, and animated graphics—among them, Paris-based Hungarian art-

```
A HOUSE OF BRICK
      IN SOUTHERN FRANCE
            USING NATURAL LIGHT
                  INHABITED BY ALL RACES OF MEN REPRESENTED WEARING PREDOMINANTLY RED CLOTHING

A HOUSE OF DUST
      ON AN ISLAND
            USING ELECTRICITY
                  INHABITED BY FRIENDS AND ENEMIES

A HOUSE OF BRICK
      IN A PLACE WITH BOTH HEAVY RAIN AND BRIGHT SUN
            USING CANDLES
                  INHABITED BY CHILDREN AND OLD PEOPLE

A HOUSE OF GLASS
      AMONG HIGH MOUNTAINS
            USING ELECTRICITY
                  INHABITED BY PEOPLE WHO EAT A GREAT DEAL

A HOUSE OF GLASS
      IN A COLD, WINDY CLIMATE
            USING ELECTRICITY
                  INHABITED BY PEOPLE WHO SLEEP ALMOST ALL THE TIME

A HOUSE OF LEAVES
      ON THE SEA
            USING NATURAL LIGHT
                  INHABITED BY VARIOUS BIRDS AND FISH

A HOUSE OF STONE
      INSIDE A MOUNTAIN
            USING ELECTRICITY
                  INHABITED BY HORSES AND BIRDS

A HOUSE OF STEEL
      IN A DESERT
            USING NATURAL LIGHT
                  INHABITED BY VEGETARIANS

A HOUSE OF DISCARDED CLOTHING
      IN DENSE WOODS
            USING CANDLES
                  INHABITED BY FRIENDS AND ENEMIES

A HOUSE OF BROKEN DISHES
      AMONG OTHER HOUSES
            USING ALL AVAILABLE LIGHTING
                  INHABITED BY PEOPLE WHO LOVE TO READ

A HOUSE OF MUD
      BY A RIVER
            USING ELECTRICITY
                  INHABITED BY PEOPLE WHO SLEEP ALMOST ALL THE TIME
```

**Figure 5.1.** Alison Knowles and James Tenney, "A House of Dust," 1967–1968. Getty Research Institute, Los Angeles (95-B3662).

ist Vera Molnár, German mathematician Théo Lutz, Italian poet Nanni Balestrini, Billy Klüver's Experiments in Art and Technology (E.A.T.), and the innovative teams at Bell Labs.[6] In the 1960s, this idea of computers as visual art machines was still generally regarded as speculative. Others had used aleatory procedures to fill slots in a textual template, as Knowles did in "A House of Dust," but the system had not previously been automated.[7] Indeed, the "new modeling of information in bytes and codes" Tenney conveyed to a community of artists for the first time in the United States made them early and unexpected founders of digital art.[8] Knowles's poem, specifically, was almost immediately recognized as a groundbreaking example of computer-generated art and was included in the watershed exhibition *Cybernetic Serendipity*, curated by Jasia Reichardt at the Institute of Contemporary Arts in London in 1968.[9]

This final chapter delves into the reconsideration of the subject, function, and distribution of language systems (poetic, visual, spatial) that Knowles initiated—through, first, a foray into computational art as a tool of critical practice and, second, the materialization of the poem "A House of Dust" in multiple textual and physical forms. Buttressed by significant archival finds,

I delineate how Knowles's "object/poem" opened new territories of artistic investigation in a dialectical relation to life in an increasingly globalized and technocratic world amid the political and aesthetic ecologies of the later 1960s and 1970s.[10]

With *The Big Book* and earlier multidimensional works such as *Bean Rolls* (plate 5), Knowles appropriated not only the themes of reading, language, objects, and information but the distribution systems of knowledge acquisition through which the self comes to understand the world. This innovative approach blossoms fully in *The House of Dust*. Parallel to the chance-based artwork explored in earlier chapters, Knowles engaged with advanced art practices (e.g., computer-generated content) that changed ideas of what art was and could be. I aim to highlight what we might call the *participatory ecologies* articulated in Knowles's computational poetics—referring only obliquely to the familiar, singular definition of *ecology*, a science concerned with the interrelationship of organisms and their ecosystems, and more pointedly to the Greek root of *eco-*, meaning house. I conclude by suggesting that this perpetually changing work, as both poem and freestanding, habitable spaces, could serve as a model to amplify the history of critically advanced art by women in the latter half of the twentieth century.

This, of course, requires reconsidering Knowles alongside artists who shared certain conceptual kinships and commitments—site-specificity, terrestrial and industrial modes of production, public-private transformations, feminist critiques of domesticity—and for whom specific site was not merely a geographically remote landscape to be permanently transformed by mobilizing colossal resources. The primary goal was, rather, the unruly modes of *participation*, even a performance politics. We may regard Knowles's contribution to contemporary art, in *The House of Dust* and related works, as exemplary of a speculative rearticulation, even reperiodization, of what we now designate "digital," "new media," "feminist," "process," and "land art" or "earthworks."[11] What fascinates me about Knowles's terms (how she wields objects and poems) is precisely the ways in which she continued to conceptualize, even systematize, her work as an open platform to be shared and realized—a seemingly infinite occasion for contingency and reuse. Her artistic sensibilities, at that time and, as we will see, in subsequent decades, is one of recycled forms, accumulations, assemblages, and participatory models of exchange generated by living environments, objects, and texts, all perpetually in flux.

## A House of Dust, First Iteration: Poem

Knowles's poem "A House of Dust" or, as it was originally titled, *Proposition No. 2 for Emmett Williams* was intended as a continuation of, and a departure from, the Fluxus scores she wrote and performed in the early 1960s. Like *Proposition #3: Nivea Cream Piece* (1962; fig.2.9) and her text-image-film projection piece *Do You Remember (für Emmett Williams)* (1968; plate 3), itself a

**Program for** Proposition No. 2 for Emmett Williams, **by Alison Knowles, realized by James Tenney.**

```
EE317M      TENNEY                                FORTRAN SOURCE LIST
            SOURCE STATEMENT

      $IBFTC ARCH     LIST,REF
            DIMENSION MAT(3,17),SIT(8,25),LIT(4,4),INH(11,22)
            INTEGER SIT
            CALL RAND1
            READ(5,101)((MAT(I1,J1),I1=1,3),J1=1,17)
      101   FORMAT(6X,3A6)
            READ(5,201)((SIT(I2,J2),I2=1,8),J2=1,25)
      201   FORMAT(6X,8A6)
            READ(5,301)((LIT(I3,J3),I3=1,4),J3=1,4)
      301   FORMAT(6X,4A6)
            READ(5,401)((INH(I4,J4),I4=1,11),J4=1,22)
      401   FORMAT(6X,11A6)
            DO 200 N=1,50
            WRITE(6,102)
      102   FORMAT(1H1)
            DO 200 M=1,12
            JM=1.+RAND(17.)
            JS=1.+RAND(25.)
            JL=1.+RAND(4.)
            JI=1.+RAND(22.)
            WRITE(6,202)(MAT(I1,JM),I1=1,3),(SIT(I2,JS),I2=1,8),(LIT(I3,JL),I3
           1=1,4),(INH(I4,JI),I4=1,11)
      202   FORMAT(1H0,5X,11HA HOUSE OF ,3A6/12X,8A6/18X,6HUSING ,4A6/24X,13HI
           1NHABITED BY ,11A6)
      200   CONTINUE
            CALL RAND3
            STOP
            END
```

**Figure 5.2.** Alison Knowles and James Tenney, a portion of the program for *Proposition No. 2 for Emmett Williams*, 1967. Reprinted in Dick Higgins, *Computers for the Arts* (1970).

duet conceived as a riposte to the poem "Litany and Response No. 2 for Alison" (1962), "A House of Dust" was dedicated to Williams, her most treasured Fluxus friend and interlocutor.[12] Knowles defined the poetic structure, a series of four-line stanzas, and composed lists of words and phrases to be randomly inserted into each line. James Tenney wrote a program to generate the quatrains, then fed the lists, keyed onto punch cards, into an IBM mainframe computer at Brooklyn Polytechnic Institute (BPI), where he held a research position in musical acoustics within the electrical engineering department. The initial run achieved Knowles's aim: "there were four hundred quatrains generated before a repetition occurred."[13]

The software used by Tenney was FORTRAN-IV, an upgraded version of the classical FORTRAN, a computer language whose flexible, modular architecture was finding applications not only among scientists, who used it to analyze computationally intensive data patterning (as in numerical weather prediction, finite element analysis, and fluid dynamics), but in libraries and other settings concerned with compiling information.[14] Tenney's program (fig. 5.2) made random selections from Knowles's lists of seventeen materials (represented in the program as MAT), twenty-five situations (SIT), four lighting sources (LIT), and twenty-two sorts of inhabitants (INH). Higgins, who accompanied Knowles and Tenney at BPI, reported that the "entire process of computing and printing out the full fifty pages of the text required only 1.93 minutes."[15] Knowles's chance-computational poem, exemplary of the period's technologically driven explorations at the intersection of cultural and industrial production, also inquires into how the *experience* of the body in the world of objects is inflected by interactions involving different texts and spaces. And how, in this instance, texts conjure speculative spaces and architectures.[16]

The poetic matter of "A House of Dust" resists both conformity and literary intentionality, revealing a quixotic world in which the actual, the possible, and the unimaginable coexist. Knowles's original lists envision homes made of plastic, discarded clothing, wood, tin, glass, steel, straw, or paper; illuminated by natural light, candles, electricity, or "all available lighting"; located in a deserted church, by a river, in an overpopulated area, in Japan, under water, among small hills, in heavy jungle undergrowth, or on an island; and inhabited by friends, vegetarians, fisherman and families, very tall people, or people who enjoy eating together. The formulaic structure, repeating with variation, achieves a paradoxical lucidity that is often fascinatingly absurd, humorous, and evocative:

A HOUSE OF DUST
  IN MICHIGAN
    USING NATURAL LIGHT
      INHABITED BY VEGETARIANS

A HOUSE OF ROOTS
  BY A RIVER
    USING NATURAL LIGHT
      INHABITED BY PEOPLE WHO SLEEP VERY LITTLE

A HOUSE OF SAND
  AMONG OTHER HOUSES
    USING ELECTRICITY
      INHABITED BY PEOPLE WHO LOVE TO READ

A HOUSE OF LEAVES
  IN A METROPOLIS
    USING ALL AVAILABLE LIGHTING
      INHABITED BY ALL RACES OF MEN REPRESENTED WEARING
        PREDOMINANTLY RED CLOTHING[17]

The poem, then, proposes and achieves an ever-shifting textual-symbolic journey through fantastical spaces of peaceful cohabitation.

The inhabitants Knowles included—"lovers," "collectors of all types," "Negroes wearing all colors," "children and old people," "American Indians," "French and German speaking people," "friends and enemies," "people speaking many languages wearing little or no clothing"—emphasize her vision of communal intimacy and connection, at a time of both global and domestic conflict and a youthful psychedelic counterculture with utopian aspirations.[18] Knowles, far from a countercultural activist, was nevertheless attuned to the pervasive discontent with traditional models of living, working, and making, and she personally supported the collective resistance to war, racial oppression, capital punishment, and environmental catastrophe.[19] In the punched-card universe of information, and the insidiously impersonal ways it was deployed for militaristic ends, Knowles's brief technological embrace can be regarded as a potential countermodel for turning the era's instrumentalized logic toward creative ends.

Around 1968, the poem physically materialized as stacks of computer printouts issued by Cologne-based curators and publishers Kasper and Walther König.[20] Knowles had met Kasper in the mid-1960s, when he was living and working in New York, and he and his brother Walther arranged to have her installation *The Big Book* exhibited in September 1968 in the Rowohlt Verlag booth at the Frankfurter Buchmesse (an event marked by mass student protests in West Germany and dubbed the "Police Fair").[21] In an interview with Hans Obrist decades later, Walther recalls receiving a large package mailed by Kasper from New York that contained magnetic tapes, technical data, and other materials related to "A House of Dust."[22] Searching for a partner to help them generate a full copy of the computer poem, the brothers convinced the Siemens Corporation in Munich to print it at no charge, and a few weeks later "an endless pile of folded paper" (in fact, three feet high) arrived in a box on Walther's doorstep.[23] A year later, he created a limited-edition portfolio by dividing this printout into twenty sections, each of which he wrapped in a clear plastic sleeve with a label screen-printed in red (fig. 5.3). A copy in the Getty Research Institute contains one of König Verlag's slices of the poem, consisting of two hundred and sixty unique stanzas on twenty accordion-folded pages.[24]

The continuous ribbon of green-and-white-lined pages emerging from a tractor-fed printer can be made to stack neatly (fig. 5.4) or allowed to sprawl haphazardly into heaps, as in Hans Haacke's contemporaneous telex installation, *News* (1969). Knowles's work differs markedly from Haacke's in inviting viewers to touch the pages, to pull them up to read—to *perform*—the poem. One cannot recite "A House of Dust" without attending to the multisensorial physicality of its linked pages. In this way, as Zabet Patterson has noted in a related context, Knowles's poem aligns with other computationally experimental art of this era, like filmmaker Stan VanDerBeek's "Poemfield" series (1965–1971). Similar to those animated works, "articulated through a cascading chain of human and machine-readable languages," Knowles's conceptualization of a series of imaginative shelters outperforming their environmental and elemental conditions produces visual epics that unfold over time.[25]

In its deployment and transmission of lists, Benjamin H. D. Buchloh has argued, "A House of Dust" attains "the formulation of an aesthetic language that considered the displacement of the conventional promises of poetry to be among its primary functions."[26] Moreover, it merges poetic, visual, and spatial impulses simultaneously. In attending to the subjective content of "A House of Dust," journeying through and out of its populous fictive environments, we recite and give form to the idea of witnessing. We observe horses and birds in

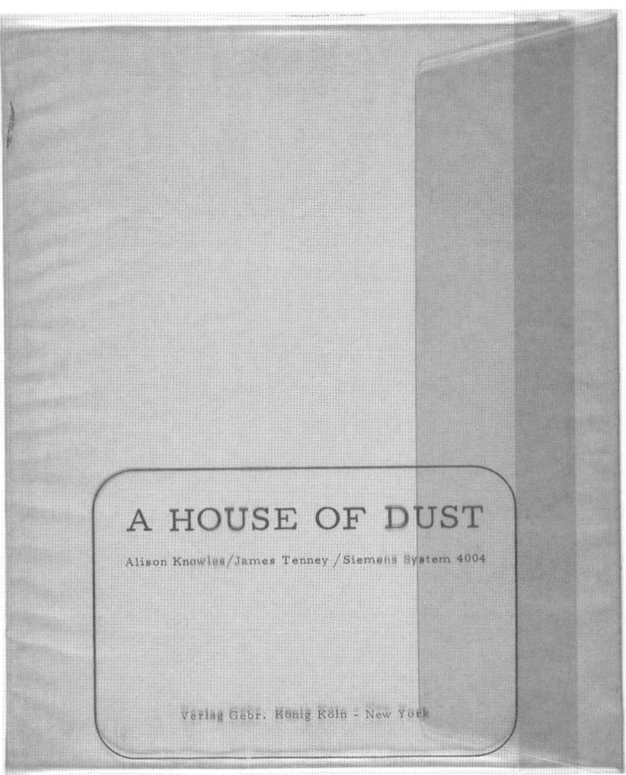


**Figure 5.3.** Alison Knowles and James Tenney, "A House of Dust," ca. 1968. Computer printout in plastic with screen print, published by Verlag Gerb. Köning, Cologne, 1968. Getty Research Institute, Los Angeles (acc. no. 95-B3662.c1).

high mountains, lovers and friends by the sea, red-clad men of all races in a hot climate. The theme of the domestic recurs. Visions of expansive connection sync up with the Summer of Love and allude to temporally distant literary sources—notably, *The Epic of Gilgamesh*, an epic poem from ancient Mesopotamia, first recorded on clay tablets dating to the third millennium BCE, that follows the story of the mythological King of Uruk and his wild friend Enkidu.[27] In tablet 7, Enkidu recounts a vivid dream of the "house of dust," where kings are stripped of their power, where patriarchy is overthrown in favor of generosity and care for others:

> On entering the House of Dust,
> everywhere I looked there were royal crowns gathered in heaps, everywhere
> I listened, it was the bearers of crowns who in the past had ruled the land,
> but who now served Anu and Enlil cooked meats,
> served confections, and poured cool water from waterskins.
> In the House of Dust that I entered
> there sat the high priest and acolyte,
> there sat the purification priest and ecstatic,
> there sat the anointed priests of the Great Gods
> There sat Etana, there sat Sumukan,

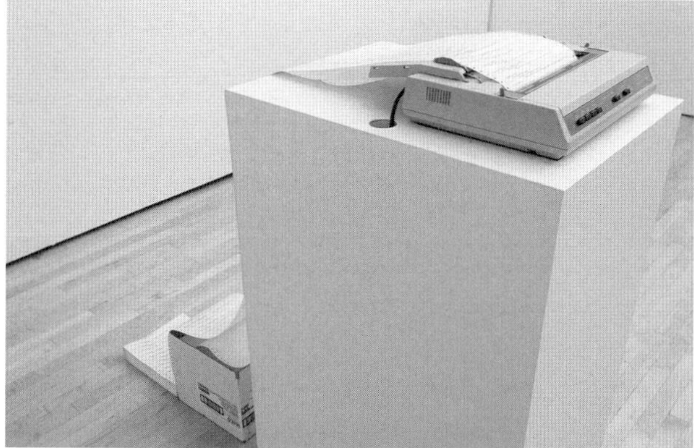

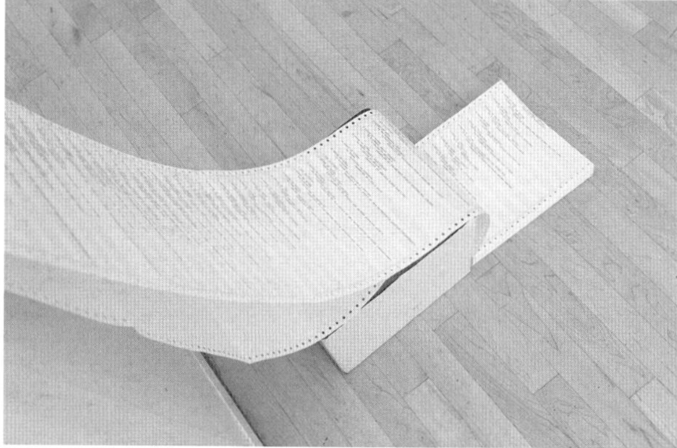

**Figure 5.4.** Alison Knowles, "A House of Dust," live computerized printout, James Gallery at CUNY Graduate Center, New York, 2016.

> there sat Ereshkigal, the Queen of the Netherworld.
> Beletseri, the Scribe of the Netherworld, knelt before her . . .[28]

Houses of glass, of roots, or of tin propose a new experience of specular and spatial reflection; there is more outside and there is no more outside. In its *incantations*, its multiple manifestations and publics, the rhetorical power of "A House of Dust" is, for me, the state of "otherness" we might occupy as it radically reimagines what a home consists of, its perceived inhabitants and future audiences. Which is to say, in the interstice between material document and computer typeface, inventive cognition, and textual transmission, "A House of Dust," like other heaps of language works of the later 1960s, refuses to announce the abolition of the paper support for merely instantaneous data; we are instead called to navigate its peculiar intentions by staying with the iterative material. With the computer organizing, systematizing, randomizing the lists, we are also caught up in the finitude of permissibility of textures.

Importantly, then, "A House of Dust" is not just a poem. It is an ever-evolving, generative artwork and an infinitely mutable score. It can be reprogrammed, reprinted, and reread in perpetuity, just as one might reperform *Proposition #2: Make a Salad*, *Proposition #6: Shoes of Your Choice*, or *The Iden-*

*tical Lunch*. So, too, the poem can be read in unlimited variation: as sequential stanzas, determined by what pages are available, or fragmented, disjointed in time and space, in public or in private, with hushed or booming voices.[29] This distinctive combination of functionality and utopian fantasy grew even more evident in the second phase of the poem, when it *transformed* from two dimensions into three.

## The House of Dust, Variation I: Object (New York)

In 1968 Knowles was awarded a Guggenheim Grant to "physicalize" "A House of Dust" as a large outdoor environment.[30] Hoping this new iteration of the work—now *The House of Dust*—would elicit participation from "performers" known and unknown, as her Fluxus propositional scores had in the early 1960s, she chance-selected (probably with some nonrandom tinkering) one of the poem's printed quatrains with the intention of building a "house" to its material specifications: A HOUSE OF PLASTIC / IN A METROPOLIS / USING NATURAL LIGHT / INHABITED BY PEOPLE FROM ALL WALKS OF LIFE.[31]

This "house of plastic" was first rendered as a pair of synthetic maquettes, biomorphic structures "made in curving, turning shapes" that "resemble a tadpole turned to stone" and that, in their full-size versions, children could play in and around (plate 7).[32] Knowles's whimsical phrasing amplifies the poem's evocation of fantastical dwellings far removed from conventional domestic architecture. The stereotypical postwar North American home promised safety, security, class, and racial homogeneity. *The House of Dust* offered no such symbolic sanctuary but, rather, "play sculptures," nested in public space between high-rise buildings.[33] Through this material shift, Knowles appears to level a criticism at austere modernist architecture, its domestic urban enclosures, the formal/cultural relationships it generates, and the conformist spaces and publics they conjure.

While developing plans to expand *The House of Dust* to an architectural scale, Knowles sought support from various individuals and institutions. In a letter to British-born critic and curator Lawrence Alloway, seeking permission to use his name as cultural capital in dealing with the city's Parks Department, she sketched the project's goals:

> On an abandoned site which I am requesting the city to clear, I will deposit a partial coating of cement. On the dirt and cement areas will be "presented" raw materials e.g. stone, wood, pebbles, etc. The sculptures, fences and forms that result are not necessarily my work, but [produced by] teams of workers (artists), children, anonymous new yorkers and anyone who cares to participate in a changing environment.[34]

Knowles also corresponded with Billy Klüver, a former engineer at Bell Labs and cofounder and president of the nonprofit organization Experiments in Art

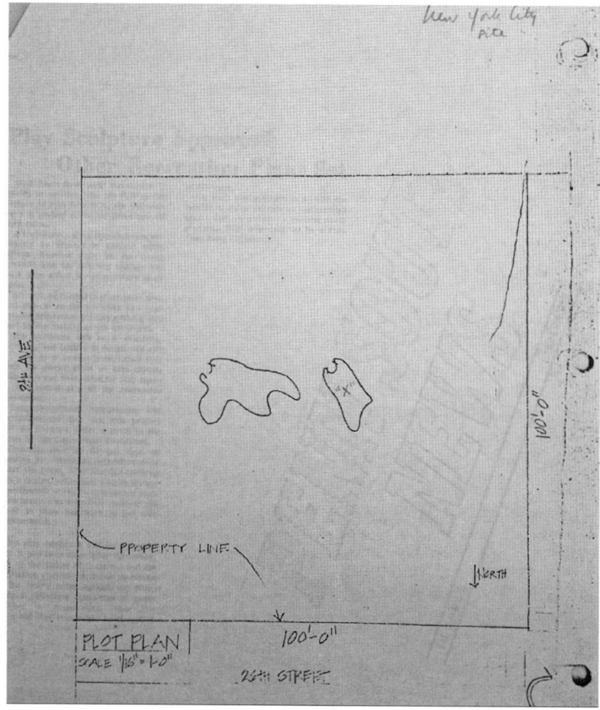


**Figure 5.5.** Alison Knowles, drawing and plans for *Chance House*, Eighth Avenue and 28th Street, New York, 1968. Alison Knowles Studio Archive.

and Technology (E.A.T.), who was unable to assist in computational operations but urged her to investigate potential municipal funding sources.[35]

More substantive and sustained advocacy came from her friend William N. Berger, an architect and teacher of aesthetics at Pratt Institute. Berger spent eight months aiding Knowles in the development process and shepherding blueprints through the New York City Building Department (fig. 5.5). After a series of failed attempts to covertly place the prefabricated environments in abandoned lots, Knowles reframed the project as a public sculpture and secured a permit to install it on an acre of public land in her Chelsea neighborhood. Knowles's "home for the houses"—a description she used interchangeably with "Chance House," "Happenings House"—would be realized at the Penn South Housing Co-op, a development between 28th Street and Eighth Avenue funded by the International Ladies Garment Workers Union (ILGWU).[36] In a letter to John Cage, Knowles noted her intention to add a collaborative aspect to the object/poem by embedding in its surfaces "discarded dishes and objects" solicited from co-op residents.[37] In an article referring to the work as a "play sculpture," the *Penn South Newsletter* focused on this openness to performative public engagement, reassuring skeptical residents that all would be "invited to place their special objects on the sculpture as permanent decoration and thus actually take part in the making of this art object."[38]

Henry Margulies, the ILGWU general manager, convinced the co-op's board of directors and recreation committee to approve placing her two irregularly shaped fiberglass tunnel domes on a plot measuring about seventy-five

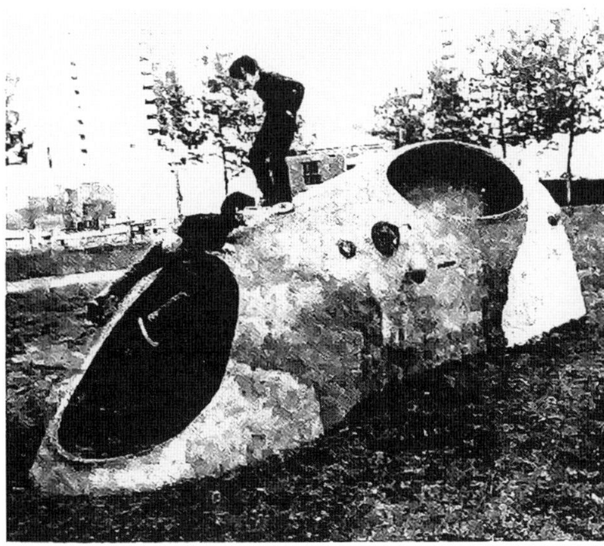

**Figure 5.6.** *The House of Dust* at Penn South, as shown on page 3 of *Chelsea Clinton News*, October 23, 1969.

by fifty feet near the power plant on 26th Street (fig. 5.6). The smaller dome, fabricated in plaster, reinforced polyester resin, and plywood by a Philadelphia foundry (George Kreier, Jr., Inc.), weighed two tons and incorporated a sonic element: Knowles commissioned her close friend (and fellow Tenney seminar participant) the new-music percussionist Max Neuhaus to add ambient sound activated by what Knowles called the house's "electric eye"—a sunlight-sensitive trigger connected to eight one-inch-square speakers inside the structure that generated a subtle acoustic murmur, most clearly audible as a "singing" element at dawn.[39] The live-weather sensor and sine-wave oscillator installed by Neuhaus, as Charles Eppley explains, "used photovoltaic cells to control amplitude and frequency variables," determining the tonal structure of the sound piece.[40] In a contemporaneous interview recorded as Knowles was repairing the work's façade with applications of resin (only the small house was ever installed in Chelsea), she described her collaboration with Neuhaus:

> You see its geared to the sun with light, and heat is activated by an electric eye that's on the other side. The more sound generated or activated [voice trails off] . . . a hot sunny day gets eight tiny speakers pulsing in there . . . it's a very light, quiet sound at best. When it's dark, you just get one or two. It's very complicated to work out . . .
>
> The small one is more of a "meditation space," and the bigger one will have no sound inside, just silence . . . [but] it can hold 12 people, and the space volume is that much bigger [so] you'll be able to get echoes.[41]

In the same interview, Knowles addressed the conceptual framework for the environment and its potential use-value:

> This is the first kind of sculpture I've done . . . and it has more to do with people sitting and being quiet in an object. In the sense that it's an enclosure with space [that] its sort of like a sculpture which I've never made before. I'm much less interested in the outside than I am in the inside . . . one of the things it's for is children playing inside.[42]

There is, indeed, a moment in the recording when children (who can be heard in the background throughout) interrupt the interviewer and bluntly ask Knowles what she is doing, how she made the work, and why. One particularly spirited exchange is worth recounting:

Child: Are you going to build something to get down from?
AK: No, I don't want to make it easy to get down from.
Child: How did you make this big thing?
AK: Uh, a little bit at a time . . . I make models that looked like this but were much smaller. I'm working with a very strong peroxide, the catalyst for the fiberglass, or else it would never harden it would stay like that for years. The catalyst is what burns, which is why I can't have you [near it] . . . I wanted very much to have water going . . . a fountain inside, [and] I wanted so much to have somehow the grass growing up the sides of the house, Linda, so it could actually grow up and almost cover over the top at random, so it seems like it has risen out of the air like a bubble.[43]

The status of the house as an actively evolving environmental experience was manifested, then, in several ways: in the sunlight-activated acoustic elements, the invitation to meditation or play, and the affixing to the work's rough shell of objects supplied by co-op residents ("the neighbors gave me so much stuff, I'm flooded") or collected by Knowles in the surrounding streets.

The placement of these found objects (scissors, buttons, shells, shoe heels, toys, etc.) was determined by chance operations derived from another computer "poem" printout, *Patina Selection* for *The House of Dust*, made in 1969 by Knowles's friend Jef Raskin. Specifying compass direction and object attributes ("weight, shape, color or category") as poetic "elements," Knowles later explained, "the computer was used again to select certain objects from the contributions for certain parts of the fiberglass houses, . . . placing them on one or another surface of the houses."[44] Using this computationally derived *score*, Knowles determined, for example, that the façade would face northeast and have ninety-two black things embedded in seven or eight areas.[45] The object chart (shared with Klüver at E.A.T.) identifies the smaller structure as the "low house" and the (unbuilt) larger one as the "high house"; specifies the processes to be used in embellishing the façades (e.g., melting, embedding, drilling); and includes notes on appropriate materials: "There will not be fabric used directly as it weathers badly and is incompatible, often forms bubbles or disintegrates, with the plastic. Paper can be collaged on the surface. . . .

There may, for instance, be a picture used showing the 17 required hats on the South East façade of the high house."[46] The visual effect of the object accretions on the houses was key. As Knowles emphasized two years later, "They resemble some beasts surfacing from the very depths of the sea. Objects collect on them like barnacles drawn from surrounding world by chance and locked onto the surface subject to change and breakage with time and the weather."[47] The material offerings amassed from friends, children, churches, and schools in the neighborhood manifested her vision of the object-poem's ability to connect disparate groups in creative collaboration.

But despite Knowles's consistent commitment to inclusion and engagement, some co-op residents—particularly those in the adjacent Building 4—regarded *The House of Dust* less as public art than as an affront to their privacy, their use of lived space, and even their safety.[48] It didn't help that they didn't know what to *call* the work. As Knowles later recalled:

> The whole previous year I'd been struggling with the Building Department. They gave it a terrible time because it *lacked a category*. You see, the object is partially inclosed [*sic*] and has only one exit. It wasn't open enough to be a sculpture . . . There's quite a difference between a sculptor doing outdoor pieces [e.g., Mark di Suvero] for a decade or more and a visual artist doing performance and intermedia looking for a place for her three-ton poem![49]

Residents may have been unsure how to meaningfully interact with a work of art that "lacked a category," but the petition they circulated against its installation and presence on their lawn focused on criticisms they could articulate: it would increase noise pollution, it would lead to misuse of the garden, and, more threatening, "it might attract unwanted strangers," provide a "convenient hiding spot for muggers" and "lend itself to hooliganism in the evening hours."[50] It gathered more than six hundred signatures, escalating pressures that would oblige the board of directors to rescind its support of the project. Frustrations mounted. The sound system was vandalized. And then, in the early morning of October 20, 1969, the complex's gardener was allegedly bribed to litter the house with kerosene-soaked trash and throw a torch into the skylight. A few days later, Knowles received a color photograph of the ensuing blaze, sent anonymously through the mail.[51] In shock and disappointment, and fearing the work was irretrievably damaged, she cast the project aside for two months, focusing more intently on her diurnal scored performance *The Identical Lunch* (figs. 3.16–3.17).[52]

In late 1969, Knowles again sought technical assistance and funding for *The House of Dust* project from Klüver and E.A.T. Klüver recommended that Knowles apply for E.A.T.'s newly created Projects Outside Art program—"outside" marking both a physical boundary and a desire to connect art making with nontraditional materials and methods in technologically savvy "realizable environments."[53] In her exhibition proposal, Knowles was careful to note that the iteration at Penn South was a "first sketch" and that *The House of Dust*'s relocation and transformation to E.A.T.'s public art context would be an apt variation for an interpretable object, fitting nicely into E.A.T.'s Recreation and Play category.[54] The computer printout she had used with the Chelsea environment would be put to service again to randomize the selection and placement of objects from fresh participants on the surface of the fiberglass shell, "like barnacles drawn from the surrounding world by chance."[55]

Underscoring the object/poem's capacity to live on discursively, even as she struggled to secure new funding, Knowles submitted a dossier of documents, preparatory drawings, press clippings, and objects related to *The House of Dust*, along with descriptions of her entanglements with the co-op tenants, to Swiss curator Harald Szeemann as her contribution to his pioneering *Happening & Fluxus*, held at the Kölnischer Kunstverein in 1970 (fig. 5.7).[56] In the exhibition, Szeemann placed Knowles's vitrine near the foyer between those for Ay-O and Ben Vautier, with the documentary ephemera she instructed him to install (including the König computer printout of "A House of Dust") hanging from hooks in vinyl sheet protectors and the plastic maquettes of *The House of Dust* stored nearby under a glass dome. Knowles's display was supplemented with over fifty discarded shoes, broken heels, and cobblers' molds collected from boxes left at public schools and shops, with the stock to be replenished by Szeemann from local sources should any of the initial items go missing.[57] In the spirit of the new ecologies of scale she was then engaged with, Knowles submitted another curatorial request to Szeemann that did not ultimately come to fruition: an entrance with "some kind of environmental flavor," like a "polyethylene tunnel for visitors to crawl through," to achieve a "wrapped effect to encounter and pass through."[58]

Knowles's decision to send very new work with an already vexed history (rather than decidedly Fluxus work like *Bean Rolls*) for a show whose curatorial aim was to historize the emergence of time-based and durational art during the previous decade posits an important shift in her artistic evolution from performance to environments. But the collection of shoes also shrewdly recalls her earlier Fluxus score *Proposition #6: Shoes of Your Choice* (1963; fig. 2.15), wherein participants are invited to describe their footwear, and signals a sustained interest in shoes, especially as they align with the human body and its movements in space, that would continue for decades to come.[59] In a German context in 1970, the mass of abstracted footwear might also evoke haunting images from the Holocaust of heaps of clothing and other personal goods stripped from their wearers, or the forced labor in the camps, which included shoe production. Like much of Knowles's work, *The House of Dust* vitrine hints at a political awareness that is present but elliptically referenced.

Beyond politics, conceptually and materially, Knowles's Cologne presentation of *The House of Dust* suggests the depth of her investment in a chance-based experimental process that, while often messy, entails generative, iterative collaboration between the artist and her various publics (other artists,

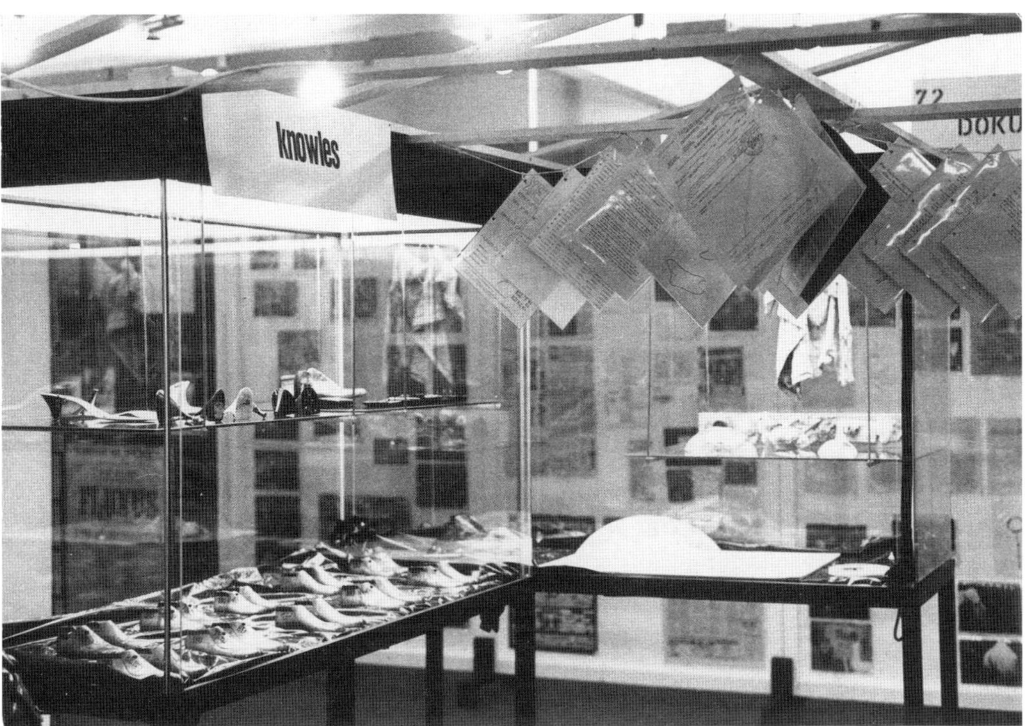


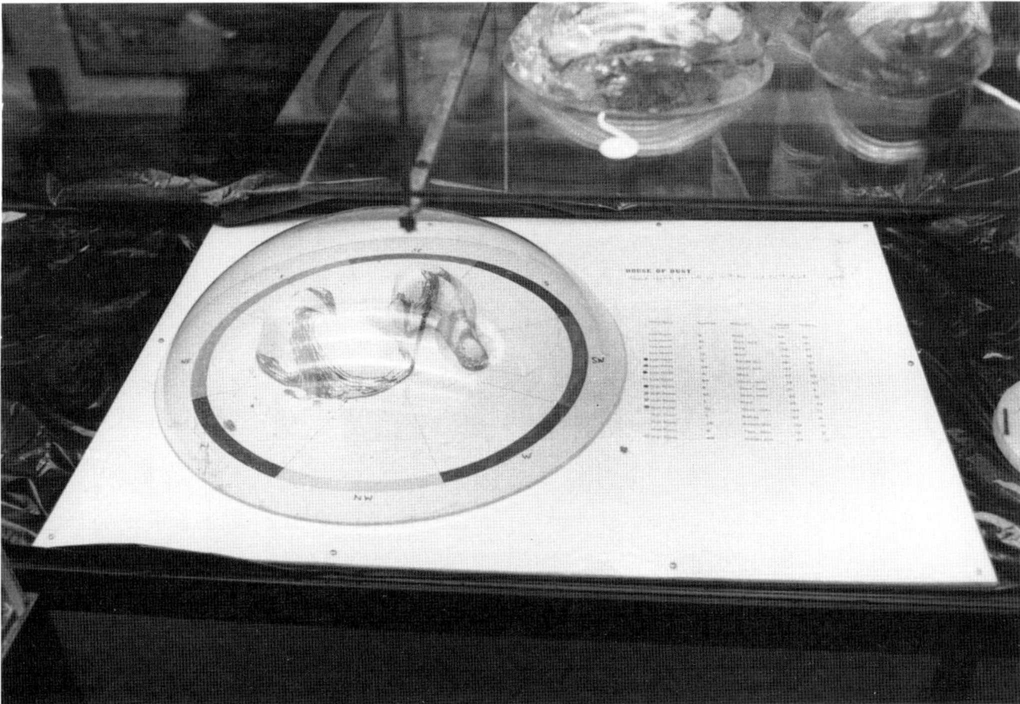

**Figure 5.7.** Alison Knowles, *The House of Dust*, 1968–1969. (*Top*) Installation view, *Happening & Fluxus*, Kölnischer Kunstverein, 1970–1971; (*bottom*) detail showing maquette. Courtesy Charles Deering McCormick Library of Special Collections, Northwestern University.

curators, NYC co-op boards, museumgoers, what have you). Unlike minimalist sculptor Richard Serra, who famously declared, "To remove the work of art was to destroy the work," when faced with legal and civic pressure to remove his monumental *Tilted Arc* in the early 1980s, Knowles translated the near-destruction and relocation of her Chelsea sculpture into expansively discursive, transatlantic archival sharing.[60] In 1970, when Knowles relocated to the West Coast to take a teaching position at the newly established California Institute of the Arts, *The House of Dust* environments were revived in yet another variation, for new uses and new publics.

## The House of Dust, Variation II: Object (California)

In 1970 Paul Brach, the first dean of studio art at CalArts, and Allan Kaprow, a recent New York transplant and CalArts's chair of studio art, recruited Alison Knowles as the first artist to direct the school's Graphic Prints Lab—a hire that recognized her deep technical training and expertise in silk-screening and other printmaking processes as well as performance and intermedia. Intent on creating an atmosphere "free of fear and repression," Brach chose as founding studio faculty "artists with professional experience in major metropolitan areas rather than those with only college art experience."[61] Sharing the long drive with artist Peter Van Riper, Knowles headed west in a large Hertz rental truck loaded with the contents of her studio and Higgins's Green Street loft, remnants of the Chelsea *House of Dust*, and a "hysterical cat."[62]

The contract Knowles negotiated promised her full rein over an acre of land on CalArts's temporary campus in Burbank (at Villa Cabrini, formerly a private Catholic girls' school), where she could reconstruct *The House of Dust* (plate 8). She based the California iteration of *The House of Dust* on a different quatrain: "A HOUSE OF DUST / ON OPEN GROUND / USING NATURAL LIGHT / INHABITED BY FRIENDS AND ENEMIES."[63] The object/poems initially sat on a patch of concrete on a disused tennis court overlooking Interstate 5. Two new environments, larger than their New York predecessor—the cavelike second dwelling unit measured twenty-three feet long by twelve feet high—sat alongside a refurbished version of the earlier incinerated work. Knowles again commissioned Max Neuhaus (who was invited as an artist-in-residence at CalArts) to add a sound element activated by "electric eye" sensors in the floor of the smaller of the two new houses; power was again supplied via underground cables to structures made of wood and fiberglass, and now laminated with reinforced polyester to make them fireproof (fig. 5.8).[64] The installation took four full days working with local forklift operators, with Knowles patching the Chelsea structure's grimy façade, "grayed up with diesel fuel from its trip west."[65]

Delighted in the distance "the poems journeyed," Knowles sketched an idea for a performance reading that would detail the objects' travels. The script—to be "spoken in a hushed voice as if describing something secret or

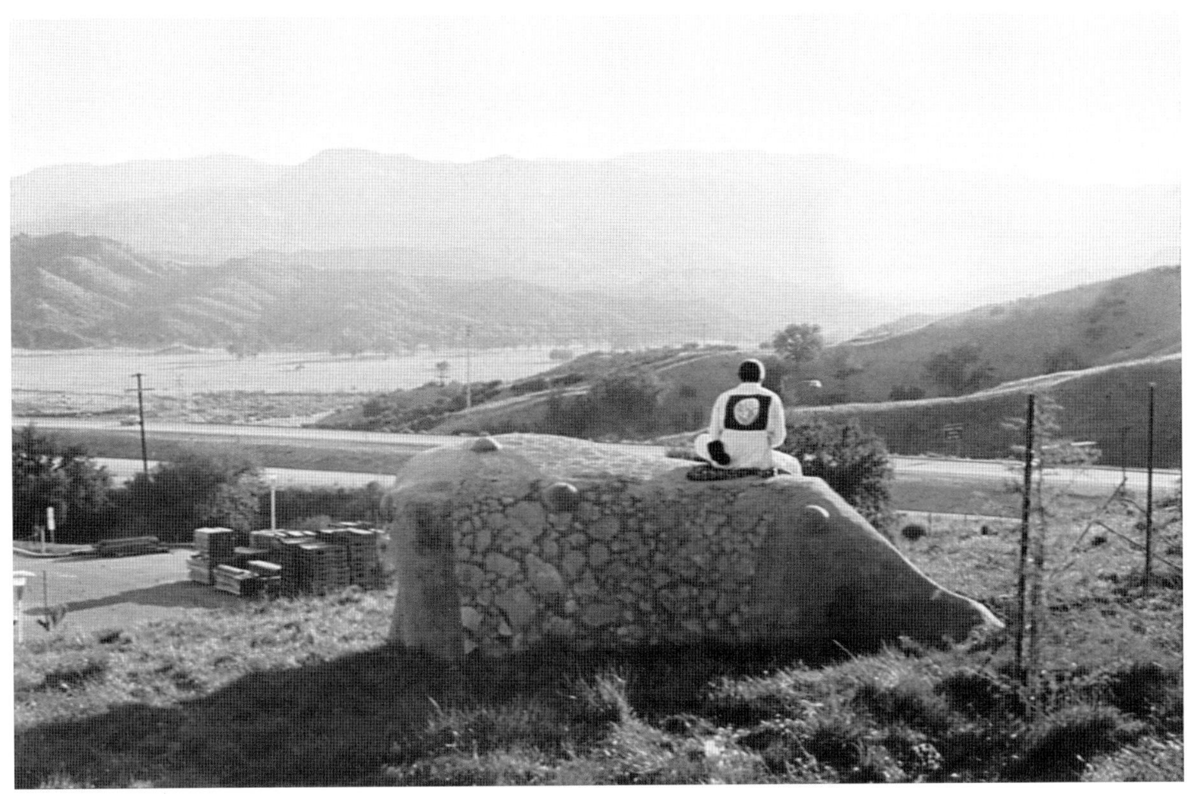

Figure 5.8. Student sitting atop *The House of Dust* structures, CalArts, ca. 1970. Courtesy of California Institute of the Arts Library & Institute Archives.

forbidden," with a cacophony of "concrete sounds relating to the event playing in the background"—reads in part:

> House of Dust arrives via flatbed truck in Newhall California / in fair shape / with crane and fork-lift adjusted onto abandoned tennis courts of the Villa Cabrini / shapes fuse instantly with landscape / hills maybe rocks / maybe small elephants / certainly prehistoric / all surfaces coated with diesel fuel from trip are allover / a scummy gray-green / ready to change position in the land / ready to be fixed in their temporary compass home / they wait for the play will be good / soon the big game will begin / nightfall / rest and meditation in the land.
>
> (background noise and/or sound fades to minimum as voice assumes normal volume and expressionless tone).[66]

It is unclear whether Knowles intended to present this reading on the site of the environments or in another space. What is clear is that the positioning of the houses was key to Knowles's intentions, performative and otherwise. The object/poems were set apart from other temporary campus buildings, but white lines radiating outward on the ground place them at the center of a sort of compass, with eight cardinal points corresponding to the *I Ching*'s eight trigrams, consistent with her original visualization in the maquettes (plate 7).

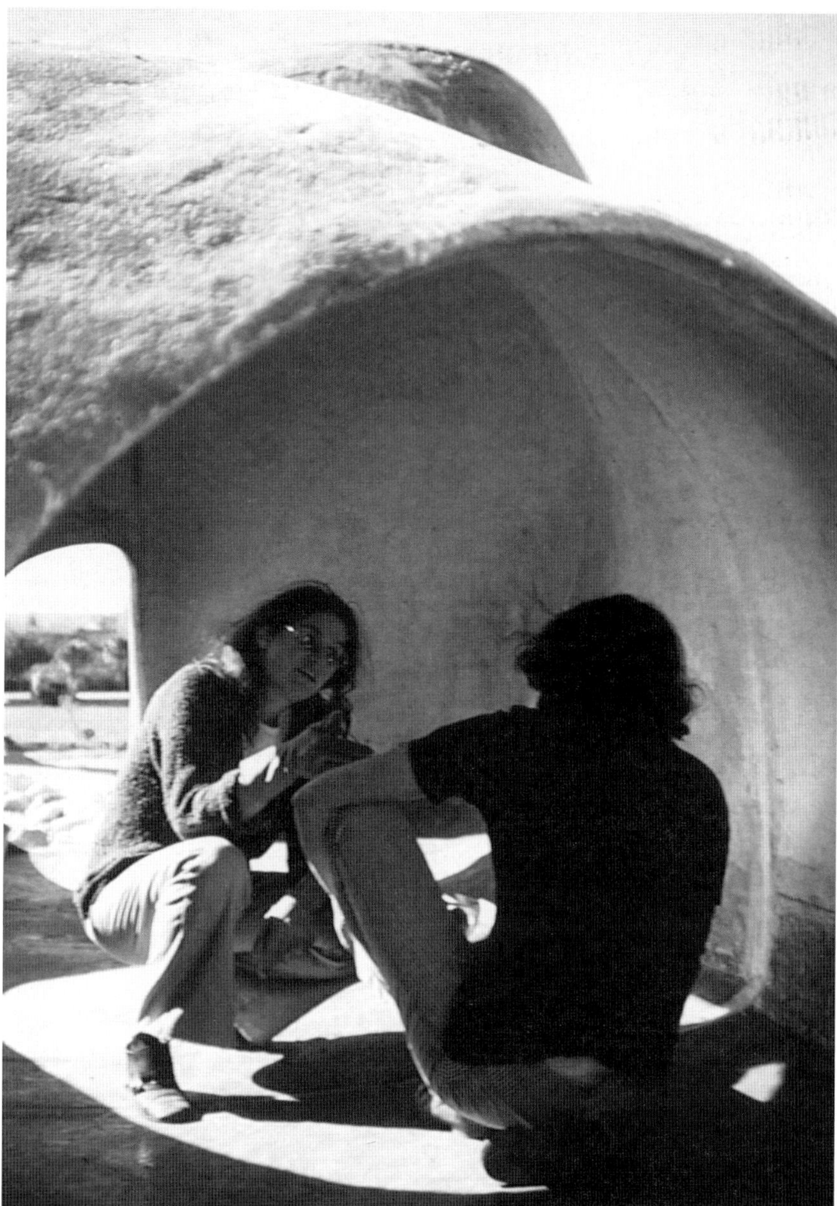

**Figure 5.9.** Alison Knowles with unidentified student in *The House of Dust*, CalArts, ca. 1970. Courtesy California Institute of the Arts Library & Institute Archives.

The compass divisions were specifically intended to "radiate out into the surrounding environment," priming it for performance events.[67] Lacking proper office space at her new post, Knowles conceived of the object/poems also as locations for thoughtful exchanges with students, colleagues, and visiting scholars and artists (fig. 5.9). Part of the site—a hill rising sharply to a plateau—was reserved for inclusion in *Space Atlas*, a compendium by artist Dana Atchley (a.k.a. Ace SpaceCo.), a forerunner of intermedia video art and "digital storytelling" whom Knowles was fond of and felt compelled to support.[68] A year later, Atchley, as artist-in-residence at California College of the Arts, proposed

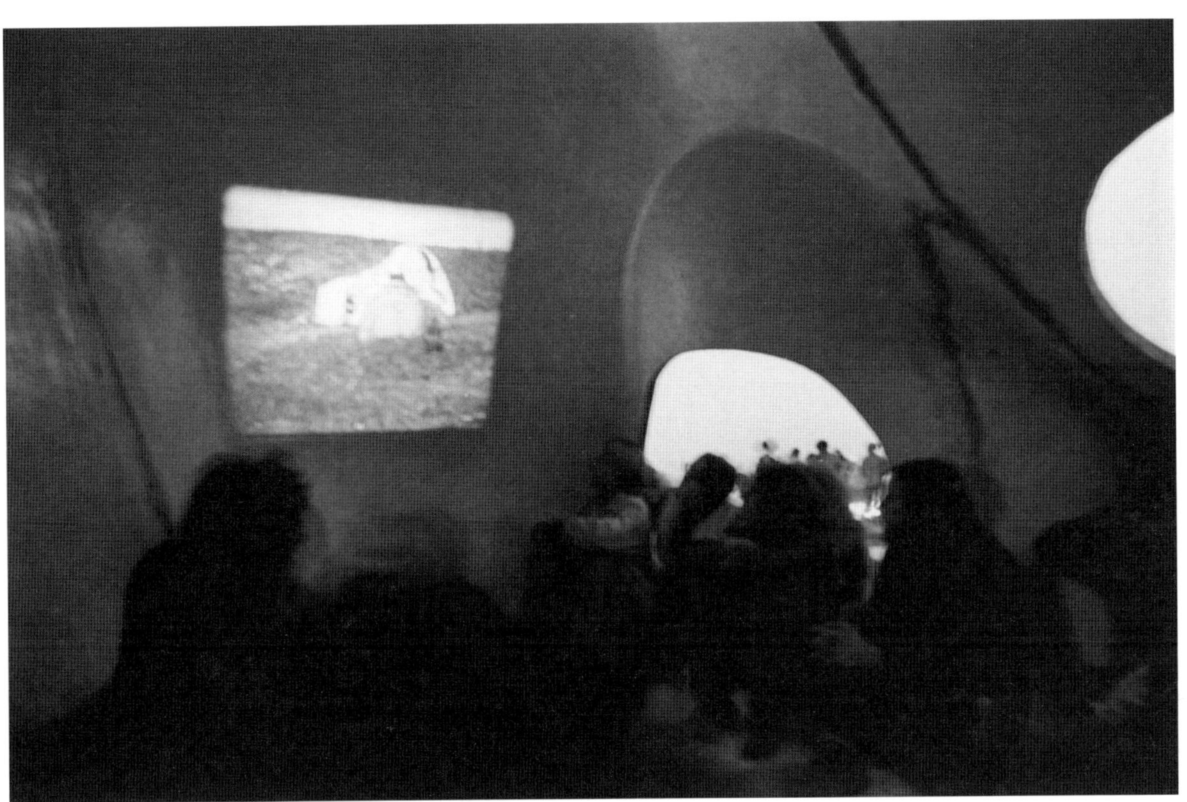

**Figure 5.10.** Students watching films in the large dome (*The House of Dust*), CalArts, ca. 1970–1971. Photo: Dan Wilt. Courtesy California Institute of the Arts Library & Institute Archives.

relocating the environments to Oakland and using the area around Knowles's "poem-in-progress" for events, installations, and happenings.

The smaller house, wired for sound, became the preferred spot for film screenings programmed by Knowles or others in the CalArts community (fig. 5.10). In turn, the visually irregular, communally active enclosures inspired local artists, including experimental filmmaker Andy Voda, who created *Chance Chants* (1979)—an animated piece derived in part from randomly selected stanzas of Knowles's poem "A House of Dust"—and Shuya Abe, who remixed Super 8 footage of *The House of Dust* using his revolutionary video synthesizer.[69] What Knowles managed to produce was a live-object, continuously performing (and being performed by) its own logic of participatory ecologies and constituencies. Acceptance of ever-shifting relations between art and its communities is central to Knowles's aesthetic. She had conceived the original "Chance House" as a gift to the New York neighborhood in which she lived and worked only to have the gift rejected and destroyed. At CalArts, she ensured the environments would live on in another variation at a site specifically chosen for a new use and public presence. Her complex use of computer-generated material worked not to merge public and private space, ultimately, but to upend that antinomy entirely.

As part of a course titled "Intermedia" at CalArts, Knowles encouraged her students to create original artworks derived from their use of *The House of Dust*. One memorable project was "Computer Poem Drop over The House of Dust," organized by Knowles and student Norman Kaplan, and advertised in the *LA Times* to celebrate CalArts's upcoming May 1971 move to its permanent campus in Valencia (fig. 5.11).[70] Postcards announcing the event quoted still another quatrain: "A HOUSE OF DUST / WAY OUT THERE / LIGHTED BY CANDLES / INHABITED BY FISHERMEN AND THEIR FAMILIES."[71] For this iteration, Raskin, by then an assistant professor at UC San Diego and a frequent visitor to CalArts, arranged with Mike Plesset at Caltech's Jet Propulsion Laboratory (JPL) to generate the first large-scale printout of the poem since König Verlag's version in 1968.[72]

In a September 1970 letter to John Cage, Knowles described the opportunities the collaboration provided, excitedly listing the computers JPL gave her access to and asking Cage to send Plesset ICHING, a subroutine composer Lejaren A. Hiller Jr. had programmed that generated *I Ching* hexagrams and translated them into musical notes. Once secured, the software was integrated with the poem-producing program and the new printout prepared in time for the poem drop.[73]

The resulting printout, a stack of connected pages over four feet high, was subsequently dropped from a rented helicopter over the Burbank installation, with Knowles orchestrating the timing from the ground via a two-way radio (fig. 5.12). Hundreds of people watched from the ground as long streamers of printer paper flipped through the air on a clear, breezy day. Kaplan rode along with the pilot while Kaprow recorded the drop from below on Super 8 film.[74]

Knowles obtained funding for the helicopter rental from the Art, Theater, and Critical Studies programs by arguing the pedagogical benefits of providing students unconventional means for presenting their art.[75] Richard (Dick) Banks, another of Knowles's students, led a Greek chorus of readers (dressed in white togas) in reciting the poem as the pages "like birds flew from the sky" and settled over the smaller *House of Dust*.[76] But the "Poem Drop Event"—publicized in a school memo as a "visual, physical, poetry experience"—also alluded to different aesthetic and sociopolitical currents.[77] Referencing other artists' works, obliquely or obviously, was standard practice for Knowles and the neo-avant-garde artists with whom she is professionally and personally associated. In that regard, the 1971 poem drop may give a wink to an absurdly theatrical performance by Knowles's close friend Ray Johnson, who in September 1969 had procured a helicopter and dropped hot dogs over the lawns and homes of Wards and Mill Rock Islands in Manhattan as his contribution to Charlotte Moorman's 7th Annual Avant Garde Festival (fig. 5.13).[78]

A second, less hermetic reference is to the war in Southeast Asia, which saw the first large-scale use of helicopters in a combat role. Helicopter formations were widely used by the US Army to locate and assault North Vietnamese ground forces and transport troops into battle, and some of the most enduring images television brought into American living rooms were of paratroopers jumping from choppers, landing with distinctive "thump-thumps."[79]

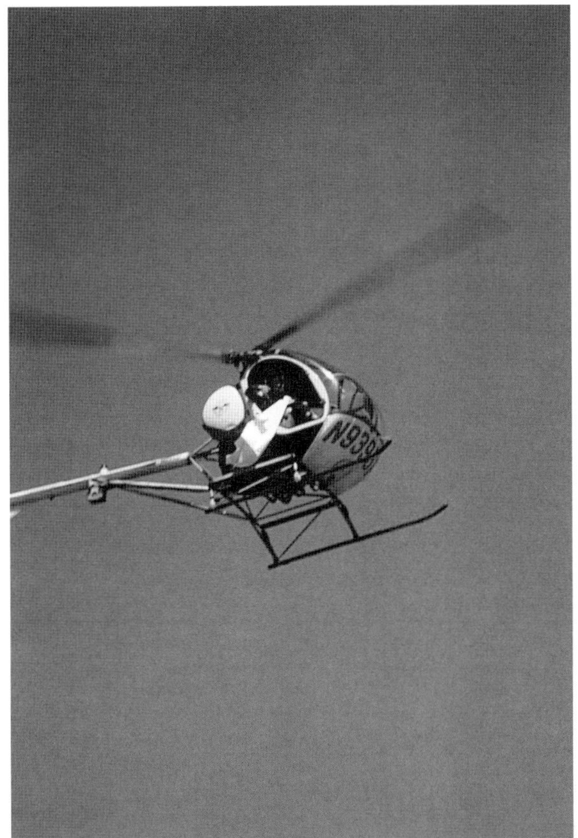


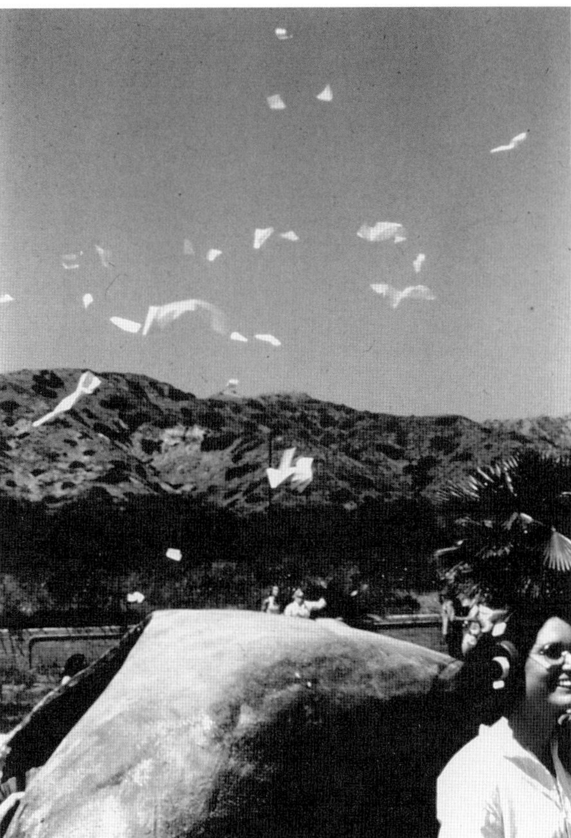

**Figure 5.11.** Alison Knowles with Norman Kaplan, *Poem Drop Event* at *The House of Dust*, CalArts, May 1971. Courtesy California Institute of the Arts Library & Institute Archives.

**Figure 5.12.** Alison Knowles with Norman Kaplan, *Poem Drop Event* at *The House of Dust*, CalArts, May 1971.

Knowles's poetic bombardment at CalArts coincided with the Spring Offensive—three weeks of antiwar protests in Washington, DC, in May 1971, by student activists, Vietnam veterans, and a coalition of more than a hundred peace and radical groups (fig. 5.14). It occurred almost exactly one year after four unarmed students were shot by the Ohio National Guard at Kent State University, and numerous protests against US foreign policy had also occurred in Los Angeles in the two years Knowles had lived there, including an August 1970 antiwar demonstration in East Los Angeles organized by the Chicano Moratorium Committee.[80] In the context of political activism among her students at CalArts and throughout the wider arts and university communities, Knowle's helicopter event might be considered a pointed critique of California as a primary driver of the US military-industrial complex.[81]

In an oppositional counternarrative, Kaprow's film and other archival images of Knowles's poem drop show a joyful event, perhaps even a reclamation of the helicopter as metaphor for peaceful liberation rather than violent aggression. For me, Knowles's antiwar stance connects to a form of pedagogical activism wherein collaborations with students constitute a politics in kind. A child of the Great Depression, Knowles was a generation older that her students, but that by no means precluded allying herself with their activ-

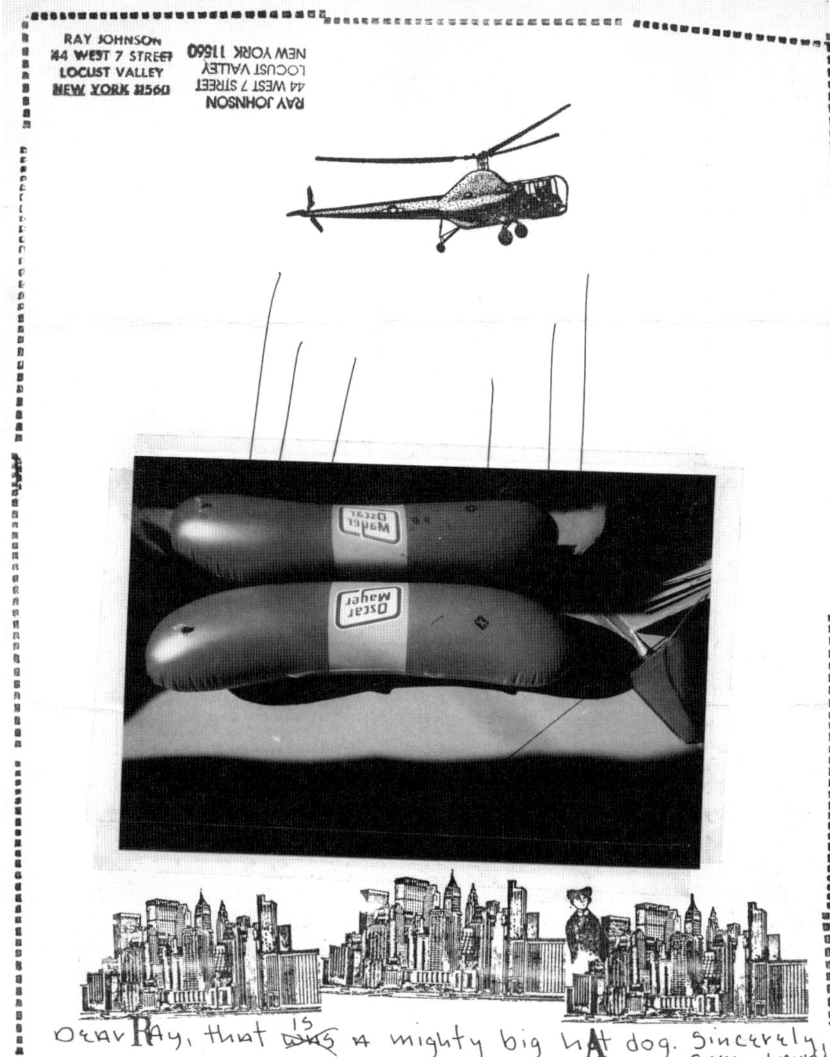


**Figure 5.13.** Ray Johnson "Helicopter Event" mailing, 7th Annual Avant Garde Festival, Wards and Mills Island, New York, 1969. This copy was signed and returned by "Gorey Laurie" (Laurel Hall). © Ray Johnson Estate, New York, New York.

ism. Whether overseeing the Graphics Print Lab, where what students produced included political posters, or dropping paper poems from a helicopter, rather than propagandistic leaflets or chemical bombs, Knowles's activities at CalArts manifest a participatory ecology of making that binds dissenting responses to American imperialism to expansive practices of art.

Like many happenings at *The House of Dust*, the poem drop displaced the routines of campus life and created a new space open to public participation. A similar openness was apparent in *99 Red North*, a performance scored by Knowles, in which ninety-nine red apples were arranged on the quadrant north of *The House of Dust* (fig. 5.15).[82] Participants in the event, organized by Knowles and several art students (including Matt Mullican), were invited to exchange any object for one of the apples.[83] Describing *99 Red North* and its

94th Year ···· No. 150 © 1971 The Washington Post Co. TUESDAY, MAY 4, 1971 Phone 223-6000 Circulation 223-6100 Classified 223-6200 10c Beyond Washington, Maryland and Virginia 10c

# 7,000 Arrested In Disruptions

## E. Germany's Ulbricht Quits

By John M. Goshko
Washington Post Foreign Service

BONN, May 3—Walter Ulbricht, the most durable of Europe's Communist leaders, today surrendered his two-decade grip on power by resigning as first secretary of East Germany's Communist Party.

In a sudden announcement from East Berlin, the East German news agency (ADN) said that the 77-year-old Ulbricht had quit for reasons of age and health.

Succeeding him as first secretary—the most powerful position in East Germany—is Erich Honecker, 58, who had long been regarded as Ulbricht's heir apparent. As secretary of the central committee, Honecker had been in charge of running the party's day-to-day affairs for the past several years.

The ADN announcement, which included long statements by both men, said that Ulbricht would retain the post of president of the Council of State, which he has held since 1960.

This means that he continues as East Germany's head of state. He also was named honorary chairman of the party, a title created especially in his honor.

However, both positions are essentially ceremonial without any real power, and the implication is that Ulbricht is falling back on the role of a largely retired elder statesman of communism.

The immediate reaction of Western observers was that Ulbricht's departure from ac-

## Court Backs Death Verdict Procedures

By John P. MacKenzie
Washington Post Staff Writer

The Supreme Court upheld yesterday the procedures used to impose the death penalty in the 38 states that allow capital punishment.

By a 6-to-3 vote the court ruled that judges need not give juries more definite standards to guide their sentencing decisions and held that states need not provide separate hearings on guilt and punishment in capital cases.

The decision came as no surprise to groups seeking to eliminate all executions in the United States. But it stirred anxiety among civil rights and civil liberties lawyers that numerous executions would soon break the court-imposed moratorium that has stayed all executions since June 1967

By Douglas Chevalier—The Washington Post

Protesters tie up traffic at 35th and M Streets NW with stalled Volkswagens placed in the intersection.

## Justify Arrests, Judge Orders Police

### Total Sets a U.S. Record

By Sanford J. Ungar and Maurine Beasley
Washington Post Staff Writers

The metropolitan police department and D.C. National Guard have been ordered into court tonight either to justify irregular procedures used yesterday

they committed their alleged offenses.

Acting on an emergency habeas corpus petition filed by the Public Defender Service, Judge Greene hinted

### Protesters Irk Citizens

By Haynes Johnson
Washington Post Staff Writer

Tom Henderson left his suburban home in Hillcrest Heights, Md., early yesterday morning to go to work. Hours later he still hadn't made it to the flower shop on Wisconsin Avenue and

for what? If this keeps up, I'm going to lose a whole week's work. I can't go to work, and I can't go home. And I can't afford it. I've got responsibilities."

## New Obstructions Threatened Today

By Paul W. Valentine
Washington Post Staff Writer

More than 7,000 persons were arrested in widespread hit-and-run skirmishes with police and federal troops in Washington yesterday as antiwar protesters made an unprecedented attempt to bring the government to a physical halt.

By most accounts, including those of protest organizers, the disruption plan generally failed.

The arrests, made while police fired tear gas through much of downtown Washington and military helicopters whirred across city skies, were greater in number than those in any single event in the nation's history, research indicated.

But Rennie Davis, spokesman for the protesters, vowed just before he was arrested by FBI agents in midafternoon on federal conspiracy charges that a new attempt would be made this morning to snarl commuter traffic.

Targets for 7:30 a.m. today will be restricted to Dupont, Scott and Thomas Circles and Mount Vernon Square, some protest leaders said. However, final strategy had not been determined.

As the dissidents took to the streets at dawn yesterday, a message from President Nixon asking that Washington be kept an open city was read over the police radio network.

Five hours later, Attorney General John N. Mitchell announced from the Justice Department, "The city is open. The traffic is flowing. The government is functioning."

To keep the city open, 4,000 troops were brought in. Another 4,000 were held in reserve nearby.

The bulk of Washington's 5,100-man police force was on duty throughout the day, supported by 1,400 D.C. National Guardsmen.

Troops with fixed bayonets occupied streets where demonstrators had been. Army trucks and jeeps rumbled through the city. Sirens wailed. Acrid tear gas floated through quiet residential streets in Georgetown and seeped into office buildings downtown.

Busloads of prisoners were shuttled to jails, including an emergency outdoor detention center hastily set up at a Washington Redskins' practice field near RFK Stadium. Later, 2,481 of them were transferred to the Washington Coliseum.

**Figure 5.14.** May Day protests against the war in Vietnam, Washington, DC. *Washington Post*, May 4, 1971.

methodology, Knowles has explained, "This particular event concerns my interest in chance operations and random structuring. . . . Apples were selected as the object for exchange. They were placed in the compass direction to answer category North, 90, red. This quadrant of the section of the abandoned tennis court where the HOUSES were located [was] painted white for the occasion [with] the number 90 stenciled on it."[84] Many people left something behind (e.g., key chain), but many of the apples sat decaying for several weeks (fig. 5.16).

A related live performance arranged by Knowles for the campus community, after *The House of Dust* environments had moved to Valencia, was a day-long presentation of poet Jerome Rothenberg's *Gift Event II (Kwakiutl)*. *Gift Event II* is a translation piece that is itself in communion with Knowles's 1963 *Proposition #16: Giveaway Construction*, which instructs, in part, that performers "Find something you like in the street and give it away."[85] Rothenberg's text was originally penned in 1960 and republished by Knowles and Higgins's Something Else Press in 1966. The poetic directives for giving are derived from "assembled statements by Indians" in potlatch ceremonies he found described in an article by anthropologist Helen Codere. The score reads, in part:

> Start by giving away different colored glass bowls.
> Have everyone give everyone else a glass bowl.
> Give away handkerchiefs & soap & things like that

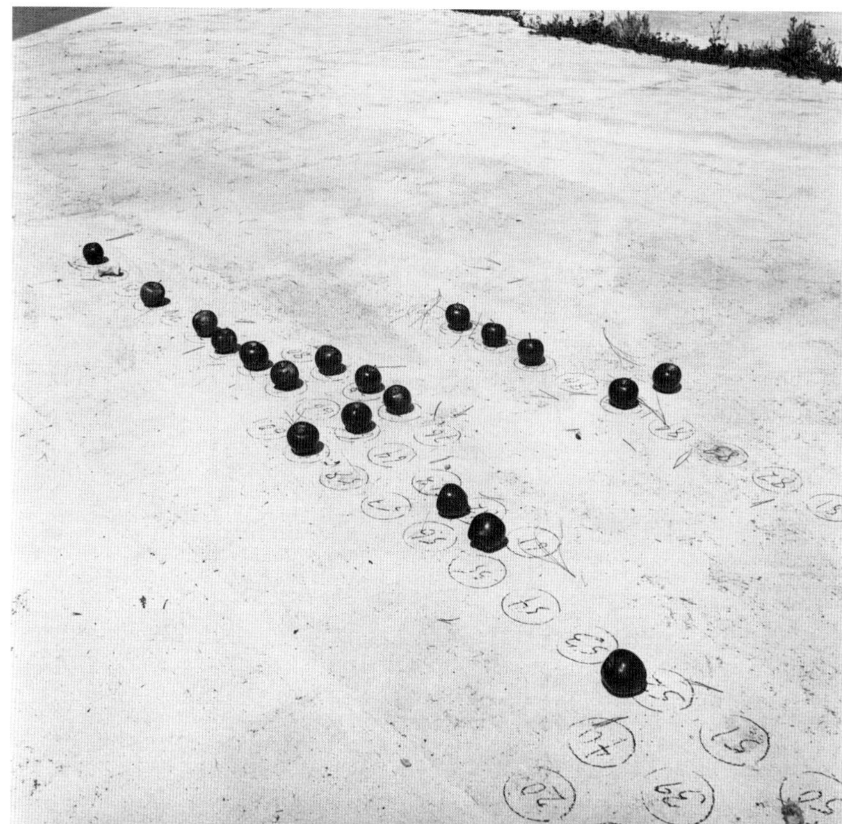

**Figure 5.15.** Alison Knowles, *99 Red North Event* at *The House of Dust*, CalArts, ca. 1970–1971. Courtesy California Institute of the Arts Library & Institute Archives.

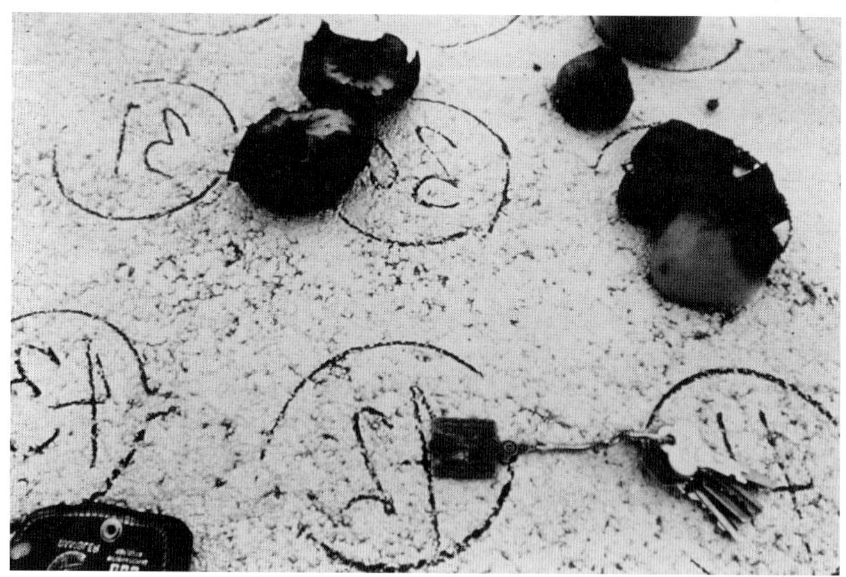

**Figure 5.16.** Alison Knowles, *99 Red North Event* at *The House of Dust*, CalArts, ca. 1970–1971.

Give away a sack of clams & a roll of toilet paper.
Give away teddybear candies, apples, suckers & oranges.
Give away pigs & geese & chickens, or pretend to do so.
Pretend to be different things.
Have the women pretend to be crows, have the men pretend
To be something else . . .[86]

The spring "new moon" 1972 iteration of *Gift Event II* was significantly expanded by Knowles into a "dawn to midnight extravaganza," including a "ritual shoe-burning after dark," all events constituting "a happening because of the panoramic scale of the displays and occurrences."[87] Participants were mostly students who interpreted the "give away" instructions as they wished. Gift exchanges of varying worth, poetry recitals, orchestral instruments, and a small graphics exhibition went on under a silk parachute rigged up for the occasion. Knowles later reported that all items mentioned in the "giving ritual" were somehow represented: "There was a roast pig that turned all day, tended by an Indonesian chef, and music by a group from Africa visiting the musical school at the time. The event had the spirit of a California swap-meet—which was a local phenomenon that interested me a great deal and around which I modeled the piece."[88] By emphasizing *use* value to students or anyone with access to the campus in the poem drop, *99 Red North*, and *Gift Event II*, as Karen Moss has also noted, Knowles's communal environments foreground social relations as temporally expansive experiments in praxis.[89] Here the artist moves between forms—textual, literary, environmental, participatory—creating potential new publics in each instance. The desire for sociability within a community of faculty and students, whoever they were, wherever they came from, was a driving force for Knowles during her brief time in California.[90]

Mutally supportive events at CalArts involving Knowles's *The House of Dust* highlight the political significance of the artist's project and provoke a deeper consideration of the dwellings as an act of generosity. The "object-poem" brings the text's inherently sociable, public character into being physically and metaphorically; its forms, that is, give shape to a space that allows the author's and the reader's subjectivity to coexist. At CalArts, *The House of Dust* served as a primary instigator for pedagogical exercises on intermedia and the body but also as an open-air stage for self-curated poetry readings, gift offerings, exhibitions, sunrise meditations, and more (fig. 5.17), including actions outside the artist's interests or CalArts's institutional control (among students, the object/poems were known, clandestinely, as "the house of lust").[91] Assertions of the right to free speech and bodily autonomy were bound up, in the left-leaning campus milieu, with a reclaiming of the cultural and intellectual means of production, and reflected a widening chasm between the politics of new and old.

Ultimately, Knowles's collaborative performance work on the CalArts campus continued the artistic themes she had been pursuing since the early 1960s: using chance to both assert and suppress her own subjective impulses

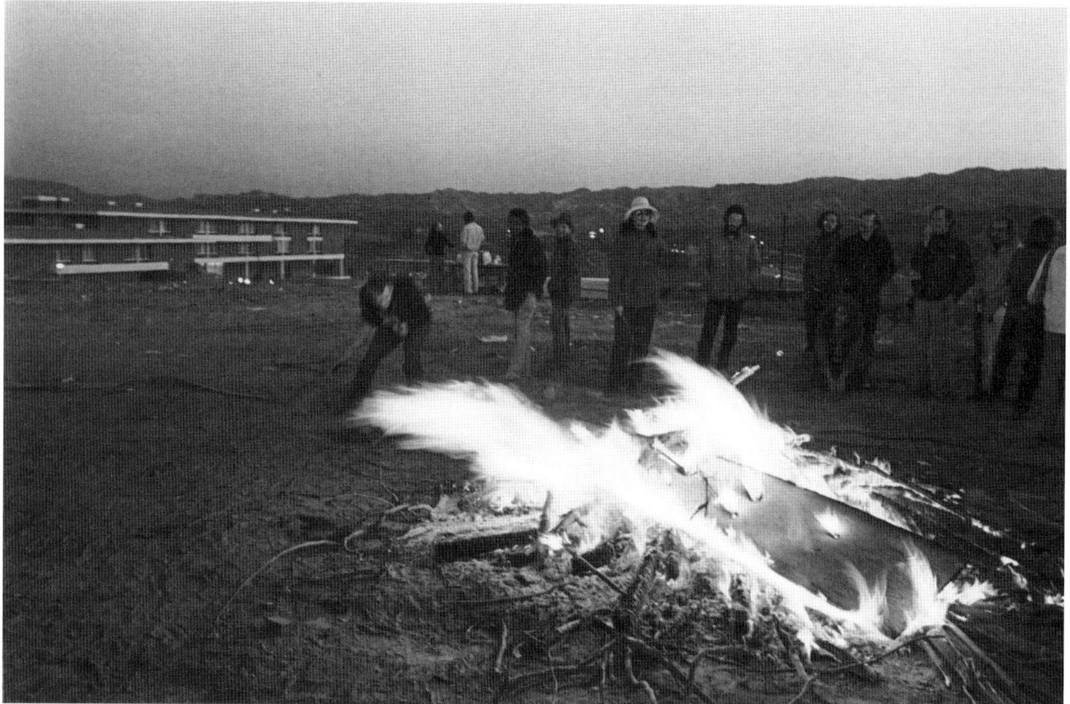

**Figure 5.17.** Alison Knowles (in hat) conducting a communal fire event at *The House of Dust*, CalArts, ca. 1972. Photo: Dan Wilt. Courtesy California Institute of the Arts Library & Institute Archives.

through an expression of the tenuousness and tediousness of life as it is lived. By encouraging an imaginatively autonomous approach to propositions, performances, objects, and spaces, Knowles consistently allowed for the slippage of any one of us into her place. As the artist later affirmed:

> The chance operations on which the poem is based, the random circuit that made the print-out, already frees it from me as an artist. Chance operations frees the work so it can find its own center outside. The participation just continues the idea. I feel apart, I am apart from the work; I adjust what goes on.[92]

In effect, "A House of Dust" and *The House of Dust* amplified the chance-based format into computational application and other expressive possibilities in the interstices between textual, literary, environmental, and object-based forms. In yet another iteration of the stanzas, Knowles commissioned "gifts to the house" from friends and collaborators inspired by the poem's domestic whimsy.[93] In at least one exhibition, the stanzas and their associated offerings were laid on Xerox copies of the objects and installed in boxes.[94] Gifts included drawings, computer cards, shoe heels, tools, erasers, and seashells—which Knowles later photographed separately, re-recycling them as individual art postcards and thus extending the chain of giving and receiving initiated in her earliest Fluxus propositions.

Nor was the raw material of the poem static. The Jet Propulsion Laboratory printout, dropped from a helicopter in 1971, was derived from a slightly altered database: among other changes, "clay" and "hair" had been added to the pool of possible materials, "wherever you find it" to the list of situations, "self-exiled Greeks" and "collectors of many types" to the potential inhabitants, and "existing in darkness" to the modes of illumination.[95] Knowles's continued reenvisioning of the original poetic text reflects certain postwar preoccupations with the agential, sensorial body and an expanded notion of art uniquely attentive to the tactile, the acoustical, and the environmental. Through *The House of Dust*, as object and as poem, Knowles again stretches the material possibilities of chance and indeterminacy toward a critique of gender as it is experienced spatially.

## Fantastic Architectures

In media of the late 1950s and 1960s, architectural historian Dianne Harris has noted, "privacy—both as a term and as a spatial imperative—became a rhetorical device, a strategy for articulating and asserting specific values that were linked to racial, class, and sexual identities."[96] Readers of popular press and shelter magazines absorbed a consistent stream of ideologically motivated images conflating corporate-capitalist consumption with idealized visions of the home. Perceptions of personal identity were increasingly bound to nationalist pride, as the home became a visual and spatial extension of the nation-state. Women were consigned to the private spheres, presumed to be (symbolically and materially) protectors of domestic space—even as their growing role in the workforce blurred socioeconomic expectations. Fascination with future-forward domestic designs, supported by corporate investment, is exemplified by the "House of the Future," manufactured by Monsanto Chemical Company for Tomorrowland, a prominent attraction at Disneyland from 1957 to 1967.[97]

Again, Knowles's visionary object/poem posited a counternarrative—a fantastical, utterly impractical vision of domestic enclosure that neither prescribed nor conformed to material or structural convention. Single-family, detached domiciles with private, fenced gardens never appealed to Knowles's aesthetic or political sensibilities. In choosing the urban (and in the early 1960s, before gentrification, gritty) neighborhood Chelsea over suburban Westchester or Scarsdale; or a commune just off US 101 in Ventura over the surrounding sprawl; or, later, another New York studio-loft and then an old barn in upstate Barrytown, she rejected the sequestration of suburban conformity. That Knowles first exhibited *The Big Book* in her and Higgins's living room qua gallery space; that the intellectual spark for "A House of Dust" was struck in that same space via Tenney's teachings; or that she sited the first iteration of the poem's sculptural rendering at a nearby housing complex—all speak to the artist's awareness of the tenuous and generative nature of domestic space, both public and private.[98] Further, the notion of performance as a unbound, liberating practice structured by chance-derived rules and instructions for play provides a compelling approach to discerning Knowles's work in the 1960s and 1970s. A free-flowing exchange between bodily enactment and randomly scored (yet still arranged) texts open to chance and manipulation serves as a conduit to more ideas, spaces, and textures, and remains her approach for decades to come.

As with the narrative imaginings of text, print, and domestic space in Knowles's book-inspired projects, we may extend our analysis of her environments through comparison to the work of another artist. Knowles admired the avant-gardists of the earlier twentieth century, their transformations of the art object and its redefined relation to commerce, politics, and Euro-American literary/visual culture. Her and Higgins's republication through Something Else Press of experimental works by Gertrude Stein, in particular, keenly reflected this persistent interest and engagement.

As detailed in chapter 1, the visual artist who spoke most authentically to Knowles, in relation to her own work, of the vitality of text, assemblage, found objects, and architecture was Kurt Schwitters. Knowles had an opportunity to view firsthand Schwitters's *Merz* pictures of the 1920s and 1930s in at least two MoMA exhibitions, *The Art of Assemblage* (1961) and *Dada, Surrealism, and Their Heritage* (1968)—shows that not only bolstered the critical reception of Schwitter's in postwar North America but grounded Knowles's own experimental sensibilities in historical assemblage and what followed—"expanded field" sculpture and the deliberate blurring of boundaries between art and architecture.[99] The 1968 exhibition, in particular, finally afforded Knowles a chance to inspect the Dadaist's major relief assemblages in person, including *Das Kreisen* (Revolving) (1919), *The "Worker" Picture* (Das Arbeiterbild) (1919), and *Merz Picture with Rainbow* (1939) as well as photographs and documents relating to his private architectural construction, the *Merzbau* (1923–1937), with which she was already familiar from reproductions in books.[100]

Schwitters's improvised environment—a dense accumulation of wood and plaster—included an inner core "formed of *Merz* agglomerations" that was only accessible through "doors" and "windows" in the surrounding structure.[101] Schwitters's radical reconceptualization of the picture plane amounted to a prototype for environmental sculpture, and in his lengthy catalog essay, MoMA curator William S. Rubin urges the reader to consider the Combines of Robert Rauschenberg, the *tableaux-pièges* ("snare pictures") of Daniel Spoerri, and the broader shift from painting to Environments to Happenings as part and parcel of the "*Merz* experience."[102]

The genealogy Rubin sketched—wherein the arts are redefined by material expansions in sculpture, installation, and performance—cohered with how many neo-avant-garde artists of the late 1960s viewed their experimentations and their place in history. For Knowles, this connective tissue was intentionally underscored when Schwitters's *Merzbau* and her own *The House of Dust* shared publishing space in *Fantastic Architecture*, a compilation of visionary architecture published by Something Else Press in 1969 (figs. 5.18–5.19). Dick Higgins and fellow Fluxus artist Wolf Vostell had begun began soliciting mate-

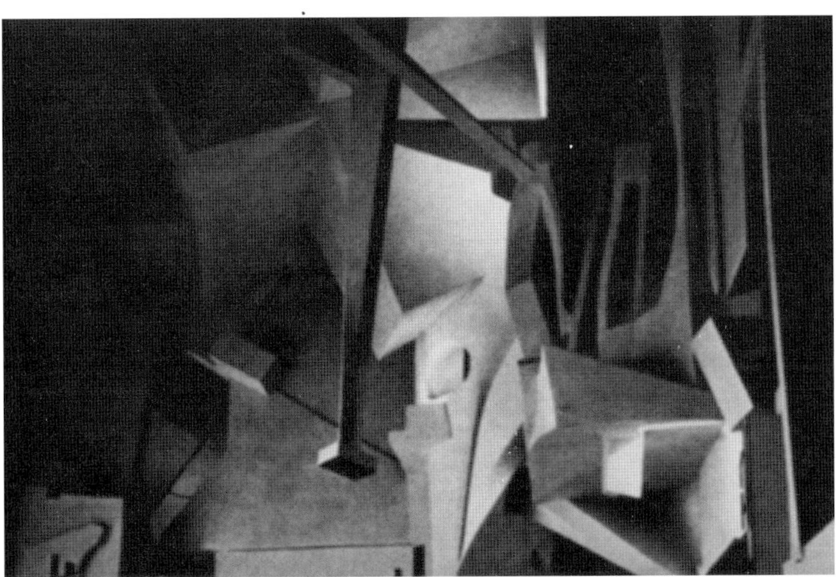

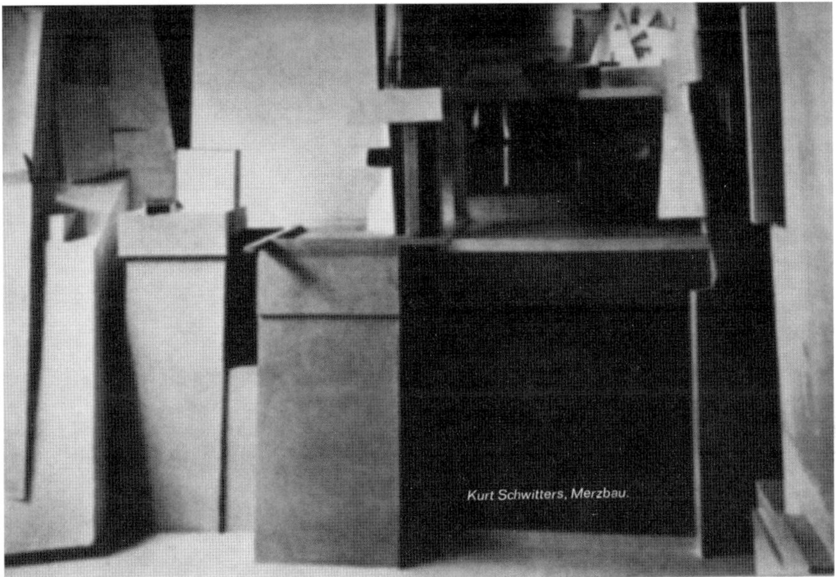


**Figure 5.18.** Kurt Schwitters's construction *Merzbau* (1927–1937), as shown in Dick Higgins and Wolf Vostell's *Fantastic Architecture* (Something Else Press, 1969).

rial for the volume in 1967, seeking articulations of an expressly utopian vision of the built environment from architects and nonpractitioners alike. Coincident with Knowles' construction of *The Big Book* and her generative poem "A House of Dust," their editorially open call invited "architectural ideas, projects and fantasies by artists, musicians, poets, constructors, philosophers, happenings makers, collagists, de-collagists and others working actively in cultural fields."[103] The types of projects they received ran the gamut from historical works of the interwar period, like Erich Buchholz's *Architectural Sculpture* (1924), to contemporaneous earthworks and urban monuments like Claes Oldenburg's *Wing-Nut Monument for Stockholm* (1966), Buckminster Fuller's

*Alison Knowles, A house of dust, computer poem*
*Gebr. König, Cologne/New York 1968*

A HOUSE OF PAPER
AMONG HIGH MOUNTAINS
USING NATURAL LIGHT
INHABITED BY FISHERMEN AND FAMILIES

A HOUSE OF LEAVES
BY A RIVER
USING CANDLES
INHABITED BY PEOPLE SPEAKING MANY LANGUAGES WEARING LITTLE OR NO CLOTHING

A HOUSE OF WOOD
BY AN ABANDONED LAKE
USING CANDLES
INHABITED BY PEOPLE FROM MANY WALKS OF LIFE

A HOUSE OF DISCARDED CLOTHING
AMONG HIGH MOUNTAINS

USING ALL AVAILABLE LIGHTING
INHABITED BY FRIENDS

A HOUSE OF DUST
IN A DESERTED CHURCH
USING ALL AVAILABLE LIGHTING
INHABITED BY PEOPLE SPEAKING MANY LANGUAGES WEARING LITTLE OR NO CLOTHING

A HOUSE OF MUD
IN AN OVERPOPULATED AREA
USING ELECTRICITY
INHABITED BY LITTLE BOYS

A HOUSE OF WEEDS
UNDERWATER
USING CANDLES
INHABITED BY VARIOUS BIRDS AND FISH

A HOUSE OF BROKEN DISHES
IN SOUTHERN FRANCE
USING CANDLES
INHABITED BY PEOPLE WHO ENJOY EATING TOGETHER

A HOUSE OF ROOTS
IN A PLACE WITH BOTH HEAVY RAIN AND BRIGHT SUN
USING ALL AVAILABLE LIGHTING
INHABITED BY PEOPLE WHO LOVE TO READ

A HOUSE OF STRAW
IN SOUTHERN FRANCE
USING NATURAL LIGHT
INHABITED BY COLLECTORS OF ALL TYPES

**Figure 5.19.** Alison Knowles's "A House of Dust" poem, as shown in Dick Higgins and Wolf Vostell's *Fantastic Architecture* (Something Else Press, 1969).

*Tetra City* (1969), Dennis Oppenheim's *Direct Seedings-Wheat* (1969), and Michael Heizer's *Coyote* (1969). Of the thirty-seven manifestos or proposals published in the book, just four represent work by women artists (Knowles, Bici Hendricks, Carolee Schneemann, and Frances Starr).[104]

Comprising sketches, texts, photographs, and photo-collages, the final version is organized around fourteen theoretical "captions." "Caption 5," for example, speculates on the relation between ecological conditions (including flows of information and social change), the human body, and the body politic, while "Caption 13" muses, "How about a city with only rumpus rooms? How about another, quiet city with only gentle sounds and gardens? And another with clang and clatter and the more boisterous order of things? Where might each be placed? Can one live in commuting distance of each?"[105] Mapping a direct lineage between early and late twentieth-century avant-gardes, Vostell's opening, in neat hand-lettering printed in black on translucent vellum, reads in part:

> This documentation of ideas and concepts of a new polymorphous reality is offered as evidence of the new methods and processes that were introduced by *Fluxus*, *Happenings* and *Pop*. A demand for new patterns of behavior—new unconsumed *environments*. The accent in all of the works in this book lies on *change*—i.e. expansion of physical surroundings, sensibilities, media, through disturbance of the familiar. *Action is architecture! Everything is architecture!* . . . Our projects—our environments are meant to free man.[106]

In the introductory text that follows, Higgins expands upon Vostell's sentiments, categorizing the strategies taken by the book's contributors:

> Some deal with the problem of consistency . . . Others deal with the expansion of the possibilities, plain and simple, into additional areas of technology and function. Some are fantasies, raising questions in the mind of the reader which hopefully will lead to new approaches towards design away from the drawing board.[107]

Clearly referencing works that act in the interstices between the built environment and the perceptual act of reading, the chance permutations of Knowles's object/poem *The House of Dust* and, slightly earlier, *The Big Book*, indeed produce a fantasy hybrid of literature and architecture. Similarly, witnesses to Schwitters's *Merzbau* (also first built in his home, in Hannover, and destroyed by Allied bombs in 1943) reported "not only formal, but also expressive significance through literary and symbolic allusions" in the three-dimensional structure whose "secret doors were opened only to initiated friends."[108] Elizabeth Thomas describes how the *Merzbau* "developed into a kind of abstract walk-in collage composed of grottoes and columns and found objects, ever-shifting and ever-expanding. It was more than just a studio; it was itself a work of art."[109]

*The Big Book* and *The House of Dust* can be reconsidered within this framework, too, as they both took root in Knowles's home/studio and marshaled—materially, spatially, and ephemerally—an epistemology of domestic space as an ever-evolving form and process. In the merging of studio/lived space with work/public space, Knowles, like Schwitters, reinterpreted her being-in-the-world through the lived experience of the everyday and called attention to the ways in which our environments are implicitly dramatized. But while the *Merzbau* has been the subject of vast and various histories, Knowles's participatory dwellings—as I have noted of other of her works—have been scarcely acknowledged, aside from curatorial efforts, in the art historical literature on the later 1960s.[110] One reason for this oversight might be in the multifarious ways, subtle and explicit, that the appropriation of language, mass-cultural images, daily rituals, and ordinary objects into her art were united by her complicated experiences as an artist, wife, and mother working outside mainstream art spaces.[111]

To better apprehend Knowles's varying approaches to the homestead and its intimacies and aspirations, we might again situate her aesthetic approach relative to that of her friend and contemporary, and Tenney's recent ex-partner, Carolee Schneemann. Knowles's contribution to *Fantastic Architecture* consists of a photoreproduction of two pages from the König version of her chance-derived poem—which nominally proposed the possibility of a visionary environment wherein one could (imaginatively) dwell in "A HOUSE OF LEAVES / UNDERWATER / USING CANDLES / INHABITED BY COLLECTORS OF ALL TYPES."[112] Schneemann's *Parts of a Body House* runs for several pages in the volume, envisioning corporeal habitation of a different type. The typed treatise, one spread of which is printed over an image of Schneemann's naked, slightly crouched body, is divided into twelve compartments, including the Lung Room, Heart Chamber/Cunt Chamber, Liver Room, Nerve Ends Room, Kidney Room, Guerrilla Gut, Genitals Play–Erotica Meat Room, and Hair and Fingers Room, as well as a Coat Room, Cat House, Bathroom, and Ice Palace.

The text provides houseguests with detailed directions: "The participants will be able to select their materials in advance; they may also build or activate parts of the environment with found materials or by using preset electronic circuits—sensory components determined by computer programs."[113] Schneemann's meticulous programming of visitors' movements recalls Knowles's attention to bodily motility and chance-based experiences in *The Big Book* and *The House of Dust*. Both installations center on the space of habitation—the body's relation to the world—inflected by each artists' sense-based activation of language systems, of everyday sounds and experiences, and of found objects. And they share, too, a history with other domestically themed artworks of the era, including, most memorably, Miriam Schapiro and Judy Chicago's collective Feminist Art Program (FAP) project at CalArts, known as *Womanhouse* (1972).

## Participatory Ecologies

At CalArts in the early 1970s, when the free speech movement, antiwar activism, and the feminist art movement were intertwining, Knowles's fantastic architectures (here, as object/poems) presented new territories to be explored. This was recognized by the prominent feminist art critic and curator Lucy R. Lippard, who viewed *The House of Dust* in situ and described the New York and California iterations as distinctive for their ability to "mak[e] stories become true occupants of the space."[114] In her survey of "women's spaces," Lippard declares that "living space is an extension of the body, and biological as well as social experience influences a woman's preoccupations with the relationships among outside, entrance, and inside."[115] Expanding her analysis of Knowles's cavelike structure, Lippard notes its direct relation to the "fictionalized" and "transformative" space of *Womanhouse*—a contemporaneous monthlong installation piece conceived, curated, and constructed by the students in the Feminist Art Program. Indeed, both *The House of Dust* and *Womanhouse* were important domains of activity for artistic, female-centered, and student-generated happenings and performances in Los Angeles, with Knowles's artist friends Shigeko Kubota and Simone Forti often joining in the object/poem events on campus (fig. 5.20). But despite having been faculty colleagues, Knowles has often recalled feeling alienated by the FAP, Chicago, and Schapiro, whom she felt blocked her bid to participate in *Womanhouse* largely because she was perceived as an artist who "only worked with men."[116] It was Chicago and Schapiro's firm view that it was the "responsibility of all older, 'established' women artists to serve as role models to their young women students: models as productive, integrated artists, as well as women."[117] As former FAP student Paula Harper later recounted, "The pressures to conform to the ideology of the community were resisted in varying degrees by many of the students, but Chicago felt them to be necessary: 'Since women have so much trouble bonding, it was very important in the early seventies to build an artificial environment which supported bonding.'"[118] Chicago and Schapiro's famous women-only admissions policies in the FAP marked a stark contrast with Knowles, who opened her graphics print and intermedia classes to all CalArts students, many of whom were male.[119]

While not adhering to any gender-specific pedagogy, as endorsed by the FAP, Knowles supported students who were active in its program and in CalArts's broader *participatory ecologies* of performance and nascent political consciousness. She evidently derived great satisfaction from her work with women art students.[120] In an interview with former student Aviva Rahmani, Knowles recalled the stimulating environment on campus:

> I had been working alone, as most women artists did then. It was new and exciting to work visually along with others . . . I hadn't had access to women of that stature. All the artists I had worked with were men . . . [but at CalArts] I found women working everywhere. It forced me to take a harder look at myself and what my own history had been.[121]

The participatory politics fostered and felt by Knowles at CalArts included working closely with student artists Suzanne Lacy, Sandra Orgel, and Rahmani, who performed the memorable and haunting *Ablutions* (1972), a meditation about rape, with Chicago. Other era-defining consciousness-raising activities were organized by various students (some of them male) at *The House*

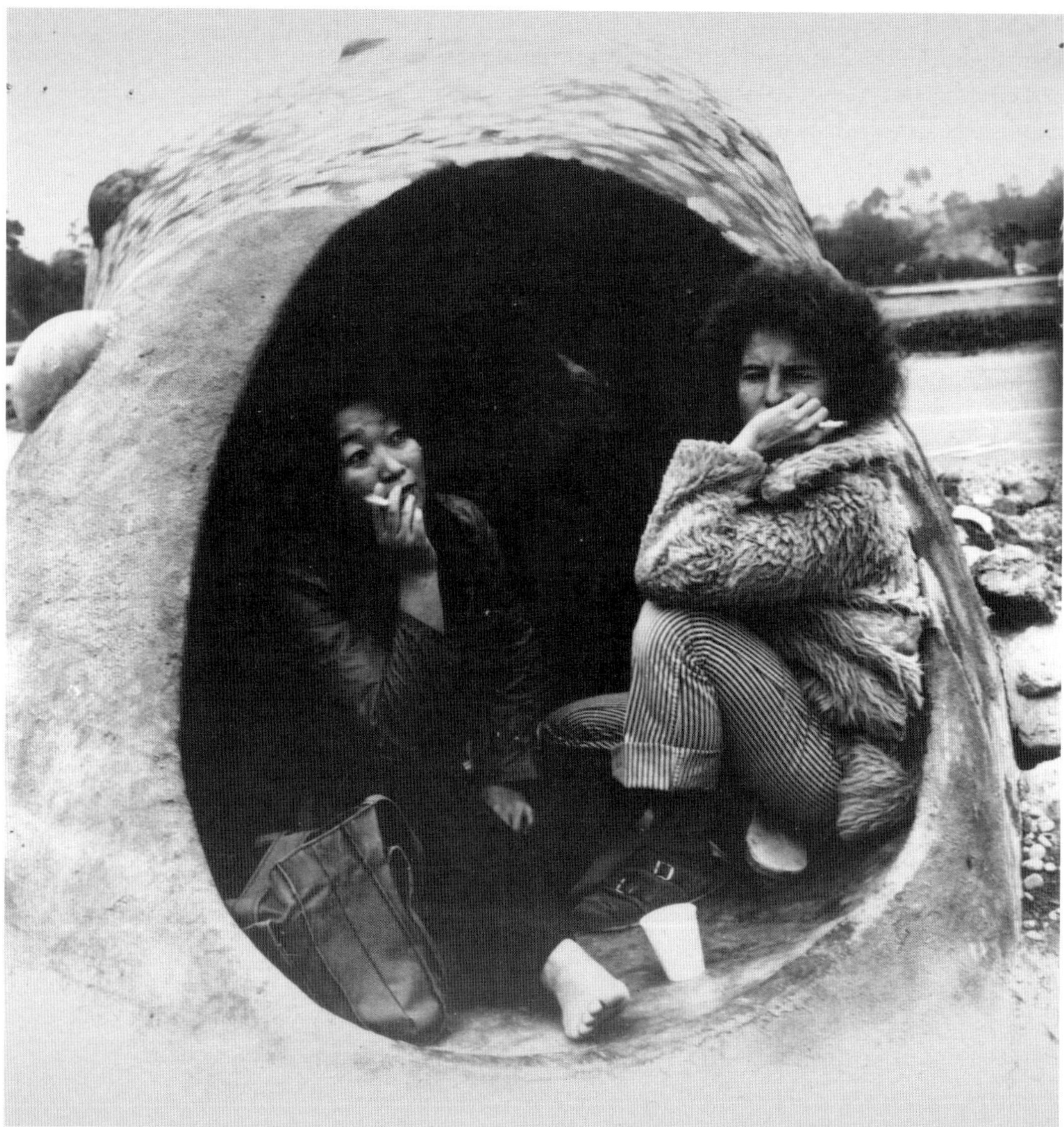

**Figure 5.20.** Shigeko Kubota and Simone Forti inside *The House of Dust*, CalArts, ca. 1971–1972. Photographer unknown.

*of Dust*, incorporating events that explored the cyclical modes of nature and the liberated body's engagement with them. One example was the "Meditation at Dawn" events organized by Knowles's student and teaching assistant Michael Bell. Following her lead to open *The House of Dust*, literally and figuratively, to anyone invested in exploring the object/poem, Bell regularly invited students into the cavelike structure, often practicing yoga (alone) while nude. He also proposed a "whole course of study" on poetry/poesy to enable, as he put it, "integrating our life experiences to make each moment an event."[122]

In retrospect, we may consider *The House of Dust* as a complement and counterpoint to *Womanhouse*. Both worked to create new models for pedagogical and public engagement; both encouraged a nonhierarchical collaborative approach to art making, including working in performance and installation; both directly or obliquely took up the domestic sphere as a source of material and critique; and both supported student work that interrogated the boundaries of ideology and institutional frameworks. Given Knowles's aesthetic of minimally produced events and environments premised on the notion of openness where performers/viewers carry out simple tasks, perhaps the struggle between Knowles and the FAP—as with her earlier demurrals from the more wildly expressionist performances of Schneemann, Kubota, and Charlotte Moorman—had less to do with what was or was not permissible for a woman artist to do than with individual taste and preference.[123] Knowles's instructional approach at CalArts was to activate aesthetics at the locus of sensorial (visual, sonic, textural) and personal experience. *The House of Dust* amplified semantic range and reach, particularly with regard to ideas about public space.

This sense of expanded publics was not lost on Knowles. In 1967, while Tenney was introducing her and her experimentalist peers to computer programming, *Sculpture in Environment*, an exhibition sponsored by New York City's Office of Cultural Affairs, was for the first time bringing large-scale artworks, temporarily, into the urban public arena. The participating sculptors were chosen precisely for the monumentality of their works: Alexander Calder's massive, welded abstractions; Marisol's protruding steel faces; Louise Nevelson's painted wood constructions. The prominent presentation of these works (and twenty-eight others) reflected an urgent interest in reviving public space, and for at least a decade, sculpture became the most fertile contemporary medium.[124] Then earth art, or Land art, emerged, casting aside the cult of personalized, transcendental expression embodied in North American postwar abstraction, including grandiose public arts projects. Process art and systems art likewise proposed reexaminations of sculpture's presumptions of isolation and purity. (Monumentalist, post-studio earth art enterprises, made in the romanticized studio, sometimes, ironically, intensify such notions.)

As with *The Big Book*'s evocation of *Alice's Adventures in Wonderland* and poetic allusions to the *Epic of Gilgamesh* in "A House of Dust," we might relate the notion of environmental offering as hospitality to desires pervasive in the culture in the decade following the publication of Rachel Carson's *Silent Spring*.[125] As (still countercultural) ideas of intervening to protect the earth gained currency, more artists were making work outdoors, often but not always site-specific. Male artists, who tended to use earth reinforced by extraneous structural supports, would in time gain great notice for their maximalist earthen excavations, mounds, piles, and markings. By contrast, Knowles, Alice Aycock, Beverly Pepper, Nancy Holt, Jody Pinto, Mary Miss, and other women were keener to construct their works—whether made with wood, metal, concrete, or other materials—in more subtle ways. Many of these artists shared a highly formalized visual language and maintained a broadly participatory aesthetic. Experiencing the environments corporeally—crawling, descending, stooping, climbing, hiding—was integral to their disparate work, and themes of domestic enclosure could be seen as both playful and protective. The physical interaction necessitated by some of these artistic enclosures recalls ancient Egyptian mastabas, labyrinthine Minoan palaces, North American Plains dwellings, rock caves and chambers, and even the visionary architectures of Buckminster Fuller and Frederick Kiesler.

In terms of *participatory ecologies*, we may well briefly compare Aycock's *The Maze* (1972; now destroyed), with Knowles's *The House of Dust*. Built on a farm in rural Pennsylvania, *The Maze* consisted of five concentric twelve-sided rings—the largest thirty-two feet across—with randomly placed openings in its six-foot-high wood-plank walls (there were three in the outer ring). Given the work's sheer scale and complex geometry, it was difficult to apprehend as a whole, a visual effect Aycock has said was inspired by Native American stockades and her experience of ancient *tholos* (beehive) tombs at Mycenae in 1970.[126]

Against the transhistorical horizon of such touchstones, we might, after Rosalind Krauss, approach *The Maze* in terms of a logical permutation of a set of culturally specific terms—sculpture, architecture, landscape—as elaborated in Western art history since the eighteenth century.[127] While conceived under very different circumstances, Aycock's "transvironment," like Knowles's, provides an interior, a place to hide, to seek shelter, to play.[128] (Recall that the fear of concealed danger was one of the more potent objections to installing *The House of Dust* at the Penn South Co-op in Chelsea.) Any viewer with access to either site is encouraged to engage with the sculpture on its own terms. There's no compulsion, but passive looking reveals little; to apprehend the work, the viewer must become a participant, physically negotiating its predetermined passages. Both works allude to domestic enclosures, to a nascent countercultural ethos of imaginative dwellings, and to an environmental *impulse* that, while not expressly activist, reveals a desire for an engagement through transformations of the earth, however ephemeral. The physical structures both, in my view, demonstrably expand the forms and relations of what we might characterize as post-studio art.

We see this over and over in the history of *The House of Dust*—the extension of its original public address to further, future publics and ecological systems. When Knowles left CalArts in late 1972, she donated the structures to the school, hoping they might continue to facilitate shared experiences in perpetuity. But, subject to time and weather, they deteriorated, and when, in 1976, an earthquake caused the larger house to split along an existing seam, the structure was abandoned. In 1977, Knowles gifted the physical remains of the smaller *House of Dust* to the Oakland Museum to be installed in an adjacent public park as a permanent outdoor sculpture. But shipping proved untenable, and the project was bogged down in bureaucracy.[129] In 1980, the tenth anniversary of the object/poem, Knowles applied for an NEA-sponsored Art in Public Space Grant to transport the CalArts fragments to a site "just at the turn of the Mississippi River" near the University of Minnesota campus. The proposal included a new computer printout that complemented earlier iterations of the poem's score in New York and California (i.e., instructions for placement, category, and color) indicating object categories or "Gifts for the House of Dust" that would be collected from friends (as in its Chelsea iteration), including Simone Forti, Malcolm Goldstein, Geoffrey Hendricks, Linda Montano, Annea Lockwood, and Knud Pedersen, who gifted a gold wedding ring.[130] She did not receive the grant funds, so the smaller house was gifted, this time to the Child Development Center at Santa Clarita Community College in California, where it was last seen, reimagined as playground equipment and painted with polka dots.[131] The perpetually new "homes for the houses" (as she referred to them) recalls Knowles's consistent and explicit uniting of the object/poem with acts of gifts and generosity. As she explained to poet Charlie Morrow, "THE HOUSE OF DUST in its inception was based on a gift. The foundation gift that enabled it to be built. Otherwise, it would have just been the poem and a couple of little plaster hand-held models. The HOUSE changes on the basis of the gifts it draws to itself."[132] This spirit of generosity, and the generative iterability at the crux of *The House of Dust*'s multiple materializations, would continue to endure for decades to come.

To commemorate the fiftieth anniversary of CalArt's founding, the curatorial team Art by Translation collaborated with faculty members Ken Erlich and Janet Sarbanes and their students, staging readings of the poem within the space of a new temporary quatrain, the "house of glass."[133] In 2021–2022, Knowles again revisited the work, drawing a shape inspired by an abalone shell on a computer printout of the poem; the image was then rendered as a 3D-printed habitable sculpture made from clay, wood, concrete, and other materials, which went on public view in Wiesbaden Kranzplatz, Germany, in celebration of the sixtieth anniversary of the founding of Fluxus in the city (plate 9).[134] Ultimately, Knowles's contribution to chance-based intermedia might lie in offering alternative ecologies for participation by multiple publics. The architectural sculptures featured in this chapter are but one instantiation of the variable, the complex, the utopian, and the fraught that manifest this focus.

## Women's Work

Three years after Knowles left CalArts to return to New York City, Miriam Schapiro, then director of the Feminist Art Program, invited her and seventy-seven other women artists to submit to the anthology *Art: A Woman's Sensibility*.[135] The publication marked the second time women artists associated with the FAP had produced a public volume of letters. For the first volume, *Anonymous Was a Woman, By . . .* (1974), artists were asked to write about themselves as a way to "repair the injustice inflicted upon women's cultural history." Now, for the second, they were asked to write introspectively about their own work; a community of women artists writing letters to another community of women artists was regarded by the organizers as a gesture of "revolutionary love."[136]

Poet and novelist Deena Metzger stated the conceit in formal terms: the first form was an invitation to write; the second was women artists coming together to make a book of women's art—distinct acts, each of which wrote a community into being. To activate these forms was a "defiant" speech act—a "new critical language" for supporting and comprehending women's artistic labor: "Nothing is excluded. The entire life is evoked, not just the moment which births the piece. The whole day and the whole night. The daily life."[137]

Knowles's contribution is telling. The photograph she submitted shows her in profile, with thick glasses and long, graying hair, in front of pantry shelves, sipping soup off a large spoon (fig. 5.21). The representative work, "Build a Bean Garden," is illustrated with another profile—a sketch of her foot lightly planted over tiny circular beans. Her statement reads, in full:

> The events I perform, the prints I have made and the environments I build are designed to put the spectator/performer in touch with him/herself and the real world. Since all feelings reside in the individual sensibility, I am interested in touching, awakening and activating certain of my own and your own personal responses. Some of this happens through sound, some through the use of found objects in a given environment, some through the glorification of daily occurrences such as eating a sandwich or examining a button. I regard simple routine activities taken for granted and materials cast off as worthless to be extraordinary, precious, magical and worthy of all kinds of perusal. My environments and performances are collections of such things. Listen as if you had never heard it; look at it as if you had never seen it before. Investigate again what you already know.[138]

To "investigate again what you already know" implies an awareness of the contingencies of lived experience—of the desire to keep learning, to keep searching.

In 1975, Knowles would continue her explorations of sound by teaming up with New Zealand–born composer Annea (Anna) Lockwood for an anthology of experimental compositions—similar to *Notations*, the book she assembled with John Cage, but dedicated exclusively to work by women. Designed by Knowles, *WOMENS WORK* (fig. 5.22) is a slim collection of notational scores by Jackie Apple, Sari Dienes, Simone Forti, Pauline Oliveros, Meiko Shiomi, Elaine Summers, and others, commissioned and edited by Knowles and Lockwood. The compendium "of beautiful scores" was eventually published in 1975 by the Print Center in Brooklyn (supported by collector Jean Brown and Aen-Jai Graphics); a sequel followed in 1978, and both were reissued by Primary Information in 2019.[139] Each was designed by Knowles, the first taking the form of a saddle-stitched magazine printed on off-white papers with brown inks, and the second a fold-out poster using photographs and drawings to announce the artists' works.

Knowles's own contribution to the first issue of *WOMENS WORK* is a two-

ART:
A WOMAN'S
SENSIBILITY

The collected works and writings
of women artists

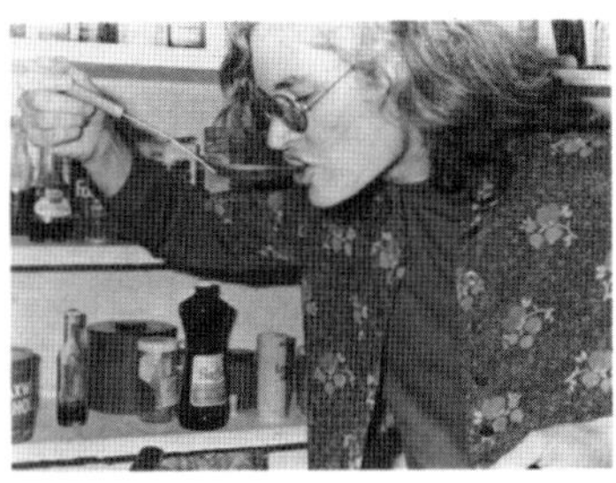

project BUILD A BEAN GARDEN

Saihoji is a garden made of mosses. Ryoanji, another garden in Kyoto has fifteen stones surrounded by white pebbles. In this garden there is also a single outdoor bell. These gardens were created in 6th century Japan and have not changed essentially since then. I had not studied them before being there and I was very impressed in their presence and decided to build a bean garden in that spirit. The environment would have white navy beans rather than pebbles, split peas for moss about the stones, and found objects would appear here and there. The bell sound would be made by the amplification of bare feet walking on the beans in the garden. The garden would exist on a wooden floor so that the beans could roll fully and resonate. It feels good to walk through beans. An attendant rakes the beans back into place in concentric circles around the rocks. The sound system is simply the feet moving on the beans travelling through the wood of the floor to two microphones plugged into simple amplifier/loudspeaker systems and translated through the resonance spectrum of two bell jars at spatial extremities from each other. The disassembling of the garden would involve its transformation into food. Several days of bean banquets would include such delicacies as white beans lamb shank, bean soup with sage, curried beans, bean cake and white beans milanese with sausage.

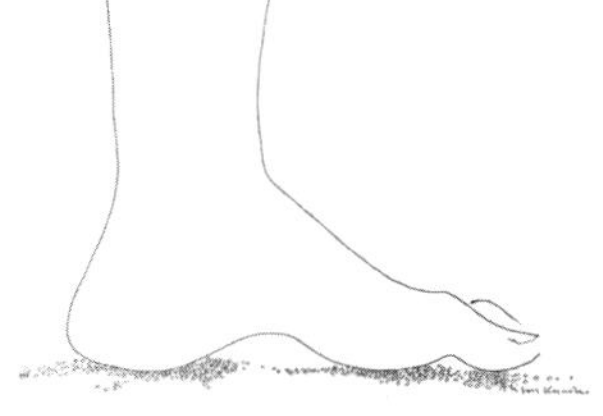

The events I perform, the prints I have made and the environments I build are designed to put the spectator/performer in touch with him/herself and the real world. Since all feelings reside in the individual sensibility, I am interested in touching, awakening and activating certain of my own and your own personal responses. Some of this happens through sound, some through the use of found objects in a given environment, some through the glorification of daily occurences such as eating a sandwich or examining a button. I regard simple routine activities taken for granted and materials cast off as worthless to be extraordinary, precious, magical and worthy of all kinds of perusal. My environments and performances are collections of such things. Listen as if you had never heard it; look at it as if you had never seen it before. Investigate again what you already know.

Alison Knowles

**Figure 5.21.** Alison Knowles's pages in *Art: A Woman's Sensibility, The Collected Works and Writings of Women Artists*, ed. Miriam Schapiro and Deena Metzger (FAP, CalArts, 1975).

page, handwritten score for *Proposition IV (Squid)*. Originally conceived as a template for events at *The House of Dust* at CalArts, *Proposition IV* comprises an intricate set of instructions to be navigated by a self-selected leader and at least four performers, engaging four predetermined quadrant categories. Each participant is directed to "make your own score card," drawing on a printout with randomized permutations of "elements" (water, air, paper, and fire), "compass-color" (red, blue, yellow, green), and "numbers":

> For example, your card might read: +7, +10, ++14, ++8, +water, +west/blue, silence. You plan what activity you will be doing in each quadrant and what tools/objects you will need. The leader begins the performance drawing a circle on the floor with chalk; or if outdoors, with a stick on the ground. . . . The leader then divides the circle into quadrants, labels them (numbers/elements/compass-color/silence). The leader also places a compass in the compass/

> color quadrant. You and the other performers enter, choose a quadrant and begin. Your activities may extend beyond the circle into the audience or the environment but the quadrants should be respected if extended. . . . Your performance is single; it does not relate to what anyone else is doing.[140]

The entire performance—open to the performers' interpretations of the script in regard to placement, transitions, movement, sound, props—is executed as one integrated piece using theatrical and visual elements unfolding in timed intervals *and* all at once. No performance is final, no experience repeatable. More complex than Knowles's propositional works in the early 1960s (e.g., *Make a Salad* or *Shoes of Your Choice*), *Proposition IV* moves from sparse, concrete prose to narratively expansive social structures and addresses its instructions to an ungendered "you." The same is true of *Monkey Shines* (1972), parenthetically dedicated to Pauline Oliveros—also a contributor to *WOMENS WORK*—"on the occasion of her fortieth birthday." Comprising a lengthy set of directions and very specific ingredients for cooking a meal together, Knowles disregards performer pronouns altogether in favor of pictographs.[141]

Both issues of *WOMENS WORK*, Knowles told a correspondent, promised an "exciting variety and vitality" that bears out "our feeling that a lot of really energetic work is going on"—that is, it is permeable in perpetuity.[142] Knowles and Lockwood envisioned their publication as an interdisciplinary enterprise derived from dance, theater, music, visual art, intermedia, and cooking to be distributed free to "people who will use it for performance."[143] Creating this infinitely generative participatory ecology, a space in which the author's and the reader's subjectivities are allowed to coexist, in published or live form that would define the next decade of artistic labor, especially for Knowles.

Indeed, Knowles's efforts in designing and securing funding for *WOMENS WORK* marks a distinctive shift in her approach to artmaking in the 1970s. While previously known (and sometimes chastised) for working "only with men," both during and after her time at CalArts, she pointedly turned to other experimentalist women artists like Lockwood, Oliveros, and Phillips to collaborate within the rapidly generative spaces of video, new media, electronic music, and sound installation. Writing to Dick Higgins in 1974, Knowles noted feeling great pleasure and satisfaction from working within supportive spaces where women artists can thrive. "One of the things in my life that is rewarding for me now is my relationships (influence [one] might say) with young women students I had at CalArts—[Barbara] Bloom and [Lisa] Mikulchik—to see how they live and what they are doing."[144] While she may have demurred from more radically engaged activism, including separatist feminism, by fusing innovative projects with a keen sense of chance, Knowles materially and symbolically articulated a critical praxis of expanded methods within a pioneering milieu of women makers, effectively dislodging male-dominated narratives that ossified around experimental art of the 1960s and 1970s.[145]

In the multitude of ways it has been (and continues to be) transformed,

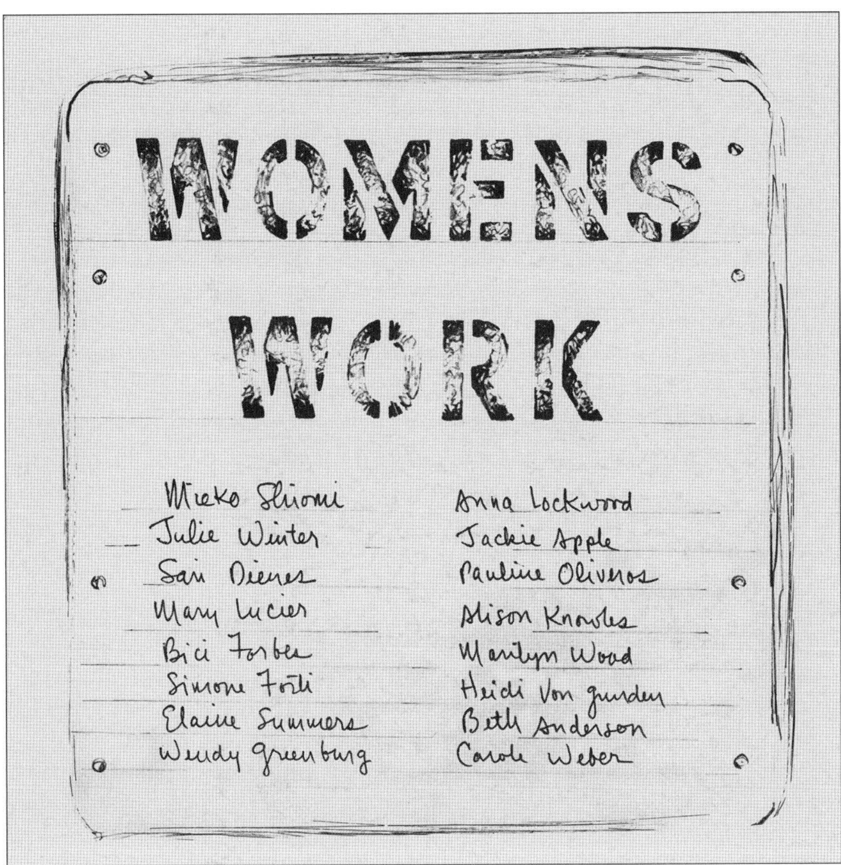


**Figure 5.22.** *WOMENS WORK*, ed. Alison Knowles and Annea Lockwood (Brooklyn, NY: Print Center, 1975).

the poem "A House of Dust" yokes the act of writing to the temporal, technological mutability of its media in the Information Age. Emmett Williams once described Knowles's efforts as intermedial "language happenings," part of an expanded poetry, concrete yet open.[146] If we understand "intermedia" to encompass site-specific sculpture; works that incorporate natural or man-made found materials; temporal, performance-based activities; and a general deflection toward process, site, and three-dimensionality, then Knowles's entire practice, from the late 1950s onward, must be included in its history. This allows us to approach her work, with its perpetually generative iterability, more holistically, underscoring the conceptual synergies that lie at the heart of a deeply heterogenous practice.

Creative play was a critical ingredient in Knowles's conceptualization of *The House of Dust* object/poem. While constrained by a defined set of parameters, it was infinitely open to different and changing outcomes. I view these variations as intentional social opportunities activated in public and private space—whether the lawn of a Chelsea housing project (where the primary objective was spirited activation—play—by its youngest residents) or a hilltop at the edge of CalArts's campus.

The multimedia projects Knowles created in the early 1970s in California entailed, not a radical break from her previous work in Fluxus, but a continued engagement with tropes intrinsic to time-based art practice: movement, memory, duration, information, experience, participation, and perception. At the same time, Knowles's letters help us situate her artistic evolution in relation to an emerging political consciousness, particularly in polemics addressing new ideas about space and subjectivity in the late 1960s. In each iteration of *The House of Dust*, for instance, the *work* of artistic practice is characterized dialectically, through a shifting set of oppositions: immediate and measured, public and private, literal and metaphorical, practical and imaginative. The scale, sensation, texture, and affective engagement of her environments demonstrate how objects perceive and are perceived in that delicate residue of human experience that seeks to make life meaningful.

# EPILOGUE

> Making an artwork is an action with its own politics. The best I can do for the ills of the world is to maintain a tight battle with the art. Art is a calling based on a need.
> **Alison Knowles**[1]

In winter 1991, Alison Knowles sat down for an interview with Aviva Rahmani, a former student who had split her time at CalArts between the Feminist Art Program and intermedia faculty members like Knowles and Allan Kaprow. Their conversation ranged from the complexities of carving out a creative existence amid professional pressures and the seductions of careerism to escalating threats of global violence. It also includes perhaps the clearest articulation of Knowles's philosophy of art. The claims she makes for art are remarkable for the *politics* they circumscribe: an attention to the habitus of social engagement and environmental consciousness wherein chance is not only a compositional technique but a life's practice. Her Fluxus pieces in the early 1960s, for example, stretched her painterly activities into the world of daily life as a series of antispectacular movements requiring cooperation (private or public) for their completion. Her engagement with the domestic everyday in and beyond Fluxus, as I argue in this book, signals an ethical demand—a questioning of the artist's sole authority as itself a social relation, an occasion of generosity and contingency.

This first in-depth study of Knowles understands her art as gesturing toward a *politics* of representation and material experimentation through an expanded formal sensibility that, in the 1960s and 1970s, brushed up against thorny questions of gender, sex, and activism. This position runs counter to certain histories of Fluxus, including the influential thesis put forth by German critic Andreas Huyssen. Writing for the indispensable exhibition catalog *In the Spirit of Fluxus* (Walker Art Center, 1993), Huyssen argues that neither Fluxus as a group nor individual Fluxus artists located their activities specifically within the political tradition of the early twentieth-century avant-garde or contemporaneous activism: "To establish a direct link between Fluxus events and the protest politics of the 1960s . . . would be to falsify the historical record."[2]

By the time Fluxus made its way back from Europe to New York in 1963–1964, radicalized youth movements such as the Student Nonviolent Coordinating Committee (SNCC) had, Huyssen correctly notes, "exploded" the territory of acceptable political discourse. But to argue that Fluxus could not be political because it did not expressly engage in 1920s-style art and politics seems to miss the crux of their experimental activities in art, music, performance, and publishing. In a 1966 letter to George Maciunas, for instance, Dick Higgins writes that he understands Fluxus in quasi-Marxist terms as "a collective, promoting a certain body of work on a mass basis, through concerts, publications; films and radio program," adding, "This was and is a model for the Something Else Press."[3] Nonetheless, claims persist that imply Knowles and other Fluxus artists consciously *disengaged* from the political scene.

Curator Valerie Cassel Oliver has rightly noted, however, that many Fluxus artists were "breaking with the conventions of society" through actions and objects "rooted in art [that] took aim at the greater sociopolitical and cultural hierarchies of the day."[4] Throughout the 1950s and 1960s, for example, Knowles, Higgins, George Brecht, Philip Corner, George Maciunas, Yoko Ono, Nam June Paik, Benjamin Patterson, and others expressed adamant opposition to the Korean conflict and the war in Vietnam.[5] (Knowles has recalled how she "marched once against the Vietnam War up Fifth Avenue playing bells" with Corner.[6]) They also supported, sometimes tacitly, sometimes explicitly, the burgeoning civil rights and antinuclear movements. In 1963, Higgins penned a letter to the editor of *Yale Alumni Magazine* arguing in favor of civil rights activism. "[African Americans] are not going to tolerate being deprived of their birthright as Americans governed by the self-same Constitution," he wrote. "If there is any violence, it is that involved in the suppression of nearly twelve million Southern people."[7] Moreover, Corner, in particular, after serving in Korea until 1961, was active with the NAACP, joined protest marches during Mississippi Freedom Summer 1964 and again in 1965, and in November 1964 organized benefit concerts at his loft for SNCC and the Council of Federated Organizations, which featured jazz saxophonist Archie Shepp.[8]

Higgins, in an April 1967 letter to Czech Fluxus artist Milan Knížák, advocates a "mass-KEEPING TOGETHER" event, which he describes as a "public KEEPING TOGETHER" modeled on the sit-ins of the civil rights movement. Elsewhere in the letter he expresses distress over how "very often the best people become mature very early because of the horror of being sent to some stupid war in which their generation, class and people have no interest whatsoever." He goes on in his characteristically sardonic tone: "Let's just hope that something happens here so poor Ken [Friedman]—and all the other Kens—don't get sent off to leave their bones in Vietnam or Bolivia, which is presumably our Deeply Honorable President's next Hell-(Ass)-Hole."[9] In still another letter two months earlier, Higgins told Knížák he was concerned that Corner and Jackson Mac Low might be "jailed for their protest against the Vietnam war."[10] In addition to activities with Higgins, Knowles volunteered in the early to mid-1950s to register voters and to work with urban schoolchildren who were to be bused to the Fresh Air Fund camp in upstate New York.[11]

As for specific Fluxus art pieces, Kristine Stiles has argued that Patterson's *First Symphony* (1964), for example, evoked social-economic-political structures challenged by the civil rights movement in the United States. He chose, she notes, to "divide," or segregate, audience members based on an informal survey of their "trust" of him (an African American male) and intended the loud, predictable "pop" of a can of vacuum-packed Maxwell House coffee to evoke militarization and social unrest, and thus "heighten the anxiety" during the performance.[12] Musicologist George E. Lewis reports that Patterson was "less sanguine about this interpretation"; while he was surely alluding to race relations, his *First Symphony* "us[ed] sound to universalize the experience of social protest, something experienced by citizens of all races at the time."[13]

Asked, decades later, "Was Fluxus political?" Patterson answered, "Of course, more or less, certainly and perhaps. (A hard 'yes' or 'no' could not be Fluxus.) I have given this answer because, given that Fluxus included so many nations, how could a singular answer be possible?"[14] While Patterson did "not see his artistic engagements with Fluxus as antithetical to the social and political issues at home," he did express disappointment with what he perceived as the lack of formal support for civil rights activism among the New York Fluxus scene.[15] Given the material evidence, however, it may have been a matter of not openly sharing engagement in political activism with every Fluxus friend or accurately recalling events long past.[16] Indeed, the issue of a Fluxus politics is tangled and fraught. It is also applied inconsistently across the many artists affiliated with the movement at one point or another.

While it is undeniable that Huyssen's retrospective account fits some Fluxus artists, I am unconvinced that all Fluxists' activities were apolitical, or that they explicitly ignored the most urgent social issues and "consciousness raising" events of their time. It simply is not borne out in the archival or artistic records I have labored to bring forth. Moreover, the very composition of Fluxus—as a transdisciplinary, transnational art movement that counted numerous women, queer, and nonwhite artists in its ranks—placed it outside the proverbial box.[17]

Nevertheless, like many women artists of her generation, and despite supporting gender equality, Knowles has been reluctant to define her artwork in an explicitly politicized way, especially regarding more activist forms of feminism. She has instead located her practice in the context of the formal experimentations of the literary and neo-avant-gardes. But her position as a woman artist creating live, anti-art performances already situates her as an aesthetic radical. And also, I maintain, a political one. An at least implicit politics is evident, especially, in her intermedial resistance to the (often male-centric) modernist project of rigidly distinguishing medium-specific working methods and materials.

Among other historical interests tied to the complexities of the era, this study has been driven by specific questions: What *kind of* politics might we imagine in Knowle's particular *forms* of art making? What desires—libidinal and affective—might these *forms* conjure? What possible viewers, performers, and readers does her work anticipate? In my view, Knowles's oeuvre institutes a politics of interaction that might be regarded as *translation in form*—by which I mean, a mechanism with which to think through a kind of participatory ecology (or generative aesthetic ecosystem) in which past, present, and future publics are called on to perform a work in perpetuity.

In scrutinizing key elements of Knowles's praxis from the late 1950s to the mid-1970s—chance, ephemerality, the event score, live performance, found objects—I have widened my interpretive scope to include physical and literary uses of the built environment and ways in which postwar ideas about public/private were inherently gendered and experientially critiqued. Overtly political or not, Knowles's work consistently *resists* dominant conceptions and expectations of gender and, in contrast to contemporaneous expressionistic performance art, refuses spectacle in favor of a visual language of and for the quotidian. This, in the context of the then-nascent feminist art movement, is one of her many contributions heretofore underexamined in the Fluxus literature. From prints (including screen-print paintings that predate Warhol's) to a sustained interest in performance as a medium of radical expressivity, Knowles's serious study of indeterminacy (or nonintentionality) as a method of making was more than an experimental strategy, a formal means to an unknowable end. On a more intimate level, her embrace of the provisional represented an emancipation from willed choice, or even from her own subject position. In attempting to remove the "self" from painting, for example, she drew attention to the limitations and limiting quality of the medium of paint and the artist subject, both of which—technique and access—are decidedly gendered in Western discourse as areas of male privilege.

I have not presumed to offer a definitive interpretation of Knowles's entire body of work from these decades, nor to account for all the diverse threads (or politics) of her practice or to insist on the tight cohesion of those I do consider. Rather, I have analyzed primary sources—including much previously unstudied archival material—and woven chronological and thematic readings around three critical practices: first, Knowles's attentiveness to everyday embodied experience (eating, talking, walking, listening, etc.), given form through found objects, performances, and installations; second, her sensitive regard for chance methods and indeterminate outcomes, and the protofeminist approach it suggests to media ecologies of production;. and, third, her disregard for the preciousness of the art object and disruption of art institutions that ascribe worth to goods that are durable, transportable, and (in more than one sense) presentable.

Knowles's oeuvre exemplifies what I term an open, or *contingent*, economy of live-art practice. Any interpretive or methodological framework—any effort to comprehend the complexities surrounding the development of her practice within the neo-avant-garde—must, then, embrace interdisciplinary sources from across art history and the humanities. My genealogical mapping of Knowles's practice does not assume either clear narrative structures or clean historical breaks, but instead contends with the changeability and contradiction inevitable in tracking, via archival materials (especially photographs), events long passed and artworks long lost, discarded, or destroyed. Ephemeral artworks predicated on the inconstancies of live iteration are in some ways no more legible, no less uncategorizable, today than they were nearly sixty years ago. My objectives throughout, then, have been to focus more sharply the conceptual lens with which I reassess the formal insights of Knowles's work in and out of Fluxus as paradigmatic of the possibilities of *new forms* of aesthetic contemplation, perceptual awareness, and personal political sympathies that sided (however obliquely) with the downtrodden and the dispossessed.[18]

Knowles's transdisciplinary artistic formation in the 1960s relates, too, of course, to the ways time and natural forces impacted environments, objects, and social relations among her artist contemporaries—a countercultural spirit often referred to as "hippie modernism."[19] In a 1967 exchange with Milan Knížák about the role of the artist in society, she privileged openness over his preferred didacticism and ambitions:

> Art does sometimes teach or instruct men how to live. but, for myself, I find "instruct" a rather tough, hard word. we are all trying to make sense to ourselves, including the broad scale of nature, the world, political issues, society, etc. <u>each action must comment on all of these. if we are the new men we feel we are, than the world will form around us and take nourishment and ideas like meat from a butcher! Art is no more important than other things,</u> so many other things. I can't but be happy, that these other things come out better for me, because I do my art. people see this. this is an influence, and infection; I would not say though, that I am instructing men to live better. <u>I am simply living better myself.</u> I think I am. I want him (man) to see that, and do the same with his own life: explore, discover and recreate in simple terms for others what you know is valid (beautiful, true). . . . the simpler the activities, the more directly it comes across. this is how people become "infected," this is what makes them feel different and change things.[20]

In envisioning the introspective self-examining Knowles conveys to Knížák as an artistic and a life practice, we might thus also note two axiomatic conclusions: first, that no artwork is made in isolation (artists in a given context respond to shared stimuli, however different their moves), and, second, that historical categories and modes of inquiry should be regarded as elastic and expandable—that is, adaptive to engaging seriously with "simpler activites" of making far outside the conventions of accepted art and political address. As abandoned and neglected archives (and artists) are uncovered or recovered, we discern, around art of the 1960s, a more intersectional, multidimensional feminist roadmap for making than has heretofore been appreciated. It is perhaps unsurprising, then, that Knowles has retrospectively defined her artistic ethos as one based on calling, a battle, a need.

If one critical determinant of Knowles's artistic production was her recognition that the aesthetic terms of advanced art had radically shifted, affirmed by her early turn toward Cage's teachings on chance and indeterminacy, another was her discontent with the intractable constraints faced by women artists in the realms of high art.[21] Knowles was never a liberation feminist, yet her work evinces a thorough self-reckoning and a consideration of broader sociopolitical concerns, notably, the quiet pervasiveness of sexism and the colonized status of women's bodies in public and private spheres (including the art circles she inhabited).

These engagements leave traces in the archive, in small but powerful moments, variously documented, that I have endeavored to bring to light. In a unpublished oral history interview from 1979, for example, Higgins recalled that in Prague in 1966 Knowles had refused, "on feminist grounds," to perform with Knížák: she "objected to Knizak and wouldn't have anything to do with him," evidently based on his reported mistreatment of his wife, Sonja Sekova, who later committed suicide.[22] Given that Higgins was the sole source characterizing this refusal, a decade later, as "feminist," we might be skeptical. But a comprehensive survey of Higgins's papers in several archives reveals the depth of his understanding of Knowles's working methods, aesthetic preferences, politics, and likes and dislikes. For her part, Knowles remarks, in the many letters she exchanged with Higgins, on very often being the only woman in a crowd of artists (even if she sometimes delighted in the singular attention).

In reexamining her art and life, Higgins's detailed remembrances, then, cannot be easily dismissed, nor should his stating Knowles's reasoning be taken as officious or presumptuous. The mass of letters reveals an arrangement of trust between the two: Knowles preferred to let her work enunciate her ideas and her politics; Higgins would be the keeper of their shared history, artistic and familial. He was not one to throw things away. He preserved Knowles's college journals and early exhibition announcements; family photographs; and sheafs of letters discussing their diverging artistic aims and ambitions, the worries and triumphs of raising their twin daughters, his wretched unhappiness leading up to their divorce in 1970—without all of which we would have little or no tangible record of Knowles's early work, her opinions, or her influences. To keep an archive as diligently as Higgins did is to understand the intimacy of historical inquiry. And, more crucially, to square that history with a complicated politics as personally lived.[23]

In the end, a close reading of Knowles's oeuvre and of her circle's archives does make her work more legible and reveals it as more complex than has generally been recognized. We see her preference for the subtle critique of institutions refracted through her daily habits—continual interrogations of how we experience and know the material world, how our bodies are articulated in processes of object-subject formation, and how these interventions are negotiated between the public and private spheres. The challenge and provocation of Knowles's neo-avant-garde work, for me, is the way her practice interpenetrates so many other practices, disciplines, genres, and materials, and yet carves out an extraordinary space of its own. It is not easily categorizable. The enigmatic, often ephemeral character of her performances and objects resides in the interstice of the enduring propositional score, which instructs performers and viewers to do something concrete, privately or in public.

Knowles's insistence on activating and transforming experience connects the body and its intricate relations to things, the body and its own aurality and rhythms, the body and its relations read as susceptible to the vicissitudes of time, use-value, and attentiveness. Webs and swaths of hurled paint, the fleshy substance of her early paintings, are replaced by chance encounters among found objects in an urban terrain; or the grain of her voice or the shuffle of her feet as she performs a score designed to heighten audience perceptivity. These new modes of making and experiencing art, centered on or within the body, signal the possibilities of merging painting and performance, by way of performing chance, into a new visual poetics of form.

# ACKNOWLEDGMENTS

The publication of *Performing Chance* is the outcome of the depth of time, generosity, and archival research that began a long time ago. First under the inimitable direction of Branden W. Joseph and Cécile Whiting, who were (and remain) my most trusted readers and whose brilliant and transformational scholarship has paved the subfields of art history to which my research lays claim. I am deeply grateful, too, for their ongoing friendship which has been a source of strength, mutual affection, and support. Simon Leung, Akira Mizuta Lippit, and Julia Bryan-Wilson were also valued readers in this book's early stages. Their collective influence is immeasurable, and I can only hope my work reflects the best of their pedagogy and erudition.

This book was enhanced by the team at the University of Chicago Press in ways I can never fully quantify. David Olsen—the editor every writer dreams of—offered patience, sage suggestions, probing questions, and enduring encouragement when delays and life's disruptions were out of our control. Joel Score's exceptionally incisive reading ensured this book could be all that it promised. James Whitman Toftness not only remained engaged with the manuscript from its start but was instrumental in securing images and permissions to reproduce them. Adrienne Meyers and Matthew Lang have been a joy to work with; Matt Avery's expert design has made this book beautiful. And Susan M. Bielstein's enthusiasm buoyed my spirits when everything felt untenable. They each deserve every accolade.

As the first monograph on Alison Knowles, this study necessarily entailed the task of piecing together scattered information from a broad spectrum of biographical and critical materials. I have had the exceptional privilege of working with a trove of primary sources, including artworks, unpublished letters and notes, photographs and rare films, out-of-print exhibition catalogs, and ephemera from Knowles's studio loft. My sincerest thanks to Alison for her unwavering cooperation, her gentle pushback on interpretations she disagreed with, her assistance in tracking down archival materials, and the countless hours of interviews (on the record and off) that made working on this book both a pleasure and an exercise in attentive listening. We also shared many meals together, including various iterations of *The Identical Lunch* and *Make a Salad*. Sadly, Alison passed away as this book was nearing publication. I am profoundly grateful for the time we spent together during her final weeks flipping through its pages, with Alison often smiling radiantly and reminiscing about friends and artworks long gone.

As the daughters born under the sign of Fluxus (biologically and allegorically), Hannah B Higgins and Jessica Higgins have contributed invaluable knowledge to the history of Fluxus and to this study in particular. Hannah is a formidable scholar on Fluxus and performance art, Jessica an intermedia artist, and both, on a more personal level, have been (and still are) endlessly willing to engage in conversation about their parents, Alison and Dick Higgins, and to share rare photographs and books. My gratitude extends, too, to their family members Joshua Selman, Joseph Reinstein, Zöe and Nathalie Reinstein, and Clara Joy Selman for their care and support of this project. I had the immense honor of working closely with Alison, Hannah, curator Karen Moss, Lucia Fabio, and Lauren Fulton on the exhibition *by Alison Knowles: A Retrospective (1960–2022)*, which debuted at the Berkeley Art Museum and Pacific Film Archive (2022–2023), then traveled Europe for three years. I am especially grateful to Karen for including me in the exhibition's conception and planning, and providing an opportunity to write about Knowles for the catalog. Each of these dazzling thinkers deserves special recognition for their contributions to my understanding of Knowles's and Higgins's lives and art. I encourage readers to seek out their work.

In revising the manuscript for publication, extensive writing and research was generously supported by timely external fellowships and grants. As the Ailsa Mellon Bruce Visiting Senior Fellow at the Center for Advanced Study in the Visual Arts, National Gallery of Art, Washington, DC, I benefited from inspiring senior scholars and curators who offered productive insights on an early draft. I am grateful to former dean Elizabeth Cropper, Peter Lukehart, Therese O'Malley, and Helen Tangires for creating a vigorous intellectual community, as well as members of my cohort—especially Babette Bohn, Lynne Cooke, Megan Holmes, and Prita Meier—for energizing my thinking about Knowles's oeuvre in relation to other models of historical inquiry. My appreciation extends to the wonderful cadre of emerging scholars, fellowship assistants, and staff at The Center and the Smithsonian American Art Museum, whom I convened with regularly during my residency in DC, including Caitlyn Beach, Catherine Quan Damman, Danielle Horetsky, Jen Rokowski, Xuxa Rodriguez, Jennifer Sichel, Jeanette Ibarra Shindell, and Abbe Schriber. I thank the Institute for Scholarship in the Liberal Arts (ISLA) at the University of Notre Dame for a publication subvention grant. Former ISLA directors

Kenneth Garcia, Thomas Merluzzi, and Alison Rice were also instrumental in funding research travel to explore dangling threads and leads. I also thank Denise Massa and Marsha Stevenson for their expert assistance in tracking down images, books, and archival documents at Hesburgh Library, and for their wonderful friendship along the way.

This project is particularly indebted to the Graham Foundation for Advanced Studies in the Fine Arts, Chicago, which awarded me an Individual Research Travel Grant to conduct late-stage work in the Archiv Sohm, Staatsgalerie, Stuttgart, at a crucial juncture. Having the opportunity to consult materials in the Sohm collection produced rare discoveries—unpublished notes, photographs, journals, letters unearthed from a trove of neglected boxes—that allowed me to cross-check and contextualize Knowles's practice (especially her slimly documented early career). I thank the knowledgeable library staff for their assistance, most especially Ilona Lütken and Katja Ellenschläger, who secured all the materials I needed from Sohm's vast Fluxus files and made other invaluable image resources available on a moment's notice. The Fondazione Bonotto, Molvena, Italy, afforded access to (then) rarely viewed film materials of Knowles's early Fluxus performances and their rich corpus of documentary ephemera and art multiples.

Over the course of this study, as I painstakingly pieced together an arc (and archive) of Knowles's life and art that did not previously exist, I conducted original research at numerous institutions and libraries across the US, including the Archives of American Art, Smithsonian Institution, Washington, DC; California Institute of the Arts Archives, Valencia, CA; Charles Deering McCormick Library of Special Collections, Northwestern University, Evanston, IL; Fayles Library, New York University; Getty Research Institute, Los Angeles; Gilbert and Lila Silverman Fluxus Collection Archives, Museum of Modern Art, New York; Emily Harvey Foundation Archives, New York (now at the Getty); Dick Higgins Estate, Chicago; Jewish Museum of Art Archives, New York; Museum of Contemporary Art Library and Archives, Chicago; Paula Cooper Gallery Archives, New York; and the Special Collections Libraries at the University of Iowa, UC Irvine, and UC San Diego. My special thanks to Ted Walbye and Marcia Reed at the Getty Research Institute and Library; Kim Conaty, Jon Hendricks, and Danielle Johnson for their help early on locating materials in MoMA's off-site storage archives in Queens; and Mary Richardson for her vast knowledge of the MCA's archive, especially its early history. At Northwestern, I am grateful to Scott Krafft, Greg MacAyeal, Abbey Maynard, Sigrid Pohl Perry, and Gary Strawn for their assistance in the archives of John Cage, Jan Herman, Dick Higgins, Peter Moore, and Charlotte Moorman (much of it still unprocessed when I initiated this project). The exceptionally helpful Alice Centamore, during her tenure at the Emily Harvey Foundation, and Evan Graham, who during his studies at Pratt Institute tracked down Knowles's student work, merit special thanks—as does Marisa Bourgoin at the Archives of American Art, and Kate Wilson, who provided key assistance in the papers of her father, William S. Wilson, before they were acquired by the Art Institute of Chicago. Lastly, I am thankful to the resource staff who made available vital materials that were languishing during the COVID-19 epidemic, when many offices and repositories were shuttered with no tangible timeline for their safe reopenings. With this publication, I am hopeful more museums and libraries will prioritize digitization of Knowles's oeuvre for future studies.

Conversations with artists, curators, scholars, composers, and film archivists have shaped this book in countless important ways over its long gestation. I sincerely thank Simon Anderson, Valerie Oliver Cassel, Doris Chon, Bridget R. Cooks, Huey Copeland, Philip Corner, Catherine Quan Damman, Meghan DellaCrosse, Simone Forti, James Fuentes, Stephen Fredman, Saisha Grayson, Suzanne Hudson, Maud Jacquin, Simon Leung, Bonnie Marranca, W. J. T. Mitchell, Barbara Moore, Liz Phillips, Sebastién Pluot, Michelle Puetz, Irene Ravell, Bruce Richards, Janet Sarbanes, Andrew Schloss, Barbara T. Smith, Kirsten Swenson, Gregory Tentler, Joyce Tsai, Gloria Sutton, Christian Xatrec, and Damon Willick for generously sharing their time and support. Vital interlocutors who passed before seeing this book in print include Anne Friedberg, Anna Halprin, Kasper König, Benjamin Patterson, Barbara Rose, Carolee Schneemann, Owen F. Smith, and Elaine Summers. Cara M. Jordan read the first draft of this manuscript and offered expert editorial and scholarly advice. Eric Crosby at the Carnegie Museum of Art was a source of information and camaraderie during the 2016 exhibition of Knowles's work in Pittsburgh. Josh Rutner came to my rescue in the final hour to elegantly map out this book's index, for which I am deeply grateful.

For opportunities to share my research on Knowles as an invited guest or contributor, I thank colleagues at the Smithsonian Institution's Archives of American Art; Aspen Art Museum; Carleton College; College Art Association; Graduate Center at CUNY; Kenyon College; Lawrence University; Midwest Art History Society; Newberry Library, Chicago; RED/CAT California Institute for the Arts; Stanford University; UC Davis; and the University of Iowa, among others. Miguel de Baca, Silvia Bottinelli, Melissa Dabakis, Erika Doss, Ross Elfline, Lauren Fulton, Amelia Goerlitz, Micol Hebron, James E. Housefield, Branislav Jakoljević, Heather Parrish, Elizabeth Pulsinelli, Xuxa Rodriguez, and Margherita d'Ayala Valva—you have my thanks for allowing me the space to think aloud (in person, or on the page) about Knowles's art and life, and for kindly offering thoughtful feedback. The roster of historians, curators, and writers on Fluxus and experimental art of the postwar period is by now quite long, but I'd be remiss if I did not acknowledge the exceptional scholarly contributions of Benjamin H. D. Buchloh, Colby Chamberlain, Natilee Harren, Hanna B. Hölling, Liz Kotz, Branden W. Joseph, Julia Robinson, Kristine Stiles, and Midori Yoshimoto—each of whom fortified my own thinking about Fluxus or its related subjects in significant ways. I am grateful, too, for Michael Filas, Hannah Higgins, Roger Rothman, Craig Saper, Dennis Summers, and all the creators and writers who gather nearly every year to discuss some aspect of Fluxus (PechaKucha style) at the Society for Literature, Science, and the Art's annual conference. You have somehow made conference-going a joy again.

Former colleagues, now dear friends, with whom I forged inestimable relationships during my time in the Midwest remain a deep source of sustenance and affection. My sincerest thanks to Emily S. Beck, Anne H. Berry, Robert (Randy) Coleman, Nooshin Hakim Javadi, Danielle B. Joyner, Tamara Kay, Jason Lahr, Sarah Edmands Martin, Martin Lam Nguyen, Robin F. Rhodes, and Maria Tomasula for their resolute care, outstanding dinner parties, pandemic porch cocktails, sparkling discourse, travel and museum companionship, and so much more. I am grateful, too, for the collegiality, support, and friendship of Pamela Butler, Korey Garibaldi, Barbara Green, Perin Gürel, Ricky Herbst, Jim Hopfensperger, Robin Jensen, Michael Kackman, Mary Celeste Kearney, Jenna and Marc Kissel, Kathleen Pyne, Tatiana Reinoza, Annie Rhodes, Charles and Carol Rosenberg, Jason Ruiz, James Searl, David Smith, Steve Tomasula, and Pamela Robertson Wojcik. I am also grateful to Mary Cecilia Mitsch, who always made sure I had a place to stay (and a cat to pet) in New York. Lastly, I wish to thank former students for their sophisticated thinking on the intersections of performance and contemporary art. A few standouts include Zachary Anderson, Christine Anspach, Ava Bloom, Meg Burns, Caroline Cox, Evan Graham, Liam Maher, Larissa Nez, Willoughby Thom, and Corey Robinson.

I had the enormous luck to pursue my doctoral studies at a decisive moment where art history, film & media studies, and critical theory productively converged. My scholarship widened and deepened because of the intellectual rigor of interdisciplinary courses offered at UC Irvine, most especially in graduate seminars and public lectures led by Étienne Balibar, Angela Davis, Elizabeth Grosz, David Joselit, Julia R. Lupton, Achille Mbembe, Fred Moten, Yvonne Rainer, Felicity D. Scott, Sally Stein, Judith Wilson-Pates, and the late Lindon W. Barrett, Jacques Derrida, Mark Poster, and Ngũgĩ wa Thiong'o. My peers helped create a generous community of sharing and reflection, and many of us forged enduring bonds along the way. My thanks to Cole Akers, Kim Beil, Heidi Rae Cooley, Tobey Crockett, Kimberly Feig, Eva Friedberg, Vuslat Demirkoparan, Laura Holzman, Stefka Hristova, Jordy Tackitt-Jones, Kelly Kirshtner, Anna Kornbluh, Ari Lee Laskin, Janet Neary, Natalie E. Phillips, Tina Rivers Ryan, Vanessa Schulman, Tim Seiber, Sami Siegelbaum, Arden Stern, Mariana Wardwell, Mary Trent, and Bahar Zaker.

Closest to my heart are cherished family and friends in my beloved California, who have eagerly anticipated *Performing Chance*'s appearance in the world. Thank you Doris Chon, the Duckworth and Goltra families, Stacey Hess Pettersson, Natalie Noble, many SJB friends, and my dear, fierce Nydia Garcia, whom we lost too soon. For their enduring cheer and emotional support, I thank my parents, the late James A. Woods, who always encouraged me to keep going even when things fall apart, and my exceptionally caring and loving mother, Maragret Woods, who sustained life in this project in every conceivable way. My siblings and their extended families have brought cheer and welcome distractions. The Williamson family has been a nurturing joy. Finally, to my daughter, Helena, and my husband, Isaac—the tight-knit twosome whose abiding love, steadfast enthusiasm, enduring patience, biggest hugs, and timely laughs have seen me through to the end—I dedicate this book.

# NOTES

Frequently cited archives are abbreviated as follows:

| | |
|---|---|
| AAA | Archives of American Art, Smithsonian Institution |
| AKS | Alison Knowles Studio Archive, New York |
| AS | Archiv Sohm, Staatsgalerie Stuttgart |
| DHP | Dick Higgins papers, 1960–1994 (bulk 1972–1993), GRI |
| EHF | Emily Harvey Foundation Archives, GRI |
| GRI | Getty Research Institute, Research Library, Los Angeles |
| JBP | Jean Brown papers, 1916–1995 (bulk 1958–1985), GRI |
| JCNP | John Cage Notations Project Collection, Northwestern University Music Library |
| MCA | Museum of Contemporary Art Library and Archives, Chicago |
| NU | Charles Deering McCormick Library of Special Collections, Northwestern University |
| SFA | Gilbert and Lila Silverman Fluxus Collection Archives, Museum of Modern Art, New York |
| UCSD | Special Collections and Archives, Geisel Special Collections, University of California, San Diego |

## Introduction

1 Knowles began constructing *The Big Book* in 1966 and previewed it that year at Something Else Gallery, on the first floor of her Chelsea home. In 1967, it was shown at the Pollock Gallery in Toronto before being transported to Chicago. I return to *The Big Book* in chapter 4.

2 "She's close in something that's far out" (Alison Knowles with *The Big Book*, Museum of Contemporary Art, Chicago), AP wirephoto and caption, 1967.

3 Edward Barry, "Museum to Give Fresh Insight into Art," *Chicago Tribune*, October 24, 1967, A5.

4 Hal Foster, "What's Neo About the Neo-Avant-Garde?" *October*, no. 70 (Fall 1994): 20. For more recent assessments of Fluxus's complicated relationship to the avant-garde, see Mari Dumett, "A Fantastic Confusion," in *Corporate Imaginations: Fluxus Strategies for Living* (University of California Press, 2017), 1–37; and Natilee Harren, "The Crux of Fluxus: In-

termedia, Rear-guard," in *Art Expanded, 1958–1978*, ed. Eric Crosby and Liz Glass, vol. 2 of *Living Collections Catalogue* (Walker Art Center, 2015), http://walkerart.org/collections/publications/art-expanded/crux-of-fluxus.

5 Written in 1965, Dick Higgins's manifesto "Intermedia" was first published in *Something Else Press Newsletter*, no. 1 (February 1966).

6 See, for example, Liz Kotz, "Post-Cagean Aesthetics and the 'Event' Score," *October*, no. 95 (Winter 2001): 54–89; Branden W. Joseph, *Beyond the Dream Syndicate: Tony Conrad and the Arts After Cage* (Zone Books, 2008); Joseph, *Experimentations: John Cage in Music, Art, and Architecture* (Bloomsbury, 2016); Julia Robinson, ed., *The Anarchy of Silence: John Cage and Experimental Art* (Museu d'Art Contemporani, Barcelona, 2009). On Cage's relation to visual art, see Caroline A. Jones, "Finishing School: John Cage and the Abstract Expressionist Ego," *Critical Inquiry* 19, no. 4 (Summer 1993): 628–65.

7 Pieces devised by Higgins for Cage's 1958 class can be found in Dick Higgins papers, The Flaming City, box 190, AS.

8 While Knowles was not enrolled in "Experimental Composition," some publications (and exhibitions) have assigned her a seat in Cage's classroom. She was, however, a regular participant in his Mushroom Identification courses (ca. 1959–1962), also at the New School. Knowles and Cage's collaborations, over several decades of friendship, included plans for a macrobiotic cookbook. Knowles, interview with author, New York, December 8, 2006. See also Stephen Montague, "John Cage at Seventy: An Interview," *American Music* 3, no. 2 (Summer 1985): 206.

9 See, for example, Benjamin H. D. Buchloh, "The Book of the Future: Alison Knowles's *The House of Dust*," in *Mainframe Experimentalism: Early Computing and the Foundations of the Digital Arts*, ed. Hannah Higgins and Douglas Kahn (University of California Press, 2012), 200–208; Mari Dumett, "Alison Knowles: Ritual and Routine," in *Corporate Imaginations*, 269–307; Julia Robinson, "The Sculpture of Indeterminacy: Alison Knowles's Beans and Variations," *Art Journal* 63, no. 4 (Winter 2004): 96–115; Kristine Stiles, "Tuna and Other Fishy Thoughts on Fluxus Events," in *Indigo Island: Art Works by Alison Knowles* (Stadtgalerie Saarbrücken, 1995), 26–35. Studies focusing on particular works include Meghan A. Della-Crosse, ed., *Alison Knowles, The Big Book* (Passenger Books, 2013). The first comprehensive museum survey of Knowles's work, *by Alison Knowles: A Retrospective (1960–2022)*, opened in July 2022 at Berkeley Art Museum and Pacific Film Archive and traveled to Europe in 2024–2026. I am very grateful to curator Karen Moss for including me in the exhibition's conception and planning, and providing an opportunity to write about Knowles for the catalog.

10 One need only gloss the literature on George Maciunas and Nam June Paik to get a sense of this imbalance. On women artists in Fluxus and related movements, see, for example, Midori Yoshimoto, *Into Performance: Japanese Women Artists in New York* (Rutgers University Press, 2005); Meredith Morse, *Soft Is Fast: Simone Forti in the 1960s and After* (MIT Press, 2016); Joan Rothfuss, *Topless Cellist: The Improbable Life of Charlotte Moorman* (MIT Press, 2014); and *Shigeko Kubota: Liquid Reality*, exh. cat. (Museum of Modern Art, New York, 2022).

11 For example, Kate Millett's *City of Saigon* (1967) and Carolee Schneemann's *Interior Scroll* (1975) are examined in Kathy O'Dell's important essay "Fluxus Feminus," although neither work was conceived or performed under Fluxus. See O'Dell, "Fluxus Feminus," *Drama Review* 41, no. 1 (Spring 1997): 43–60. Schneemann, in a June 1992 letter to Walker Art Center curator Elizabeth Armstrong, describes herself as "Flux-affiliated"—that is, "based within and configuring the community aesthetic—projects, editions, collaborations, performances." Schneemann personal archives, cited in Rebecca Schneider, *The Explicit Body in Performance* (Routledge, 2013), 189n24. To be clear, I am not arguing for a strict definition of who should and should not count as Fluxus at any given time. The coalition was, as it were,

always fluid. This book does aim, however, to put Knowles for the first time squarely at the center of Fluxus.

12 On Maciunas's "excommunication" activities, see O'Dell, "Fluxus Feminus," 44.

13 Knowles, interview with author, New York, December 8, 2006. On the "dirty games" Higgins and Maciunas played following their return from Europe, see Cuauhtémoc Medina, "The 'Kulturbolschewiken' I: Fluxus, the Abolition of Art, the Soviet Union, and 'Pure Amusement,'" *RES: Anthropology and Aesthetics* 48 (Autumn 2005): 184–85. Between 1966 and the end of 1967, for example, Maciunas omitted Knowles and Higgins from the distribution list for an official newsletter and from the inventory of "all [Fluxus] projects; past, present and future." George Maciunas, "Fluxnewsletter, March 18, 1967," reproduced in *Fluxus, Etc., Addenda 1*, ed. Jon Hendricks (New York: Ink &, 1983), 172–75. For a reassessment of the conflict between Maciunas and Higgins, especially as it related to Fluxus's internal politics and the narratives driving each, see Colby Chamberlain, *Fluxus Administration: George Maciunas and the Art of Paperwork* (University of Chicago Press, 2024), 136–45.

14 Higgins, letter to Maciunas, August 17, 1966, JBP. See also Higgins, letter to Jeff Berner, August 22, 1966 (JBP), wherein he elaborates on the quarrel with Maciunas and cites the issues around founding Something Else Press (originally to be called "Fluxus Annex"), including Knowles's role in persuading him to "call it something else."

15 Higgins, letter to Maciunas, August 23, 1966, JBP. The 1963 performance in Stockholm is referenced later in the chapter. In 1974, Higgins sent a long, reflective missive to Maciunas in which he acknowledges "missing" the spirit of Fluxus in founding the press and missteps in organizing performances: "No, George, you were right and I was wrong when I took off on my tangent of professionalism. That much has become crystal clear . . . partly it was in my background, these false ambitions and the fact of being born privileged in a society which I could not respect." Higgins, typed letter to Maciunas, November 19, 1974, DHP.

16 In a 1966 letter to Maciunas, Knowles criticizes his "rigid, 'this is mine,' 'that is yours'" approach to Fluxus content, noting it put her "in a very tight spot" but affirming that the "important thing George, is that the work keep coming." Maciunas Archive, Alison Knowles Correspondence, JBP.

17 Knowles, interview with author, Boston, November 9, 2009. See also correspondence between Knowles and Higgins, boxes 18–19, DHP.

18 See, for example, Jerome Rothenberg, ed., *Technicians of the Sacred: A Range of Poetries from Africa, America, Asia, Europe and Oceania* (University of California Press, 1968); Rothenberg, *Shaking the Pumpkin: Traditional Poetry of the Indian North Americas* (Doubleday, 1972); Ronald Gross and George Quasha, eds., *Open Poetry: Four Anthologies of Expanded Poems* (Simon & Schuster, 1973).

19 Knowles, interview with author, New York, December 15, 2006; unpublished interview with Higgins, DHP.

20 Knowles's books include *by Alison Knowles* (Something Else Press, 1965); *Journal of the Identical Lunch* (Nova Broadcast Press, 1971); *Gem Duck* (Pari & Dispari Edition, 1977); *More by Alison Knowles* (Printed Editions, 1979); *Natural Assemblages and the True Crow* (Printed Editions, 1980); *A Bean Concordance* (Printed Editions, 1983); *Event Scores* (Left Hand Books, 1992); *Spoken Text* (Left Hand Books, 1993); *Bread and Water* (Left Hand Books, 1995); *Footnotes: A Collage Journal 30 Years* (Granary Books, 2000); *A Common Boat (Phaseolus vulgaris)* (Brisbane, Australia: Edition 1000, 2004); *Plah Plah Pli Plah* (Chicago: Sara Ranchouse Publishing, 2009); and, with Rirkrit Tiravanija, *Clear Skies All Week* (Paris: Onestar Press, 2011).

21 My essay "Do You Remember? Alison Knowles in Context," in the exhibition catalog *by Alison Knowles: A Retrospective (1960–2022)*, revisits the tricky and limited nature of the archive within art historical discourse. I return to this point in the epilogue.

22 See Elizabeth Armstrong and Joan Rothfuss, eds., *In the Spirit of Fluxus* (Walker Art Center, 1993); Ken Friedman, ed., *The Fluxus Reader* (Academy Editions, 1998); *What's Fluxus? What's Not! Why* (Centro Cultural Banco do Brasil, 2002); Dick Higgins, *Postface/Jefferson's Birthday* (Something Else Press, 1964); Hannah Higgins, *Fluxus Experience* (University of California Press, 2002); Larry Miller, "Transcript of the Videotaped Interview with George Maciunas" (1978), in Hendricks, *Fluxus, Etc.*, 11–28; Johan Pijnappel, ed., "Fluxus: Today and Yesterday" (special issue), *Art & Design* 28 (1993); Owen F. Smith, *Fluxus: The History of an Attitude* (San Diego State University Press, 1998); Astrit Schmidt-Burkhardt, *Maciunas' Learning Machines: From Art History to a Chronology of Fluxus* (Vice Versa Verlag, 2003); Emmett Williams and Ann Noël, *Mr. Fluxus: A Collective Portrait of George Maciunas, 1931–1978* (Thames & Hudson, 1997).

23 See Schneemann, "The Obscene Body/Politic," *Art Journal* 50, no. 4 (Winter 1991): 28–35; Midori Yoshimoto and Alex Pittman, eds., "An Evening with Fluxus Women: A Roundtable Discussion," *Woman & Performance* 19, no. 3 (December 2009): 369–89.

24 See Chamberlain, *Fluxus Administration*; Valerie Cassel Oliver, *Benjamin Patterson: Born in the State of FLUX/us* (Contemporary Arts Museum, Houston, 2012); Hanna Hölling, *Paik's Virtual Archive: Time, Change, and Materiality in Media Art* (University of California Press, 2017); Julia Robinson and Alfred Fischer, eds., *George Brecht Events: A Heterospective* (Verlag der Buchhandlung Walther König, 2005); and Robinson's forthcoming book *George Brecht, the Event, and the Duchamp Paradigm (1940s–1950s)* (October Books/MIT Press, 2026).

25 "Dr. Edwin Knowles, a Pratt Professor," *New York Times*, May 19, 1967, 39. Her mother, Lois Beckwith Knowles, had died the year before, on May 12, 1966. "Deaths—Knowles, Lois Beckwith," *New York Times*, May 15, 1966, 89. Chapter 1 provides more detail on Knowles's upbringing and her close relationship with her father.

26 *Cahiers d'Art* 1, no. 1–2 (May 1936). Gabrielle Buffet-Picabia's essay "Cœurs Volants," a study of Duchamp's optical works, appears in this issue.

27 SEP announcement card for *Coeurs Volants*, Dick Higgins Correspondence folder, Duchamp Coeurs Volants folder, AS. The prints measured approximately 45 × 59 cm. Higgins kept detailed contemporaneous notes of the 1967–1968 collaboration between Knowles and Duchamp. See Higgins papers, Duchamp Coeurs Volants folder, AS. Several sources date the Williams book to 1967, but Higgins's own "SEP History, 1963–1973" dates it to February 1968. See Higgins, typed SEP chronology, SFA I.504.

28 Higgins, typed page dated January 9, 1968, Higgins papers, Duchamp Coeurs Volants folder, AS.

29 Knowles, quoted in "Notes Toward an Indigo Island: A Conversation Between Alison Knowles and Hannah Higgins, 1994," in *Indigo Island*, 101–102. See also Richard Hamilton, "Letter to Alison Knowles" (December 1972), in his *Collected Words: 1953–1982* (Thames & Hudson, 1982), 236–37. Knowles describes a second visit to Duchamp's apartment in a 1968 letter to Cage. John Cage Ephemera, Correspondence Files, University Music Library, Northwestern University.

30 Knowles, interview with author, New York, December 15, 2006.

31 Higgins to Schwarz, May 22, 1968, Higgins papers, Duchamp Coeurs Volants folder, AS. On Schwarz's assessments of what should be included in Duchamp's official oeuvre, see Francis Naumann, "Arturo's Marcel," *Art in America* 86, no. 1 (January 1998): 35–39.

32 Knowles, quoted in "Flux Generations," a roundtable with Janet A. Kaplan, Bracken Hendricks, Geoffrey Hendricks, Hannah Higgins, and Knowles, *Art Journal* 59, no. 2 (Summer 2000): 10.

33 Alan Jones, "Carte Blanche," *Arts Magazine*, February 1991, 25. The *I Ching* translation was by Richard Wilhelm; *The Book of the Hopi*, by Frank Waters. Knowles also listed Waters's

*The Portable Jung* (1971); Rothenberg's *Technicians of the Sacred* (1968); Shunryu Suzuki, *Zen Mind, Beginners Mind* (1970); *The Complete Works of Chuang-Tzu* (1968); Peter Matthiessen, *Cloud Forest: A Chronicle of the South American Wilderness* (1961); and the L. L. Bean catalog.

34 A project inspired by Thoreau's journals, for example, yielded a book, audiotapes, and sculptures (found objects collected outdoors in various lived spaces), plus word collages and screen prints. See Alison Knowles, *Natural Assemblages and the True Crow* (Printed Editions/Visual Studies Workshop Press, 1980).

35 Knowles maintains a modest archive in the SoHo studio loft she's inhabited since 1972. Most, if not nearly all, material evidence of her life and work is contained within Higgins's vast collection of letters, photographs, compositions, notes, and films, which is dispersed across multiple archives in the US and Germany.

## Chapter 1

1 Dick Higgins, "Alison Knowles in Context, 1959," caption for photograph no. 27 in Higgins, *1959/60* (Verona: Edizioni Pari & Dispari, 1979), 36–37. An album of personal photographs and remembrances, *1959/60* includes images taken by Higgins of Allan Kaprow's *18 Happenings in 6 Parts* (1959) and *Below Zero* (1959), Reuben Gallery, New York; GRI.

2 Hannah B. Higgins offers accounts of the relationship between Knowles and Higgins, which spanned more than five decades, in "Love's Labor's Lost and Found: A Meditation on Fluxus, Family, and Somethings Else," *Art Journal* 69, nos. 1–2 (Spring–Summer 2010): 8–22, and "Eleven Snapshots of Dick Higgins," in *Intermedia, Fluxus, and the Something Else Press: Selected Writings of Dick Higgins*, ed. Steve Clay and Ken Friedman (Siglio Press, 2018), 327–45. Other sources recall Knowles and Higgins meeting in 1960, but personal letters between Higgins, Knowles, and even his father show they first met sometime in 1959 (or even late 1958) and by New Years Eve 1959, "first began the process of living together." Higgins, Correspondence Files, ca. 1959–1974, boxes 15, 18, 19, DHP.

3 Edwin Blackwell Knowles received his PhD in English at New York University in 1938 with a thesis titled "The Influence of Don Quixote on English Literature, 1605–1660." He was active in the Renaissance Society of America, serving on its editorial board and as treasurer throughout the 1950s and 1960s. See Edwin B. Knowles, "Thomas Shelton, Translator of *Don Quixote*," *Studies in the Renaissance* 5 (1958): 160–75, and Edwin Blackwell Knowles papers, 1957–1967, Columbia University Archives, New York.

4 Extracurricular activities included attending (and later waiting tables at) the Von Trapp Family Music Camp in Stowe, Vermont, and singing in the choir at the Reformed Protestant Dutch Church of Greenville, New York. Knowles, interview with author, New York, December 15, 2007. See also Alison Knowles Correspondence Files, JBP. Other bios, scattered in various archives, verify these details, but many dates are misattributed or erroneous.

5 Richards, "Oral History Interview with Alison Knowles," AAA.

6 Knowles, interview with author, New York, March 15, 2007.

7 While Knowles's bios from the early 1970s list 1952 as her high school graduation date, Scarsdale High School transcripts confirm that the date was 1951.

8 The Blake term paper, dated May 22, 1953, was for Fine Arts 25; a few notebooks from the seminar are in Alison Knowles Juvenilia folder, AS. For more on Knowles's time at Middlebury College (1952–1954), see Richards, "Oral History Interview with Alison Knowles," AAA.

9 For more on Healy, see Correspondence Files, box 44, folders 23–25, Macbeth Gallery records, 1838–1968, bulk 1892–1953, AAA. The brochure for a 1946 exhibition at Macbeth

includes a foreword by Healy's close friend, the poet Robert Frost. See Macbeth Gallery Exhibition Catalogs, Metropolitan Museum of Art, New York.

10 Alison Knowles, interview with author, New York, November 6, 2008. See also Higgins, "Love's Labor's Lost and Found," 13.

11 German-born Richard Lindner (1901–1978), North American–born Roger L. Crossgrove (1921–2016), and Finnish-born Leander Fornas (1925–2014) all taught at Pratt in the 1950s. Children's book writer and illustrator Tomie DePaola was a 1956 graduate in Illustration with Knowles at Pratt. Pratt Institute awarded Knowles an honorary doctorate in 2015.

12 According to Pratt records, Adolph Gottlieb (1903–1974) taught evening classes from 1955 through the 1958–1959 school year. These would have been the fall and spring semesters, as the Gottliebs spent their summers outside of New York City. My thanks to Sanford Hirsch, executive director of the Adolph and Esther Gottlieb Foundation, for clarifying these details.

13 Knowles, interviews with author, New York, March 15 and December 15, 2007; Dorothy Seiberling, "Women Artists in Ascendance," *Life*, May 13, 1957, 74–75.

14 Knowles, interview with author, New York, March 15, 2007.

15 Knowles, interview with author, New York, March 16, 2007.

16 On studio lofts and the arts community in SoHo, see Aaron Shkuda, *The Lofts of SoHo: Gentrification, Art, and Industry in New York, 1950–1980* (University of Chicago Press, 2016); Richard Kostelanetz, *Artists' SoHo: 49 Episodes of Intimate History* (Fordham University Press, 2014); Kostelanetz, *SoHo: The Rise and Fall of an Artists' Colony* (Routledge, 2003); and James R. Hudson, *The Unanticipated City: Loft Conversions in Lower Manhattan* (University of Massachusetts Press, 1987).

17 *ADLIB*, no. 4 (1956), Pratt Archives, Brooklyn, New York. The contributors write, "This is a collection of etchings, wood, and linoleum cuts. It is an attempt by seventeen senior illustrators, through experiment with these graphic techniques, to create a book as a group." The list of artists includes Knowles, Richard ("Dick") Giglio, Ted Lewin, Roy Superior, Hugh Hirtle, and Kathy Mosedale. The production staff dedicated the issue to Fornas, who served as advisor. I am grateful to Evan Graham for his research assistance in the Pratt Archives. A copy of *ADLIB* can also be found in the New York Public Library, Schwarzman Building, Rare Book Collection, room 328.

18 Carl Sandburg, "Upstream," from *Slabs of the Sunburnt West* (Harcourt, Brace and Company, 1922), 30. Sandburg also penned the prologue to Edward Steichen's infamous *The Family of Man* exhibition at the Museum of Modern Art, New York (1955). Knowles recalls viewing the exhibition in late winter 1955. Knowles, interview with author, New York, December 15, 2007.

19 The poem first appeared on vinyl LP on *Sandburg Reads Sandburg*, track b1, recorded in 1953, Decca, Gold Label Series 7541.

20 Knowles, interview with author, New York, March 15, 2007, and Pittsburgh, PA, May 20, 2016.

21 Knowles, interview with author, New York, December 15, 2007.

22 "Alison Knowles—The Nonagon, 99 Second Avenue. Paintings," April–May 1958. See "Fifty Art Shows Slated for Week: Highlights to Be Displays at Brooklyn, Whitney, City and Jewish Museums," *New York Times*, April 27, 1958.

23 Charles Mingus Quintet, *Jazz Portrait: Mingus in Wonderland* (United Artists, 1959), recorded January 16, 1959, at the Nonagon Art Gallery, New York; produced by Alan Douglas. For a review of the concert, and descriptions of Nonagon's gallery space (a narrow room of "brooding beams, heavy chandeliers, and dark woodwork carved with unicorns"), see Whitney Balliett, "Mingus Among the Unicorns," *New Yorker*, January 24, 1959, 103–5.

24 Guin Hall, "All the Arts in One House: Gallery Shows Music," *New York Herald Tribune*, No-

vember 19, 1958, A2. On Richards's April 1958 show at Nonagon Gallery, see Jenni Sorkin, "The Pottery Happening: M. C. Richards's 'Clay Things to Touch . . .' (1958)," *Getty Research Journal*, no. 5 (November 2013): 197–202. Knowles's spring show opened one week before Cage's exhibition of notational scores at the nearby Stable Gallery. See Dore Ashton's review, "Cage, Composer, Shows Calligraphy of Note," *New York Times*, May 6, 1958, 33.

25 The paintings appear to measure roughly four by four to six by four feet. On the scale of her 1950s paintings, see a draft interview between Knowles and George Myers, ca. 1977, DHP. An edited copy can be found in Knowles's artist file, EHF. The condensed published version is included in George Myers, "Alison Knowles: To See Clearly and Afresh Each Moment," in *Alphabets Sublime: Contemporary Artists on Collage and Visual Literature* (Paycock Press, 1986), 42–52.

26 "Nuptials on June 2 for Alison Knowles," *New York Times*, February 18, 1956, 12; "Alison Knowles Wed," *New York Times*, June 3, 1956, 94.

27 All quotations from Robert Warren Dash, "Alison Knowles" *Arts* 32, no. 8 (May 1958): 56.

28 See Hubert Crehan, "Fortnight in Review: Rauschenberg," *Arts Digest*, January 1, 1955, 30. For a now-famous reassessment of Rauschenberg in contrast to formalist readings, see Leo Steinberg, "Reflections on the State of Criticism," *Artforum* 10, no. 7 (March 1972): 37–49.

29 Other artists in *8 Painters* included George Dworzan, Ruth Kukonis, William Sebring, Barbara Silbert, and Beate Wheeler. To my knowledge, the only extant documentation of the show is a gallery notice in the *New York Times* (June 1958) and the hand-drawn announcement poster in the Estate of William S. Wilson, which I first inspected in New York in June 2019. My thanks to Kate Wilson for generously allowing access to her father's archive before much of it was acquired by the Art Institute of Chicago as the William S. Wilson Collection of Ray Johnson.

30 Albers taught at the Bauhaus from the early 1920s to 1933, then at Black Mountain College from 1933 to 1949, moving to Yale University in 1950. Before retiring from Yale in 1960, he taught summer classes at Syracuse in 1958 and 1959. See "Curriculum Vitae and Bibliography, 1966–1970," box 1, folder 1, Josef Albers papers, 1929–1970, Series I: Biographical Material, 1957–1970, AAA. On his rigorous teaching methods, see Eva Díaz, *The Experimenters: Chance and Design at Black Mountain College* (University of Chicago Press, 2015), 15–52.

31 Knowles, interview with author, New York, March 15, 2007.

32 Knowles, interview with author, New York, March 15, 2007.

33 Figurative drawing, especially portraits of close friends, beans, and other subjects (and matter) important to her, would nevertheless persist as a practice throughout Knowles's life. See, for example, her elegant line drawing of Benjamin Patterson (1965), GRI, and her drawings collected in *Footnotes: Collage Journal 30 Years* (Granary Books, 2000).

34 Knowles recalls feeling both isolated and contingently accepted at the Cedar Tavern (also known as the Cedar Tavern Bar) and other watering holes shared with the abstract expressionists, and being deeply saddened by Jackson Pollock's tragic death in August 1956, just a few months after she graduated from Pratt. Knowles, interview with author, New York, March 15, 2007. Lette Lou Eisenhauer, a later friend and collaborator of Knowles, remembers witnessing shockingly violent behavior toward women artists at the Cedar Tavern. See Joan Marter, ed., *Off Limits: Rutgers University and the Avant-Garde, 1957–1963* (Newark Museum/Rutgers University Press, 1999), 150–51.

35 Ann Eden Gibson, *Abstract Expressionism: Other Politics* (Yale University Press, 1999), xx. See also Joanne Meyerowitz, ed., *Not June Cleaver: Women and Gender in Postwar America, 1945–1960* (Temple University Press, 1994); Serge Guilbault, *How New York Stole the Idea of Modern Art: Abstract Expressionism, Freedom, and the Cold War*, trans. Arthur Goldhammer (University of Chicago Press, 1983).

36 "I think the whole feeling [of the art world in that era] engendered in me a desire to go in a more radical direction, as proper for me . . . even though Gottlieb wanted me to continue painting." Knowles, interview with author, New York, March 16, 2007.

37 Knowles quoted in Ellen Pearlman, "Interviews with Alison Knowles, July–October 2001, New York City," *Brooklyn Rail*, January–February 2002. https://brooklynrail.org/2002/01/art/interviews-with-alison-knowles-july-october-2001-new-york-city.

38 Having frequented MoMA in midtown New York, Knowles was, by the late 1950s, familiar with complex investigations of color, texture, and form, including Jackson Pollock's *Full Fathom Five* (1947), with its encrusted skeins of swirling lines of paint and bits of the everyday world, such as keys, cigarette butts, coins, glass, and other detritus. *Full Fathom Five*, first exhibited in a 1953 summer exhibition of new acquisitions at MoMA, remained a work Knowles greatly admired. Knowles, interview with author, New York, March 15, 2007.

39 See, for example, Clement Greenberg's "American-Type Painting" (1955), wherein the influential critic celebrates Pollock's canvases for their "capacity to bind the canvas rectangle and assert its ambiguous flatness." *Partisan Review*, Spring 1955, 187.

40 Knowles and James Ericson separated in 1958 and were divorced in May 1959 in Juárez, Mexico. Precisely when she first met Higgins is murky; personal correspondence indicates sometime in 1959, but it may have been late 1958. Higgins Correspondence Files, ca. 1959–1974, boxes 15 and 18, DHP. For an account of Knowles's divorce and Ericson's alleged gambling and later suicide, see Knowles, letter to Emmett Williams, July 1967, Emmett Williams Archives, Alison Knowles Correspondence, JBP; and Hannah Higgins, "Love's Labor's Lost and Found," 13.

41 Hannah Higgins, "Eleven Snapshots," 335. Podber was an activist, performance artist, and raucous downtown denizen, recently released, at the time of the party, from the Women's House of Detention on Sixth Avenue, where she had been jailed for arranging abortions for women. She would become infamous in 1964 for shooting a stack of Andy Warhol's *Marilyn* paintings. See Randy Kennedy, "Dorothy Podber, 75, Artist and Trickster Is Dead," *New York Times*, February 19, 2008, A22; Alice Centamore and Christian Xatrec, eds., *Call It Something Else: Something Else Press, Inc. (1963–1974)* (Museo Reina Sofia, 2023), 220. Ray Johnson, an artist and founder of the New York Correspondence School, was an early and ardent supporter of Knowles's work and a regular visitor to her downtown loft. They remained close friends and collaborators until his death in 1995.

42 Knowles, interview with author, New York, March 16, 2007.

43 Dick Higgins, quoted in Hannah Higgins, "Eleven Snapshots," 335. Higgins repeated the plumbing metaphor in his poem "The Women in Your Life Are Buried in a Pillar of Salt," *Gay Liberator* 21 (October 1972): 11.

44 See "Miss Knowles Wed to Richard Higgins," *New York Times*, June 1, 1960, 35; "Higgins-Knowles Wedding Takes Place in New York," *Worchester Evening Gazette*, May 31, 1960, C1. Painter Lawrence (Larry) Poons served as best man.

45 Interview with author, New York, March 15, 2007. See also letters between Knowles and Higgins and Jan Herman, dating from the late 1960s to early 1970s (DHP, NU).

46 Knowles, interview with author, New York, December 15, 2007. See also Hannah Higgins, "Eleven Snapshots," 335, 342.

47 Carole Pateman, *The Sexual Contract* (Stanford University Press, 1988), 132.

48 Desire aside, Knowles's dedication to her career, the demands of parenting, and Higgins's mental health struggles became a source of bickering in the later 1960s. The couple divorced in 1970, reconnected in 1974, and remarried in 1984 in an open partnership that continued until his death in 1998. Interviews with author, New York, April 23 and December 15, 2007. See also Hannah Higgins, "Eleven Snapshots," 335, 342.

49 Daniel Kane, *All Poets Welcome: The Lower East Side Poetry Scene in the 1960s* (University of California Press, 2003), xiii–xiv.

50 P. K. Thomajan, "500 More Printers: Manhattan School of Printing Offers Well-Rounded Training," *American Printer and Lithographer* 136 (May 1955): 25–27.

51 Interview with author, New York, March 15, 2007. References to her early design work appear, for example, in Dick Higgins's letter to his father, Carter Higgins, December 17, 1961, DHP. In another letter, Dick updates the elder Higgins on a hand injury Knowles suffered at work after a chrome poisoning accident. See also Alison Knowles, Benjamin Patterson, Tomas Schmit, and Philip Corner, *The Four Suits* (Something Else Press, 1965); William S. Wilson, "The Big Book," *Art in America* 56, no. 4 (July–August 1968): 100–103.

52 I detail Knowles's time at CalArts in chapter 5. For more on Warhol's move to silk-screen canvases in 1962, see Andy Warhol and Pat Hackett, *POPism: The Warhol '60s* (Harcourt Brace Jovanovich, 1980). Higgins also took courses at the Manhattan School of Printing, training that enabled him to handle the complex printing and design tasks undertaken by his and Knowles's publishing house Something Else Press (1960s–early 1970s) and subsequent operations including Unpublished Editions (1970s) and Printed Editions (1980s). See Alice Centamore, "The Making of Something Else Press, Inc.," in *Call It Something Else: Something Else Press, Inc. (1963–1974)*, ed. Alice Centamore and Christian Xatrec (Museo Reina Sofia, 2023), 14–29.

53 Greenberg, "Modernist Painting" (1960), in *Modernism with a Vengeance, 1957–1969*, vol. 4, *The Collected Essays and Criticism*, ed. John O'Brien (University of Chicago Press, 1993), 85–94.

54 Franz Kline, quoted in Caroline A. Jones, "The Romance of the Studio," in *Machine in the Studio: Constructing the Postwar American Artist* (University of Chicago Press, 1996), 23, 383n75.

55 New York City in the late 1950s was far from a liberal bastion; like many northern cities, it still practiced both de facto and de jure racialized segregation, especially in housing, transportation, and education. See Matthew F. Delmont, "The Origins of 'Antibusing' Politics: From New York Protests to the Civil Rights Act," in *Why Busing Failed: Race, Media, and the National Resistance to School Desegregation* (University of California Press, 2016), 23–53.

56 Walter Benjamin, "A Short History of Photography" (1930), in *Classic Essays on Photography*, ed. Alan Trachtenberg (Leet's Island Books, 1980), 204 (italics in original).

57 Jill Johnston, "Alison Knowles," *ARTnews* 60, no. 10 (February 1962): 17.

58 The entire suite of the *Notations* project is housed in JCNP. In addition to her own *Blue Ram*, Knowles helped to design and edit Cage's compilation of new musical scores. See John Cage and Alison Knowles, eds., *Notations* (Something Else Press, 1969). Knowles's *Blue Ram* score was reprinted in *Scenarios: Scripts to Perform*, ed. Richard Kostelanetz (Assembling Press, 1980), 503. Chapter 4 returns to the *Notations* project.

59 See Knowles and Myers, draft interview, ca. 1977, DHP. SFA erroneously dates the Judson solo show to 1961 (series I, folder 73). An announcement card giving the show's dates as January 12–31, 1962, can be found in Knowles's exhibition files, AS. The painting was also included in *Object Poems* (1966) at Something Else Press Gallery, discussed further in chapters 3 and 4. The Judson Gallery opened in the basement of Judson Memorial Church in 1958 and offered exhibition space to many then-unknown artists, including Knowles, Claes Oldenburg, Jim Dine, Red Grooms, and Robert Rauschenberg. Under Reverend Howard Moody and assistant minister Bud Scott, the church supported a radical arts ministry that took shape by serving its local community. On Moody's progressive mission, which he simply named "the political, the social, and the artistic," see Robert E. Haywood, *Allan Kaprow & Claes Oldenburg: Art, Happenings, and Cultural Politics* (Yale University Press, 2017), 42–50.

60 Johnston, "Alison Knowles," 17.

61 Knowles, interview with author, New York, March 15, 2007. Kline regularly projected small drawings and photographs, which he then rendered large with painterly brushstrokes. On this practice, see Elaine de Kooning, "Franz Kline," in *Franz Kline Memorial Exhibition*, exh. cat. (Washington [DC] Gallery of Modern Art, 1962), 14–15; "Franz Kline: Painter in His Own Life," *ARTnews* 61, no. 7 (November 1962): 28–31, 64; and Harry F. Gaugh, *Franz Kline* (Abbeville, 1985), 83–100.

62 Johnston, "Alison Knowles," 17.

63 See my essay "Do You Remember? Alison Knowles in Context," in *by Alison Knowles: A Retrospective (1960–2022)*, ed. Karen Moss and Lucia Fabio (University of California, Berkeley Art Museum and Pacific Film Archive, 2022), 31–43. Williams's poem was first published in *Underground* in 1966 and appeared the following year in *An Anthology of Concrete Poetry* (Something Else Press). In this work, Knowles again recycled imagery from *Blue Ram*, including a cropped negative-transfer portrait of Off-Broadway actress and friend Florence Tarlow (1922–1992), who appeared in many of Higgins's happenings and experimental films of the late 1950s and 1960s. For more on Tarlow, see Florence Tarlow professional files, 1949–1985, Billy Rose Theater Division, New York Public Library for the Performing Arts.

64 Leo Steinberg, "The Flatbed Picture Plane," excerpt from *Other Criteria: Confrontations with Twentieth Century Art* (Oxford University Press, 1972), 88–89. Decades later, Knowles told an interviewer, "What separates me from Robert Rauschenberg is that he would go to a studio and point out what he wanted in a very hands-off approach. I had no access to an art world that would fund or promote me. I didn't have a gallery. I was out there alone." See Harry J. Weil, "Sandwiches, Silkscreens, Swatches, and Scores: A Conversation with Alison Knowles," *Afterimage* 38, no. 5 (March–April 2011): 19.

65 Knowles, email exchange with author, December 28, 2008.

66 Knowles approximates her time at the department store as between 1958 and 1962. Knowles, interview with author, New York, April 23, 2007. For window displays at Bloomingdale's, she also recalls using the Bell-Opticon to "project tiny flowers" on the walls. Knowles, interview with author, New York, March 16, 2007.

67 *Object Poems* is discussed further in chapters 3–5. In addition to *Mother, or the Great Train Robbery* painting, Knowles exhibited a 1964 found object sculpture (block of wood with rope). Dick Higgins papers, Something Else Gallery folder, AS.

68 Knowles, interview with author, New York, March 15, 2007.

69 Contrary to many accounts of this era, Knowles had not yet met Higgins in 1958, and she has expressed regret that she never had the opportunity to take Cage's course. See, for example, Judith Olch Richards, "Oral History Interview with Alison Knowles," June 1–2, 2010, AAA. For an account of Cage's course content, see George Brecht, *Notebooks*, vol.1 (1958), GRI; Dick Higgins, *Postface/Jefferson's Birthday* (Something Else Press, 1964), 48–52; Higgins, "June–July 1958," in *John Cage*, ed. Richard Kostelanetz (Praeger, 1970), 122–24; Branden W. Joseph, "Chance, Indeterminacy, Multiplicity," in *Experimentations: John Cage in Music, Art, and Architecture* (Bloomsbury, 2016), 133–72; Rebecca Y. Kim, "The Formalization of Indeterminacy in 1958: John Cage and Experimental Composition at the New School," in *John Cage*, October Files 12, ed. Julia Robinson (MIT Press, 2011), 141–70; and Benjamin Piekut, *Experimentalism Otherwise: The New York Avant-Garde and Its Limits* (University of California Press, 2011). For photographs of the class taken by Harvey Gross, including Higgins, Allan Kaprow, George Brecht, and others performing individual works, see Al Hansen, *A Primer of Happenings & Time/Space Art* (Something Else Press, 1965), 95–101.

70 Hannah Higgins, *Fluxus Experience* (University of California Press, 2002), 1–2. Dick Higgins and Al Hansen have described their experiences in Cage's New School class, emphasizing

the free-form elements inherent in Cage's democratic teaching style. See Higgins, *Postface/ Jefferson's Birthday*, 51; Hansen, *Primer of Happenings*, 96.

71 Cage, interview with Barbara Rose, Barbara Rose papers, 1940–1993 (bulk 1960–1985), "American Artist Speak II: The Sixties," GRI. Save for Higgins and Toshi Ichiyanagi, who had formally trained as composers, Cage's class was a motley group of painters, poets, filmmakers, and actors, among others.

72 Knowles remembers that dates with Higgins included mushroom hunting trips with Cage beginning in late 1959. While not a student in "Experimental Composition," she was a regular participant in Cage's "Mushroom Identification" course at the New School between 1960 and 1962. In 1965, she and Higgins, along with Cage, became official members of the New York Mycological Society. Knowles, interviews with author, New York, March 15–16, 2007.

73 Knowles, interview with author, New York, March 16, 2007.

74 Knowles and Cage regularly cooked macrobiotic meals together during their nearly four-decade friendship. In 1987, they appeared in Cage's New York kitchen for "Cooking with Cage," episode 15 of *SWITCH*, an arts television program produced by artists in Western Massachusetts. In a March 2018 interview with author, Knowles recounted the details of Cage's "small kitchen" at 326 Monroe Street and her delight in cooking with him there with the "sounds from the street below" keeping them company.

75 Kurt Schwitters, "Merz (1920)," in *The Dada Painters and Poets: An Anthology*, ed. Robert Motherwell (1951; G. K. Hall, 1981), 59. For more recent analyses, see Christoph Zeller, "Aus Müll Gold gesponnen: Kurt Schwitters' Merzkunst und die Inflation," *German Studies Review* 31, no. 2 (May 2008): 345–67; Megan R. Luke, *Space, Image, Exile* (University of Chicago Press, 2014), 92–93. I return to Schwitters's influence on Knowles in chapter 5.

76 Knowles, email exchange with author, December 28, 2008. Knowles made similar points in other of our interviews, for example, November 2009, Boston, a conversation that centered on her early influences, especially the work of Schwitters and Duchamp.

77 Higgins also felt Schwitters's pull: "The rediscovery of Kurt Schwitters was the big thing in the late 1950s . . . [His] name was always a name that was around." Robert C. Morgan, "Interview with Dick Higgins" (cassette tape), New York, December 23, 1977, Robert C. Morgan Collection on Conceptual Art, Rare Books and Special Collections, Hesburgh Libraries, University of Notre Dame.

78 Photographs of Knowles in the "Ray Gun Spex" Happenings have not previously been published. See "First Judson Memorial Church Happening," Robert R. McElroy Collection, GRI. Announcement card for "The Poets Theater at Judson," March 3–5, 1962, is in Dick Higgins papers, AS. For *Stacked Deck*, see "Electronic Music Makes Debut," *Villager*, January 12, 1961, in Dick Higgins Scrapbooks, SFA, III.1. See also Mildred L. Glimcher, *Happenings New York, 1958–1963* (New York: Monacelli Press, 2012), 90–103; Dick Higgins and Letty Lou Eisenhauer, "Graphis," *Tulane Drama Review* 10, no. 2 (Winter 1965): 123–31; Higgins, "The Origins of Happenings," *American Speech* 51, nos. 3–4 (Autumn–Winter 1976): 268–71; Judith F. Rodenbeck, *Radical Prototypes: Allan Kaprow and the Invention of Happenings* (MIT Press, 2011), 1–28.

79 The dice have been misattributed to Takako Saito, a Japanese Fluxus artist and friend of Knowles. To my knowledge, the only remaining cube is in the collection of the Estate of William S. Wilson, New York. Two images printed on the Wilson cube were reused by Knowles for other projects, including *Blue Ram* (1966), *The Big Book* (1966–1969), and *Do You Remember (für Emmett Williams)* (1968). Photographs by Peter Moore of *The Tart* (1965) are in the Dick Higgins Archive, MS132, NU.

80 Johanna Drucker, "Collaboration Without Object(s) in the Early Happenings," *Art Journal* 52, no. 4 (Winter 1993): 53.

81 Drucker, "Collaboration Without Object(s)," 52. In addition to dance performances by Judson Theater Group, the basement gallery at Judson Memorial Church presented visual arts from 1958 to 1962 and again from 1969 to 1976 under the direction of artist-curator Jon Hendricks. Florence Tarlow, one of only two women auditing Cage's New School course, costarred in Higgins's elaborate Happenings at The Living Theater and Sunnyside Gardens. My thanks to Hendricks for discussing the contributions of Knowles, Tarlow, and Higgins in early Happenings, New York, 2016.

82 Knowles, interview with author, New York, December 15, 2007. Her design work is cited in Knowles, *The "T" Dictionary*, in *The Four Suits* with Tomas Schmit, Benjamin Patterson, Philip Corner (Something Else Press, 1965), xii. Knowles also later designed and screen-printed a clear cover jacket for Kaprow's spoken-word vinyl LP *How to Make a Happening*, published by Mass Art and distributed by Something Else Press in 1966. See Peter Frank, *Something Else Press: An Annotated Bibliography* (McPherson & Co., 1983), 78.

83 Barbara Haskell locates the Ergo Suits performances in Woodstock, East Hampton, and Bridgehampton, NY, August 18–25, 1962; Harald Szeemann's *Happening & Fluxus* exhibition (1970) places Knowles's event in East Hampton. To my knowledge, no photographs of Knowles's performance have been unearthed, though based on interviews with the artist I strongly suspect that the Happening indeed involved burning her remaining abstract expressionist canvases. Knowles, interview with author, New York, December 15, 2007. See Haskell, *Blam! The Explosion of Pop, Minimalism, and Performance, 1958–1964* (Whitney Museum of American Art, 1984), 147; Szeemann, "Chronologie 1959–1970," in *Happening & Fluxus: Materialien* (Kölnischer Kunstverein, 1970), n.p.

84 Unpublished manuscript, Emmett Williams Archives, Correspondence Files, JBP.

85 In interviews over the years, Knowles has said the burnings happened at "an event" at her father's house *and* at her brother's house on Long Island (Larry, a fisherman, lived in East Hampton). It is possible the two versions refer to a shared family home. For documentation of John Baldessari's *Cremation Piece* (1969), a performative burning of his "accumulated paintings" (dating from 1953 to 1966), see *Software*, exh. cat. (Jewish Museum, New York, 1970), 28–31.

86 Knowles, interview with author, New York, March 15, 2007.

87 John Cage, "Composition as Process," in *Silence: Lectures and Writings by John Cage* (Wesleyan University Press, 1961), 38–39.

88 Cage, "Composition: To Describe the Process of Composition Used in *Music of Changes and Imaginary Landscape No. 4* (1952)," in *Silence*, 59.

89 Cage, quoted in Kyle Gann, *No Such Thing as Silence: John Cage's 4′33″* (Yale University Press, 2010), 4. See also Calvin Tompkins, "John Cage," in *The Bride and the Bachelors: Five Masters of the Avant-Garde: Duchamp, Tinguely, Cage, Rauschenberg, Cunningham* (Penguin, 1965), 118–19; James Pritchett, "What Silence Taught John Cage: The Story of *4′33″*," in *The Anarchy of Silence: John Cage and Experimental Art*, ed. Julia Robinson (Museu d'Art Contemporani, Barcelona, 2009), 166–77.

90 Barbara Haskell, "Happenings," in *Blam!*, 31. Breton first articulated the idea of objective-chance in his novel *L'Amour Fou* (Gallimard, 1937), 32–38.

91 See Natilee Harren, "Diagramming Form, from Graphic Notation to the Fluxus Event Score," in *Fluxus Forms: Scores, Multiples, and the Eternal Network* (University of Chicago Press, 2020), 36–44; Julia Robinson, "John Cage and Investiture: Unmanning the System," in *Anarchy of Silence*, 101–3.

92 Aviva Rahmani, "Alison Knowles: An Interview," in *M/E/A/N/I/N/G: An Anthology of Artists' Writings, Theory, and Criticism*, ed. Susan Bee and Mira Schor (Duke University Press, 2000), 366.

93 Knowles, typed artist's statement, ca. 1971, unmarked folder, AKS.

94 Julia Robinson, "The Sculpture of Indeterminacy: Alison Knowles's Beans and Variations," *Art Journal* 63, no. 4 (Winter 2004): 98–99.

95 The Circle in the Square premiere took place on March 7, 1960. Announcement card, Dick Higgins papers, AS. According to the John Cage Trust, "This work was originally used as music for the choreographed piece by Merce Cunningham of the same title. Theatre Piece is a composition indeterminate of its performance. It is one of Cage's earliest works to use time brackets. These time brackets indicate a segment within which an action may be made. The actions are taken from a gamut of 20 nouns and/or verbs, chosen by the performer. The compositional means were the materials of Fontana Mix. Parts are provided for 1–8 performers, which may be used in whole, in part, or in any combination." Peters Edition EP 6759a-h.

96 Branden W. Joseph, "The Social Turn," in *Beyond the Dream Syndicate: Tony Conrad and the Arts After Cage* (Zone Books, 2011), 76.

97 On Cage's Asian influences, see David W. Patterson, "Cage and Asia: History and Sources," in *The Cambridge Companion to John Cage*, ed. David Nicholls (Cambridge University Press, 2002), 41–59. Knowles was also influenced by seventeenth-century Japanese poet Matsuo Bashō's poetic diary, *The Narrow Road to the Deep North (Oku no hosomichi)*. Knowles, interview with author, New York, March 15, 2007.

98 Rahmani, "Alison Knowles: An Interview," 366.

99 Cage invited Knowles to serve as coeditor of the compendium in 1967. More on *Notations* and their shared appreciation for the work of Henry David Thoreau can be found in chapter 4. Chapter 5 discusses their excited use of ICHING, a newly programmed computer subroutine, in the late 1960s and early 1970s.

100 Myers, "Alison Knowles: To See Clearly," 46.

101 Myers, "Alison Knowles: To See Clearly," 46–47. Knowles is paraphrasing Alan Watts's characterization of D. T. Suzuki's notion of reaching Zen enlightenment. See Alan Watts, *The Way of Zen* (New York: Vintage, 1957), 22. Alexandra Munroe contextualizes the "flood of English translations and commentaries on Zen Buddhism" available in the 1950s–1960s to American artists and writers "coming of age in the wake of nuclear and politically facilitated holocausts." See Munroe, "Buddhism and the Neo-Avant-Garde: Cage Zen, Beat Zen, and Zen," in *The Third Mind: American Artists Contemplate Asia, 1860–1989* (Guggenheim Museum Publications, 2009), 199–215. On the impact of Cage's modeling of Zen theories in his compositional aesthetic, see Branden W. Joseph, *Random Order: Robert Rauschenberg and the Neo-Avant-Garde* (MIT Press, 2003).

102 Rahmani, "Alison Knowles: An Interview," 366 (emphasis mine).

103 For more on Brecht, see Liz Kotz, "Post-Cagean Aesthetics and the 'Event' Score," *October*, no. 95 (Winter 2001): 55–89; Julia Robinson, "From Abstraction to Model: George Brecht's Events and the Conceptual Turn in Art of the 1960s," *October*, no. 127 (Winter 2009): 77–108; and Harren, *Fluxus Forms*, 101–9.

104 Knowles's expansion of the event-score format as propositions is explored in chapter 2.

105 George Brecht, *Chance-Imagery* (Something Else Press, 1966), 12–14. The text first appeared in *Collage* (Palermo), nos. 3–4 (December 1964). Brecht consistently hyphenated "chance-imagery" in his writings.

106 Brecht, *Chance-Imagery*, 14. See also Harren, *Fluxus Forms*, 71–100.

107 Knowles would repurpose the same scissors imagery in her *Blue Ram* piece (1966).

108 Among Knowles's papers, a press release for *Vintage Themes: Alison Knowles*, an exhibition at Gracie Mansion Gallery, New York, January–February 1998, is the only document to itemize the authorship. See SFA, I.738. Knowles has also confirmed in interviews her scissors contri-

bution and that she solely screen-printed the canvases and assorted objects. Knowles, interview with author, December 15, 2007, New York City.

**109** Knowles, letters to Oscar (Emmett) Williams, dated 1963, describing the objects and her process of making them. Emmett Williams Archives, Alison Knowles Correspondence, JBP. The *BLINK* stamps were reused on ephemera that Knowles created and distributed to friends announcing the birth of her twin daughters, Jessica and Hannah, in August 1964. A version intended for Ray Johnson can be found in the William S. Wilson Archive.

**110** *Sissor Bros. Warehouse*, at the Rolf Nelson Gallery, Los Angeles, October 7–November 2, 1963. See Rolf Nelson Gallery records, 1953–1937, GRI. A brief review in *Artforum* deemed the exhibition a "Pop event" and emphasized the role of anonymity in the production process. See Rosalind G. Wholden, "BLINK," *Artforum* 2, no. 6 (December 1963): 11. My reading of the *BLINK* canvases and ephemera comes from analyzing original versions in Knowles's studio loft in New York.

**111** Materials related to the Pasadena Museum of Art's exhibition, *Marcel Duchamp*, held October 8–November 3, 1963, can be found in AAA.

**112** Art Seidenbaum, "Anti-Art Goes Out on a Limb," *Los Angeles Times*, October 3, 1963, n.p.; Wholden, "BLINK," 11. Simon Anderson notes that the trio "out-Fluxused George Maciunas's contemporaneous efforts at collectivity and alternative commodity distribution." See Anderson, "Living in Multiple Dimensions: George Brecht and Robert Watts, 1953–1963," in Marter, *Off Limits*, 109.

**113** Knowles, quoted in Weil, "Sandwiches, Silkscreens, Swatches, and Scores," 17.

**114** The *BLINK* exhibition also anticipated the now-famous Pop art exhibition *The American Supermarket* (Bianchini Gallery, 1964), which featured art-as-commodity works by Watts, Oldenburg, Andy Warhol, Tom Wesselman, Roy Lichtenstein, James Rosenquist, and others. Warhol acquired a set of *BLINK* stamps, which can be found in his time capsule (TC21.90); see *Andy Warhol's Time Capsule 21* (Andy Warhol Foundation/Dumont, 2003), 220. Watts, letter to Emmett Williams, October 22, 1963, Emmett Williams Archives, Robert Watts Correspondence, JBP. Incidentally, Oldenburg's then wife, Patty Mucha, attended the opening of the Sissor Bros. show.

**115** "3rd Rail" (or "Third Rail") refers to an alternative space founded by Al Hansen in his loft at 49 E. Broadway, where Knowles indicates the *BLINK* canvases were intended to be exhibited. Ferus Gallery was in Los Angeles. See Knowles, two letters to Williams, both dated 1963, Emmett Williams Archives, Alison Knowles Correspondence, JBP.

**116** See Peter Frank, "New York Fluxus," in *New York—Downtown Manhattan: SoHo* (Berlin: Akademie der Künste, 1976), 151–79; Sally Banes, "The Reinvention of Community," in *Greenwich Village 1963: Avant-Garde Performance and the Effervescent Body* (Duke University Press, 1993), 33–80; Piekut, *Experimentalism Otherwise*, 102–39.

**117** Knowles, interview with author, New York, March 15, 2007. Podber's illegal activities are briefly mentioned in her 2008 obituary. Kennedy, "Dorothy Podber, 75," A22.

**118** Knowles, interview with author, New York, March 15, 2007.

**119** On the beginnings of Cage's anarchist ethos, see his "Defense of Satie (1948)" and "Form Is a Language (1960)," in *John Cage: An Anthology*, ed. Richard Kostelanetz (Praeger, 1970), 78–81; 135. Knowles's complex response to feminism is discussed in later chapters.

**120** Knowles, interview with author, New York, December 15, 2007. For an account of Cage's own anarchist politics, see Joseph, *Experimentations*, 182–87.

## Chapter 2

1 Alison Knowles quoted in George Myers, "Alison Knowles: To See Clearly and Afresh Each Moment," in *Alphabets Sublime: Contemporary Artists on Collage and Visual Literature* (Paycock Press, 1986), 52.

2 *Make a Salad* is listed as *Proposition #2* in her book of scores, *by Alison Knowles* (Something Else Press, 1965), 2. *Make a Salad* was her first written score, but *Shuffle Piece* was erroneously listed as *#1* in the text. Interview with author, New York, December 15, 2007. To avoid confusion, I have retained the original published version throughout this study.

3 Victor Musgrave, quoted in *Evening News*, October 16, 1962. Musgrave and Spoerri had previously collaborated when the latter brought *Editions MAT ("Multiplication d'art Transformable")* to Gallery One in 1959. The flyer for "The Festival of Misfits" curiously omits Knowles's name from the list of performers. According to Simon Anderson, the festival was "originally to be called the Misfits Fair, a rather more punning title." See Anderson, "Fluxus Publicus," in *In the Spirit of Fluxus*, ed. Elizabeth Armstrong and Joan Rothfuss (Walker Art Center, 1993), 45, 61fn13.

4 Musgrave, quoted in Carmen Juliá, "You saw it here first: Gallery One, New Vision Centre, Signals and Indica at Tate Britain," *Tate Etc.*, no. 24 (Spring 2012): 15.

5 Spoerri explicitly noted to a local reporter that the aim was "to involve the audience." See Jeremy Hornsby, "The Day I Stumbled on Neti Neti—Not to Mention a Kicking Machine," *Daily Express*, October 19, 1962, 10. Musgrave recounts British artist Robin Page performing his *Guitar Piece* (1962), which involved Page kicking a guitar from the stage into the audience and then outside onto Dover Street. The audience was encouraged to follow him as he continued to kick the instrument around the block, back inside, then onto the stage again. It was performed again on the streets of New York (with Knowles, Patterson, Higgins, and others) during George Brecht and Robert Watts's Yam Festival in May 1963. See Musgrave, "The Unknown Art Movement," *Art and Artists* 7, no. 7 (October 1972): 12; Brecht, "Interview with Robin Page and Carla Liss" in the same issue, 28–33.

6 Quoted in Estera Milman, "Road Shows, Street Events, and Fluxus People: A Conversation with Alison Knowles," *Visible Language* 26, nos. 1–2 (1992): 103. In a contemporaneous letter to Allan Kaprow, Higgins observed the multisensory pleasures of the original performance. Dick Higgins papers, Correspondence Files (KA–KE), AS. Julia Robinson discusses the sonic element in a subsequent staging in "The Sculpture of Indeterminacy: Alison Knowles's Beans and Variations," *Art Journal* 63, no. 4 (Winter 2004): 97–98.

7 In January 1963, before returning to New York, Knowles and Higgins had a belated honeymoon in Turkey—in Istanbul, in Ankara, and along the Black Sea. See Knowles, letter to Emmett Williams, January 1963, JBP; Alison Knowles Correspondence Files, and Higgins's letter to his father and stepmother, February 9, 1963, DHP; Dick Higgins Scrapbooks, SFA, III.1. On the delayed honeymoon, see Higgins, *Postface/Jefferson's Birthday* (Something Else Press, 1964), 68, 73.

8 A postcard announcing Higgins's *Graphis 82* event (1960) verifies Knowles's participation in at least one proto-Fluxus performance at The Living Theater (along with Florence Tarlow, Lette Lou Eisenhauer, and Michael Hall), as do contemporaneous letters to George Maciunas. George Maciunas Correspondence Files, and Dick Higgins Announcement Files, JBP. She was also cast in a program featuring Corner's music (January 1961) at Judson—a last-minute change from its original location in Ono's Chambers Street loft. See SFA, IV.B.1.

9 Like Fluxus later, the New York Audio-Visual Group was a loose confederation of diverse practitioners who arranged public programs of "new music" as a means of "encourag[ing]

experimentation in all the arts." Dick Higgins papers, untitled manuscript dated August 5, 1959, AS.

10 See Henry Flynt, "La Monte Young in New York, 1960–62," in *Sound and Light: La Monte Young, Marian Zazeela*, ed. William Duckworth and Richard Fleming, *Bucknell Review* 40–41 (1996): 44–97.

11 Knowles, interview with author, New York, December 28, 2008. Forti, then known under her married name of Morris, confirmed their meeting in 1961 and a friendship that flourished first in New York and then while both were living in Southern California in the early 1970s. Forti, interview with author, Los Angeles, July 10, 2019.

12 The concert series ran from March through July 1961; its third installment included work by Higgins as well as Cage, Young, Jackson Mac Low, Flynt, Joseph Byrd, and others. See Emmett Williams and Ann Noël, eds., *Mr. Fluxus: A Collective Portrait of George Maciunas* (Thames & Hudson, 1998), 39–41; Colby Chamberlain, *Fluxus Administration: George Maciunas and the Art of Paperwork* (University of Chicago Press, 2024), 60–66; Natilee Harren, *Fluxus Forms: Scores, Multiples, and the Eternal Network* (University of Chicago Press, 2020), 88–99. For Kuenstler's contemporaneous poetry, see his volume *LENS* (New York: Film Culture, 1964).

13 See Jackson Mac Low, "How Maciunas Met the New York Avant-Garde," *Art & Design*, no. 28, special issue, "Fluxus: Today and Yesterday" (1993): 17, 38; Maciunas, "This Is George Maciunas Speaking: Talking About Fluxus History," typed transcript of a recording made April 20, 1978, SFA, I.855.

14 A miniature mockup of the anthology, as well as handwritten notes between Maciunas, Mac Low, and Young, can be found in the Jackson Mac Low papers, UCSD. For a contextualized history of Maciunas's "unorthodox design strategies," see Liz Kotz, "Poetry Machines," in *+-1961: Founding the Expanded Arts*, ed. Julia Robinson and Christian Xatrec (Museo Nacional Centro de Arte Reina Sofía, 2013), 51–68.

15 The Living Theater's 1962 benefits, on January 8 and February 5, featured scores by Brecht, Brown, Cage, Ono, Higgins, Walter De Maria, Nam June Paik, James Waring, Emmett Williams, and others. Typed notices found in Emmett Williams Archives, La Monte Young Correspondence, JBP; Dick Higgins Scrapbook, 1959–1962, SFA, III.1; and Judson Memorial Church Archives, Fales Library and Special Collections, New York University. According to Benjamin Piekut, architect Paul Williams "eventually paid the outstanding printing bill for *An Anthology*, but he asked that copyright on the final publication be held by both Young and Mac Low, to which condition Maciunas agreed. In the end, therefore, we say that Young edited it, Maciunas designed it, and Young and Mac Low copublished it." See Piekut, "La Monte Young, ed.: *An Anthology of Chance Operations* (1962–63)," in *The Scores Project: Experimental Notation in Music, Art, Poetry, and Dance, 1950–1975*, ed. Michael Gallope, Natilee Harren, and John Hicks (Getty Research Institute, 2025).

16 Mac Low, "How Maciunas Met the New York Avant-Garde," 40. See also Chamberlain, *Fluxus Administration*, 66–72.

17 See letters exchanged between Maciunas and Higgins in spring 1962, George Maciunas Files, JBP.

18 Individual Fluxus editions began in 1963. Seven yearbooks were proposed, each to cover a particular location or perceived historical ancestor of Fluxus (e.g., Dada). Only *Fluxus 1* was ever completed; it included Knowles's contribution of a thin plastic medical glove. See the plans for yearboxes reprinted in Jon Hendricks, ed., *Fluxus Codex* (Harry N. Abrams, 1988), 103–22.

19 "Fluxus" is first used in reference to a Lithuanian cultural journal to be published by Maci-

unas and Salcius. See Mats B, "Birth of Fluxus: The Ultimate Version," *Kalejdoskop*, no. 3 (1979): n.p. Reprinted in Williams and Nöel, *Mr. Fluxus*, 32–33.

20 Higgins, *Postface/Jefferson's Birthday*, 68. *The Flaming City* was screened in spring 1962 in his loft at 359 Canal Street and again in December 1963. See Dick Higgins, folder 1962, AS; Dick Higgins Scrapbooks, SFA, III.1; Jonas Mekas, "Movie Journal," *Village Voice*, June 20, 1963; Mekas, "On Dick Higgins" (1963), reprinted in *Movie Journal: The Rise of the New American Cinema, 1959–1971* (Macmillan, 1972), 110. Materials related to its production, including intertitles, can be found in Dick Higgins papers, AS, and in a typed manuscript, "About My Films by Dick Higgins" (1995), Dick Higgins Archive, MS132, NU. *The Flaming City* is preserved at the Film-Makers' Cooperative, New York. My thanks to Lauren Fulton for many conversations about her original research on Higgins's films. See Fulton, "Centers of Emanations of Experience: Tracing Dick Higgins' Autobiography Through Boredom and Danger, c. 1956–76" (PhD diss., Stony Brook University, 2024).

21 Watts recalled, "At that time [Maciunas] was in a hospital with asthma, so I thought to make events for George to be performed in the hospital while he was sick. This was my first connection with Maciunas." See "Robert Watts," in *Encyclopedia of the Word: Artist Conversations 1968–2008*, ed. Achille Bonito Oliva (Milan: Skira Rizzoli, 2010), 169–70. See Philip Corner, *NY 60s: Scenes from the Scene* (Frog Peak Music, 1995), 23.

22 In a mock interview, Williams and Patterson playfully bantered about what an audience could expect. See Emmett Williams, "Way Way Way Out," *Stars and Stripes*, August 30, 1962, 11. US military presence in West Germany was significant during the early years of Fluxus. Williams traveled an hour from Darmstadt to Wiesbaden to perform in the festival. Maciunas was employed by the US Air Force Exchange, and Patterson sold encyclopedias to US Army families in Paris. Higgins had failed his military exams and was classified "draftable only in case of a dire emergency." See Williams and Noël, *Mr. Fluxus*, 55; Valerie Cassel Oliver, "The Curious Case of Benjamin Patterson," in *Benjamin Patterson: Born in the State of FLUX/us* (Contemporary Arts Museum, Houston, 2012), 16–33; Hannah B. Higgins, "Eleven Snapshots of Dick Higgins," in *Intermedia, Fluxus, and the Something Else Press: Selected Writings of Dick Higgins*, ed. Steve Clay and Ken Friedman (Siglio Press, 2018), 336.

23 See Dick Higgins, "Fluxus: Theory and Reception," in *Modernism Since Postmodernism: Essays on Intermedia* (San Diego State University Press, 1997), 167–70; Knowles, "Fluxus Survival Fundamentals: Find Shelter," typed statement, ca. 1966, AKS. In this document Knowles recalls learning that Maciunas was forced to live out of his car before procuring the house in Ehlhalten from a potato farmer who kept a room in the basement.

24 Knowles, "Belief in Actions of the Everyday," *PAJ: A Journal of Performance and Art* 34, no. 1 (January 2012): 20.

25 Higgins, letters to Maciunas dated April and August 1962, George Maciunas Correspondence Files, JBP. According to the spring letter, Knowles was already thinking up scores and other artworks, including prints, to contribute to the Fluxus concerts.

26 Knowles, statement found in the Correspondence Files, DHP.

27 In 1964, when Higgins was preparing to publish her book of scores, *by Alison Knowles* under the Great Bear Pamphlet Series for Something Else Press, she gave him the handwritten instructions, which he then typed up. Higgins returned the notes to Knowles, who at some point around 1967 gave them to Cage for the *Notations* project. For Knowles's spiral notebook of handwritten propositions, see JCNP; for Higgins's typed pages, SFA, I.739.

28 Alison Knowles, *Salad*, 1962, B-42, JCNP. Despite the surprisingly detailed notes dictating each moment of its realization, the idea for the salad was reportedly spurred, in part, by chance. In an interview for the Archives of American Art, she recalls "riding with Dick in a

cab in London and a [Fluxus] performance was going to be the next day and I think I was expected to come up with a lot of the pieces for the program. . . . I said, 'What can I do? Why don't I do something with food? Why don't I make a salad?'" Knowles, quoted in Judith Olch Richards, "Oral History Interview with Alison Knowles," June 1–2, 2010, AAA.

29 Higgins, handwritten letter to Allan Kaprow, Dick Higgins papers, Correspondence (KA–KE), AS. "Parallele Aufführungen Neuster Musik" took place in Amsterdam, October 5, 1962.

30 During Knowles's time in the UK, newspaper headlines were dominated by the Cuban Missile Crisis. See for example, "Blockaders Ready—Kennedy Sends Jets for Top Congressmen, Net Closes on Castro," *Daily Express*, October 23, 1962, 1.

31 Letter from Maciunas to Tomas Schmit, November 8, 1963, reprinted in *What's Fluxus? What's Not! Why* (Centro Cultural Banco do Brasil, 2002), 160.

32 Letter from Maciunas to Schmit, January 1964, reprinted in *What's Fluxus?*, 163 (emphasis in original).

33 In his lecture "The Creative Act," presented in spring 1957 to the Convention of the American Federation of Arts in Houston and published two years later in a widely circulated monograph, Marcel Duchamp argues against the autonomy of the artwork by recognizing the "chain of reactions accompanying the creative act." Knowles has affirmed that she was aware of the essay by early 1961. Interview with author, Cambridge, MA, November 5, 2009. See Robert Lebel, *Marcel Duchamp*, trans. George Heard Hamilton (Paragraphic Books, 1959), 77–78.

34 Aviva Rahmani, "Alison Knowles: An Interview," in *M/E/A/N/I/N/G: An Anthology of Artists' Writings, Theory, and Criticism*, ed. Susan Bee and Mira Schor (Duke University Press, 2000), 367. The openness Knowles desires was very close to my experiences of *Make a Salad* performances at Aspen Art Museum (2018) and Disney Concert Hall, Los Angeles (2019). Audience members gave wildly different responses to its execution, including political and aesthetic observations.

35 This may account for the seemingly disinterested presentation of Knowles's scores in Maciunas's early performance cards devised to keep track of Fluxus concerts, which in turn led early Fluxus chroniclers to downplay her significance and contribution. In some of the contemporaneous documentation, her name was also misspelled as "Allison" or given as "Alison Higgins," which was not her professional preference.

36 On Higgins's meticulous saving of their contemporaneous ephemera, Knowles remembers: "Dick was keeping a concert roster, a record of the events, so he was [always] writing them all down with the idea of publishing them later." Knowles, interview with author, March 16, 2007. See also, George Maciunas Correspondence Files, JBP. Some of the dating and numbering is incorrect (e.g., *Make a Salad*).

37 The Café au Go Go was a large coffeehouse owned by Howard and Elly Solomon that purportedly sat three to four hundred people in its basement. Andy Warhol premiered his film *Harlot* there on January 10, 1965. Nam June Paik screened one of his earliest video works, *Electronic Video Recorder*, and performed in Charlotte Moorman's *Human Cello*, both in October 1965. See Nam June Paik, *Electronic Video Recorder, Café au Go Go, October 4 and 11, 1965*, electrostatic print on paper, Collection San Francisco Museum of Modern Art; Peter Moore, *Charlotte Moorman and Nam June Paik performing Human Cello at Café au Go Go, October 5, 1965*, Peter Moore Photography Archive, NU. For a firsthand account of Jackson Mac Low's 1965 performance at the Café of Robert Filliou's *Ample Food for Stupid Thought*, see Mac Low's jacket notes, "Some Unsystematic Reflections for Filliou and Others (23 Feb. & 21–4 March 1965)," in Filliou, *Ample Food for Stupid Thought* (Something Else Press, 1965).

38 While Monk collaborated more regularly with Higgins, she and Knowles were both invested in art as a practice of lived experience. Monk mentions these events in remarks made at Higgins's memorial service at Judson Memorial Church. He passed very unexpectedly in Québec, Canada, in 1998. See Meredith Monk, "I Remember Dick Higgins," *PAJ: Performance Art Journal* 21, no. 2 (May 1999): 18.

39 "Notes on Chance" are three pages of undated typescript notes found among Alison Knowles's studio papers, which she often used when delivering guest lectures. During a November 2009 conversation with the author in Boston, Knowles read these notes aloud.

40 Knowles, interview with author, Boston, November 9, 2009.

41 Higgins, *Postface/Jefferson's Birthday*, 67–68. I return to Fluxus politics in the epilogue.

42 Dick Higgins, *Selected Early Works 1955–1964* (Herausgeber Verlag Edition ARS VIVA & Berliner Künstlerprogramm das DAAD, 1982), 8; Fluxus West Collection, University of Iowa Libraries.

43 Richard O'Regan, "There's Music—and Eggs—in the Air," *Stars and Stripes*, October 21, 1962, 33.

44 See Higgins, *Postface/Jefferson's Birthday*, 69. Nam June Paik later noted the pamphlets. See Calvin Tomkins, "Video Visionary," *New Yorker*, May 5, 1975, 51. I return to Higgins's "Strike for Peace!" activism in the early 1960s with The Living Theater in the epilogue.

45 See Dick Higgins "Boredom and Danger," *Something Else Newsletter* 1, no. 9 (December 1968): 1–4; Ina Blom, "Boredom and Oblivion," in *The Fluxus Reader*, ed. Ken Friedman (Academy Editions, 1998), 63–90.

46 Stiles, "Between Water and Stone, Fluxus Performance: A Metaphysics of Acts," in Armstrong and Rothfuss, *In the Spirit of Fluxus*, 72.

47 Timothy Scott Brown notes that many early Fluxus performances overtly referenced the Nazis, including Joseph Beuys's performance at the Technische Hochschule in Aachen on July 20, 1964, wherein he and his group read a passage from Joseph Goebbels's infamous 1943 "total war" speech. See Brown, *West Germany and the Global Sixties: The Antiauthoritarian Revolt, 1962–1978*, New Studies in European History (Cambridge University Press, 2013), 200–203. For more on Fluxus in Germany, see Claudia Mesch, *Modern Art at the Berlin Wall: Demarcating Culture in the Cold War Germanys* (Tauris Academic Studies, 2008), 165–85.

48 Knowles performed *Danger Music No. 2* with Higgins again during Charlotte Moorman's 4th Annual Avant Garde Festival, September 9, 1966, and with Max Neuhaus in May 1968, shaving his head for a Tone Roads Chamber Ensemble concert in New York City. Tone Roads was a performance series/group formed by experimental composers Neuhaus, Philip Corner, Malcolm Goldstein, and James Tenney. Photo documentation of Neuhaus before and after the performance appears in "Max Neuhaus: A Max Sampler," *Source: Music of the Avant-Garde*, no. 5 (January 1969). I return to Knowles's collaborations with Neuhaus and Tenney in chapter 5.

49 Another exception followed Beuys's performance in Aachen. See "Ein Professor wurde geschlagen . . . ," *Die Zeit*, no. 31, July 31, 1964.

50 Higgins, *Postface/Jefferson's Birthday*, 70.

51 See Owen F. Smith, *Fluxus: The History of an Attitude* (San Diego State University Press, 1998), 241.

52 David Doris, "Zen Vaudeville: A Medi(t)ation in the Margins of Fluxus," in Friedman, *Fluxus Reader*, 101.

53 Doris, "Zen Vaudeville," 108.

54 In a typed yellow chart of performances for the Nordic Festum Fluxorum, under "Noninstrumental action music," Maciunas included "Alison's new piece: Proposition . . . with on-

ions, carrots, tomatoes, lettuce, oil" listed under "equipment and items needed." See Maciunas, George Brecht Correspondence Box I-R, Alison Knowles Folder, AS; SFA, IV.B.55.

55 Knowles, taped interview for *The Misfits: 30 Years of Fluxus*, Cinnamon Film (distributed by Electronic Arts Intermix, 1993). Organized by the directors of the Royal Art Library, the Young Tonal Artists' Society, and Danish artist Arthur Køpcke, the Nordic Festum Fluxorum made use of a neglected old church, the Nikolaj Kirke in central Copenhagen. See Peter van der Meijden, "Fluxus, Eric Andersen and the Communist East," in *A Cultural History of the Avant-Garde in the Nordic Countries 1950–1975*, ed. Tania Ørum and Jesper Olsson (Brill Rodopi, 2016), 324–35.

56 Knowles, in *Performance Artists Talking in the Eighties*, compiled by Linda Montano (University of California Press, 2000), 173.

57 *Publics*, plural; I make this distinction because the work lives on discursively in documentation photos, reviews, later performances, scores, etc.

58 Cooking food in a gallery space and then turning the leftovers into works of art, as in the work of Rirkrit Tiravanija, has become par for the course in contemporary art. For an overview of his early food performances, see Janet Kraynak, "Rirkrit Tiravanija's Liability," *Documents* 13 (Fall 1998): 26–40.

59 Andrea Fraser, "How to Provide an Artistic Service: An Introduction" (1994), in *Theory in Contemporary Art Since 1985*, ed. Zoya Kocur and Simon Leung (Wiley-Blackwell, 2012), 69–75.

60 On Judson Dance Theater and how Yvonne Rainer's dance work refashioned spectatorship, see Carrie Lambert-Beatty, *Being Watched: Yvonne Rainer and the 1960s* (MIT Press, 2008). Knowles met Rainer in the early 1960s when the latter performed in a Happenings events composed by Dick Higgins. Over the years, Knowles would also work closely with Simone Forti and Judson dancer and filmmaker Elaine Summers. For more context, including Higgins's relation to Judson and the intermedia work of Summers, see Gloria Sutton, "Elaine Summers's Intermedia," in *Judson Dance Theater: The Work Is Never Done*, ed. Ana Janevski and Thomas Lax (Museum of Modern Art, New York, 2018), 82–88. My thanks to the late Elaine Summers for sharing her memories of this era with me.

61 Knowles, *by Alison Knowles*, 3. She performed the piece again in New Jersey in 1963 and Madrid in 1966.

62 Knowles, *by Alison Knowles*, 3. The male pronouns also reflect the practical reality that most Fluxus performances utilized male performers.

63 This is a variant written by Knowles. See Knowles, *by Alison Knowles*, 3.

64 For detailed descriptions of *Meat Joy*, see Carolee Schneemann, *More Than Meat Joy* (Documentext, 1979), 63–87; Harriett Curtis, "Fifty Years Since Carolee Schneemann's *Meat Joy* (1964), *Performance Research* 20, no. 2 (March 2015): 118–20; Elise Archias, "Concretions: Carolee Schneemann," in *The Concrete Body: Yvonne Rainer, Carolee Schneemann, Vito Acconci* (Yale University Press, 2016), 77–121.

65 See Midori Yoshimoto, *Into Performance: Japanese Women Artists in New York* (Rutgers University Press, 2005), 181–82. Other (mostly male) artists also objected to Kubota's metaphorical equation of the processes of bodily excretion with painterly actions.

66 Yoshimoto, *Into Performance*, 182.

67 Knowles, interview with author, Boston, November 9, 2009.

68 Published in *dé-coll/age* 3 (Cologne, 1962), reprinted in Wulf Herzogenrath, ed., *Nam June Paik: Werke 1946–1976, Musik-Fluxus-Video* (Kölnischer Kunstverein, 1977), 50.

69 Documentary film footage of the 1962 event is housed the Collection of Fondazione Bonotto, No. FXC1583-3. Higgins describes the evening in detail in *Postface/Jefferson's Birthday*, 70–72. Knowles performed the piece at least one more time in November 1962 at the

Nordic Festum Fluxorum in Copenhagen. See Petra Stemann, ed., *"The Lunatics Are on the Loose . . .": European Fluxus Festivals, 1962–1977* (Down with Art!, 2012), 123–42, 163–82.

70 Knowles quoted in Kristine Stiles, "Anomaly, Sky, Sex, and Psi in Fluxus," in *Critical Mass: Happenings, Fluxus, Performance, Intermedia and Rutgers University 1958–1972*, ed. Geoffrey Hendricks (Rutgers University Press, 2003), 69. Paik's *Serenade for Alison* was also performed by Knowles for the Festum Fluxorum in Düsseldorf, February 1963—an iteration with no Korean robe or added accountrements. Knowles's interpretation of *Serenade* stands in contrast to Yoko Ono's infamous "strip-tease" performance *Cut Piece* (1964–1966), in which audience members were invited to cut away pieces of her clothing as she knelt silently on stage. See Ono, "To the Wesleyan People (Who Attended the Meeting)," in *The Stone* (Judson Gallery, 1966). On the profound ethical and geopolitical implications of Ono's action, see Julia Bryan-Wilson, "Rembering Yoko Ono's *Cut Piece*," *Oxford Art Journal* 26, no. 1 (2003): 99–123.

71 Paik's score, quoted in Stiles, "Between Water and Stone," 98n77.

72 For a description of the "sexy underwears" that were to be paired with a sound track of national anthems, see Tomas Schmidt, "Exposition of Music," in *Nam June Paik: Wërke 1947–1976*, 70. A framed article about the Cuban missile crisis, published in a German newspaper in 1961, hung next to the four stained flags of Germany, Turkey, the UK, and Denmark. See photographs of the flags by Manfred Montwé in the Nam June Paik Art Center collections, https://njpart.ggcf.kr/collections/141. I am grateful to Saisha Grayson for sharing her original research on Paik's collaborations with women artists. See Grayson, "Cellist, Catalyst, Collaborator: The Work of Charlotte Moorman" (PhD diss., City University of New York, 2018).

73 In *by Alison Knowles*, she identifies it as the score *Proposition #13: Composition for Paik*, which premiered at the Café au Go Go in 1964 during her "Assorted Night Riders" event (part of Brecht and Watts's "Monday Night Letters" series). Throughout her career, Knowles dedicated scores and artworks to favored friends. Another example is *The Danish Proposition*, a "great management game" presented to Danish artist and Fluxus-adjacent poet Knud Pedersen, who first met the Fluxus troupe when he helped Arthur Køpcke organize the November 1962 events in Copenhagen at Nikolaj Kirke. Knowles's sent Pedersen detailed instructions (enumerated as parts A–C) to analyze "a sick company." In "B: Human Exploration," for example, "all the workers in the terminal company sick area are taken off the job and isolated from each other and the world to make one audio tape." See Knowles, *The Danish Proposition*, 2-page typed letter to Pedersen, SFA, I.741. For the Café au Go Go event flyer, see Fluxus West Collection, University of Iowa Libraries.

74 As Julia Robinson has noted, the "institutional sphere of subjection of the socially inscribed body" (here, writing) is "arguably at the heart of Fluxus." See Robinson, "Maciunas as Producer: Performative Design in the Art of the 1960s," *Grey Room* 33 (Fall 2008): 71.

75 Knowles, interview with author, New York, March 16, 2007. See typed performance roster for "Happenings, Danger Music, Fluxus," Allé Teatern, Stockholm, Sweden, March 1, 1963, Collection of Fondazione Bonotto, No. FXC1660. Higgins and Maciunas bickered about the couple's involvement in the event, with Maciunas angered by Higgins's not performing a "complete fluxus festival," arguing that "fluxus is a 'collective' & should not be associated with any particular fluxus individual." See letters exchanged between Higgins and Maciunas, February–March 1963, Dick Higgins papers, AS.

76 Two pages from *CC V TRE* (January 1964), from the Walker Art Center collection; reprinted in Armstrong and Rothfuss, *In the Spirit of Fluxus*, 164–65.

77 *Child Art Piece* is included on the Yam Day schedule of performances for May 11, 1963, at the Hardware Poets' Playhouse. It is unclear which child may have performed. Benjamin

Patterson's son, Ennis, executed the score at a Fluxus concert held in the Carnegie Recital Hall in New York City on June 27, 1964. For the Yam Day schedule, see Jackson Mac Low papers, George Brecht Correspondence (1962–1965), UCSD.

78 Of the "failing piece," Knowles reported that at Douglass College she "got no volunteer after two repetitions and five minutes of waiting . . . so said that the piece could not be performed today." Knowles, letter to Maciunas, April 16, 1963, George Maciunas Correspondence Folder A–M, AS. Knowles's propositions on the list of performances at Douglass College included, along with *Shoes of Your Choice*, *Nivea Cream Piece*. Knowles recounts offering *Shoes of Your Choice* in October 1962 at the ICA's Festival of Misfits, with a memorable performance by British Pop artist Richard Hamilton. While there is little doubt she conceived the work abroad, I have not been able to corroborate Hamilton's presence at the event in multiple archives, firsthand accounts, Hamilton's writings, or correspondence with Knowles. See Robinson, "Sculpture of Indeterminacy," 99.

79 Knowles, *by Alison Knowles*, 5.

80 Robinson, "Sculpture of Indeterminacy," 100.

81 Letty Lou Eisenhauer, "A Version of Trace in 2008; An Interpretation of Scores," in *Fluxus Scores and Instructions: The Transformative Years*, ed. Jon Hendricks (Gilbert and Lila Silverman Collection, 2008), 34.

82 The Zaj Group, founded in Madrid in 1964, was deeply influenced by the work of John Cage. Members included Ramón Barce, José Luis Castillejo, Esther Ferrer, Juan Hidalgo, and Tomás Marco. Higgins and Hidalgo began exchanging letters in July 1966. In 1967, Higgins published *A Zaj Sampler*, a collection of experimental poetry, as part of Something Else Press's Great Bear Pamphlet series.

83 The evening also included Knowles's performance of several other propositions. While a program was never printed, Juan Hidalgo recounted the events in a history of the Zaj Group and Tomás Marco published a contemporaneous overview. Hidalgo, "Zaj," *Revista de Letras* 1, no. 3 (1969): 424–44; Marco, "Teatro musical," *S. P. Revista de información mundial*, December 4, 1966, 71.

84 Henar Rivière Rios, "Fluxus-Concert, Berlin, 4 October 1966," in Stegman, "*The Lunatics Are on the Loose . . .* ," 378. In Berlin, Knowles also performed *Proposition #12: Simultaneous Bean Reading* (1964), *Proposition #10a: Variation (String Piece)* (1964), and *Newspaper Music* (1965) with Juan Hidalgo, along with scores of works by John Cage and Fluxus artists. In the Fluxus Concerts in Prague, 1966, she enacted *Proposition #8: Performance Piece* (1965) with Ben Vautier and Serge Oldenbourg.

85 Audience member, quoted in Rivière Rios, "Fluxus-Concert, Berlin," 378.

86 Unnamed performer, quoted in Dan Sullivan, "Avant-Garde Day in Park Goes On and On," *New York Times*, September 10, 1966, 19.

87 Nam June Paik, "Postmusic, An Essay for the New Ontology of Music," reprinted in *What's Fluxus?*, 103–4. A footnote cites *The Monthly Review of the University for Avant-Garde Hinduism*, a Fluxus publication edited by Paik, as the original source.

88 In the second, Knowles, atop the Eiffel Tower, "cut her beautiful long hair in the winter wind," again with no witnesses—except "Sorry, Dick Higgins saw it. It is just the unavoidable evil. He is her husband." Paik, "Postmusic," 103.

89 Umberto Eco, "The Poetics of the Open Work" in his *Opera Aperta* (The Open Work), trans. Anna Cancogni (1962; Harvard University Press, 1989), 3–4 (emphases in original).

90 Knowles, "Notes on Chance," AKS.

91 See, for example, Sol LeWitt, "Sentences on Conceptual Art," *0–9* (January 1969): 4. George Brecht's 1959 show *Toward Events*, at Reuben Gallery, and his subsequent development

of the event-score, as well as Henry Flynt's notion of art as "concepts," articulated in his 1961 essay "Concept Art" for *An Anthology of Chance Operations*, had profound effects on Knowles's work. Interview with author, Cambridge, MA, November 5, 2009. On Brecht's influence, see Robinson, "Sculpture of Indeterminancy," 98–102.

92 On the "impersonal" nature of her early performances, see Emmett Williams Archive, Alison Knowles Correspondence, JBP.

93 Knowles, "Alison Knowles Interview," April 17, 1977, New York City; unpublished interview, Dick Higgins Archive, MS132, NU.

94 There is ample writing on exhibiting and collecting time-based art, including critiques of the institutional practices as potentially exploitative of artists. See, for example, Claire Bishop, "Outsourcing Authenticity? Delegated Performance in Contemporary Art," in *Double Agent*, ed. Bishop and Silvia Tramontana (ICA, London, 2008): 110–25; Carmelia Cutugno, "Archiving Performance: 'Reenacting' Creativity," *Mantichora* 4 (December 2014): 2–10; Rebecca Schneider, "Performance Remains," *Performance Research* 6, no. 2 (2001): 100–108; André Lepecki, "Not as Before, but Simply: Again," in *Perform, Repeat, Record: Live Art in History*, ed. Amelia Jones and Adrian Heathfield (University of Chicago Press, 2012), 137–70; Carrie Lambert-Beatty, "Against Performance Art," *Artforum* (May 2010): 208–13; Polly Savage, "Playing to the Gallery: Masks, Masquerade, and Museums" *African Arts* 41, no. 4 (Winter 2008): 74–81.

95 Knowles, "Notes for Proposition #2: Make a Salad," performance kit, AKS. Knowles has described feeling "put out" by certain institutions, including those that sold tickets to her performances or excluded the public in favor of "art world insiders"—actions she finds inherently opposed to the spirit of generosity in her work. Interviews with author, New York, December 8, 2014, and Aspen, July 16, 2018.

96 I am grateful to Lauren Fulton and Heidi Zuckerman for their invitation to witness a performance by Knowles of *Make a Salad* and to give a lecture contextualizing the piece in 2018 at the Aspen Art Musuem. https://aspenartmuseum.org/program/alison-knowles-proposition-2-make-a-salad-plein-air-variation/.

97 Knowles, quoted in Tom Johnson, "New Music," *High Fidelity* (June 1975): 12–13.

## Chapter 3

1 Alison Knowles, interview with author, New York, December 15, 2007. An earlier version of this chapter appears as Nicole L. Woods, "Provisional Objects: Alison Knowles's Bean Rolls," in *The Taste of Art: Cooking, Food, and Counterculture in Contemporary Practices*, ed. Silvia Bottinelli and Margherita D'Ayala Valva (University of Arkansas Press, 2017), 263–78.

2 On Moorman's festivals, see Joan Rothfuss, *Topless Cellist: The Improbable Life of Charlotte Moorman* (MIT Press, 2014), 53–108; 167–74; and Hannah B. Higgins, "Live Art in the Eternal Network: The Annual Avant-Garde Festivals," in *A Feast of Astonishments: Charlotte Moorman and the Avant-Garde, 1960s–1980s*, ed. Lisa G. Corrin and Corinne Granof (Northwestern University Press, 2016), 61–90. The Hardware Poets' Playhouse is remembered more for events it hosted (e.g., La Monte Young's 1965 *Theater of Eternal Music* and Meredith Monk's early solo choreography) than the resident company's productions; it closed in 1966. See Stephen Bottoms, *Playing Underground: A Critical History of the 1960s Off-Off-Broadway Movement* (University of Michigan Press, 2006), 65. On the events at Douglass College, see Geoffrey Hendricks, ed., *Critical Mass: Happenings, Fluxus, Performance, Intermedia and Rutgers University, 1958–1972* (Rutgers University Press, 2003). Among other events, Knowles participated in Kaprow's happening *Calling* (1965), a two-day performance carried out in

New York City and the woods of George Segal's farm. See Jeff Kelley, *Childsplay: The Art of Allan Kaprow* (University of California Press, 2004), 106–7.

3 Williams's *Voice Piece for La Monte Young* was included in a book version of *Fluxus Yearbox 1* (1964) and recorded by Giorno Poetry Systems, New York, December 1968.

4 Two decades later, Knowles and Vautier again performed *Two Inches* on the street, after a press conference outside of Hotel Prindsen, Roskilde, Denmark, May 24, 1985. According to reports, the action, this time using a cash-register tape, "brought cars and trucks to a halt, while cyclists simply ducked underneath while other impatient drivers drove through the temporary barrier." See the Festival of Fantastics online archive, http://www.festivalof fantastics.com/1985/05/press-conference/ (accessed January 2018).

5 Higgins to Allan Kaprow: "On Sunday at the theater we did a 'solo for dancer'—Alison slung a rope over a beam & hoisted herself up as high as possible—terribly exciting." See Dick Higgins papers, Correspondence Files, AS; Higgins, *Postface/Jefferson's Birthday*, 75.

6 A letter from Knowles to Maciunas, dated April 16, 1963, describes the Douglass College performance; Allan Kaprow and Roy Lichtenstein also gave the rope piece a "noble try," she reports, but ultimately failed to get off the ground. George Maciunas Correspondence, Folder A–M, AS. See also Hendricks, *Critical Mass*; Marter, *Off Limits*. With Patterson, Knowles performed (wearing a *BLINK* sweatshirt) the "examinations" in his *Seminar* (1964) during *Fully Guaranteed 12 Fluxus Concerts*, Canal Street, New York, May 1964. The multipart piece instructed the participants "to sit facing each other. Three symmetrical events involving the fingers, eyes and ears of both are agreed upon and enacted, once each." A photograph of the artists rubbing each other's ears was published in "Fluxus Foldout," *Tulane Drama Review* 10, no. 2 (Winter 1965): 9–10.

7 Fellow Fluxus artist Robert Watts, who shares some of the closest affinities with Knowles's object-based works, makes a related point. See Watts, "In the Event, 1964," *Times Literary Supplement*, Thursday, August 8, 1964.

8 I first referenced Knowles's food-based artworks as "provisional" in chapter 3 of my dissertation, "Performing Chance: Alison Knowles, Fluxus, and the Enigmatic Work of Postwar Art, 1962–1975" (University of California, Irvine, 2010). The term *provisional* has since taken on new currency. See, for example, Natilee Harren, "The Provisional Work of Art: George Brecht's Footnotes at LACMA, 1969," *Getty Research Journal*, no. 8 (2016): 177–97; Anna Dezeuze, "In Search of the Insignificant: Street Works, 'Borderline Art' and Dematerialisation," in *Objets en process: Après la dematerialization de l'art, 1960–2010*, ed. Ileana Parvu (Geneva: Métis-presses, 2012), 35–63.

9 George Brecht, "Something About Fluxus, May 1964." Originally published in *Fluxus cc fiVe ThReE*, no. 4 (June 1964). Subsequent quotes are from this source.

10 SEP's operations relocated in 1968 to the Chelsea brownstone at 238 West 22nd Street that Higgins and Knowles shared with their twin daughters, Hannah and Jessica, and a revolving troupe of Fluxus friends who rented rooms for various stretches.

11 Knowles, interview with author, New York, December 15, 2007. In a March 1967 letter to Tjeena Deelstra, Higgins writes, "I went home to Alison Knowles . . . I told her we founded a press. She asked what its name was. It said it was 'original Fluxus.' She said that was too aggressive, and why didn't I call it 'something else.' So I did." Dick Higgins papers, Correspondence Files, AS. A 1966 letter from Higgins to Jeff Berner, cited by SEP vice president Barbara Moore in 1991, recalls "Fluxus Annex" as another proposed name. See JPB; GRI; Barbara Moore, "Some Things Else About Something Else Press," brochure accompanying the exhibition *Something Else Press* (Granary Books, New York, 1991), 2. References to "Shirtsleeves Press" can be found in Higgins, "Around the World in a Minesweeper, or a Few Observations on Fluxus" (1982), in *Wiesbaden Fluxus, 1962–1982: Eine Kleine Geschichte von*

*Fluxus in Drei Teilen*, ed. René Block (Harlekin Art/Berliner Künstlerprogamm des DAAD, 1983), 130; "Two Sides of a Coin: Fluxus and the Something Else Press," *Visible Language* 26, nos. 1/2 (1992): 144–52; *Intermedia, Fluxus, and the Something Else Press: Selected Writings of Dick Higgins*, ed. Steve Clay and Ken Friedman (Siglio Press, 2018). See also two invaluable recent publications: *A Something Else Press Reader*, ed. Dick Higgins, assembled by Alice Centamore (Primary Information, 2022); Alice Centamore and Christian Xatrec, eds., *Call It Something Else: Something Else Press, Inc. (1963–1974)* (Museo Reina Sofia, 2023).

12 See Hannah B. Higgins, *Fluxus Experience* (University of California Press, 2002), 33–45; David Joselit, "The Readymade Metabolized: Fluxus in Life," *RES: Anthropology and Aesthetics*, nos. 63–64 (Spring–Autumn 2013): 190–200; Natilee Harren, "Fluxus and the Transitional Commodity," *Art Journal* 75, no. 1 (2016): 44–69.

13 On Maciunas's crucial role as collector and designer, see Julia Robinson, "Maciunas as Producer: Performative Design in the Art of the 1960s," *Grey Room* 33 (Fall 2008): 56–83; Natilee Harren, "George Maciuns, Fluxusboxes, and the Transitional Commodity," in *Fluxus Forms: Scores, Multiples, and the Eternal Network* (University of Chicago Press, 2020), 133–53; and Colby Chamberlain, *Fluxus Administration: George Maciunas and the Art of Paperwork* (University of Chicago Press, 2024).

14 Letter from Maciunas to Schmit, reprinted in *What's Fluxus? What's Not! Why* (Centro Cultural Banco do Brasil, 2002), 55.

15 Brecht, "Something About Fluxus, May 1964."

16 Knowles, interview with author, New York, March 15, 2007. See also Knowles, "Why I Work with Beans" (April 30, 1981), typed statement, AKS.

17 Rodenbeck relates this point to Knowles's work in general during this era, including *Make a Salad* and *The Identical Lunch*. Judith F. Rodenbeck, "Alison Knowles," in "The Artist as Experience Maker," in *Work Ethic*, exh. cat., ed. Helen Molesworth (Pennsylvania State University Press, 2003), 185.

18 See, for example, Cage's *Water Music* (1952).

19 Duchamp, interview with James Johnson Sweeney, National Broadcasting Company, January 1956. Reprinted in *The Writings of Marcel Duchamp*, ed. Michel Sanouillet and Elmer Peterson (Da Capo, 1973), 134–45.

20 Knowles, interview with unknown author, AKS.

21 Knowles, *by Alison Knowles* (Great Bear Pamphlet, Something Else Press, 1965), 10. It is unclear who this first performer was. Knowles performed *Proposition #12* at Events y New Music, Escuela Técnica Superior de Arquitectura, Madrid, November 12, 1966. Other performances by Knowles at the Café au Go Go include Emmett Williams's *Opera* (1963) with Ben Patterson, Ay-O, and Williams in January 1965. For more on the Café au Go Go events, see Emmett Williams Archives, Correspondence, JBP; Fluxus West Collection, University of Iowa Libraries.

22 Higgins, *Fluxus Experience*, 118.

23 Knowles, *Proposition X: Build a Bean Garden* (1971), in *More by Alison Knowles* (Printed Editions, 1979). After the 1972 Avant Garde Festival, Knowles featured the *Bean Garden* sound environment for the Meet the Woman Composer series at the New School for Social Research, November 5, 1976. Knowles and her daughters recall many pounds of leftover beans after these performances, which she stored near the elevator shaft on the sixth floor of her studio loft. They would wash and eat the beans for years. See "Alison Knowles Bean Garden Folder," AS; Knowles, interview with author, New York, March 16, 2007.

24 *The Bean Garden* has since been remade for exhibitions at the Block Museum of Art at Northwestern University (2016); the Carnegie Museum of Art, Pittsburgh (2016); and Berkeley Art Museum and Pacific Film Archive (2022).

25 Knowles recalls Nam June Paik telling her that he kept *Bean Rolls* "beside the toilet for his morning contemplative reading." See "Notes Toward Indigo Island: A Conversation Between Alison Knowles and Hannah Higgins, 1994," in *Indigo Island: Art Works by Alison Knowles* (Stadtgalerie Saarbrucken, 1995), 105. This linking of vitality and nourishment distinguishes my reading of text-object-performance from the excellent approaches of art historians Liz Kotz and Julia Robinson.

26 See George Maciunas, *Bean Kit (Homage to Alison Knowles)* (1964); Jackson Mac Low, "A Bean Diastic for Alison Knowles from an Earlier Bean Poem," in *Stanzas for Iris Lezak* (Something Else Press, 1972); Mac Low, "Bean Phonemicon for Alison Knowles" (1984), Jackson Mac Low Papers, UCSD; John Cage, "Where Are We Eating? And What Are We Eating? (Thirty-Eight Variations on a Theme by Alison Knowles)," in *Merce Cunningham*, ed. James Klosty (New York: Limited Editions, 1975), 55–62; Anne Tardos, "Bean Snow (for Alison Knowles)" (1984), Anne Tardos papers, UCSD.

27 The poem was published in *Bean Rolls* and later reprinted in its entirety, including updated information from a 1978 New York City telephone book, in *More by Alison Knowles*. This edition differs from *More by Alison Knowles* (Unpublished Editions, 1976). In the 1979 version, she added *Three New Bean Events* (1976), *The Shoemaker's Assistant* (1976), *Bean—See also Bein for George Maciunas* (1978), and *Monkey Shines (for Pauline Oliveros on the occasion of her fortieth birthday)* (1972). I return to *Monkey Shines* in chapter 5.

28 Knowles considered *The Big Book*, *The Book of Bean*, and *The Boat Book* (2014–2015) a sort of trilogy. I return to *The Big Book* in chapter 4. For a richly descriptive feature on *The Book of Bean*, see "Alison Knowles, Visual Artist, *The Book of Bean*," *Aperture* 93, Esalen Arts Symposium: Photography 1982 (Winter 1983): 36–39. Her vinyl LP *Sounds from the Book of Bean* (2021) is an assemblage of texts and audio material related to its construction in 1980, originally published in 1982 for Charlie Morrow's New Wilderness Audiographics. I am very grateful to Knowles and Joshua Selman for sharing a copy of the LP with me.

29 Knowles, "It Really *Is* a Book," in *Talking the Boundless Book: Art, Language, and the Book Arts*, ed. Charles Alexander (Minnesota Center for the Book Arts, 1995), 117. See also Lucia Fabio, "Touch, Listen, Smell, Eat, Look: Intersensory Perception in the Work of Alison Knowles," in *by Alison Knowles: A Retrospective (1960–2022)*, ed. Karen Moss and Lucia Fabio (University of California, Berkeley Art Museum and Pacific Film Archive, 2022), 55–69; images on 164–67. Since its debut, Knowles's daughter Jessica Higgins has been the most frequent performer of *Loose Pages*.

30 "The scrolls were all the same and they were run offset, and we would cut them meticulously. We didn't get to two hundred because my mother and I were simply worn out." Knowles, interview with author, New York, March 16, 2007.

31 As noted in chapter 2, Knowles's food-based pieces may be seen as precursors of, for example, the "free food" events created by Rirkrit Tiravanija in the early 1990s. Knowles and Tiravanija later collaborated on an editioned book scroll, *Men and Women Commonly Dress Alike* (Paris: Three Star Books, 2011), GRI.

32 Knowles, interview with unknown author, AKS. On protofeminist aspects of Knowles's work in the late 1960s–1970, see also Nicole L. Woods, "Object/Poems: Alison Knowles's Feminist Archite(x)ture," *X-TRA* 15, no. 1 (Fall 2012): 7–25.

33 Knowles, "Why I Work with Beans." Another bean work, *Twenty-Eight Pole Limas*—performed for the Maciunas-organized Flux-Harpsichord Recital at 80 Wooster Street, New York, in 1975—involved tossing lima beans over a harpsichord bed covered with paper and then picking them up with tweezers.

34 Jill Johnston, "Flux Acts," *Art in America* 82, no. 6 (June 1994): 79 (emphases mine).

35 Knowles's relation to Broodthaers is argued differently by Julia Robinson in "The Sculp-

ture of Indeterminacy: Alison Knowles's Beans and Variations," *Art Journal* 63, no. 4 (Winter 2004): 96–115. For a survey of food's prominence within Fluxus, see Hannah Higgins, "Food: The Raw and the Fluxed," in *Fluxus and the Essential Questions of Life*, ed. Jacquelynn Baas (University of Chicago Press, 2011), 13–22. On Maciunas, see Colby Chamberlain, "Prescribed Performances: Fluxus and Disability," *October*, no. 177 (Summer 2021): 24–51.

36 Rachel Haidu, "Laughter," in *Part-Object/Part-Sculpture* (Wexner Center for the Arts; Pennsylvania State University Press, 2005), 131–35. In the context of North America, beans were, of course, a staple for many during the Great Depression of the 1930s, and for those stockpiling canned goods in home bomb shelters during the Cold War. See Elaine Tyler May, *Homeward Bound: American Families During the Cold War* (Basic Books, 1988).

37 On gender and post–World War II US cookbooks, see Marjorie L. DeVault, *Feed the Family: The Social Organization of Caring as Gendered Work* (University of Chicago Press, 1991); Sherrie A. Inness, "Of Casseroles and Canned Foods: Building the Happy Housewife in the Fifties," in *Dinner Roles: American Women and Culinary Culture* (University of Iowa Press, 2001), 141–64; Harvey Levenstein, *The Paradox of Plenty: A Social History of Eating in Modern America* (Oxford University Press, 1993); and Jessamyn Neuhaus, "The Way to a Man's Heart: Gender Roles, Domestic Ideology, and Cookbooks in the 1950s," *Journal of Social History* 32, no. 3 (Spring 1999): 529–55.

38 Some scholars have written that the noontime meditation began in 1969, when Philip Corner first observed and recorded the ritual; others date the work to 1968. Knowles affirms it began in 1967. The confusion may arise from her early publication of journal entries dated to 1968. The narrative arc in this chapter derives from original research in my dissertation on Knowles (2010), with some material previously published in Woods, "Taste Economies: Alison Knowles, Gordon Matta-Clark and the Intersection of Food, Time and Performance," *Performance Research: A Journal of the Performing Arts* 19, no. 3 (2014): 157–61.

39 Knowles, "The Identical Lunch," *The Outsider* 2, nos. 4–5 (Winter 1968–1969): 182–84.

40 Knowles, quoted in Kristine Stiles, "Tuna and Other Fishy Thoughts on Fluxus Events," in *Indigo Island*, 26. Corner first mentions the lunch in notes dated August 1969, SFA, I.186. See also Higgins, *Fluxus Experience*, 46–48; Mari Dumett's chapter on Knowles in *Corporate Imaginations: Fluxus Strategies for Living* (University of California Press, 2017), which analyzes *The Identical Lunch* and the artist's "aesthetic of routinization" in relation to American labor and cooking practices; Emily Ruth Capper, "*The Identical Lunch* (late 1960s–early 1970s)," in *The Scores Project: Experimental Notation in Music, Art, Poetry, and Dance, 1950–1975*, ed. Michael Gallope, Natliee Harren, and John Hicks (Getty Research Institute, 2025); Lucia Fabio, "Alison Knowles Make a Salad and Identical Lunch: Communal and Sensory Performance Through Open Scores" (master's thesis, University of Southern California, 2015); Megan R. Fizell, "Gastronomic Body: Sensory and Sociocultural Dimensions of Food Art" (PhD diss., UNSW Sydney, 2021); Jessica Santone, "Circulating the Event: The Social Life of Performance Documentation, 1965–1975" (PhD diss., McGill University, 2010).

41 Aside from a few photographs (including portraits Knowles would later use for silk-screened canvases) and program announcements for the Annual Avant Garde Festivals, scant documentation is preserved from the October 28, 1972, and November 16, 1974 performances. Other occasions include "Performance 10: Alison Knowles," Museum of Modern Art, New York (2011); and *Feast: Radical Hospitality in Contemporary Art*, Smart Museum, University of Chicago (2012). While she was a fellow at the Radcliffe Institute for Advanced Studies at Harvard (2009–2010), Knowles made the lunch for me with all the ingredients from the original score, "conducting," as it were, the conditions for a "robust discussion and feast." Knowles, interview with author, Cambridge, MA, November 5, 2009.

42 With the establishment of large canneries in the early twentieth century, the humble tuna

fish sandwich became a staple of the North American diet (notably, pre- and postwar childhood lunches) and an important economic generator, especially for the California fishing industry. For more on the industry, including controversies around dolphin mortality and mercury contamination, see Andrew F. Smith, *American Tuna: The Rise and Fall of an Improbable Food* (University of California Press, 2012).

43 Knowles, artist's talk at Goddard College, Vermont, March 1973; transcribed by the author from audiotape, Jan Herman Archive, MS51, NU. Composer Malcolm Goldstein, a friend and frequent collaborator of Knowles in the 1970s, invited her to perform the lunch and speak to his class, "Practices of Music Improvisation and Music of Noise." See Malcolm Goldstein Papers, Fales Library and Special Collections, New York University.

44 Knowles, "Introduction," in Philip Corner, *The Identical Lunch: Philip Corner Performances of a Score by Alison Knowles* (Nova Broadcast Press, 1973), 1.

45 The *Journal* was published by writer Jan Herman's Nova Broadcast Press. Knowles, letter to Jan Herman, December 21, 1971, Jan Herman Archive, MS51, NU. Other performers documented include Tony Anderson, Susan Harnett, Bici Hendricks, Debbie Hollingworth, Lynn Lonidier, Jim Maya, Michael McClanathan, Max Neuhaus, Jeffrey (Jef) Raskin, Tom Wasmuth, and Ken Werner.

46 See Moore's contact sheets documenting performance of the lunch by Knowles and friends in June 1969 in Jan Herman Archive, MS51, NU.

47 Knowles, letter to Jan Herman, December 21, 1971, Jan Herman Archive, Correspondence, NU.

48 Santone, "Circulating the Event," 92.

49 Anna Dezeuze, "What Is a Fluxus Score? (Some Preliminary Thoughts)," *Fluxus Scores and Instructions: The Transformative Years* (Gilbert and Lila Silverman Collection, Detroit; Museum of Contemporary Art, Roskilde, Denmark, 2008), 28.

50 Bici Hendricks's entry in Knowles, *Journal of the Identical Lunch*, n.p.

51 Knowles, artist's talk at Goddard College, Vermont, March 1973.

52 For exhibitions taking "information" as a point of departure, see K. G. Pontus Hultén, *The Machine: As Seen at the End of the Mechanical Age* (Museum of Modern Art, 1968); Kynaston McShine, *Information* (Museum of Modern Art, 1970); Jack Burham, *Software, Information Technology: Its New Meaning for Art* (Jewish Museum, 1970). David Joselit has examined George Maciunas's food works in relation to what he calls the "bio-readymade," which he defines as a post-Duchampian readymade "to be literally metabolized both in organic bodies and consumer networks." His rich theorization of "vestigial artworks" focuses nearly exclusively on Maciunas and mentions Knowles and others only briefly. See Joselit, "Readymade Metabolized," 190–200.

53 Knowles, *Journal of the Identical Lunch*, 10–32. The first pages of entries are reproduced from *The Outsider* (1968). Later entries recount lunches eaten at Riss Diner in June–July 1969 and in other locations, including Raskin in San Diego, California. The March 6 entry (fig. 3.18) refers to Knowles and Raskin's collaborative printing of her computer poem "A House of Dust" at the Jet Propulsion Laboratory, May 1971.

54 Knowles, *Journal of the Identical Lunch*, 15. See also Nicholas von Hoffman, "174 Arrested in Second Battle of Columbia: Rebels Who Seized Building Routed," *Washington Post*, May 23, 1968, A1, A14.

55 At the end of 1968 there were 536,100 US troops in Vietnam, with American fatalities nearing 17,000.

56 On the political meaning of newspaper fragments in Picasso's Cubist collages ca. 1912–1913, see Rosalind E. Krauss, "The Circulation of the Sign," in *The Picasso Papers* (MIT Press, 1999), 25–88.

57 Grace Glueck, "Art Community Here Agrees on Plan to Fight War, Racism and Oppression," *New York Times*, May 19, 1970, 30. See also Julia Bryan-Wilson, *Art Workers: Radical Practice in the Vietnam Era* (University of California Press, 2009); Mignon Nixon, "What's Love Got to Do, Got to Do With It? Feminist Politics and America's War in Vietnam," *Artists Respond: American Art and the Vietnam War, 1965–1975*, ed. Melissa Ho (Smithsonian American Art Museum/Princeton University Press, 2019,) 325–47.

58 Corner, "Philip Corner Lunch," in Knowles, *Journal of the Identical Lunch*, n.p.

59 Corner, letter to Knowles, in *Journal of the Identical Lunch*, n.p. (emphases in original). "Digger" refers to an anarchist street theater troupe, active in San Francisco 1966–1968, that took its name from a group of English dissenters who, in 1649–1650, advocated for commonly held agrarian land. See Bradford D. Martin, *The Theater Is in the Street: Politics and Performance in Sixties America* (University of Massachusetts Press, 2004), 86–124.

60 See Corner's book *NY 60s: Scenes from the Scene* (Lebanon, NH: Frog Peak Music, 1995), 19; Steve Courtney, "Peekskill's Days of Infamy: The Robeson Riots of 1949," *Reporter Dispatch* (White Plains, NY), September 5, 1982, n.p.; Paul Robeson Jr., *The Undiscovered Paul Robeson: Quest for Freedom, 1936–1976* (John Wiley and Sons, 2010), 168–169.

61 See Cecilia Novero, "Introduction," in *Antidiets of the Avant-Garde: Futurist Cooking to Eat Art* (University of Minnesota Press, 2010), vii-xxxvii.

62 Knowles, *Journal of the Identical Lunch*, 4 (Higgins), n.p. (Corner and Hartung).

63 Writer Nancy Kricorian recounts, in a wholly different context, a harrowing and hilarious childhood tale in which her mother demands she eat a pureed tuna fish sandwich. See Kricorian, "Tuna," *Heresies* 21 (Food Is a Feminist Issue) (1987): 50.

64 Hannah Higgins, "Art and the Senses: The Avant-Garde Challenge to the Visual Arts," *A Cultural History of the Senses in the Modern Age*, ed. David Howes (Bloomsbury, 2014), 213. Maciunas's well-known taste for processed food has been linked to his unstable income. See Joselit, "Readymade Metabolized"; Chamberlain, "Prescribed Performances."

65 See Arthur Danto, *The Transfiguration of the Commonplace: A Philosophy of Art* (Harvard University Press, 1981). The relation between Pop art and Fluxus is reevaluated in Iñaki Estella Noriega, "The Impossible Performance of Mass Commodity: George Maciunas, Herman Fine, and Robert Watts' Implosions Inc. (ca. 1967)," *Culture & History Digital Journal* 5, no. 2 (December 2016), https://doi.org/10.3989/chdj.2016.019.

66 Knowles describes the series in her performance at Goddard College, Vermont, March 1973. Maciunas organized the New Year's Eve event and Knowles prepared the tuna fish lunch and a "shit bean" porridge for the dinner. See Maciunas, "Invitation to Participate in New Year's Eve's Flux-Feast (Food & Drink Event)," 1969, SFA, V.F.11. On Knowles and Maciunas's shared investment in the subject, see Chamberlain, *Fluxus Administration*, 209–19.

67 The entire suite of prints from *The Identical Lunch* at the Museum of Modern Art, New York, include images of Anne Brazeau, Ay-O, Michael Cooper, Humphrey Evans, Jan Herman, Hannah Higgins, Jessica Higgins, John A. Kimm, Shigeko Kubota, Brian Jacobs and Ron Jenkins, George Maciunas, "unidentified woman," and Stephen Varble.

68 Knowles, quoted in Higgins, "Notes Toward Indigo Island," 101. Knowles noted (in her 1973 talk at Goddard College) that she later met another StarKist representative in San Diego. Bogdanovich would go on to study business at Boston University and to produce Jamaican reggae and dancehall music with enterprises including DownSound.

69 Roth, quoted in Sue Reilly, "All in the Duchamp Mood: UCI Festival Salutes Art Anarchist," *Los Angeles Times*, November 8, 1971, F11–12. Oral history interview with Moira Roth, April 22–24, 2011, AAA. My thanks to the late Barbara Rose for sharing her memories of the festival. Rose, email exchange with author, September 23, 2019.

70 Rose, email exchange with author, September 23, 2019. The ceramics building also hosted screenings of René Clair's short film *Entr'acte* (1924) and Hans Richter's *8 × 8: A Chess Sonata in 8 Movements* (1957).

71 "Art News: Festival at UC Irvine," *Los Angeles Times*, November 7, 1971, 61–62. Rose, who often used videotapes in her classes, arranged for the lectures to be taped on a reel-to-reel Sony industrial video recorder. The tapes, lost for decades, have been rediscovered by artist and UCI professor Miles Coolidge and, to my knowledge, are awaiting digital transfer. Coolidge, email correspondence with author, June 2016. The one lecture that has been digitized is Richard Hamilton's "A Lecture on Duchamp's *The Large Glass*." My thanks to Miles for sharing this file with me.

72 Moira Roth, "Appendix B: Duchamp Festival, University of California, Irvine, 1971," *West Coast Duchamp*, ed. Bonnie Clearwater (Grassfield Press, 1991), 116.

73 See Peter Frank, "Context, Attitude, Community: The Early Years of the UCI Art Department," in *Best Kept Secret: UCI and the Development of Contemporary Art in Southern California, 1964–1971*, ed. Grace Kook-Anderson (Laguna Art Museum, 2011), 19–31. See also Maurice Stein and Larry Miller, *Blueprint for Counter Education* (Doubleday, 1970); Janet Sarbanes, "A Community of Artists: Radical Pedagogy at CalArts, 1969–72," eastofborneo.org, June 4, 2014. My thanks to artist Bruce Richards for sharing his experiences as a student at UCI (1966–1973) with me. Email exchange with author, July 5, 2019.

74 My thanks to Barbara T. Smith for discussing her time at UCI with me. Interview with author, July 22, 2019, Pasadena, CA. Burden's *Five-Day Locker Piece* was originally intended for inclusion in the festival, but it was performed instead in April 1971 as part of his MFA graduate thesis project. In a 2009 interview, Burden recalled wanting to perform his infamous *Shoot* piece at the Duchamp Festival. http://www.artinfo.com/news/story/28002/chris-burden/.

75 Roth, "Appendix B," 116.

76 During her time at CalArts, Knowles lived on a commune for a time, was in the throes of a breakup with Higgins, and regularly traveled up and down the state for projects, including a radio program for KPFK in Berkeley. I return to this context in chapter 5.

77 Knowles, letter to George Maciunas, 1971. George Maciunas Correspondence, Alison Knowles folder, AS. Peter Van Riper was an adjunct professor at CalArts, Knowles's then-partner, and a pioneer of laser technology and holographic art. It is unclear from archival records whether Van Riper's contribution indicated these were new documentary photographs of people performing the lunch or ones Knowles already had in her possession in California. For more on holography in the early 1970s, see Jeff Berner, *The Holography Book* (Avon, 1980).

78 Knowles, "The Identical Lunch for Video," unpublished typed proposal to the New York State Council on the Arts, 1973, AKS. On the UCSD performance, see Knowles, letter to Jan Herman, September 11, 1971, Jan Herman Archive, MS51, NU; and Knowles, letter to curator Pat Baxter detailing her request for materials, November 1971, Alison Knowles (Performance November 5, 1971) folder, University Art Gallery Records, UCSD.

79 Knowles, letter to Jan Herman, December 4, 1971, Jan Herman Archive, MS51, NU. See also Knowles's recounting of the UCI event in letters to Maciunas, 1971, George Maciunas Correspondence, Alison Knowles folder, AS.

80 Knowles, "Identical Lunch for Video" proposal. To my knowledge, no definitive images documenting this portion of the Duchamp Festival exhibition have been found.

81 Knowles, letter to Higgins, dated December 1971, Dick Higgins papers, Correspondence Files (KI–KN), AS.

82 Knowles, "The Identical Lunch for Video" proposal. In an artist's talk two years after the

UCI performance, Knowles notes that it was in San Diego where she met a representative from StarKist.

83 The photograph included here as figure 3.22 has been reproduced in many accounts of *The Identical Lunch*, but it is difficult to determine precisely when and where it was taken. It is possible that the photograph can be attributed to performances at UCI or UCSD in 1971, but my research also points to Knowles's solo exhibition at Galerie Inge Baecker in Bochum, Germany, May–June 1973. See announcement card in Alison Knowles Identical Lunch files, AS, as well as letters between Knowles and Higgins, dated October 1973 (also AS). Graphic prints, black-and-white photographs, and color-in-color photocopies of the lunch can be found in the Collection Staatsgalerie, Stuttgart. See, for example, https://www.staatsgalerie.de/de/sammlung-digital/the-identical-lunch-5.

84 I am specifically thinking of Eleanor Antin and Vito Acconci, both of whom Knowles had met at avant-garde poetry readings in New York and counted as close friends.

85 In contrast to other, contemporaneous works connecting eating and the social body, Knowles did not directly engage dieting, for instance, as a repressed form of heteronormative domination of the image (and psyche) of woman, nor was she overtly invested in critiquing the fishing industry. I am currently working on an essay in which I reconsider *The Identical Lunch* with and against Eleanor Antin's *CARVING: A Traditional Sculpture* (1972), Adrian Piper's *Food for Spirit* (1971), Bonnie Sherk's *Public Lunch* (1971), and Christine Kozlov's *Eating Piece* (1969), among others.

86 Mari Dumett has connected *The Identical Lunch* with Andy Warhol's earlier *Tuna Fish Disaster* series (1963). Warhol's series famously documented the death of two suburban Detroit women who died of canned-tuna botulism that same year using photographs sourced from *Newsweek*. See Dumett, "Ritual and Routine," 305–6. Natilee Harren makes the case for the parallels of Knowles's practice with ecofeminist theories and activism emergent in the mid-1970s. See Harren, "The Eternal Metabolic Network: Fluxus, Food, and Ecofeminism," originally published in *Living Matter: The Preservation of Biological Materials in Contemporary Art*, proceedings of a conference held in Mexico City, June 3–5, 2019 (J. Paul Getty Trust, 2022), https://www.getty.edu/publications/living-matter/.

87 Knowles, "Identical Lunch for Video" proposal. The "Blind Lunch" proposition is also included in *More by Alison Knowles*. Black-and-white photographs of Knowles staging the "Step On Lunch" ca. 1972–1973 (wearing six different pairs of shoes) can be found in the Staatsgalerie, Stuttgart; for example, https://www.staatsgalerie.de/de/sammlung-digital/the-identical-lunch-3. See also Alison Knowles Boxed Publications, Identical Lunch album, AS.

88 Knowles and Phillips would collaborate on multimedia video performances in the 1970s, including Phillips's *TV Dinners* (1973), produced in Estabrook's studio; https://vimeo.com/1092658164. Estabrook was a news producer who set up a studio in Greenwich Village to teach television production in the mid-1960s and 1970s. See Lillian Africano, "Is It Home or TV Studio?" *The Villager*, September 12, 1974, 6. I return to Phillips in chapter 5.

89 Knowles, "Identical Lunch for Video" proposal. Subsequent quotes are from this source.

90 In late spring 1973, Knowles performed *The Identical Lunch*, *Blind Lunch*, *Drawn Out Lunch*, and *Step-Up Lunch* at Galerie Inge Baecker in Bochum, her first solo exhibition in Germany. Her fellow performers are unnamed on the announcement card. Alison Knowles Identical Lunch Folder, AS.

91 Jim Maya's entry in Knowles, *Journal of the Identical Lunch*, n.p.

92 Higgins's entry in Knowles, *Journal of the Identical Lunch*, n.p. Higgins and Knowles's remarks were written on index cards and reproduced in the journal in their original form. Knowles's reply is particularly interesting as she crosses out sentences to make her point more concise.

93 Hendricks, in "Artists Talk on Art," a SoHo20 Gallery panel series featuring a discussion,

recorded in April 1989, between art critic Robert C. Morgan, Knowles, Higgins, Hendricks, Philip Corner, and Ay-O. Robert C. Morgan Conceptual Art Collection, Special Collections, University of Notre Dame (transcribed by the author, June 2016). The story of the naked lunch comes around the 16:47 mark. To my knowledge, the photographs, along with much of Higgins's personal archive, were destroyed in a flood at the Barton (West Glover) farm later in the 1970s.

**94** Hendricks later recalled his first meeting with Higgins: "In '63 when the group of Fluxus artists came back from Europe, Maciunas had set up this Flux Shop down on Canal Street in a loft, and I was there a few times. The first time I was there, Dick Higgins afterwards took me to the bar downstairs and began to explain to me all the things about George Maciunas and what I had to watch out for, and about what was going on within Fluxus and the situation of the Flux-tour, because he had had this big split and fight with George. It was subliminal at that point, certainly not expressed with either of us, but a quiet queer male bonding, unrecognized, un-visualized, was beginning to take place. He was the other queer Fluxus artist." Elizabeth Stephens and Annie Sprinkle, "Interview with Geoff Hendricks," *Total Art Journal* 1, no. 1 (2011): 11. By the early 1970s, Higgins was living openly as a gay man and began publishing work that specifically addressed sexual desire, including *Amigo* (Unpublished Editions, 1972). On his friendship with Hendricks, see *A 22 Year Old Manuscript Found in Attic of Artist's New York Residence 1977* (New York: Money for Food Press, 1999).

**95** As noted in chapter 1, Knowles and Higgins divorced in 1970. Geoff Hendricks and the artist and writer Bici Hendricks (later Nye Ffarrabas) divorced in 1971—an event of personal and sexual transformation symbolically documented that year by Hendricks in *Ring Piece*, a twelve-hour performance during Moorman's 8th Annual Avant Garde Festival at the New York City Armory. See Hendricks, *Ring Piece* (Something Else Press, 1973); David Getsy, "The Spectacle of Privacy: Geoffrey Hendricks's *Ring Piece* and the Ambivalence of Queer Visibility," *Art Bulletin* 104, no. 3 (August 2022): 117–45.

**96** Knowles, "Artists Talk on Art," at 18:29.

**97** Self-care, a radical idea in the hands of Audre Lorde and Michel Foucault, has, through a corporatist rebranding as "self-help," a cheap replacement for social care, been largely stripped of its politics. See Lorde, *A Burst of Light and Other Essays* (Firebrand Books, 1988); Foucault, *The Care of the Self*, vol. 3 of *The History of Sexuality*, trans. Robert Hurley (Vintage Books, 1986).

**98** Knowles, *Indigo Island*, 10 (emphases mine).

**99** *Three Songs* comprises three scrolls with sepia ink prints: *Shoestring Song*, *Silk Thread Song*, and *Onion Skin Song*.

**100** Knowles, typed statement, "Back to the Real Onion: Notes on 'Song #1' of Three Songs," November 11, 1978, Artists Files, JBP. The scrolls are hung either vertically or horizontally, dependent on the site. Knowles, for example, still hangs hers vertically in her SoHo loft.

**101** Knowles, "Song #1," in *Three Songs* printed score (Edition René Block, 1973), Alison Knowles Files, Estate of William S. Wilson, New York. Stepping on the layered plastic is how Knowles performed the work with students during a two-week residency at the San Francisco Art Institute in 2003. Kenneth Baker, "Peeling Away the Layers of an Artwork with Music," *San Francisco Chronicle*, April 1, 2003, D5, col.1.

**102** Knowles, artist's statement, *A Performance/Exhibition of Works by Alison Knowles* (Bowdoin College Museum of Art, Brunswick, Maine, December 1980), 1.

**103** Knowles, artist's statement, *A Performance/Exhibition*, 2; Knowles, "Back to the Real Onion: Notes on 'Song #1' of Three Songs."

**104** The theme of food recurs over decades in Knowles's oeuvre. For example, in *Bread and Water* (1992), a series of cyanotypes and palladium prints made in collaboration with artists

Bryan McHugh and Catherine Harris, Knowles electrographically imaged the bottoms of bread loaves she baked. In the larger palladium prints, their cracked and creviced topographies are visually paired with specific rivers (e.g., Yangtze, Dnieper, Amazon, Santa Clara). See Knowles, "Bread and Water," typed notes, u.d., EHF.

## Chapter 4

1 Alison Knowles quoted in Emmett Williams, "Alison in Wonderland," *BOOKS* (September 1966): 12.

2 Howard Junker, "Pandora's Book," *Newsweek*, April 29, 1968, 88. *The Big Book*, Junker noted, would be on view at the Frankfurter Buchmesse in September 1968. It is unclear precisely where he first experienced the installation.

3 Junker, "Pandora's Book," 88. A similar point is made by Johanna Drucker, who notes that Knowles "made the concept of the book into an environmental *experience* in ways which broke new and familiar ground." See Drucker, "The Codex and Its Variations," in *The Century of Artists' Books* (Granary Books, 2004), 152–53 (emphasis mine).

4 Junker, "Pandora's Book," 88.

5 See Nicole L. Woods, "Object/Poems: Alison Knowles's Feminist Archite(x)ture," *X-TRA* 15, no. 12 (Fall 2012): 6–23.

6 *The Big Book* was destroyed shortly after its last exhibition at the Jewish Museum in 1969. The history and interpretive framework presented in this chapter rely on Knowles's personal papers, unpublished photographs, Dick Higgins's 16mm film of the work (1966–1967), studio notes, recollections, a series of long interviews with the artist, and endless hours in numerous archives. The bulk of the archival material comes courtesy of the Getty Research Institute, Los Angeles (GRI); the Jewish Museum Archives, New York; Emily Harvey Foundation Archives (EHF); Gilbert and Lila Silverman Collection Fluxus Archives, Museum of Modern Art, New York (SFA); Archiv Sohm, Staatsgalerie Stuttgart (AS); Museum of Contemporary Art Archives, Chicago (MCA); Special Collections Libraries, Northwestern University (NU); and Special Collections & Archives, Geisel Special Collections, University of California, San Diego (UCSD).

7 Higgins, "Statement on Intermedia," in *dé-coll/age* 6 (1965), ed. Wolf Vostell. Rosemary Furtak Collection, Walker Art Center Library. See also Higgins's 1966–1967 version, reprinted in *In the Spirit of Fluxus*, ed. Elizabeth Armstrong and Joan Rothfuss (Walker Art Center, 1993), 172; Dick Higgins, "Intermedia" (1965), reprinted with an appendix by Hannah Higgins, *Leonardo* 34, no. 1 (2001): 49–54. For compelling reconsiderations and histories of Higgins's "intermedia," see Trevor Stark, "Passionate Expanse of the Law: Intermedia and the Problem of Discipline," in *Call It Something Else: Something Else Press, Inc. (1963–1974)*, ed. Alice Centamore and Christian Xatrec (Museo Reina Sofia, 2023), 48–60; and Natilee Harren, "The Crux of Fluxus: Intermedia, Rear-Guard," in *Art Expanded, 1958–1978*, ed. Eric Crosby and Liz Glass (Walker Art Center, 2015), https://walkerart.org/collections/publications/art-expanded/crux-of-fluxus.

8 SEP was founded by Higgins in 1963, but Knowles was an equal financial partner as well as a coeditor, secretary, and book designer/page setter. Knowles, interview with author, New York, December 8, 2006. See also Alice Centamore, "The Making of Something Else Press, Inc.," in Centamore and Xatrec, *Call It Something Else*, 14–29.

9 For more on Beat literary culture in downtown Manhattan, see Steven Clay, *A Secret Location on the Lower East Side: Adventures in Writing, 1960–1980, A Sourcebook of Information* (New York Public Library/Granary Books, 1998).

10 Knowles, quoted in Williams, "Alison in Wonderland," 10.

11 See *Andy Warhol's Time Capsule 21* (Andy Warhol Foundation/Dumont, 2003), 220.

12 Knowles, letter to Williams, April 1963, Emmett Williams Archive, JBP. Al Hansen auctioned off the hats (with Lette Lou Eisenhauer modeling them) in "Yam Hat Sale," May 9–10, 1963. Photographs of the auction taken by Peter Moore can be found in AS.

13 Knowles picks up the nautical theme—an homage to her (now late) brother Larry Knowles, a career fisherman on Long Island—in *The Boat Book*, created in 2014–2015 with artist Kari Miller, first exhibited at Art Basel Miami Beach by New York gallerist James Fuentes, and featured in a retrospective at the Carnegie Art Museum, Pittsburgh, in 2016 and the Berkeley Art Museum and Pacific Film Archive in 2022.

14 Knowles, "Big Book Data," typed notes, n.d., SFA, I.740.

15 Jan van der Marck, "Pictures to Be Read/Poetry to Be Seen," *Journal of Typographical Research*, July 1968, 270.

16 William S. Wilson, "The Big Book," *Art in America* 56, no. 4 (July–August 1968): 100, 102. Van der Marck also notes the work's allusions to "unpretentious Manhattan loft living in the 1950's and early 1960's" in "Pictures to Be Read," 272.

17 Knowles quoted in Williams, "Alison in Wonderland," 11.

18 The artists—Shusaku Arakawa, Gianfranco Baruchello, Mary Bauermeister, George Brecht, Öyvind Fahlström, Ray Johnson, Allan Kaprow, R. B. Kitaj, Knowles, Jim Nutt, Gianni-Emilio Simonetti, and Wolf Vostell— shared, a press release said, "an interest in expanding the boundaries of their medium and pictorializing, in original ways, highly complex information structures." Knowles and Kaprow were the only two invited to exhibit large-scale works. Press release, "Museum of Contemporary Art Opens Doors with Pictures to Be Read/Poetry to Be Seen" (1967), Exhibition Files, MCA.

19 Contemporaneous reviews relating Knowles's *Big Book* to Duchamp's *Large Glass* include Alfred Frankenstein, "Pictures to Be Read, Poetry to Be Seen," *San Francisco Sunday Examiner & Chronicle*, November 5, 1967, 36.

20 Van der Marck, "Pictures to Be Read," 262.

21 Knowles, speaking with Charlie Morrow, in "A Dialogue: The House of Dust," *New Wilderness Letter* 8 (Spring 1980): 22. The gallery page included works on paper by Higgins, Brecht, Takako Saito, Carolee Schneemann, Wolf Vostell, Emmett Williams, and seventeen others. In letters to friends over the years, Knowles sometimes misidentified the animal as a "mountain elk." See, for example, George Brecht Correspondence Files, AS.

22 Ken Friedman "lived" in *The Big Book* for two weeks in fall 1966 while visiting Knowles and Higgins. One of his clearest memories, which he penned at the time, was the book's containment of "every kind of light available on the commercial market—neon, fluorescent, electric, incandescent . . ." See Ken Friedman Collection, Alison Knowles Folder, UCSD. Knowles's inclusion of an equipped kitchen in *The Big Book*, as with performances of *Make a Salad* and *Make a Soup*, evidence how often she prioritized a space for making and serving food.

23 Harold Rosenberg, *Artworks and Packages* (New York: Horizon Press, 1969), 150. During the run of *Pictures to be Read/Poetry to be Seen* at the MCA, *The Big Book*'s telephone connected to the museum's switchboard. Edward Barry, "Museum to Give Fresh Insight into Art," *Chicago Tribune*, October 24, 1967, A5.

24 See Hans Christian Adam, ed., *Eadweard Muybridge: The Human and Animal Locomotion Photographs* (Taschen, 2010).

25 Knowles, "Big Book Data," SFA, I.740.

26 Emmett Williams, "The Big Book of Alison Knowles" (1967), Emmett Williams Archives, Alison Knowles Correspondence, JBP. Knowles confirmed the intentional mimicry in an email exchange with author, April 9, 2010.

27 Among the sundry items, one reviewer also noted a "loaf of bread, a half-empty bottle of wine, a strainer . . . a German-English dictionary . . . and a tape recorder [that] played continuous music." See Nancy Wheelock, "Heard Any Good Paintings Lately?" *Junior League News*, May 1968, 27.

28 Wilson, "Big Book," 100–103. See also *ICA Bulletin* 163 (November 1966): 12.

29 Knowles, quoted in Williams, "Big Book of Alison Knowles."

30 In Higgins's audiorecording detailing *The Big Book*'s move from upstairs to downstairs, he mentions that Canadian media theorist Marshall McLuhan happened to be visiting their house. Something Else Press published McLuhan's *Verbi-Voco-Visual Explorations* in 1967. Higgins, "Big Book," audiotape reel, ca. 1967–1968. Audio Visual Materials, Reel-to-reel audiotapes, 1965–1987, R7, JBP.

31 Grace Glueck, "Between Media," *New York Times*, March 20, 1966, 22. The subsequent SEG shows would be *Intermedia* and *The Arts in Fusion*. Works by Knowles listed on the spring 1966 card announcing *Intermedia* include *The Alphabet Shirt*, *Railroad Shirt*, and *Car Crash Shirt for Wolf Vostell*. See Higgins papers, Something Else Gallery folders, AS.

32 Joe Jones helped Knowles "bolt, screw, and electrify" the installation. See contemporaneous letters in which she updates Emmett Williams and George Brecht (AS) and a photograph of Jones inside *The Big Book* (SFA, I.740). In 1963, Knowles had assisted Jones with his "self-playing" mechanized instruments in a performance at the Pocket Theater. See Ross Parmenter, "Music: Mechanical Star: A Self-Playing Percussion Assemblage at Pocket Theater Concert," *New York Times*, August 27, 1963, 28.

33 On USCO, see Gerd Stern, "From Beat Scene Poet to Psychedelic Multimedia Artist in San Francisco and Beyond, 1948–1978," an oral history interview conducted by Victoria Morris Byerly (1996), Bancroft Library, University of California, Berkeley. For Warhol's EPI events, see Branden W. Joseph, "'My Mind Split Open': Andy Warhol's Exploding Plastic Inevitable," *Grey Room* 8 (Summer 2002): 80–107.

34 Another account of the press previews quipped, "She is very polite and gracious. How does a girl like that get mixed up in art like this?" See "New in Art," *Chicago Tribune*, October 21, 1967. During *The Big Book*'s 1969 exhibition at the Jewish Museum, a critic reported that while the "meaning of it all" escaped them, "a group of young teenagers [were] mesmerized by the 'Book,' staring at it silently, with an occasional 'Wild,' 'Fabulous,' and 'Groovy' heard above the taped narrative." See Jo Martin, "They Have Art Appeal," *Daily News*, May 2, 1969, 54.

35 Knowles, quoted in Rosenberg, *Artworks and Packages* (Horizon Press, 1969), 150.

36 Michael Fried, "Art and Objecthood," *Artforum* 5 (June 1967): 12–23.

37 On Drop City, a southeastern Colorado "hippie commune" founded in 1965 by Gene Bernofsky, JoAnn Bernofsky, Richard Kallweit, and Clark Richert, see Felicity D. Scott, *Architecture or Techno-utopia: Politics After Modernism* (MIT Press, 2007), esp. chap. 6, "Revolutionaries or Dropouts," 151–84.

38 *The Big Book*'s audio collage was not the first Knowles sound piece to include her daughters. See, for example, *This Bath Is Finished* (ca. 1965), whose score reads: "Two children in the same tub with toys before understandable speech recorded from tub filling until the bath is finished." Knowles recorded the twins using magnetic tape and presented it at "Continuous Performances of New Music," an event at New York University in 1967 funded by Experiments in Art & Technology. See typescript score, Collection of Fondazione Bonotto, No. FX0675.

39 See the abbreviated transcription of the audio collage in *Alison Knowles: The Big Book*, ed. Meghan DellaCrosse (Passenger Books, 2013), 26–30.

40 "Bill Wilson Interviews Alison Knowles," unpublished cassette tape recording, 1967. Col-

lection of the author. My sincere thanks to Kate Wilson for locating this tape in her father's archive and allowing me to digitize the recording; to Robert Simon, music librarian at the University of Notre Dame, for expertly converting the tape for this project; and to Hannah Higgins, who graciously shared notes from an unpublished manuscript wherein she recalls (in detail) playing in *The Big Book* with her sister Jessica, and who has, in conversations over several years, helped clarify my understanding of the environment.

41 "It plays eternally once the juice (electricity) is turned on . . . [I'm] taking Steve Reich as my sound man." Knowles, letter to Emmett Williams, July 9, 1967, Emmett Williams Archives, Alison Knowles Correspondence, JBP. Reich also assisted Knowles with the audio collage for a performance at York University before she traveled to Chicago for the MCA exhibition.

42 Knowles quoted in Williams, "Big Book of Alison Knowles," 11.

43 Bill Wilson, "The Big Book of Alison Knowles," *dé-coll/age* 6 (July 1967), n.p.

44 Jorge Luis Borges, "The Library of Babel," in *Labyrinths: Selected Stories and Other Writings*, ed. Donald A. Yates and James E. Irby, trans. James E. Irby (New Directions, 1962), 54–59.

45 Borges, "Library of Babel," 54–59.

46 See Andrew Blauvelt, ed., *Hippie Modernism: The Struggle for Utopia* (Walker Art Center, 2015); Simon Sadler, "Drop City Revisited," *Journal of Architectural Education* 59, no. 3 (February 2006): 5–14.

47 See Reyner Banham, "A Home Is Not a House," *Art in America* (April 1965): 109–18.

48 Betty Friedan, *The Feminine Mystique* (Norton, 1963), 15–32; Sigmund Freud, "Family Romances" (1909), in *Collected Papers*, vol. 5, ed. James Strachey (Hogarth Press, 1952), 74–78.

49 Beatriz Colomina, *Domesticity at War* (MIT Press, 2007), 12.

50 Philippa Tristam, *Living Space in Fact and Fiction* (Routledge, 1989), 2 (emphasis in original).

51 Knowles quoted in Williams, "Alison in Wonderland," 10 (emphasis mine). A version of her typed notes on *The Big Book* can be found in Knowles, "Big Book Data," SFA, I.740.

52 Alexander Lavrentiev, *The Complete Works of Varvara Stepanova*, ed. John Bowlt (MIT Press, 1988), 104–7.

53 Lavrentiev, *Complete Works*, 109, 112.

54 On Stepanova's optical fabric designs in service to revolutionary ideals, see Christina Kiaer, "The Constructivist Flapper Dress," in *Imagine No Possessions: The Socialist Objects of Russian Constructivism* (MIT Press, 2005), 89–142.

55 Elizabeth Grosz, *Architecture from the Outside: Essays on Virtual and Real Space* (MIT Press, 2001), 157. Viewer-readers who documented their experiences of *The Big Book* were predominately male (e.g., Higgins, Williams, Friedman, Wilson, Van der Marck). The paradox of males viewing her highly personalized "female space" was evidently apparent to Knowles. Conversation with author, December 2007.

56 Viewing the film has been crucial to my understanding of the work and its meaning. I am grateful to Knowles for screening a copy with me and the late Elaine Summers in December 2007 at the Emily Harvey Foundation, New York. My thanks to film archivist Michelle Puetz, too, for a second viewing in 2015.

57 Rosenberg, *Artworks and Packages*, 150.

58 *The Fluxus Exhibition + Flux Concert* at UCSD ran February 12–March 22, 1969, in collaboration with Antin and curator Lawrence Alloway, then at New York State University at Stonybrook; Knowles's *The Big Book* opened on March 5 and included five *BLINK* canvases and *Bean Rolls* from a *Fluxkit*. A related event, Flux-Parade, was organized by John Baldessari and Robert Watts on March 4. Oliveros was a professor and cofounder of the Electronic Music Program at UCSD at the time. For the concert, she was assisted by Watts and Bertram Turetzky. See Lawrence Alloway Papers, Fluxus Ephemera, 1959–1965, GRI; "UCSD Gallery Plans 'Big Book,'" *La Jolla Light-Journal*, February 27, 1969, plus photographs and other

documentary materials in University Art Gallery Records, UCSD. For unknown reasons, the SUNY Stony Brook show was delayed and then canceled.

59 Knowles, letter to Friedman, July 30, 1967. Ken Friedman Collection, Alison Knowles Folder, UCSD. Much of Knowles's correspondence during this time mentions her struggles with the work—even her desire to destroy it in frustration. See also Knowles, letter to Emmett Williams, July 9, 1967, Emmett Williams Archives, Alison Knowles Correspondence, JBP.

60 Knowles was consistently forced to repair *The Big Book*, which was also badly damaged when first shipped to Toronto. To avoid further damage, she personally drove it from Toronto to Chicago.

61 Knowles has, in interviews over many years, expressed a sense of being done with (perhaps even exhausted by) particular works, subjects, practices, or materials, as well as an acceptance that works will change in ways beyond her control. For example, after work by Knowles and other Fluxus artists was damaged following the UCSD exhibition (due, according to correspondence between David Antin, Barbara Moore, and UCSD insurance representatives, to the crates being stored under shoddy conditions at SUNY Stony Brook), Knowles regarded the sparser version of *The Big Book* shown in *Superlimited* at the Jewish Museum as a second edition. See Knowles, letter to Robert Filliou, 1969, Robert Filliou Correspondence Box (I–P), AS; "Fluxus and the Big Book (1969 March)" files, University Gallery Records, UCSD.

62 Van der Marck, introductory essay, in *Pictures to Be Read/Poetry to Be Seen*, n.p.

63 Critics reviewing the show often made note that Kaprow and Knowles were "discreetly sealed off from the main exhibition area." See, for example, Hilton Kramer, "Mixing the Media," *New York Times*, October 29, 1967, D33. For the Duchamp references, see Marcel Duchamp, "The Creative Act" (1957), reprinted in Robert Lebel's monograph *Marcel Duchamp*, trans. George Heard Hamilton (New York: Paragraphic Books, 1959), 77–78. Knowles has affirmed her awareness of his essay at that time. Knowles, interview with author, Boston, November 9, 2009.

64 Rosenberg, "Museum of the New," *New Yorker*, November 18, 1967, 224–35.

65 Harold Rosenberg Papers, 1923–1984, GRI. Another reviewer of the show claimed Knowles's *Big Book* "would rank among the most inventive items in almost any show." See Edward Barry, "They Make You Wonder," *Chicago Tribune*, November 5, 1967, H8.

66 Rosenberg, *Artworks and Packages*, 150.

67 Van der Marck, executive meeting notes, dated October 7, 1967. See *Pictures to be Read/ Poems to be Seen*, Exhibition Files, MCA. A newspaper announcement for the event, held at Second City theater, at 1616 North Wells Street in Chicago, omitted mention of Kaprow. "Concerts and Recitals," *Chicago Tribune*, October 22, 1967, F16.

68 Copies of Higgins's playbill, a very small, folded booklet that also included program notes, can be found in "Chicago Gig 1967" folder, DHP.

69 Knowles, interview with William Fetterman, 1989. Some of the details in their exchange are incorrect; for example, in editorial parentheses Fetterman dates *The Big Book* to 1964. See Fetterman, *John Cage's Theater Pieces*, Contemporary Music Studies (Routledge, 1996), 202.

70 "Museum of Contemporary Art Sponsors Art Program at Second City October 23," news release, *Pictures to Be Read/Poems to Be Seen*, Exhibition Files, MCA.

71 Van der Marck, "Pictures to be Read," 270.

72 Mieko Shiomi's *Spatial Poems* (ca. 1965–1975), Stan VanDerBeek's *Poem Fields* series (1967), and Robert Smithson's *A Heap of Language* (1966) could be apt comparisons.

73 John Cage and Alison Knowles, eds., *Notations* (Something Else Press, 1969). Cage had begun soliciting manuscripts from composers, visual artists, and writers in 1965. When he invited Knowles to collaborate, she was charged with editing and designing the anthology and often corresponding with contributors. Higgins managed the paperwork related to copyright

issues. Knowles and Cage collected a total of 274 works, which can be found in JCNP. Cage continued to add to the collection for nearly a decade after the SEP publication.

**74** Cage, preface to *Notations*, n.p. Knowles and Cage exchanged long letters and memograms over two years as they began to receive the contributions from composers. See JCNP. Knowles's contribution to the Notations Project comprised notes for "Salad: Proposition No. 1" (discussed in chapter 2) and *Blue Ram* (1966), which was published in the book.

**75** Knowles, artist's statement, *A Performance/Exhibition of Works by Alison Knowles* (Bowdoin College Museum of Art, Brunswick, Maine, December 1980), 1–2. On how Knowle's investment in pattern, repetition, and models for categorization has borne fruit in particular works, see Nicole L. Woods, "Do You Remember? Alison Knowles in Context," in *by Alison Knowles: A Retrospective (1960–2022)*, ed. Karen Moss and Lucia Fabio (University of California, Berkeley Art Museum and Pacific Film Archive, 2022), 31–43; and George Quasha, "Auto-Dialogue on the Transvironmental Book: Reflections on 'The Book of Bean,'" *New Wilderness Newsletter*, no. 11 (December 1982): 41–44.

**76** Alison Knowles, Benjamin Patterson, Tomas Schmit and Philip Corner, *The Four Suits* (Something Else Press, 1965).

**77** Knowles, *The "T" Dictionary*, in *The Four Suits*, n.p. All quotes that follow also come from this source. Nineteen silver prints from *The "T" Dictionary* were exhibited in *Intermedia* at Something Else Gallery, April–May 1966, along with "work shirts" silk-screened with various imagery. See Higgins papers, Something Else Gallery folders, AS. Knowles created elegant line-drawing portraits of herself, Corner, Patterson, and Schmit, which Higgins reproduced for the "Prospectus" of *The Four Suits* (1965), offset print, SEP Collection, EHF. A gelatin-silver photographic print of Patterson's portrait sketch can be found in the GRI collection.

**78** This text also appears in Knowles, *by Alison Knowles* (Great Bear Pamphlet, Something Else Press, 1965), 7.

**79** Ray Johnson mentions Alison's "silk screen teeth" design in a letter to artist May Wilson (Bill Wilson's mother), May 12, 1964. A paper version of the floating teeth can also be found in the papers of William S. Wilson. As mentioned in the introduction, Knowles also silk-screened the *Coeurs Volants* image onto T-shirts and baby onesies. Knowles, interview with author, New York, December 8, 2006. Knowles's *Blue Ram* materials can be found in the JCNP. In a 1965 letter to Barbara Moore, Knowles mentions exhibiting *The "T" Dictionary* prints at the Fischbach Gallery the same year, SFA, I.739.

**80** Cage, *Writing Through Finnegans Wake & Writing for the Second Time Through Finnegans Wake* (University of Tulsa Press, 1978). Cage's editor found the first iteration—115 pages with 862 mesostics—too long, which prompted a second pass. Curiously, Cage does not credit Knowles in the introduction to the 1978 book. But in an acrostic poem announcing its publication, which he circulated to friends, Cage acknowledges "the position of punctuation designed and realized by John Cage and Alison Knowles." Jackson Mac Low Papers, Correspondence Files (John Cage, 1958–1992), Special Collections and Archives, UCSD. Cage used the *Finnegans Wake* mesostics in *Roaratorio: An Irish Circus on Finnegans Wake*, October 22, 1979, for WDR in Cologne, Germany. Knowles would also create hörspiels (radioplay or ear-play) for WDR in the 1980s. On Cage's *Roaratorio*, see Richard Kostelanetz, "John Cage and Richard Kostelanetz: A Conversation About Radio," *Musical Quarterly* 72, no. 2 (1986): 216–27. On Knowles's WDR works, see Lauren Fulton, "Sonic Possibilities, Meditations on Being, and the Mysterious Wisdom of Alison Knowles," in *by Alison Knowles: A Retrospective*, 63–69.

**81** Ellen Pearlman, "Interviews with Alison Knowles, July–October 2001, New York City,"

*Brooklyn Rail*, January–February 2002, https://brooklynrail.org/2002/01/art/interviews-with-alison-knowles-july-october-2001-new-york-city.

**82** See Carman Moore, "Magic and Ritual," *Village Voice*, March 30, 1967. Judson Memorial Church Archive, Fayles Library and Special Collections, New York University. Rothenberg's event was adapted from his *Ritual: A Book of Primitivizing Rites and Events* (Something Else Press, 1966).

**83** Jack Anderson, "Dance/Poetry/Music Judson Memorial Church, March 21 & 22, 1967," *Dance Magazine* (May 1967), n.p. See also Flyer announcing Judson Dance Theater events of March 21–22, 1967, DHP.

**84** For *Gift Event III* cast, script, and performance notes, see Jerome Rothenberg, ed., *Technicians of the Sacred: A Range of Poetries from Africa, America, Asia, Europe and Oceania* (University of California Press, 1968), 376–82. For a recording of the 1967 performance of "PoorManMusic" at Judson, see Philip Corner, *PoorManMusic*, vinyl LP (Alga Marghen, 2016), and https://www.youtube.com/watch?v=ChFiFzjhA-U.

**85** Rothenberg, ed., *Technicians of the Sacred*, 451. Rothenberg, ed., *Shaking the Pumpkin: Traditional Poetry of the Indian North Americas* (Doubleday, 1972), xxii. Knowles offered *Gift Event II* as a daylong performance at CalArts in 1972. I return to this piece in chapter 5.

**86** See Rothenberg, *Technicians of the Sacred*, 116; Rothenberg, *Shaking the Pumpkin*, 188. *Giveaway Construction* cited in *Shaking the Pumpkin*, 435. *Proposition #16: Giveaway Construction* was first published in *by Alison Knowles* (Great Bear Pamphlet), 12. It is unclear whether Knowles had any personal experiences with Kwakiutl potlatch ceremonies.

**87** Rothenberg borrowed the phrase from poet Robert Duncan's influential essay "Rites of Participation," first published in *Caterpillar* 1 and 2 (1967, 1968). For a reconsideration of Rothenberg's promotion and appropriation of Indigenous literature, see Stephen Fredman, "Jerome Rothenberg's *Technicians of the Sacred*: Transactions Between the Indigenous and the Avant-Garde," in *American Poetry as Transactional Art* (University of Alabama Press, 2020), 30–45.

**88** Knowles's artistic activities after 1978 are beyond the scope of this book, but it is my sincere hope that other scholars will take up her later works in future studies.

**89** Knowles, *Newspaper Music* (1965), reprinted in *The Fluxus Performance Workbook*, ed. Ken Friedman (El Djardia Magazine/Editions Conz, 1990), 34. Knowles's best-known performance of this piece, at the Stuttgart Club Voltaire in 1966, was photographed by Hanns Sohm. See Hanns Sohm Performer Files, AS. She has performed it repeatedly over the decades since, including a performance I witnessed at James Gallery, CUNY, September 7, 2016. I briefly discuss *Simultaneous Bean Reading* in chapter 3.

**90** See, for example, Maggie Nelson, *Women, The New York School, and Other True Abstractions* (University of Iowa Press, 2007). Something Else Press books by Stein: *The Making of Americans; Being a History of a Family's Progress* (1966); *Matisse, Picasso and Gertrude Stein* (1972); *A Book Concluding with As a Wife Has a Cow: A Love Story* (1973).

**91** Annea (or Anna) Lockwood, Ruth Anderson, and Jean Rigg helped facilitate the readings, though contemporaneous accounts credit Knowles as the main organizer. Rigg (misnamed John in one review) was a law student and former manager of the Merce Cunningham Dance Company. Announcement cards for the New Year's Eve readings, ca. 1976–1978, can be found in Alison Knowles Announcements and Invitations folder, JPB. See "Going Out Guide," *New York Times*, December 31, 1975, 12; Thomas Lask, "Stein Reading to Go On and On," *New York Times*, December 31, 1976, 37; Tom Johnson, "Shoe Strings, Shoes, and Gertrude Stein," *Village Voice*, January 6, 1978. Paula Cooper Gallery continued to host the New Year's Eve readings until 2000, with Knowles often participating.

92 "The Reading," Talk of the Town, *New Yorker*, January 17, 1977, 26.

93 Knowles recalls homeless men from the neighborhood sleeping near the back of the gallery for several hours at a time. Interviews with author, December 2007 and December 2012, New York.

94 Jean Rigg, quoted in Lask, "Stein Reading to Go On and On," 37.

95 While it's true that her work has never been explicitly political, and (unlike many women artists of her generation) she does not consistently view it as such even retrospectively, she concedes that there are feminist inflections in her overall practice. I address this issue and its relation to the archive in chapter 5 and in my essay in *by Alison Knowles: A Retrospective*, 31–43.

96 Helen Molesworth, "Work Avoidance: The Everyday Life of Marcel Duchamp's Readymades," *Art Journal* 57, no. 4 (Winter 1998): 50–61.

97 While first assembling *The Big Book*, Knowles did, however, direct a short film of her twin toddlers sitting on the beach for *Fluxfilms II*. See Knowles, *(Untitled) Fluxfilm No. 21*, 16 mm, b/w, silent, 1966, Collection Centre Pompidou, #F1267 (21); Maciunas, August 1966 letter to Higgins mentioning his inclusion of Knowles's "baby film" in a *Fluxfilm* program, George Maciunas Correspondence Files, JPB.

98 Knowles, "It Really *Is* a Book," 117. See *by Alison Knowles: A Retrospective*, 171. The *FingerBook of Ancient Language* was produced in collaboration with Kari Miller in two versions, the first of which Knowles premiered at Lighthouse for the Blind in New York in 1986. I am grateful to the Emily Harvey Foundation for pulling *Fingerbook* out of storage to allow me to experience the work firsthand when it was still onsite in December 2007.

99 Knowles, interview with author, Cambridge, MA, November 5, 2009. See also Knowles, "Notes on Chance," typed manuscript, n.d., AKS.

## Chapter 5

1 Alison Knowles, letter to Emmett Williams describing *The House of Dust*, June 1967, JBP; Emmett Williams Archives, Alison Knowles Correspondence, GRI. As with chapter 4, this chapter significantly builds upon Nicole L. Woods, "Object/Poems: Alison Knowles's Feminist Archite(x)ture," *X-TRA* 15, no. 1 (Fall 2012): 7–25.

2 See Steve Reich, "Tenney," *Perspectives of New Music* 25, nos. 1–2 (Winter–Summer 1987): 547–48; Douglas Kahn, "Interview with James Tenney," *LEA* 8, no. 11 (November 2000).

3 Philip Corner (with Larry Polansky), "Delicate Computations," *Perspectives of New Music* 25, nos. 1–2 (Winter–Summer 1987): 473.

4 Tenney responded in kind, composing *Scorecard No. 6: Swell Piece for Alison Knowles (1967)*, DHP. The work comes from a 1965–1971 suite of "postal pieces" that he typed on postcards and mailed to friends. The piece for Knowles gives simple instructions for sustaining and swelling tonal pitches (e.g., "Each performer plays one long tone after another . . . each tone begins as softly as possible, builds up to maximum intensity, then fades away again"). When both taught at CalArts in the early 1970s, Knowles helped Tenney print out the postcards in the Graphic Prints Lab. See Larry Polansky, *The Early Works of James Tenney*, Soundings #13 (1983). For more on Tenney's oeuvre, see Robert Wannamaker, *The Music of James Tenney*, vol. 2, *A Handbook to the Pieces* (University of Illinois Press, 2021).

5 In Knowles's contemporaneous notes, the title "A House of Dust" is used interchangeably with "Chance House," "Happenings House," and "sound houses." Her more expansive object-environment *The House of Dust* is the focus of the second part of this chapter.

6 See Jack Burnham, "Systems Esthetics," *Artforum* 7, no. 1 (September 1968): 30–35; Johanna Gosse and Timothy Stott, eds., *Nervous Systems: Art, Systems, and Politics since the 1960s* (Duke University Press, 2022).

7 On this "programmed slot-system," see Christopher T. Funkhouser, *Prehistoric Digital Poetry: An Archaeology of Forms, 1959–1995* (University of Alabama Press, 2007), 60–61. For surveys of digital art and literature, see, for example, Jack Burnham, "The Aesthetics of Intelligent Systems" (1969), in *On the Future of Art*, ed. Edward F. Fry (Viking, 1970), 95–122; and Scott Rettberg, *Electronic Literature* (Polity Press, 2019).

8 Hannah B. Higgins, *The Grid Book* (MIT Press, 2008), 247–48. In retrospect, as Higgins, Douglas Kahn, and other scholars have noted, Tenney's sessions provided a foundational model for the intersection of computational poetics, cybernetic applications, globalized media, and associated technologies in the late modernist era. See Douglas Kahn, "James Tenney at Bell Labs," in *Mainframe Experimentalism: Early Computing and the Foundations of the Digital Arts*, ed. Hannah Higgins and Douglas Kahn (University of California Press, 2012), 131–46. See also the transcript of Tenney's and Knowles's remarks at "The House of Dust Symposium," held at UC Davis in 2003 and organized by Kahn.

9 *Cybernetic Serendipity* was wildly popular and, after its London run, toured the US in 1969. See Jasia Reichardt, ed., *Cybernetic Serendipity: The Computer and the Arts* (Praeger, 1969).

10 In several papers related to *The House of Dust* (both text and environment), Knowles refers to the works as "object/poems," a descriptor that recalls the exhibition *Object Poems*, held at Something Else Gallery (her home) in spring 1966. I retain this usage throughout, as well as environment(s) and sculpture(s), terms she applies interchangeably in contemporaneous notes and in public interviews about *The House of Dust*.

11 Here I rely on work by scholars also invested in charting models of conceptual art, computational work, performance, site-specificity, institutional critique, land art, etc. See, for example, Caroline A. Jones, *Machine in the Studio: Constructing the Postwar American Artist* (University of Chicago Press, 1996); Miwon Kwon, *One Place After Another: Site-Specific Art and Locational Identity* (MIT Press, 2002); Pamela Lee, *Chronophobia: On Time in the Art of the 1960s* (MIT Press, 2004); Liz Kotz, *Words to Be Looked At: Language in 1960s Art* (MIT Press, 2007); James Nisbet, *Ecologies, Environments, and Energy Systems in Art of the 1960s and 1970s* (MIT Press, 2014); *Critical Landscapes: Art, Space, Politics*, ed. Emily Eliza Scott and Kirsten Swenson (University of California Press, 2015).

12 The computer printout of the poem appears as *Proposition No. 2 for Emmett Williams* in Dick Higgins, *Computers for the Arts* (Abyss Publications, 1970), 13; as "The House," *Studio International* (special issue, "Cybernetic Serendipity: The Computer and the Arts"; 1968): 56; and as "A House of Dust, Computer Poem," in *Fantastic Architecture*, ed. Dick Higgins and Wolf Vostell (Something Else Press, 1970), n.p. I write about Knowles and Williams's duet piece *Do You Remember* in Nicole L. Woods, "Do You Remember? Alison Knowles in Context," in *by Alison Knowles: A Retrospective (1960–2022)*, ed. Karen Moss and Lucia Fabio (University of California, Berkeley Art Museum and Pacific Film Archive, 2022), 31–43.

13 Higgins, *Grid Book*, 248. The structural matrices for generating the average number of quatrains before all possibilities have been represented is known in mathematics as the "coupon collector's problem." See, for example, Brian Dawkins, "Siobhan's Problem: The Coupon Collector Revisited," *American Statistician* 45, no. 1 (February 1991): 76–82.

14 FORTRAN (FORmula TRANslating System), a programming language developed in the mid-1950s at IBM by a team led by John W. Backus, quickly became a vital structure for the early evolution of compiling technology (now seen in C++ and Java software). See Elliot I. Organick, *A Fortran IV Primer* (Addison-Wesley, 1966); William D. Orr, *Conversational Computers* (Wiley & Sons, 1968).

15 Higgins, *Computers for the Arts*, 14. In 1968, Knowles and Higgins were photographed admiring IBM's room-size computer while visiting Toby Spiselman (whose name is incorrectly spelled on the back of the photograph). Spiselman, one of the few female mathematicians

who worked at IBM in the 1960s, was an ancillary member of the downtown avant-garde scene and a friend of Knowles, Higgins, Tenney, and Ray Johnson. She is perhaps best known for her role as "acting secretary" for Johnson's New York Correspondence School. See Dick Higgins Archive Photographs, 1970–1973, series 132, NU. *Computers for the Arts* includes Higgins's detailed annotations of the programs underlying Knowles's "A House of Dust" and his own computer-generated poem "Hank and Mary, a Love Story, a Chorale" (1967), also realized with Tenney at BPI.

**16** Several pioneering museum shows naïvely or semicritically surveyed the nexus of contemporary art and technology in the late 1960s–early 1970s, including *Cybernetic Serendipity: The Computer and the Arts* (ICA London, 1968), *The Machine as Seen at the End of the Mechanical Age* (Museum of Modern Art, New York 1968), *Software, Information Technology: It's New Meaning for Art* (Jewish Museum, New York, 1970), E.A.T.'s Pepsi-Cola Pavilion (Osaka World's Fair, 1970), and *Art and Technology* (Los Angeles County Museum of Art, 1971). The Howard Wise Gallery in New York was also instrumental in supporting new media projects. See Tina Rivers Ryan, "Wise Lights," *Art in America* 102, no. 9 (October 2014): 148–55.

**17** Knowles, "A House of Dust," 1968, GRI. Early publications of the poem's printout varied; for example, twelve stanzas were reproduced in the *Cybernetic Serendipity* exhibition catalog, thirty-six in Higgins, *Computers for the Arts*. This study has deeply benefited from my own ongoing inspection of the König Verlag version in my own collection and at the GRI. I am also a grateful recipient of Knowles's generosity in tearing off pages, of even stacks, of the poem as a parting gift.

**18** See Joan Didion, *Slouching Towards Bethlehem* (Farrar, Straus and Giroux, 1968); Theodore Roszak, *The Making of a Counterculture: Reflections on the Technocratic Society and Its Youthful Opposition* (University of California Press, 1995). For more recent art historical studies, see Elissa Auther and Adam Lerner, eds., *West of Center: Art and the Counterculture Experiment in America, 1965–1977* (University of Minnesota Press, 2011); James Meyer, *The Art of Return: The Sixties and Contemporary Culture* (University of Chicago Press, 2019); and Thomas Crow, *The Artist in the Counterculture: Bruce Conner to Mike Kelley and Other Tales from the Edge* (Princeton University Press, 2023).

**19** Beginning in the late 1950s, Knowles and Higgins marched in peace parades in New York City, as well as protests against capital punishment and the military draft. Knowles would continue marching against other US conflicts in later decades (e.g., the 2003 leadup to the war in Iraq). See correspondence with Carter and Mary Higgins (1959–1961), DHP. Knowles, interview with author, December 15, 2007, New York City. I return to their politics in the epilogue.

**20** Some studies date this initial printout (a small edition of twenty-one pages) to 1967. While that is certainly possible, as the brothers first printed art books under the name Gebrüder König Verlag that year, it is more likely the poem was printed in 1968.

**21** That year the Peace Prize of the German Book Trade was awarded to Senegal's controversial first president, Léopold Senghor, also a renowned poet and intellectual. Frankfurt SDS protesters denounced the award, citing Senghor's increasing authoritarian rule, and violently clashed with police forces outside the exhibition hall. See Henry Raymont, "Police Guards Leave the Book Fair in Frankfurt," *New York Times*, September 24, 1968, 15; Timothy Scott Brown, *West Germany and the Global Sixties: The Antiauthoritarian Revolt, 1962–1978*, New Studies in European History (Cambridge University Press, 2013), 116–54.

**22** Hans Ulrich Obrist, interview with Walther König, *032c 21*, March 26, 2012, 190–97, https://032c.com/2012/walther-koenig-cologne/.

**23** Obrist, interview with König, *032c 21*. A postcard to me from Kasper König in October 2016 confirmed sending the original tapes to his brother. On König's important relationship to Knowles, Fluxus, intermedia, and conceptual art, see Benjamin H. D. Buchloh, "Kasper König (1943–2024)," *October*, no. 190 (Fall 2024): 11–16.

**24** Reviewing the König printout under his alias Camille Gordon, Dick Higgins suggested that editions could be rendered in five hundred, fifteen-page poems. See Higgins, "Camille Reports #3" (1970), Dick Higgins papers, 1958–1997, AAA.

**25** Zabet Patterson, "Poemfields," in *Peripheral Vision: Bell Labs, the S-C 4020, and the Origins of Computer Art* (MIT Press, 2015), 76. See also Gloria Sutton, "Words within Words: The Poetics of Computer-Generated Film," in *The Experience Machine: Stan VanDerBeek's Movie-Drome and Expanded Cinema* (MIT Press, 2015), 161–89.

**26** Benjamin H. D. Buchloh, "The Book of the Future: Alison Knowles's *The House of Dust*," in Higgins and Kahn, *Mainframe Experimentalism*, 204; reprinted in *by Alison Knowles: A Retrospective*, 259–62.

**27** Knowles, "The House of Dust: A Chronicle," *New Wilderness Letter* 8 (Spring 1980): 18.

**28** *The Epic of Gilgamesh*, trans. Maureen Gallery Kovacs (Stanford University Press, 2016). The "Dream of Enkidu" appears in Jerome Rothenberg, *Technicians of the Sacred: A Range of Poetries from Africa, America, Asia, Europe, and Oceania* (University of California Press, 1968), 65–66. Curator Maud Jacquin found historical precedent for Knowles's environments in "hospitable texts" and "architectural poems," including Stéphane Mallarmé's *Le Livre*, on the panel "Ecologies: Material, Social and Feminist" (with myself and Hannah Higgins) at "Reframing The House of Dust: A Symposium," Roy and Edna Disney/CalArts Theater, Los Angeles (2018). I am grateful to Maud and Hannah (as well as Sara Mameni, Karen Moss, and Janet Sarbanes) for their generous feedback and vibrant discussion when I presented an early version of this chapter.

**29** Knowles has been invited to recite the poem many times in museums, galleries, and other settings; her voice and pacing is always a distinctive feature of the live experience of the text. See, for example, her May 2011 reading of "A House of Dust" at a "A Celebration of American Poetry," hosted by the Obama White House, http://www.youtube.com/watch?v=-68Z708lFsY.

**30** Knowles asked Cage to "sponsor" her Guggenheim application, and he enthusiastically wrote a supportive letter. In one exchange with Cage, she adds another quatrain for the application: "a house of broken dishes among other houses in place with both heavy rains and bright sun, etc." See 1967–1969 letters between the two in John Cage Ephemera, Correspondence Files, University Music Library, Northwestern University. In art historical publications related to *The House of Dust*, the Guggenheim award date is often misstated as 1969. Knowles's use of the term "physicalize" is from an unpublished typed statement, dated October 3, 1977, House of Dust Files, AKS.

**31** In letters to Billy Klüver of E.A.T. about the Chelsea siting, Knowles cites the quatrain "A HOUSE OF ABANDONED MATERIALS / IN A METROPOLIS / USING NATURAL LIGHT / INHABITED BY PEOPLE FROM MANY WALKS OF LIFE." In a slightly later note to her friend and collector Wolfgang Hahn, she quotes yet another quatrain: "A HOUSE OF PLASTIC / IN A METROPOLIS / LIGHTED BY NATURAL LIGHT / INHABITED BY CHILDREN AND OLD PEOPLE." See Knowles, "Request for Technical Services," ca. 1968, Experiments in Art and Technology Records (E.A.T.), General Correspondence, Jan–March 1969, GRI; letter to Galerie Tobiés & Silex, July 23, 1969, Collection Museum moderner Kunst Stiftung Ludwig Wien, Vienna.

**32** Knowles, in conversation with Charlie Morrow, "A Dialogue: The House of Dust," *New Wilderness Letter* 8 (Spring 1980): 21; Knowles, "House of Dust History," typed notes, House of Dust Files, AKS. Knowles's forms bear a remarkable resemblance to architect Frederick Kiesler's *Endless House*, included in MoMA's 1960 exhibition *Visionary Architecture*, which Knowles surely saw. See Frederick J. Kiesler, *Inside the Endless House* (Simon & Schuster, 1966).

33 Knowles, letter to John T. O'Neill, Commissioner of New York City Building Department, April 25, 1969. In this letter, Knowles mentions being "most eager to have these enclosures well underway by the time school is out for the summer." See House of Dust Files, AKS. My deepest thanks to Knowles for providing a suite of documentary materials related to all facets of *The House of Dust* over the course of several years.

34 Knowles, letter to Alloway, June 26, 1968, Lawrence Alloway papers, Topics and Artists Files, GRI. Knowles met Alloway as early as 1965 as he was assembling notes for a planned retrospective of Fluxus, and later an exhibition of *The Big Book* and Fluxus at SUNY Stony Brook and UC San Diego (more on this show in chapter 4). See Lawrence Alloway papers, Fluxus Ephemera, 1959–1965, GRI. In January 1967, Alloway was also listed as an editorial staff member of *Intermedia*, a new bimonthly magazine to be published by Knowles and Higgins's Something Else Press. See, *Call It Something Else: Something Else Press, Inc. (1963–1974)*, ed. Alice Centamore and Christian Xatrec (Museo Reina Sofia, 2023), 173, 230.

35 See the exchange of letters (1967–1969) between Knowles and Klüver in the Experiments in Art and Technology Records (E.A.T.), General Correspondence, GRI.

36 Penn South, also known as ILGWU Cooperative Village, was established in the 1950s by the United Housing Foundation (UHF) to address the city's urgent need for moderate-income housing. The ILGWU was drawn to the limited-equity co-op model and used pension funds to support its construction. It was dedicated on May 19, 1962, by President John F. Kennedy, Governor Nelson A. Rockefeller, former first lady Eleanor Roosevelt, urban planner Robert Moses, ILGWU president David Dubrinsky, and other dignitaries. See Abraham E. Kazan, "ILGWU Cooperative Village: A Dream Come True," undated flyer published by the UHF, ILGWU Publications, Kheel Center for Labor-Management Documentation & Archives, Cornell University Library; Tony Schuman, "Labor and Housing in New York City: Architect Herman Jessor and the Cooperative Housing Movement," in *Constructed Identity: Proceedings of the 86th ACSA Annual Meeting & Technology Conference*, ed. Craig Barton (1998): 622–62.

37 In several letters (1967–1969), Knowles updated Cage on the project's progress. John Cage Ephemera, Correspondence Files, University Music Library, Northwestern University.

38 "Play Sculpture Approved: Other Recreation Plans Set," *Penn South Newsletter* 2, no. 5, March 1969.

39 Like Tenney, Neuhaus was an artist-in-residence at Bell Labs in 1968, where he experimented with acoustics and electronics. His work, consistent with Knowles's objectives in this project, often sought to expand visual phenomena into acoustical material keyed to "chance" operations like the rising and setting of the sun. See Knowles, "The House of Dust: A Chronicle," *New Wilderness Letter* 8, 17; Knowles, letter to Cage, October 1968, John Cage Ephemera, Correspondence Files, University Music Library, Northwestern University. Power for the sound circuits reached the object/poem via underground cables; speakers were placed at four- to five-foot intervals. Knowles, "Happening House (physical description)," E.A.T. Records, Artists' Membership Forms (1967–1969 K–L), GRI.

40 Charles Eppley, "Soundsites: Max Neuhaus, Site-Specificity, and the Materiality of Sound as Place" (PhD diss., Stony Brook University, 2017), 143.

41 Knowles, "House of Dust," audiotape reel, February 18, 1970. Audio Visual Materials, Reel-to-reel audiotapes, 1965–1987, R7, JBP. In an April 12, 1970, letter to her friend Carl Weissner, a German writer and translator of experimental fiction whom she met while he was living in New York, Knowles describes the "House of Dust" tapes as "an amazing bunch of on

the site interviews after the explosion. I hope I can make something out of them. The houses themselves arrive in L.A. around May 20." Alison Knowles, 1968–1971, Correspondence, Series 1, Carl Weissner Archive, MS22, NU.

42 Knowles, "House of Dust," audiotape reel, February 18, 1970, JBP.

43 Knowles, "House of Dust," audiotape reel, February 18, 1970, JBP. Neither the recording itself nor related documentation at the Getty give the full name of Knowles's interlocutor. My best guess is that "Linda" is performance artist Linda Montano, a lifelong friend of Knowles beginning in the late 1960s in New York. Knowles and Montano (who was the partner of Pauline Oliveros in the early 1970s when all three were based in California) frequently wrote to each other about their lives and work. See Correpondence with Alison Knowles (1965–1987), Pauline Oliveros papers, JPB 94–5, Music Division, New York Public Library for the Performing Arts.

44 Knowles, quoted in "The House of Dust by Alison Knowles," *Experiments in Art and Technology Bulletin* 7 (January 1971): 9. On the poetic "elements" see Knowles, typed notes, House of Dust Files, AKS. On Raskin, see Knowles, "Dialogue: The House of Dust," 22.

45 Knowles, "House of Dust History," typed notes, House of Dust Files, AKS; Knowles, "House of Dust," audiotape reel, February 18, 1970, JBP. There is no hint on the tape on how she affixed the objects to the fiberglass surface, aside from embedding them with more coats of resin. This printout (and later a third version) would act as a structuring device for performances at CalArts around the *House of Dust* environments, as discussed in the next part of this chapter.

46 Knowles, "Happening House (physical description)," E.A.T. Records, Artists' Membership Forms (1967–1969 K–L), GRI.

47 Knowles, quoted in "House of Dust by Alison Knowles" (*Experiments in Art and Technology Bulletin*), 9. Much of the material published in this E.A.T. bulletin is collaged fragments from typed notes and visual materials I have found in Knowles's House of Dust Files, AKS. Some of the notes and summaries she wrote pop up as photocopies in other archives (Higgins, AS; JBP; GRI; EHF, etc.) or were collated by Knowles when preparing funding applications for the environments' new uses in the later 1970s and 1980s.

48 "Bldg. 4 Petitions Against Sculpture," *Penn South Newsletter* 2, March 1969.

49 Knowles, "The House of Dust: A Chronicle," *New Wilderness Letter* 8, 21.

50 See "Bldg. 4 Petitions Against Sculpture," *Penn South Newsletter*, no. 2, March 1969; "Play Sculpture Site May be Changed," *Penn South Newsletter*, no. 7, June 1969; "Sculpture Is Burned on Penn South Lawn," *Chelsea Clinton News*, October 23, 1969, 3. On contentious reactions to public art more generally, see Miwon Kwon, "Sitings of Public Art: Integration Versus Intervention," *One Place After Another: Site-Specific Art and Locational Identity* (MIT Press, 2004), 56–99.

51 Knowles, "The House of Dust: A Chronicle," *New Wilderness Letter* 8, 18. In another summary of events after the fire, she notes, "They say the explosion lifted the sculpture several feet off the ground. The stench of burning plastic remained in the area for weeks." Knowles, House of Dust Files, AKS.

52 Knowles, interview with author, December 15, 2007, New York City. The remains were shipped by flatbed truck back to Philadelphia and redipped in fiberglass in preparation for her 1970 move to California.

53 Initial contact letter proposal from Knowles to E.A.T.'s "Projects Outside Art" includes the news clipping that describes the lawn fire and other documentation. "Projects Outside Art" Proposals, E.A.T. Records, GRI. For a brief history of the "Projects Outside Art" program, see Michelle Kuo, "No Limits" in *E.A.T. Experiments in Art and Technology*, ed., Sabine Breitwieser (Salzburg, Vienna: Museum der Moderne, 2015), 163–81.

54 Knowles, letter to Klüver, July 25, 1970, sent from her new Los Angeles address. Knowles, "Request for Technical Services Form," January 23, 1968, E.A.T. Records, GRI.

55 Knowles, quoted in "House of Dust by Alison Knowles" (*Experiments in Art and Technology Bulletin*), 9. I return to this quote as it relates to the CalArts iterations of environments.

56 Szeemann's 1970 exhibition was the first examination of Fluxus by a major art institution. Previously, as detailed in chapter 2, Fluxus was a self-curating operation based on sharing and performing each other's works that traversed national borders but elicited limited critical response. See the collection of documents reprinted in Szeemann's *Happening & Fluxus* (Kölnischer Kunstverein, 1970); Magdalena Holdar, "Doing Things Together: Objectives and Effects of Harald Szeemann's *Happening & Fluxus*, 1970," *Journal of Curatorial Studies* 6, no. 1 (2017): 90–114; and Hans Ulrich Obrist's interview with Szeemann in *A Brief History of Curating* (JPR/Ringier, 2008), 112–13. Other archival materials related to the exhibition are in the Archiv Sohm, Staatsgalerie Stuttgart; Dick Higgins Archive, MS132, Charlotte Moorman Archive, AS9, NU; and Harald Szeemann Archive, GRI.

57 Knowles noted the potential issue with missing or stolen shoes by adding, "The nature of my contribution to the show will entail just a little concern setting up and maintaining it." See Knowles letter to Szeemann, August 4, 1970, Happening & Fluxus (1970) binder, Harald Szeemann papers, 1800-2011 (bulk 1949–2005), GRI. The mention of fifty-eight pairs of shoes collected from PS11 and PS38 in New York on view at the Kunstvervein is cited by Knowles in *Experiments in Art and Technology Los Angeles*, January 1971, 8.

58 Knowles, letter to Szeemann, August 4, 1970. Happening & Fluxus (1970) binder, GRI.

59 I am specifically thinking of the broken shoe parts in Knowles's *Gentle Surprises for the Ear* (1974–1975); collaged information about shoes in her opera *Gem Duck* (1977); screen prints from burned shoes found on the Bay of Naples in *Leone d'Oro* (1978); paper shoes in *Lentils Over Cotton Slippers* (1986–1988); and a cyanotype made from shoe heels dedicated to her son-in-law Joseph Reinstein in *For Joe* (2002).

60 Richard Serra, letter to Donald Thalacker, Director, Art-in-Architecture Program, General Services Administration, Washington, DC, January 1, 1985. Reprinted in Clara Weyegraf-Serra and Martha Buskirk, eds., *The Destruction of Tilted Arc: Documents* (MIT Press, 1991), 38.

61 Paul Brach, "Cal Arts: The Early Years," *Art Journal* 42, no. 1 (Spring 1982): 28.

62 Knowles, letter to Jan Herman, July 4, 1969. Correspondence, Series 1. Jan Herman Archive, MS51, NU. Higgins also taught briefly at CalArts. But he and Knowles had begun divorce proceedings by late 1969, and he permanently returned to the East Coast after the 1971 San Fernando earthquake. Knowles lived in various communities in and around Los Angeles, including Fillmore, Newhall, Hollywood, and Piru, where she shared a home with Van Riper, Simone Forti, Charlemagne Palestine, Nam June Paik, Shuya Abe, Richard Teitelbaum, Josef Bogdanovich, and sometimes, students who rented rooms. See Knowles's contemporaneous exchanges of letters with Herman and Weissner (NU), Higgins (Dick Higgins papers, AS), and Williams (Emmett Williams Archive, Alison Knowles Correspondence, JBP).

63 The poem's thousands of possible randomized permutations allowed for as many physical manifestations. Author's email exchange with Knowles, May 2, 2012.

64 In a December 1971 letter to Higgins, Knowles notes the high cost of the *House of Dust* sound system (over $400) and "stiff" city regulations governing the use of underground cables. A September 1971 letter mentions that the environments were added as a "legitimate course" with a budget, approved by the School of Art for the Environments, Happenings, and Conceptual Art, under which Knowles taught her classes. See Higgins Correspondence Files (KI–KN), AS; School of Art Records, 1969–1976, California Institute of the Arts Library &

Institute Archives. In House of Dust files (AKS), Knowles describes the sound-circuit box being moved to the floor in this iteration: "for at least a year the Sun Song was heard at the original CalArts campus in Burbank."

65 Knowles, letter to Higgins, August 11, 1970, Higgins Correspondence Files (KI–KN), AS.

66 Knowles, untitled statement, August 1970, House of Dust Files, AKS.

67 Knowles, typed notes, September 1970, House of Dust Files, AKS.

68 In the 1970s, Dana Winslow Atchley III toured the US as "Ace the Colorado Spaceman" and published, as Ace Space Co., *Space Atlas: Visions, Charts, Maps, Plans, Reflections* (1971), a copy of which can be found in JBP. In *Space* Pack* 2 (Winter Solstice Newsletter, 1971), he writes of *The House of Dust*, "Ace Space Co. has been invited to coordinate one of eight sections radiating from the center; section 7; West to Northwest; quantity 19; weight 124 (refer to hexagrams 19 and 20 from the *I Ching*). I would like to request all correspondents to consider this space (which is situated along a sharply rising hill and onto a plateau) and to contribute whatever they wish to the House of Dust." Alison Knowles, House of Dust Folder, AS. Atchley's connection to *The House of Dust* is noted by reporter Thomas Albright in "Correspondence Art," *Rolling Stone*, no. 107, April 27, 1972, 28–29. Albright also interviewed Fluxus-West artist Ken Friedman at length for the article.

69 Voda's *Chance Chants* can be found online at https://www.youtube.com/watch?v=QchceC3rV2k (accessed June 10, 2014). Knowles, letter to Higgins, May 25, 1972, describes Abe's use of "another" of his video synthesizers. Higgins Correspondence Files (KI–KN), AS. Knowles remembers attending a screening of Voda's film in autumn 1979 at Anthology Film Archives, New York. Knowles, interview with author, New York, March 18, 2018.

70 "Poetry Drop at CalArts," announcement, *Los Angeles Times*, May 1971. See also school memoranda announcing the event to editors and assignment desks at local newspapers. The public relations contact noted the possibility of interested participants' "acquiring a canto of the sky poem." CalArts Library Special Collections & Institute Archives.

71 Poem-drop announcement postcards (with various quatrains) can be found in the collections of GRI, SFA, AS, and UCSD. An earlier edition of postcards depicting single images with different overlaid quatrains was published in Heidelberg (1968) drawing on König Verlag's printout of the poem. In July 1971, Knowles mailed the poem-drop postcards to family and friends, including her twins, Hannah and Jessica, who were then living in Vermont with Higgins. She would continue mailing HOD postcards to friends in the 1970s and 1980s.

72 Michael Rosanoff Plesset was director of computing and information systems at JPL in the 1970s. In more recent interviews, Knowles has misidentified James Tenney as her contact and collaborator at JPL. See, for example, Janet Sarbanes, "A School Based on What Artists Wanted to Do: Alison Knowles on CalArts," *East of Borneo*, August 7, 2012, https://eastofborneo.org/articles/a-school-based-on-what-artists-wanted-to-do-alison-knowles-on-calarts/.

73 "I'll use it in my environments class and in the ongoing House of Dust project." Knowles, letter to Cage, September 20, 1970. "Guess what? . . . We'll never have to toss another coin!" Cage had written to Knowles, September 25, 1967, telling her of ICHING. For both letters, and related correspondence, see John Cage Ephemera, Correspondence Files, Music Library, Northwestern University. Cage's is reprinted in *The Selected Letters of John Cage*, ed. Laura Kuhn (Wesleyan University Press, 2016), 373. Hiller, who founded the Experimental Music Studios at the University of Illinois at Urbana-Champaign, arranged an academic residency there for Cage. Beginning in 1967, the two collaborated on Cage's computer-assisted multimedia event-spectacle *HPSCHD* (pronounced "harpsichord"), which was first staged at UIUC on May 16, 1969, using the school's ILLIAC II supercomputer. In an interview with Larry Austin, Cage recalled it had taken six weeks to produce an operable subroutine to

"[teach] the computer to toss coins" and Hiller detailed how they combined such tosses to "generate a number between one and sixty-four," from which they then derived amplitude and time-scale values. Austin, "John Cage and Lejaren Hiller, *HPSCHD*" (1968), in *Source—Music of the Avant-Garde, 1966–1973*, ed. Larry Austin and Douglas Kahn (University of California Press, 2011), 150, 158. See Lejaren A. Hiller Jr., "Programming the *I-Ching* Oracle," *Computer Studies in the Humanities and Verbal Behavior* 3 (1970): 130–43; Tiffany Funk, "John Cage and Lejaren A. Hiller, Jr., *HPSCHD*," in *Coded: Art Enters the Computer Age, 1952–1982*, ed. Leslie Jones (Delmonico Books/Los Angeles County Museum of Art, 2023), 206–9; Branden W. Joseph, "*HPSCHD*—Ghost or Monster?" in Higgins and Kahn, *Mainframe Experimentalism*, 147–69.

74 Kaprow's film (now in Allan Kaprow papers, GRI) was screened in the exhibition *by Alison Knowles: A Retrospective* (BAMPFA, 2022). I greatly benefited from many previous viewings at GRI.

75 Knowles, "A Summary of Performance Events for the HOUSE OF DUST," attachment B, typed, undated, House of Dust Files, EHF. On the role of experimental pedagogy in this era, see Karen Moss, "Performance into Pedagogy: Anna Halprin, Allan Kaprow, and Alison Knowles' Score-Based Events in Experimental Arts Education" (PhD diss., University of Southern California, 2016).

76 Knowles, "Poem Drop Event" (1977), typed summary, House of Dust Files, EHF. Knowles continues: "It was a very successful event and received five minutes of coverage on the evening news from Los Angeles. Maintenance people had expected to work overtime to clean the poetry from the grounds. There was none left. Everybody took a scrap home."

77 Stephen Fredman, a scholar of postwar art and poetry, now professor emeritus at the University of Notre Dame, was a student at CalArts during Knowles's tenure. My sincere thanks to Steve for sharing his personal trove of CalArts syllabi, memoranda, and other archival materials with me.

78 For more on Moorman's festivals, including Knowles's involvement, see the Charlotte Moorman Archive, AS9, NU. For photo documentation of Johnson's *Hot Dog Drop*, see https://www.rayjohnsonestate.com/performance-art#tab:slideshow;slide:5.

79 See Michael J. Arlen, *Living-Room War: Writings About Television* (Viking, 1969). Al Hansen and Wolf Vostell, Knowles's close Fluxus friends, also made reference to the Vietnam War using imagery of military aircraft. See Hansen, "Lettuce Manifesto" (e.g., "Lettuce drop planeloads of ham sandwiches in cellophane, and mirrors and beads on the Viet Cong"), in *Manifestos* (Great Bear Pamphlet, 1966), 18; Vostell, *B2 Lipstick Bomber* (1968), Museum of Modern Art, New York, #609.2016.

80 See Amy Scott, Luis Garza, and Colin Gunckel, eds., *La Raza* (Autry Museum of the American West/UCLA Chicano Studies Research Center Press, 2020).

81 In the 1960s, California received 25 percent of all Defense Department contracts. Gary Wills, *Reagan's America* (Penguin, 1988), 376–77. During the week of the helicopter poem-drop, various political events were happening in the LA area, including, at CalArts, a speech by a Senegalese Liberation Front activist, a lecture on "The Politics of Equality" by James Hurtak, and a protest promoting a boycott of Standard Oil by the Peace Action Council. The school's calendar also listed an off-campus event at the Hollywood Bowl: "Acting in Concert to End Genocidal War and Repression," presented by the Entertainment Industry for Peace and Justice, with Jim Brown, Sammy Davis Jr., Jane Fonda, Sally Kellerman, Donald Sutherland, George Takei, and others scheduled to appear. See Knowles, House of Dust Folder, AS. On student activism in California, see, for example, Todd Gitlin, *The Sixties: Years of Hope, Days of Rage* (Random House, 1989); Gerard J. De Groot, "Ronald Reagan and Student Unrest in California, 1966–1970," *Pacific Historical Review* 65, no. 1 (1996): 107–29; and

Francis Franscina, *Art, Politics and Dissent: Aspects of the Art Left in Sixties America* (Manchester University Press, 1999).

**82** The computational basis for *99 Red North* derived from Knowles and Raskin's compass printout with an added element by Andrew Schloss, whose contributions are discussed later in this chapter.

**83** References to compass and color directions for *The House of Dust* can be found in Matt Mullican's contemporaneous student notebooks. See, for example, Mullican, "CalArts, Early Conceptual Work" (1972), box 2, folder 7, Matt Mullican papers, circa 1968–2017, AAA. Knowles's "Summary of Performance Events for the HOUSE OF DUST" (EHF) lists another event by Mullican: "He performed alone with the direction North/yellow/5. At five o'clock he drove his yellow pickup truck adjacent to the House of Dust and parked for a while. He did this for one week. (No documentation.)"

**84** See Knowles, "Apple Exchange Event by Alison Knowles," typed notes, u.d., House of Dust Files, EHF. For photos of the quadrant at *The House of Dust*, see *by Alison Knowles: A Retrospective*, 127–28.

**85** A poster announcing Knowles's *Gift Event II* (1972) reads, "House of Dust—Spring Event—April 28—2 o'clock at House of Dust. Gift Event II is from the Book of Events section of SHAKING THE PUMPKIN. . . . The event is attributed to Kwakiutl Indians." Alison Knowles House of Dust Folder, AS. See also Knowles, *by Alison Knowles* (Great Bear Pamphlet, 1965), 12; Rothenberg, *Poems For the Game of Silence: 1960–1970* (Dial Press, 1971), 131; Rothenberg, *Shaking the Pumpkin: Traditional Poetry of the Indian North Americas* (Doubleday, 1972), 188. Many studies on *The House of Dust* erroneously list or presume *Gift Event II* as a work conceived exclusively by Knowles. Chapter 4 discusses Knowles and Rothenberg's other collaborations.

**86** See Jerome Rothenberg, *Ritual: A Book of Primitive Rites and Events* (Great Bear Pamphlet, 1966), 8; Helen Codere, "The Amiable Side of Kwakiutl Life: The Potlatch and the Play Potlatch," *American Anthropologist* 58, no. 2 (April 1956): 334–51.

**87** See Knowles, "Gift Event II" in "A Summary of Performance Events for the HOUSE OF DUST," EHF; "Alison Knowles: House of Dust," in *The Amazing Decade: Women and Performance Art in America, 1970–1980*, ed. Moira Roth and Mary Jane Jacob (Astro Artz, 1983), 108; Knowles, "Dialogue: The House of Dust," 23.

**88** Knowles, "Gift Event II"; MCA (supplemental materials given by Knowles to curator Mary Jane Jacob for *The Amazing Decade*). There are many more images documenting this event than can be reproduced here. I encourage others to seek them out in AKS and in CalArts's photo archives.

**89** Moss, "Performance into Pedagogy," 223.

**90** See Janet Sarbanes, "A School Based on What Artists Wanted to Do: Alison Knowles on CalArts," *East of Borneo*.

**91** Stephen Fredman, conversation with author, October 12, 2016, Notre Dame, IN. Fredman recalled students' practical and illicit uses of *The House of Dust* as a regular feature of the sculptures' use. Norman Kaplan, instigator of the "Poem Drop," recounted a similar memory in a conversation following a talk I gave on Knowles at the Graduate Center, City University of New York, September 2016.

**92** Knowles, "Dialogue: The House of Dust," 22–23.

**93** Knowles, interview with author, Cambridge, MA, November 5, 2009. Exhibitions of the object/poem gifts documentation and photographs were included in the traveling exhibition *The Amazing Decade: Women and Performance Art in America, 1970–1980*, organized by Mary Jane Jacobs and Moira Roth. Knowles first collaborated with Roth at the Duchamp Festival at UC Irvine in 1971 (see chapter 3).

**94** The works were installed in precisely this format in *The House of Dust by Alison Knowles*, James Gallery, CUNY Graduate Center, September 2016. Knowles also included commissioned works by friends and interlocutors in other key works, including *The Big Book*, *The Book of Bean*, and *The Boat Book*.

**95** Ever faithful to the "fluxed nature of chance," Knowles is not only unbothered by such changes, but eagerly welcomes them. Students made still more changes, she reports, during her 2016 exhibition at CUNY, including the addition of "Inhabited by Indigenous people wearing all colors." Knowles, conversation with author, September 10, 2016, New York.

**96** Dianne Harris, *Little White Houses: How the Postwar Home Constructed Race in America* (University of Minnesota Press, 2013), 113.

**97** See Stephen Phillips, "Plastics" in *Cold War Hothouses: Inventing Postwar Culture, from Cockpit to Playboy*, ed. Beatriz Colomina, Annemarie Brennan, and Jeannie Kim (Princeton Architectural Press, 2004), 91–123.

**98** In the late 1960s, Knowles maintained a consistently attentive focus on domesticity, urban housing, and the idea of her home as a chance-based performance space. See, for example, her letters to Milan Knížák, Emmett Williams, and Dick Higgins, ca. 1967, Dick Higgins Correspondence Files, AS.

**99** See Rosalind Krauss, "Sculpture in the Expanded Field" *October*, no. 8 (Spring 1979): 30–44.

**100** Schwitters assembled at least three versions of the sprawling, accumulative *Merzbau*, starting the first in Hannover in 1923. The third iteration (ca. 1947), supported by a stipend from MoMA while he was living in Great Britain, was left unfinished when Schwitters died on January 8, 1948.

**101** William S. Rubin, *Dada, Surrealism, and Their Heritage* (Museum of Modern Art/New York Graphic Society, 1968), 56.

**102** Rubin, *Dada, Surrealism*, 57. Knowles, Higgins, Joseph Beuys, and other Fluxus artists were invested in Schwitters's art, and so too Rauschenberg, Jasper Johns, and the Nouveau Réalistes. See Gwendolen Webster, *Kurt Merz Schwitters: A Biographical Study* (University of Wales Press, 1997); Wolf Vostell and Dick Higgins, eds., *Fantastic Architecture* (Something Else Press, 1969).

**103** For a copy of the call for projects, see AS. For correspondence between Higgins and contributors, see DHP.

**104** In order of appearance, the book features contributions by Vostell, Gerhard Rühm, Jean Tinguely, Raoul Hausmann, Claes Oldenburg, Schwitters, Erich Buchholz, Geoffrey Hendricks, Hans Hollein, Pol Bury, Stefan Wewerka, Addi Koepcke (Arthur Køpcke), Lawrence Weiner, Vostell, Buckminster Fuller, Joseph Beuys, Oldenburg, Carolee Schneemann, Jan Jacob Herman, Vostell, Michael Heizer, Dennis Oppenheim, Heizer, Jan Dibbets, Higgins, John Cage, Douglas Huebler, Alison Knowles, Geoffrey Hendricks, Bici Hendricks, Richard Hamilton, Diter Rot, Robert Filliou, Ay-O, Milan Knížák, Frances Starr, Philip Corner, Ben Vautier, Vostell, Franz Mon, Hollein, K. H. Hoedicke, Oldenburg, Hausmann, and Hamilton.

**105** Caption 5: Ecology, Caption 13: Systems, in *Fantastic Architecture*, n.p.

**106** Vostell, *Fantastic Architecture*, n.p. (emphases in original).

**107** Higgins, introduction, *Fantastic Architecture*, n.p. These aesthetic and material questions would flourish well into the late 1970s, as documented in another anthology with the same title: Michael Schuyt and Joost Elffers, eds., *Fantastic Architecture: Personal and Eccentric Visions* (Harry N. Abrams, 1980). Buckminster Fuller, Kurt Schwitters, and Jean Tinguely are included in this survey.

**108** Kate Steinitz, quoted in *The Art of Assemblage*, 50.

**109** Elizabeth Thomas, "In Search of Lost Art: Kurt Schwitters's *Merzbau*," MoMA blog post,

July 9, 2012, https://www.moma.org/explore/inside_out/2012/07/09/in-search-of-lost-art-kurt-schwitterss-merzbau/.

**110** Notable exceptions include Johanna Drucker's discussion of Knowles's book projects in *The Century of Artist's Books* (Granary Books, 2004), 152–53, 345–47; and the collection of primary source materials related to *The Big Book* in Meghan DellaCrosse, ed., *Alison Knowles: The Big Book* (Passenger Books, 2013).

**111** Knowles, interview with author, Cambridge, MA, November 5, 2009. On intergenerational Fluxus performance and its historical explication and reception, see Jennie Klein, "Fluxus Familias," *PAJ: A Journal of Performance and Art* 26, no. 3 (September 2004): 128–35.

**112** Knowles, stanza from "A House of Dust" reproduced in *Fantastic Architecture*, n.p. Tenney and Schneemann secretly married in 1956 and worked closely together through their split in early 1968.

**113** Schneemann, "The Nerve Ends Room," *Parts of a Body House*, in *Fantastic Architecture*, n.p. Schneemann later expanded *Parts of a Body House* into an artist's book (published in an edition of sixty by Felipe Ehrenberg's Beau Geste Press, 1972), which she explicitly conceptualized as a "prototype for [her] 'big book' . . . each element culled from mounds of related material." Pages of the artist's book are reproduced in Sabine Breitwieser, ed., *Carolee Schneemann: Kinetic Painting* (Museum der Moderne, Salzburg/Prestel, 2015), 214.

**114** Lucy R. Lippard, "Centers and Fragments: Women's Spaces," in *Women in American Architecture: A Historic and Contemporary Perspective*, ed. Susana Torre (Watson-Guptill, 1977), 187. Most previous accounts of *The House of Dust*'s reception have neglected Lippard's essay, or the work's inclusion in the influential anthology *Open Poetry*, ed. George Quasha (Simon & Schuster, 1972).

**115** Lippard, "Center and Fragments," 187.

**116** Knowles, interview with author, November 11, 2009, New York City.

**117** Miriam Schapiro, "The Education of Women as Artists: Project Womanhouse," *Art Journal* 31, no. 3 (Spring 1972): 270.

**118** Paula Harper, "The First Feminist Art Program: A View from the 1980s," in *Entering the Picture: Judy Chicago, the Fresno Feminist Art Program, and the Collective Visions of Women Artists*, ed. Jill Fields (Routledge, 2012), 97.

**119** Schapiro, "Education of Women," 270. Knowles suspected the technical nature of the Graphic Prints Lab might attract more male students and took care to emphasize the collaborative aspect of her artistic ethos in her "Silk Screen" course syllabus, which encouraged all students to engage in "live performance" and proposed two related off-campus events for students ("Recycling Event" and "Swap Meet Event"). "The emphasis of the workshop," she explained, "is on printed images. . . . The other aspect of the shop is its concern with events and happenings, relating two-dimensional art into experiential art." A copy of the syllabus is in my collection, generously shared by Steve Fredman from his personal CalArts materials.

**120** See Knowles, letter to Higgins, August 11, 1974, DHP.

**121** Aviva Rahmani, "Alison Knowles: An Interview," in *M/E/A/N/I/N/G: An Anthology of Artists' Writings, Theory, and Criticism*, ed. Susan Bee and Mira Schor (Duke University Press, 2000), 364. In the interview, Rahmani calls Knowles the "most supportive" of all her teachers at CalArts and acknowledges the importance of her mentorship.

**122** Bell, "Programs, Projects, and Offerings," typed course proposal to Maurice Stein. The early morning poetry class took place Wednesdays at *The House of Dust*, then sited on the Burbank campus. See Knowles, House of Dust Files, AKS. Stein was the founding dean of CalArts' School of Critical Studies and coauthor, with Larry Miller, of *Blueprint for Counter Education* (Doubleday, 1970), a defining work of experimental pedagogy valued by Knowles.

**123** This sensibility was once directly observed by Knowles. In an interview with George Myers, she noted, "The art that interests me isn't solving any problems or even hoping to make things better, but has the quality of lightening, brightening, questioning and a kind of tropic turn is given to reality." Knowles, unpublished interview with George Myers, ca. 1977, Dick Higgins Archive, NU.

**124** The exhibition *Primary Structures* at the Jewish Museum (1966), the huge survey *American Sculpture of the Sixties* at LACMA (1967), and the establishment of new federal programs like the NEA's Art in Public Places Program attest to this valuation.

**125** "Widespread desire for non-traditional forms of behavior and art, surging feminist solidarity, and nascent environmentalism moved innovative women artists (especially sculptors) who worked in nature into a new presence in the art world." Suzaan Boettger, "Excavating Land Art by Women in the 1970s," *Sculpture*, November 2008, 39.

**126** Howard Risatti, "The Sculpture of Alice Aycock and Some Observations on Her Work," *Woman's Art Journal* 16, no. 1 (Spring–Summer 1985): 28–38; Alice Aycock, "Work 1972–1974," in *Individuals: Post-Movement Art in America*, ed. Alan Sondheim (E. P. Dutton, 1977), 104–7.

**127** Krauss, "Sculpture in the Expanded Field."

**128** I borrow this descriptor from George Quasha's essay on Knowles's *The Book of Bean* environment reprinted as the "Transvironmental Book," in *The Book, Spiritual Instrument*, ed. Jerome Rothenberg and David Guss (Granary Books, 1996), 1–13; and in *by Alison Knowles: A Retrospective*, 241–44.

**129** In 1972, Knowles asked Nam June Paik to sponsor her application for a second Guggenheim Grant to build still another *House of Dust*. Nam June Paik Archive, K Correspondence, Smithsonian American Art Museum, Washington, DC. In 1976, she wrote to David Antin inquiring about the possibility of transferring the smaller house to UC San Diego, ideally to be sited next to "a rocky environment. . . . I want to give this piece a whole new framework, properly meditative, etc." A 1979 letter from Knowles to Linda Burnham, editor of *High Performance*, notes her frustration with the Oakland Museum's unwillingness to transport and reinstall the work. See Knowles's letters to Burham, late 1970s, High Performance Magazine Records, Correspondence Files, GRI; Knowles, typed letter to Antin, July 10, 1976, David Antin papers, Correspondence Files, GRI.

**130** For the 1980 NEA grant application and correspondence between Knowles and various curators, directors, and contractors, see Knowles, "A Summary of Gift Objects & Donors for the HOUSE OF DUST," attachment C, typed, n.d., House of Dust Files, EHF.

**131** Letter to Knowles from Joan Waller, director of the Child Development Center, June 21, 1982, House of Dust Files, AKS. The Santa Clarita placement corresponded with Knowles's original intentions; while still in Chelsea, she had shared with Robert Filliou "the good news" that "the HOUSE OF DUST project was approved for a children's park here." It was "meant to have children clambering all over and in it" and, before the fire, was reportedly "extremely popular among the children." Knowles, 1969 letter to Filliou, Dick Higgins archive, Robert Filliou Correspondence (I–P), SA; "Sculpture Is Burned on Penn South Lawn," *Chelsea Clinton News*, October 23, 1969, 3.

**132** Knowles, "Dialogue: The House of Dust," 23.

**133** For the CalArts reactivation, see https://blog.calarts.edu/2018/03/16/alison-knowles-house-of-dust-to-be-celebrated-with-calarts-performances-and-redcat-symposium/; Thomas Aguila, "Reframing the House of Dust: An Interview with Janet Sarbanes and Ken Ehrlich," https://eastofborneo.org/articles/reframing-the-house-of-dust-an-interview-with-janet-sarbanes-and-ken-ehrlich/. I delivered a talk sharing details from this chapter at BAMPFA for "*by Alison Knowles*: A Symposium," a panel organized by the exhibition's guest curator,

Karen Moss, October 15, 2022, Berkeley, CA. Other iterations of the poem and environments include reactivations by Art by Translation (curators Maud Jacquin and Sébastien Pluot) for Knowles's 2016 exhibition at the James Gallery, CUNY Graduate Center, New York (2016), as well as *Shelter or Playground* exhibition at the Schindler House, MAK Center for Art and Architecture, Los Angeles (2019). See also Jacquin and Pluot, "*The House of Dust*, a Work in Translation," in *by Alison Knowles: A Retrospective*, 71–79. My thanks to Maud and Sébastien for inviting me to speak on Knowles's practice in connection with the James Gallery show and on *The House of Dust* for "Reframing the House of Dust: A Symposium," Roy and Edna Disney/CalArts Theater, Los Angeles (2018).

**134** For the Wiesbaden iteration, see https://www.tinybe.org/artists/alison-knowles/. The traveling exhibition *by Alison Knowles: A Retrospective (1960–2022)* opened at the Wiesbaden Museum in September 2024 and featured programming related to this version of the *House of Dust*.

**135** Miriam Schapiro and Deena Metzger, eds., *Art: A Woman's Sensibility, The Collected Works and Writings of Women Artists* (FAP, CalArts, 1975). Contributors to the volume include Eleanor Antin, Lynda Bengalis, Judith Bernstein, Sherry Brody, Audrey Flack, Harmony Hammond, Grace Hartigan, Joyce Kozloff, Lee Krasner, Sylvia Mangold, Alice Neel, Lil Picard, Howardena Pindell, Adrian Piper, Betye Saar, Carolee Schneemann, Barbara Smith, Nancy Spero, and Hannah Wilke, among other artists whose names are less familiar today.

**136** Schapiro, "FAP Letter to Women Artists," 2. The radicality of the act seems premised on such a move being a reversal of the formal, analytical literary style and figural manifestation associated with the "man of letters" in Western literature.

**137** Deena Metzger, "Letter of Introduction," *Art: A Woman's Sensibility*, 1.

**138** Knowles, *Art: A Women's Sensibility*, 36.

**139** Alison Knowles and Annea Lockwood, eds., *Womens Work*, no. 1 (self-published, 1975); Knowles and Lockwood, eds., *Womens Work*, no. 2 (self-published, 1978). The first issue featured Beth Anderson, Jackie Apple, Sari Dienes, Nye Ffarrabas (as Bici Forbes), Simone Forti, Wendy Greenberg, Heidi Von Gunden, Knowles, Lockwood (as Anna Lockwood), Mary Lucier, Pauline Oliveros, Mieko Shiomi, Elaine Summers, Carol Weber, Julie Winter, and Marilyn Wood. Issue Two featured Ruth Anderson, Barbara Benary, Françoise Janicot, Knowles, Christina Kubisch, Lisa Mikulchik, Carol Law, Lockwood, Ann Nöel (as Ann Williams), Takako Saito, and Carolee Schneemann. Primary Information is a nonprofit arts organization devoted to publishing artists' books and art historical documents. With support from Knowles and Lockwood, *WOMENS WORK* was reproduced in a facsimile edition by artist/curators James Hoff and Irene Revell. My thanks to Irene for conversing about experimental art, sound, and intermedia in email correspondences in 2019.

**140** Knowles, *Proposition IV (Squid)* in *WOMENS WORK*, n.p. The score is also reproduced in Knowles, *More by Alison Knowles* (Printed Editions, 1979). The randomized list was programmed and generated by Andrew Schloss, an expert in electronic and computer music and percussive acoustics, who as a student at Bennington College had "unlimited free access" to a mainframe computer via the Dartmouth Time Sharing System. (Schloss is often misidentified as a CalArts student in the literature on *The House of Dust*.) Schloss recalls performing *Proposition IV (Squid)* with Knowles and Yoshimasa (Yoshi) Wada during the Computer Arts Festival at The Kitchen, 240 Mercer Street, New York, April 9, 1973 (see the festival program, which describes it as a "Performance piece for four voices," https://www.eai.org/supporting-documents/278/a.8654.35; and John Rockwell, "A Diverse Program of Computer Arts," *New York Times*, April 11, 1973, 40). "Squid" refers to Schloss's beloved dog, to whom he dedicated the score and his later dissertation. I am grateful to Andrew for a generous series of exchanges clarifying his collaboration with Knowles, an underresearched topic in the critical literature on *The House of Dust*. Email correspondence with author, June 4–10, 2025. Schloss had been introduced to Knowles in 1969 by his friend and roommate Liz Phillips, a young interactive sound and installation artist with deep ties to the New York avant-garde scene. In 1970–1971, Phillips was an artist-in-residence working with Serge Tcherepnin and Nam June Paik at CalArts and living with Knowles and others in their communal space. On behalf of Knowles, she asked Schloss to help in programming *Proposition IV (Squid)*. Phillips, telephone conversation with author, June 5, 2025. After CalArts, Knowles and Phillips collaborated on several media projects, including *Sum Time* (with Wada) at the Everson Museum of Art, Syracuse, New York (November 1973), and the Pratt Graphics Center (February 1974). See Charlie Morrow, "Sum Time: Alison Knowles & Liz Phillips at the Pratt Graphics Center," *SoHo News*, March 10, 1974, 18. They also performed, for Moorman's Annual Avant Garde Festivals, food-based works (Knowles's *The Identical Lunch* and Phillips's *Electronic Banquet*) in 1972, aboard the riverboat *Alexander Hamilton*, and sound pieces (Knowles's *Process Picture* and Phillips's *Sound Fields*) in the 1973 Festival, in Penn Station baggage cars at Grand Central Station.

**141** See Knowles, *Monkey Shines*, in *More by Alison Knowles* and *Ear Magazine of New Music* 2, no. 1 (February–March 1976). Knowles's handwritten score for *Monkey Shines* can be found in Special Collections Library, UCSD.

**142** Knowles, undated letter to Jean Brown, JBP. Knowles also performed *Proposition IV (Squid)* for KPFK Radio in 1971 and at Charlotte Moorman's 13th Annual Avant Garde Festival, held at the World Trade Center, in June 1977. Nigerian American dance artist Ogemdi Ude interpreted the score in a dance film as part of the With Womens Work series, April 22, 2021. See https://issueprojectroom.org/event/womens-work-ogemdi-ude-368.

**143** Knowles, letter to Jean Brown, early 1970s, JBP. On the making of *WOMENS WORK*, especially its relation to Oliveros, see Irene Revell, "Speculating on the 'Feminist Performance Score': Pauline Oliveros, Womens Work, and Karen Barad," *Contemporary Music Review* 41, nos. 2–3 (May 2022): 281–94. I am grateful to Irene for our email correspondence in 2019 and her curation and scholarship on this important anthology.

**144** Knowles, letter to Higgins, August 11, 1974, DHP.

**145** Knowles, of course, continued to work with male artists and composers (most frequently Philip Corner, Bill Fontana, Malcolm Goldstein, and Yoshi Wada). However, my research also uncovered many projects with women artists in the mid- to late 1970s (outside the temporal scope of this book), including Lockwood, Oliveros, Beth Anderson, Julia Hayward, Elaine Hartnett, Jill Kroesen, Elaine Summers, and Anne Tardos. See, for example, Knowles and Oliveros's *Postcard Theater* (Aenjai Graphics, 1974); Meet the Woman Composer series at the New School for Social Research (1975–1976); and events by the women's ensemble Sounds Out of Silent Spaces (which included Knowles), organized by Summers for her Experimental Media Foundation (1971–1979). This reflects a more capacious history of time-based and media arts in the 1970s, especially in New York City, where the emergence of nonprofit art centers like The Kitchen (1971), Artists Space (1972), Franklin Furnace (1976), and Grommet Studio (1976) provided alternative spaces for women artists to exhibit, perform, and collaborate.

**146** Williams, undated manuscript, Emmett Williams Archives, JBP.

## Epilogue

**1** Aviva Rahmani, "Alison Knowles: An Interview," in *M/E/A/N/I/N/G: An Anthology of Artists' Writings, Theory, and Criticism*, ed. Susan Bee and Mira Schor (Duke University Press, 2000), 363–64.

2 Andreas Huyssen, "Back to the Future: Fluxus in Context," in *In the Spirit of Fluxus*, ed. Elizabeth Armstrong and Joan Rothfuss (Walker Art Center, 1993), 143.

3 Higgins, letter to Maciunas, August 17, 1966, JBP. Higgins is referring to a March 1963 letter from Maciunas to Knowles and Higgins wherein he argues, "Fluxus is a 'collective' & should not associate with any particular fluxus individual." On "political motives" underlying the attraction to the quotidian in Fluxus art, see Sally Banes, *Greenwich Village 1963: Avant-Garde Performance and the Effervescent Body* (Duke University Press, 1993), 126–29.

4 Valerie Cassel Oliver, "The Curious Case of Benjamin Patterson," in *Benjamin Patterson: Born in the State of FLUX/us* (Contemporary Arts Museum, Houston, 2012), 21.

5 The March 8, 1967, *Fluxus Policy Newsletter*, written and distributed by Maciunas, includes at least three supplemental "1966 & 1967 events" under George Brecht and others: "A Strategy for Vietnam (flux-atlas)," "Fail Matches" by Danish Fluxus artist Eric Andersen, and "Futile Box" with Robert Filliou—each ostensibly devised to mark resistance to the war. Newsletter reproduced in Wolf Vostell, *dé-coll/age* 6, July 1967.

6 Knowles, quoted in Rahmani, "Alison Knowles: An Interview," 368. The Fifth Avenue Vietnam Peace Committee coordinated events and demonstrations opposing the war in the mid-1960s. For other Fluxus artists' explicit responses to the American war in Southeast Asia, see, for example, *Manifestos* (Great Bear Pamphlet, 1966); George Maciunas, *U.S.A. Surpasses All the Genocide Records* (1966), Museum of Modern Art, New York, #3001.2008. x1-36; Wolf Vostell, *Miss Vietnam: And Texts of Other Happenings*, trans. Carl Weissner (Nova Broadcast Press, 1968); and Higgins's poem "Where is Vietnam?" (1966) and *The Thousand Symphonies* (1967), a performance in which he fired a submachine gun at music paper, filmed by Knowles, at the South Brunswick, New Jersey, Police Rifle Range, November 1968. The text accompanying this last work also refers to "USA police seem[ing] to have nothing better to do than to chase down teenagers for possessing miniscule amounts of marijuana and throwing them in jail, thus ruining their lives." Higgins, *The Thousand Symphonies: Their Story* (self-published, 1991), 2–3.

7 Richard C. Higgins, "Disagreement," *Yale Alumni Magazine* (December 1963), 3. Higgins also referred to participating with Knowles and Corner in The Living Theater's Strike for Peace! demonstrations and protests against nuclear war organized by Julian Beck and Judith Malina in New York, 1962–1963. See Dick Higgins Archive, boxes 40, 76, NU. On the Becks' General Strike for Peace events, see John Tytell, *The Living Theater: Art, Exile and Outrage* (Grove Press, 1995), 170–84.

8 Corner, email exchange with author, May 4, 2019. Of his army service, he says he "refus[ed] any kind of responsibility [for the war] and as a result never [received] a promotion. Not even the automatic first stripe!" On the concerts, see also Benjamin Piekut, "On and Off the Grid: Music for and Around Judson Dance Theater," in *Judson Dance Theater: The Work Is Never Done*, eds. Ana Janevski et al. (Museum of Modern Art, 2018), 74, 75n29.

9 Higgins, typed letter to Milan Knížák, dated on Knowles's thirty-fourth birthday, April 29, 1967. Dick Higgins Correspondence Files (KI–KN), AS.

10 Higgins, typed letter to Milan Knížák, February 25, 1967, SFA, I.701.

11 Knowles and Hannah Higgins, conversation with author, Chicago, April 26, 2019. Knowles remembers feeling dispirited after being told her primary job would be to check the children's heads for lice before letting them on the bus. A biographical CV dating to the 1980s includes Knowles's work as a counselor for the Fresh Air Fund in the early 1950s. Alison Knowles Files, EHF. The organization was founded in 1877 to coordinate rural summer vacations for city children. In recent years, it has come under scrutiny for its mistreatment of African American children, especially during the civil rights era. See Tobin Miller Shearer,

*Two Weeks Every Summer: Fresh Air Children and the Problem of Race in America* (Cornell University Press, 2017).

12 Patterson, quoted in Kristine Stiles's indispensable essay "Race, Gender and Sex in Fluxus Events," in *Women in Fluxus and Other Experimental Tales: Eventi, Partiture, Performance*, ed. Elena Zanichelli (Skira, 2012), 208. See also Gillian Turner Young, "An Audience Is Divided: Benjamin Patterson, Clifford Owens, and the Politics of Representation," *Drama Review* 58, no. 2 (Summer 2014): 115–31.

13 George E. Lewis, "In Search of Benjamin Patterson: An Improvised Journey," in *Benjamin Patterson: Born in the State of FLUX/us*, 123.

14 Patterson, "I'm Glad You Asked Me That Question," in *Benjamin Patterson: Born in the State of FLUX/us*, 113.

15 Patterson, "I'm Glad You Asked Me That Question," in *Benjamin Patterson: Born in the State of FLUX/us*, 114. In this self-interview, Patterson submitted himself to a type of question/answer parody, which allows, within its unusual framework (there is no direct interlocutor asking questions or driving the conversation), a revealing candor. Recently Philip Corner expressed surprise at Patterson's sweeping characterizations given his own activist role in the NAACP at that time. Email exchange with author, May 4, 2019. Patterson, who lived with Knowles and Higgins for a time in their Chelsea townhouse in the mid-1960s, also once described their friendship as mutually sustaining in terms of the aesthetics, but also ethics and politics. Patterson in conversation with author, Los Angeles, July 10, 2006.

16 Emmett Williams's sparse but elegiac *White for Governor Wallace* (1963) is another example of addressing political violence. Originally titled *Brown for Cassius Clay*—an "Americanized" version of his *Blue for Yves Klein*—Williams changed the title after reading an account "of the tragic bombing of negro schooldchildren in Birmingham. One night soon afterwards, I dreamed I was performing *Brown for Cassius Clay* for the mourning parents of the murdered children. In the middle of the dream, I interrupted the piece, apologized to the parents, and started over as White for Governor Wallace." When the word "white" is read at the end of the piece, a candle is "snuffed out," leaving the audience in darkness. See Williams, typed pages detailing key works of the early 1960s. In a letter to Williams, Knowles described the evening when Patterson, Higgins, and Mac Low performed the piece at the Café au Go Go, January 1965. For both documents, see Emmett Williams Archive Works, JBP.

17 Huyssen, however, wholly neglected Knowles and Patterson in his accounting of the founding members of Fluxus. See also Kristine Stiles, "Uncorrupted Joy: International Art Actions," in *Out of Actions: Between Performance and the Object, 1949–1979*, ed. Paul Schimmel (Thames & Hudson, 1998), 227–329. Maciunas's complex sexuality and penchant for cross-dressing is noted in several sources, including Kathy O'Dell, "Fluxus Feminus," *Drama Review* 41, no. 1 (Spring 1997): 43–60; Stiles, "Between Water and Stone, Fluxus Performance: A Metaphysics of Acts," in Armstrong and Rothfuss, *In the Spirit of Fluxus*, 62–99; and Colby Chamberlain, *Fluxus Administration: George Maciunas and the Art of Paperwork* (University of Chicago Press, 2024), 219–23.

18 Knowles, interview with author, New York, December 15, 2006.

19 On "hippie modernism" in countercultural art, architecture, music, and design, see curator Andrew Blauvelt's preface and introductory essays in *Hippie Modernism: The Struggle for Utopia* (Walker Art Center, 2015), 11–43.

20 Knowles, 2-page typed letter to Knížák, July 1, 1967, SFA, I.741.

21 In 1989, Knowles added her name to the poster *Guerilla Girls' Identities Exposed!* for the screenprint edition series *Guerrilla Girls Talk Back* (1990), Tate Modern Collection #P78816.

22 Dick Higgins, unpublished, typed transcript, oral history interview with Michael Oren (1979). Dick Higgins papers, AAA, 1979, 8. I address the historical complexities of research-

ing Knowles's life and art when much of her archive was saved in Higgins and other Fluxus friends' papers in Woods, "Do You Remember? Alison Knowles in Context," in *by Alison Knowles: A Retrospective (1962–2022)*, ed. Karen Moss and Lucia Fabio (University of California, Berkeley Art Museum and Pacific Film Archive, 2022), 31–43.

**23** As noted in chapter 1, Knowles and Higgins became companions again in the late 1970s and remarried in an open partnership in 1984, which continued until his untimely death in 1998. Knowles kept the SoHo loft she had been living in since she returned to New York City after CalArts, and Higgins relocated to Barrytown in the Hudson River Valley in 1980. In a 1988 interview, Knowles complimented the unusual but productive arrangement as it related to her work: "My family respects me enough to let me have my solitude 4 days of the week. I go to the country the other 3. I have a lucky balance of things that gives me most of my time to do the work I wish. It's quite interesting how this has been possible as a wife and mother. This is where I have had a lot of luck." See exhibition brochure featuring the interview and her multimedia piece *North Water Song*, November 1988, Benhhaus, Lübeck, Germany. Alison Knowles Files, EHF.

# INDEX

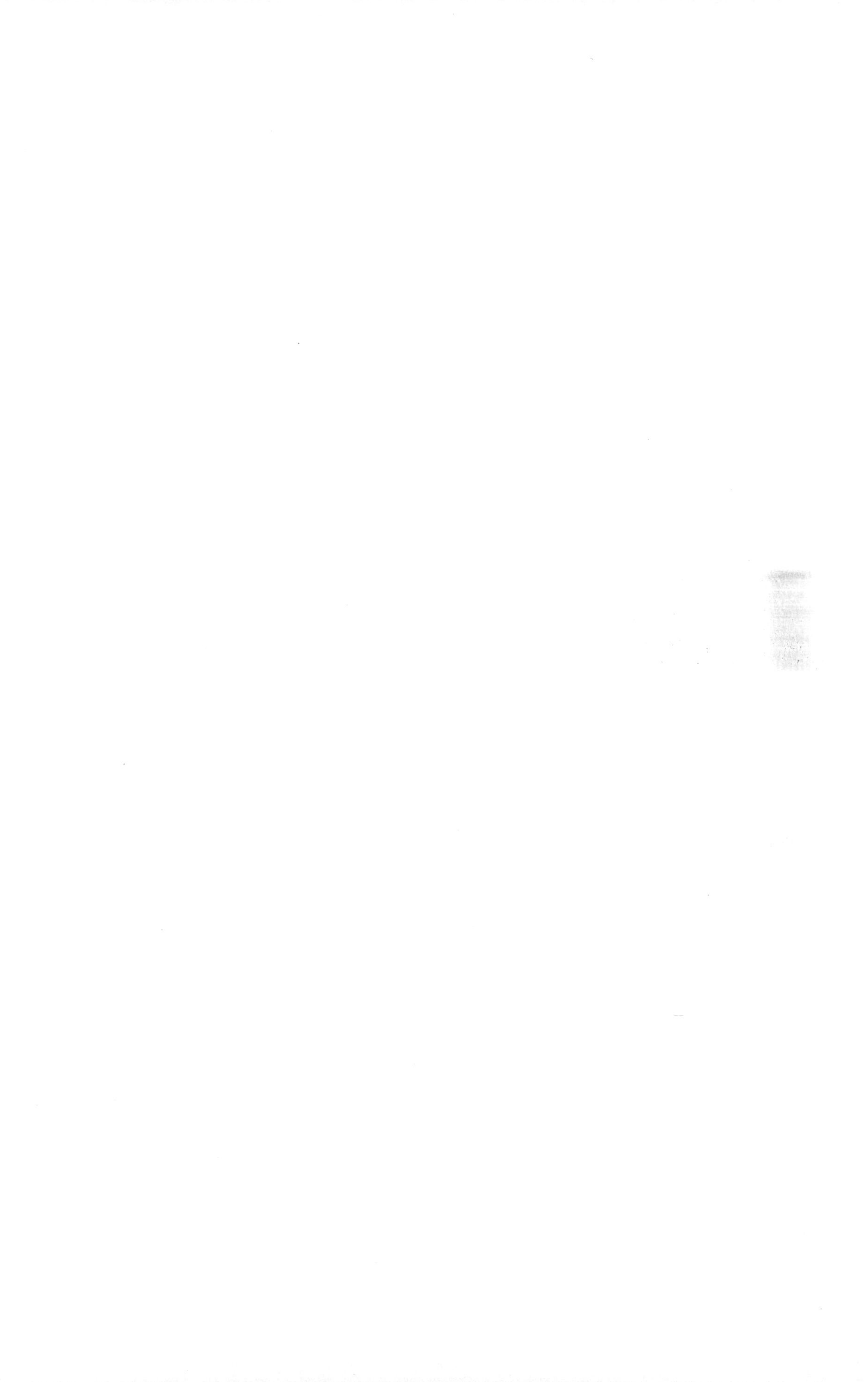